W9-ACW-572

NAM

NAM

A PHOTOGRAPHIC HISTORY

Leo J. Daugherty
Gregory Louis Mattson

MetroBooks

MetroBooks

An Imprint of the Michael Friedman Publishing Group, Inc.

Library of Congress Cataloging-in-Publication Data
available upon request.

ISBN 1-58663-083-0

Editorial and design by:
Amber Books Ltd
Bradley's Close
74-77 White Lion Street
London N1 9PF

Additional caption material by Will Fowler.
Box material by Chris McNab.

Project editors: Lee Johnson, Charles Catton, and Tom Jenkins
Editor: Judith Millidge
Art director: Kevin Ullrich
Design: Neil Rigby at www.stylus-design.com
Picture research: Stasz Gynch, Lee Johnson, and Lisa Wren

Printed in Singapore

1 3 5 7 9 10 8 6 4 2

For bulk purchases and special sales, please contact:

Friedman/Fairfax Publishers
Attention: Sales Department
230 Fifth Avenue
New York, NY 10001
212/685-6610 FAX 212/685-3916

Visit our website:
www.metrobooks.com

Endpapers:©Walter Bibikow/Folio

Contents

Chapter 1: **The Background**   8

Chapter 2: **1965**   38

Chapter 3: **1966**   84

Chapter 4: **1967**   130

Chapter 5: **1968**   210

Chapter 6: **1969**   350

Chapter 7: **1970**   410

Chapter 8: **1971**   450

Chapter 9: **1972**   486

Chapter 10: **1973**   516

Chapter 11: **1974**   536

Chapter 12: **1975**   552

Chapter 13: **The Aftermath**   564

Timeline   598

Index   602

1940

1964

The French Legacy

The origins of the Vietnam War can be traced to the French colonial occupation of the present-day states of Cambodia, Laos, and Vietnam, the area known as French Indochina. The Japanese Army occupied the mineral-rich area during World War II, and afterward France agreed to grant the states self-government within the French Union.

Vietnamese nationalists were dissatisfied with this arrangement and the independence struggle between the French and the nationalist forces of the Vietminh broke out less than a month after the end of World War II in September 1945.

The League for the Independence of Vietnam, the Vietminh, was founded in 1941 by Nguyen Ai Quoc (later known as Ho Chi Minh) the leader of the small, though very active, Vietnamese Communist Party. He drew up a program that appealed to both intellectuals and peasants alike: relief from taxes, redistribution of land, and the abolition of forced labor and military conscription.

Throughout the Japanese occupation, the Vietminh organized and trained for the anticipated independence struggle with colonial French forces. Impressed by the United States' policy promising colonial self-determination at the end of the war, Ho supported the U.S. war effort. The Vietminh recovered American pilots shot down by the Japanese, and carried out sabotage and intelligence-gathering missions against the Japanese Army. In turn, American OSS (Office of Strategic Services – the forerunner to the Central Intelligence Agency) officers trained the Vietminh and supplied them with arms and equipment. For a brief period, the United States and Ho Chi Minh's Vietminh were united against a common foe. The Vietminh seized control from the Japanese in August 1945 in what was virtually a bloodless coup d'etat, but the rapprochement with the U.S. broke down with the return of the French later in 1945.

The Vietminh established a political infrastructure throughout Indochina, particularly in Tonkin (northern Vietnam), linking villages through provincial rule, all under the leadership of the Vietminh Central Committee. By the end of 1944, over 500,000 people had joined, an estimated 200,000 in Tonkin, with 150,000 members further south in Annam and Cochin China (South Vietnam).

Ho and his military commander, Vo Nguyen Giap, set out to organize the Vietminh's military capability to resist the French. At each administration level, a "Committee of Resistance" was established to direct the war effort and other political activities in each district. At the provincial levels and below, Hanoi instructed all committees of resistance to recruit and

---

ABOVE: An officer of the Imperial Japanese Navy surrenders his ceremonial sword to a Royal Navy officer during the surrender of the occupying Japanese forces in Saigon at the close of World War II.
RIGHT: Under the steady downpour of the monsoon rain in Indochina, a French colonial soldier uses a looted umbrella for shelter as he guards bails of stores captured from the Vietminh.

train a local militia, as well as local security units. Collectively known as "popular troops," the militia consisted of an auxiliary military group of men and women of all ages, and a part-time combat power group of men aged between 18 and 45. In addition, villages were required to provide porters for the regular army units. At the district, provincial, or inter-zone levels, there were battalion-sized units, know as "regional troops." At the provincial level there was a complex known as "technical cells," which reported to the provincial military command on intelligence, special espionage, political affairs, propaganda, arms production, communications, and military administration.

Regional troops trained recruits for the regular units, but their primary task was to protect the area and population by launching small guerrilla attacks.

Local militia or "popular" troops served part-time, without interrupting their civilian tasks. The main responsibility of the auxiliary

LEFT: Sgt Phillip C. Kellison, a U.S. Army Signals Corps attached to the Nationalist Chinese forces who were operating in northern Indochina in July 1945. The Chinese had just captured the town of Malung Tsi from the Japanese. The OSS and U.S. Army missions were involved with operations by the Chinese and Ho Chi Minh's forces in Indochina at the close of the war.

BELOW LEFT: Still bearing its U.S. Army insignia from World War II, an M5 light tank precedes a Howitzer Motor Carriage M8 as French troops clear the countryside near Saigon in October 1945. Though impressive, this armor was not best suited to fighting the type of guerrilla war undertaken by the Vietminh in southern Indochina.

arm of the village popular troops was intelligence-gathering, guarding local arms caches and supplies, building bases, repairing roads, fortifying villages, and acting as porters for regular army units. These troops also undertook some guerrilla actions, though on a small scale. At the top of the Vietminh military structure was the regular army known as the Liberation Army.

After 1950, as the war with France intensified, these units were oftentimes increased at the expense of the regional forces. The mission of the regular army was to participate in a "war of movement," or to be used in what Vo Nguyen Giap called a "mobile war."

In sum, the Vietminh's leadership organized its military forces along the same lines as that of the party, with distinct local, regional, and national arrangements. There were irregular local guerrilla units, composed of peasants and other civilians; regional military units; and a hard-core of well-disciplined and trained

troops organized nationally. All three military levels coordinated their activities in a flexible and efficient system.

The activities of the Vietminh were all directed toward resisting a re-installation of French rule, rather than launching a Communist "revolution." In essence, Ho and his followers realized that the greater danger to Vietnamese independence came from the French, not from capitalists.

The war between the Vietminh and the French began on December 19, 1946 with attacks on French garrisons in Hanoi and throughout the country. The French were able to field a well-armed and well-trained army and faced a force of some 60,000 men led by Vo Nguyen Giap, a master tactician and the author of one of the best known works on guerrilla warfare.

A sympathetic populace provided the Vietminh military forces with accurate intelligence and logistics support. Over a period of

ABOVE: A French soldier guards a group of Vietnamese taken prisoner outside Saigon as a convoy opens up mined or destroyed roads. The prisoners would probably be used as forced labor and remain attached to the unit.

several months, the Vietminh continued to harass and demoralize the French forces, while at the same time transforming its army from a rag-tag band of guerrillas into a highly modern conventional military force of battalions, regiments, and divisions of 10,000 fighters each.

The Vietminh's leadership surmised that France would grow tired of a stalemated colonial war if pacification – and ultimate victory on French terms – was nowhere in sight. In order to make this clear to French public opinion at home, Giap realized that the Vietminh needed to inflict a series of military defeats on the French. By 1950, Giap had successfully implemented two parts of his overall strategy to defeat the French. First, the Vietminh had successfully carried out a number of hit-and-run raids against French troops while avoiding a major defeat; second, they had penetrated and broken the French defensive line along the Sino–Vietnamese border.

As a part of his third phase, Giap turned his attention toward a series of general counteroffensives which would eventually defeat France. He needed to consolidate his forces for more and larger offensive actions in preparation for a general counteroffensive.

The guerre mobile, or "war of movement," was characterized chiefly by the "absence of fixed fronts and rear areas, quick concentrations for action, and immediate disengagement after fighting." It was a war of attrition, in the sense that all efforts, military and nonmilitary, were aimed at wearing down the French.

LEFT: Regular soldiers from the Vietminh display radio equipment as well as loudspeakers captured from the French Army after the battle of Dien Bien Phu in 1954. The boxes have markings showing the equipment was part of a consignment of U.S. government aid which had been sent to the French. The French colonial forces also used a vast array of surplus U.S. weapons, aircraft, uniforms, and artillery in the war in Indochina.

Vietminh attacks on isolated French outposts began in the fall of 1950 along the Sino–Vietnamese border in the Red River Delta area. One by one, these border outposts fell, so that by January 1951 northern Vietnam, except for the Red River Delta which the French fought desperately to hold, had fallen to Giap's forces and provided an excellent conduit to receive military supplies from the Chinese Communists.

Both Ho Chi Minh and Giap regarded 1951 as a decisive year in the Vietminh's overall strategy to defeat the French. In January 1951, Giap prepared his forces for a general counteroffensive that included capturing Hanoi. He knew that the French suffered from a lack of reinforcements and were at the end of a precarious supply line. The Vietminh's campaign to seize control of the Red River Delta and to drive the French out of northern Vietnam began with a series of set-piece battles. The French could use superior firepower against the Vietminh, so Giap reverted to the first phase of guerrilla warfare: ambushes, hit-and-run raids, and assaults that had brought the Vietminh great success against the French line along the Chinese border. Giap also instituted what he called "human sea" attacks, with

ABOVE: Legionnaires from the French Foreign Legion watch as an M5 light tank passes a demolished bridge near Ninh Hoa in January 1946. The tank bears the battle honor El Alamein, where the Free French brigade, the 13th DBLE of the Foreign Legion, fought in 1942. The M5 was armed with a 37 mm (1.47 in.) gun and two .3 in. machine guns, and this tank has spare tracks fixed to the turret as extra protection against antitank weapons.

Uncle Ho

Ho Chi Minh wasn't his first name, but it was the one by which the world would know him. He was born Nguyen Sinh Cung on May 19, 1890 in Hoang Tru, northern Annam. Ho's rural childhood was tough and impoverished. His father, Nguyen Sinh Huy, was a scholar – not the easiest way to make a living – so money was scarce. Learning and aspiration, however, were in abundance. At the age of 14 Ho entered a grammar school in Hue and showed that he had a bright and perceptive mind. After successfully studying for four years he rolled through a couple of academic jobs. But he was restless, so in 1911 he took a job as a cook on a French steamer.

He stayed at sea for three years, soaking up foreign cultures and ways of thinking. Places visited included Boston and New York, and various ports in Africa. His wanderlust eventually took him to live in France for six years. Here he started to cut his teeth on politics, mixing a deep interest in French Socialism with an involvement in Paris' large Vietnamese community. This set the course for his future. By the time he left Paris he was a committed communist, and he spent much of the 1920s and 1930s in Russia and China under the name of Nguyen Ai Quoc ('Nguyen the Patriot') advising the regimes there on colonial affairs, and forming the Indochinese Communist Party in 1930 in Hong Kong.

The name Ho Chi Minh – meaning 'He Who Enlightens' – was adopted when he returned to his homeland of Indochina in 1941. In the Far East, war was raging with the Japanese, and Ho gained his first military experience leading guerrilla units against the Japanese occupiers. When the Japanese were finally defeated, Ho declared an independent Vietnamese state, fulfilling his dream of Indochinese reunification following decades of French rule. It didn't last. The old French colonial masters returned and took control, and Ho returned to the jungles. Ten years of war resulted – in effect the first Vietnam War. Ho showed brilliance in tactics, attacking the French militarily while undermining them with political maneuvers. Having spent so much time abroad, he knew what actions would hurt the West psyche, and in 1954 the French surrendered.

Yet the West was not happy with a communist Vietnam. The country was split into a communist North – ruled by Ho – and a democratic South backed by the U.S. with the promise of reunificatory elections. The elections didn't happen, and Ho wanted the South back. From then on the U.S. was dragged into an expanding conflict which effectively turned into outright war in the 1960s. Ho was both ruthless and cunning. He played politics with Europe, China, and the Soviet Union, while sending thousands of NVA and Viet Cong into action over the border in one of the longest and bloodiest wars since 1945.

The result is history. In 1975 the whole of Vietnam fell to the communist powers. Ironically, however, Ho was not there to see it. He died in 1969 in his beloved Hanoi. Ho Chi Minh had said that the war with the U.S. would be like the clash between a tiger and an elephant. In open battle, the elephant would crush the tiger. Yet if the tiger every once in a while crept out of the jungle to tear chunks off the elephant's hide, the elephant would slowly bleed to death. History showed Ho to be correct.

BELOW: Ho Chi Minh, the architect of Vietnamese independence. His ability to outfox both the French and American governments undoubtedly was helped by his personal experience of those two countries before World War II. He died before the end of the Vietnam War.

wave after wave of Vietminh soldiers throwing themselves against the French lines.

The French forces, commanded by the veteran Marshal de Lattre de Tassigny, attempted to salvage a campaign that prior to 1950 had been mismanaged and poorly led.

Marshal de Lattre launched a vigorous recruiting campaign of French and pro-French South Vietnamese civilians into auxiliary combat units in order to free front-line French army and Legionnaire units. He set up defense units along the Vietminh's infiltration routes straddling the Red River Delta. The French had superiority in the air and in artillery, so Giap avoided major confrontations. When Vietminh forces did attack en masse, the French repelled them with the help of fighter-bombers, heavy artillery, and the use of para-troops dropped behind enemy positions.

De Lattre employed two further types of operations against the Vietminh. One was the "meat grinder" operation, by which the French attempted to draw into battle and then destroy the enemy's regular units in one great battle. This was largely unsuccessful because Giap

refused to be baited into a large battle with the French. The second was a brief counterattack launched either to destroy a Vietminh position in Vietminh territory, or to cut off Vietminh units from northern bases. This was more successful, particularly at Hoa-Binh, a garrison 20 miles (32 km) inside Vietminh territory.

While most of the French mobile forces were concentrated in the northern areas of Vietnam, French operations in southern Vietnam slowed down as the French-trained Vietnamese security forces conducted a vigorous and successful counter-terrorist campaign. There were no major terrorist incidents in Saigon between 1952 and 1954.

De Lattre died in December 1952 and despite his efforts, the French position remained tenuous. As the Vietminh tied the French down in static warfare, the situation had reached stalemate. General Henri Navarre succeeded as French commander-in-chief and tried to reorganize French units to increase their mobility, beginning a series of counteroffensives designed to break the Communist forces by 1955. Navarre attempted to meet

ABOVE: A Vietminh crew in training with a former British Army 3 in. (76.2 mm) mortar. Despite their unsophisticated appearance, the crew are still looking very business-like, with one man adjusting elevation and cross leveling, while behind the mortar, men pass more bombs forward. Local protection comes from a rifleman close to the tree. The medium mortar was an ideal weapon for guerrilla forces since it could be carried in the jungle and a good crew could fire five or six bombs into a French, or later American, base and quickly withdraw before the enemy had a chance to respond.

every threat posed by the Vietminh. As a result, the French troops were essentially run ragged as they were unable to pin down the Vietminh into a decisive set-piece battle. In November 1953 Navarre launched Operation Castor to cut off Laos, which eventually led to the climatic battle at Dien Bien Phu. He hoped to employ the "meat grinder" tactics against the bulk of the Communist battle force far from the vital Red River Delta, while the French high command would concentrate the remainder of its forces upon mopping up the delta. He also intended to use the airstrip to interdict supplies flowing into the Red River Delta from Laos.

Three French parachute battalions were dropped over the valley of Dien Bien Phu on November 20, 1953. While the operation itself was a tactical surprise, a Vietminh mortar unit and several rifle companies then training at the drop site inflicted heavy casualties on the paratroops before withdrawing into the hills.

Despite the strong French presence (which eventually included seven paratroop battalions and six artillery groups) the French were in a weak defensive position, a fact which Giap adroitly exploited. Situated away from the

ABOVE: French Foreign Legion soldiers man a blockhouse covering the city of Moncay. Static defenses were intended to protect vulnerable targets like bridges, railways, and towns and cities. While effective, they could also become targets in their own right.

FAR LEFT: A young Legion signaller or "radio" from a parachute battalion sits drafting a signal prior to transmission. He is dressed in distinctive M1943 ex-U.S. Marine Corps camouflaged clothing.

LEFT: The crew of an M24 Chaffee light tank talk to soldiers in a convoy before it heads into the interior. The tank, armed with a 2.95 in. (75 mm) gun and two machine guns, would have provided protection against the Vietminh ambushes.

LEFT: Men of a French parachute battalion plod through flooded low lying land during Operation Citron Mandarine. The minimal equipment of the officer on the right suggests that this group are conducting a short range patrol in order to set up an ambush or establish a cordon during the operation. Despite the wealth of ex-U.S. Army equipment made available to the French, though Colonial paratroops might jump into action, they more often relied on marching in order to move out of an area in the aftermath of any major operations.

coastal plain and major highway networks, Dien Bien Phu was dependent almost entirely on air support, and was a poor site for a set-piece confrontation.

The Vietminh opened up their attack on Dien Bien Phu with a terrific artillery and mortar barrage which coincided with an extensive tunneling campaign that brought them close to the French positions. While Giap had access to an uninterrupted network of supplies, the French had to rely upon aircraft dropping supplies to their now beleaguered garrison. As the situation at Dien Bien Phu became critical, the French asked the United States to intervene on their behalf, but General Matthew B. Ridgway, the Army Chief of Staff, eventually convinced President Eisenhower that the French position was untenable, and that the commitment of U.S. ground troops would inevitably lead to a wider U.S. commitment.

After a heroic stand, the French garrison surrendered on May 7, 1954, just as peace negotiations at Geneva, Switzerland got underway. The Dien Bien Phu defeat hastened France's disengagement from Indochina.

After the French defeat at Dien Bien Phu and the signing of the Geneva Accords,

Vietnam was split into two ideologically different zones at the 17th parallel, pending a national referendum. North of the 17th parallel was the Democratic Republic of Vietnam or DRV led by Ho Chi Minh. In the south, in the Republic of Vietnam or RVN, an anti-Communist regime had been established, briefly under the titular head of the Emperor Bao Dai with Ngo Dinh Diem, a Roman Catholic and one-time French colonial administrator serving as prime minister.

As the Cold War grew more intense, the Eisenhower administration re-evaluated its policy and began a slow but steady involvement in Vietnam by dispatching military advisers to the South Vietnamese military. Initially, a group of 342 American military advisers were attached to the Military Assistance Advisory Group Vietnam (USMAAG) at the request of the Diem regime in 1955. They began a thorough re-organization and training of the Army of the Republic of Vietnam (ARVN).

Diem pursued a vigorous anti-guerrilla campaign against the remnants of the Vietminh and his political opponents, but in these early years the real failure to destroy the Communist infrastructure in South Vietnam came from the

LEFT: U.S. Army General J. "Lightning Joe" Lawton Collins visiting Hanoi with General Jean de Lattre de Tassigny, the High Commissioner of French Indochina. De Lattre's black armband is worn in honor of his son, a platoon commander in Indochina, whose death devastated him.

BELOW: A 4.7 in. (120 mm) mortar line of the 1ere CEPML 1st Foreign Para Heavy Mortar Company in action during Operation Castor, the initial landings in the valley in Dien Bien Phu. The native houses in the background were torn down to clear fields of fire and to build defenses.

NEXT PAGE: Patrice de Carfort, medecin-lieutenant of the 1er Battalion de Etranger de Parachutistes, the 1st Battalion of the Foreign (Legion) Parachutists, in a front line aid post during operations in 1953.

Diem regime's neglect of political, social, and economic reforms. The leaders of southern guerrilla movement began to urge their northern compatriots to sanction a new armed struggle against Diem and his American advisers.

Diem's government was ill-prepared to wage an effective campaign against what now became known as the Viet Cong, partly because U.S. military advisers concentrated on training the ARVN to meet a conventional invasion from the North, rather than deal with the guerrilla tactics of the VC. As the ARVN pursued the Vietminh, who had been identified as hard-core Communists, the guerrillas began to rebuild their infrastructure. Disbanded in 1954, the Vietminh were succeeded by the Viet Cong, a term devised by Diem for his Communist opponents. The Viet Cong, now organized along military lines into companies and battalions, launched a series of attacks

against the South Vietnamese paramilitary forces, and occasionally against the ARVN. Their activities expanded from the area around Saigon to the Central Highlands, where VC agents began a vigorous recruiting campaign among the Montagnard tribesmen. In order to recruit disaffected non-Communists in South Vietnam, in 1960 Hanoi created the National Liberation Front of South Vietnam, or NLF.

Quite simply, the majority of U.S. advisers were not trained to cope with the guerrilla tactics and organization of the Viet Cong. ARVN-trained and armed civil guard and self defense groups were poorly equipped and led, and were riddled with enemy agents. The VC, by contrast, adopted the all-embracing political and military organization of the Vietminh, utilizing local, provincial, and national forces. Communist political officers approved missions and often outranked a unit's military commander. Party policy, discipline, and unit cohesion were inculcated and reinforced by three-man party cells in every unit.

As the Viet Cong's control over the population increased, their military forces grew in number and size. While much of this military

TOP LEFT: In a clearing on the edge of a bamboo grove, French paratroop officers pay their last respects at the grave of a comrade killed in action.
LEFT: Vietnamese soldiers from the French Army open fire with a Chatellerault M1924/29 light machine gun. The weapon weighed 20 lb. (9.24 kg) and had a 25 round box magazine.
TOP RIGHT: A French Army film cameraman waits for the paratroops manning a .3 in. (7.62 mm) Browning machine gun to establish themselves on the edge of a dry paddy field before he starts filming.
RIGHT: A French officer examines weapons which have been captured from the Vietminh: Japanese 3.2 in. (81 mm) Mortar Type 99 barrels and 0.25 in. (6.5mm) Heavy Machine Gun Type 3s.

LEFT: A Vietminh psychological warfare poster which urges that French soldiers demand repatriation to France when they have returned back at their base. The poster explains that the situation is grave everywhere in Indochina for the French Expeditionary Forces and that General Henri Navarre is sending soldiers into combat for his own personal ambition. He makes the soldiers fight "for his (rank) stars" but Dien Bien Phu risks becoming the soldiers' grave. This idea has been a recurrent theme of propaganda and psychological warfare; later in Vietnam African American soldiers were told by North Vietnam that they were dupes fighting the White Man's war.

ABOVE RIGHT: The elegant and aristocratic commander at Dien Bien Phu, the cavalryman Brigadier General Christian Marie Ferdinand de la Croix de Castries, in his underground command post in 1954. Under the pressure of the Vietminh attacks he would remain in the bunker, rarely emerging outside and failing to give firm leadership and direction to the French and Vietnamese garrison. Command of the garrison passed to the "parachute Mafia," a small group of tough para colonels who fought for 55 days. After the defeat, de Castries survived three months in captivity and died in July 1991 aged 88.

BELOW RIGHT: With the drop zone at Dien Bien Phu secured, landed paratroops watch as their comrades land in waves on the dry paddy fields. Many commentators believed the fortified base deep in enemy territory would grind down Vietminh forces. For Ho Chi Minh and Vo Nguyen Giap, the challenge was one that, with Chinese backing, they were confident they could win.

ABOVE: At the beginning of Operation Castor, as parachutes descend on the valley of Dien Bien Phu, casualties are loaded aboard a Sikorsky H-19 helicopter. Helicopters and fixed wing aircraft were used for casualty evacuation from the base until Vietminh 4.1 in. (105 mm) artillery fire closed the airstrip.

RIGHT: Loaded with huge panniers of rations and camouflaged with vegetation, a column of Vietminh porters move supplies on modified bicycles, which allowed transportation of two or three times the weight a man carried on his back. Huge armies of porters supplied the Vietminh at Die Bien Phu.

remained under the overall authority of the southern Communists, North Vietnamese leaders in Hanoi funneled supplies down to their comrades in the south, and sent former southern Vietminh soldiers back home to join or train Viet Cong units. Eventually, regular North Vietnamese soldiers went south to join local Viet Cong units and senior officers manned the expanding Viet Cong command systems, including the political headquarters of the Viet Cong in South Vietnam, the Central

Office South Vietnam, or COSVN. Subordinate to the Central Committee in Hanoi, COSVN's senior commanders were high ranking officers of North Vietnam's Army. In order to equip its forces in the south, the Viet Cong came to rely heavily on captured armaments from the ARVN, and by 1964, weapons and equipment began to arrive from the People's Republic of China and later the Soviet Union and other Communist-bloc nations.

BELOW: A Vietnamese soldier receives first aid for wounds from shell fragments in the bombardment of Dien Bien Phu. The French Army medical orderly has a field dressing in the elastic around his helmet. In the event of a serious wound, all soldiers would apply the field dressing to themselves or their comrade and then be moved back to an aid post behind the front line.

RIGHT: Victorious Viet Minh troops enter Hanoi following the partition of Vietnam and the withdrawal of France from its Southeast Asian colonies.

BELOW LEFT: Lt Boissey of the 1/2e REI Foreign Legion Infantry, wounded during the fighting in Dien Bien Phu, looks out of a bunker after he has had his injuries dressed. Many men who would normally have been evacuated to a rear hospital were trapped at Dien Bien Phu and, rather than leave their comrades, returned to their units.

BELOW RIGHT: In a scene re-enacted for propaganda after the battle at Dien Bien Phu was over, French North African troops emerge to surrender to a Vietminh soldier.

From a strength of approximately 5,000 at the start of 1959, the Viet Cong's ranks swelled to about 100,000 by the end of 1964. Approximately 41,000 infiltrators alone came from North Vietnam along the infamous Ho Chi Minh Trail stretching from North Vietnam through Laos and Cambodia and into South Vietnam. As the ARVN failed to uproot the local VC cadre from the villages, the Viet Cong were able to expand in adjacent areas that Saigon deemed "safe."

Among the more burning foreign policy issues that Eisenhower passed on to John F. Kennedy was the war in Vietnam. Determined to prove his administration's "toughness" in dealing with Communist expansion, largely due to Soviet General Secretary Nikita Khruschev's pronounced support for "wars of national liberation," President Kennedy began a slow but steady build up of the number of American advisers in South Vietnam. Despite

NGO DINH DIEM
President of Disaster

On November 2, 1963, President of the Republic of South Vietnam, Ngo Dinh Diem, was assassinated during a coup d'état by Vietnamese generals. Few in the country mourned. Diem's nine-year reign brought Vietnam nothing but conflict, mismanagement, and despair, and certainly precipitated the onset of the Vietnam war. He was born to a noble family in 1901, in Quang Binh province, northern Vietnam. Social status led to him being appointed Vietnamese minister of the interior under Emperor Bao Dai in 1933, though he resigned from this post in protest at French autocracy. He only returned 12 years later. Having turned down an offer from Ho Chi Minh to join the northern government, he was installed with U.S. backing as the president of South Vietnam in 1954. Then began a reign of incompetence and bias. He was a Roman Catholic who ostracized and persecuted the Buddhist majority, his unimaginative military tactics were useless against the Viet Cong, and his army had little affection for him. Eventually, the U.S. tired of his behavior and withdrew their support. Now isolated and widely hated, his end was assured.

LEFT: U.S. Adviser Capt. Linton Beasley, along with South Vietnamese 1st Lt Nguyen Tien, inspect the weapons of the Vietnamese officer's platoon. The men of the Vietnamese Lieutenant's platoon are almost completely dressed and armed by the United States, and their weapons included the M1 Thompson sub machinegun and M1 carbines. The role of adviser was difficult in the early days, requiring tact and courage.

BELOW LEFT: A strategic hamlet, where a village in South Vietnam has been surrounded by ditches, barbed wire, and panji stakes, and the male population enrolled as a self defense force. The theory was that guerrillas would be unable to receive supplies from the population or exercise control over them if they were kept out of the hamlets. Terror, corruption, and inefficiency resulted in the program being less than effective, and those hamlets that excluded the Viet Cong ran the risk of suffering a nocturnal assault.

RIGHT: A cyclist looks on in shock, and a policeman in apparent indifference, as a young Buddhist monk who has set fire to himself in a protest against the government policies of President Ngo Dinh Diem sits calmly in flames. The protest on October 5, 1963 was the sixth that year. The Diem family, who were Catholics, including the fearsome wife of the President, Madame Nhu, referred to the fiery suicide protests as "barbecues."

ABOVE: Using a scale model in his demonstration, a Viet Cong commander briefs his soldiers before an attack which is due to be carried out in October 1964 on Ben Cau strategic hamlet near the provincial capital of Tay Ninh, about 60 miles (96 km) northwest of Saigon.

OPPOSITE TOP: U.S. sailors at Pearl Harbor watch a warship approach. The U.S. Navy's 7th Fleet had forces on the Yankee Station off of the coast of North Vietnam, while the Dixie Station to the south covered South Vietnam from 1965 to 1966.

LEFT: Cradling his 5.56mm (0.22 in.) Armalite rifle, a U.S. Army adviser on a patrol boat watches the river banks during an operation in June 1964.

the young president's emphasis on preparing the army (and other services) to fight in a counterinsurgency environment, his administration lacked not only a coherent operational strategy, but also a clear doctrine on how to fight in such wars.

The United States' conventional forces received an impressive boost in strength and capabilities, including the creation of special units to fight in a counterinsurgency environment. For the U.S. Army, this meant the creation of Special Forces, or the "Green Berets," named for their head covers. In Vietnam, the "Green Berets" organized the various highland tribes, particularly the Montagnards, into the Civilian Irregular Defense Groups (CIDGs). They also implemented self-defense and village development programs. By 1964, there were an estimated 60,000 Montagnard tribesmen serving in the CIDGs. The Green Berets also sponsored offensive guerrilla activities, border surveillance, and implemented control measures at key locations along the Laotian and Cambodian borders.

Kennedy and his successor, Lyndon B. Johnson, greatly expanded the American advisory effort from a total of 700 U.S. advisers in 1960, to a record 24,000 by 1964, as it became obvious that the ARVN was still incapable of defeating the insurgency. The dubious battlefield capability of the ARVN was clearly demonstrated in January 1963 at the battle of Ap Bac, where Viet Cong forces annihilated an ARVN battalion in a conventional battle.

As the strength and audacity of the Viet Cong grew, the South Vietnamese army,

GREEN BERETS
Jungle Warriors

They were the first in and some of the last out of the Vietnam War: U.S. Army Special Forces Group, otherwise known as the Green Berets. Formed in the early 1960s as a specialist behind-the-lines counterinsurgency unit, the Green Berets became legends in the folklore of the Vietnam War. By 1960, men of the 77th Special Forces Group were in the heart of Vietnam, training the local soldiers and civilians in defense techniques. History and the media tends to portray the Green Berets as hardened killers. They could be when needed, but often overlooked is the Green Beret spending months in a Vietnamese village building up trust and delivering medical care. They were intelligent, rounded individuals who came to know Vietnam and its people better than most. Yet they terrified the Viet Cong. Their snipers, assassins, and demolitions experts would disappear into the foliage, returning days later having visited death and violence upon the enemy who were bewildered by their elusive presence. Many Special Forces camps were isolated in remote corners of the Vietnamese/Laotian border or the Central Highlands, forgotten places now remembered as sites of incredible combat and bravery. The full extent of their impact on the conflict in Southeast Asia may never be known.

ABOVE: A shattered M151 light truck stands outside the Brinks Hotel. This particular hotel was known to have been taken over as U.S. Army bachelor officers' quarters in Saigon, and therefore became a potential target for the enemy. Two Viet Cong agents disguised as South Vietnamese soldiers had left a car bomb outside the building on December 24, 1964, which exploded, killing two Americans and wounding 65 South Vietnamese and Americans. Maxwell Taylor, General Westmoreland, and senior U.S. officials tried to persuade President Johnson to respond with retaliatory raids against North Vietnam, but the President refused and, in his reply to Taylor, said that he was considering committing U.S. combat troops to Vietnam.

despite the growing number of US advisers and influx of American weapons and equipment, became increasingly reluctant to respond to guerrilla outrages in the countryside. If anything, the battle of Ap Bac made the ARVN more cautious, much to the consternation of their American advisers. The Viet Cong meanwhile, concentrated on destroying strategic hamlets, showing that it was the Viet Cong, not Diem's forces, who controlled the countryside.

After a series of violent anti-Diem demonstrations, led primarily by Buddhist monks, a group of South Vietnamese generals decided that the president was a liability in the fight against the Viet Cong. With the encouragement and probable knowledge of the American government, Diem was ousted on November 1, 1963, and then brutally murdered. Kennedy himself was assassinated three weeks later, and the political turmoil that followed in Saigon emboldened the Viet Cong to launch more attacks against ARVN and, for

the first time, American advisers. North Vietnamese leaders decided to intensify the armed struggle against ARVN and further undermine the country's political authority before the United States could intervene militarily and rescue the situation.

As the South Vietnamese political and military situation deteriorated, a series of high level meetings between senior U.S. military and political officials began to explore ways in which to increase the military pressure against North Vietnam. While General Maxwell D. Taylor, the U.S. Ambassador to Saigon, advocated a direct air campaign against North Vietnam as the only means to pressure Hanoi from withdrawing from South Vietnam, others urged the Johnson administration to send a limited number of ground troops to guard U.S. air bases and other facilities. They also advanced the idea of using U.S. forces to repel any attack against the demilitarized zone which separated North and South Vietnam. This, they believed, would give

Saigon a breathing space to put its political and military houses in order, and would also enable it to carry out the war against the Viet Cong.

As the year developed, the likelihood of a direct confrontation between the United States and North Vietnam increased. This crisis came in August 1964 in the Gulf of Tonkin when North Vietnamese patrol boats attacked two U.S. naval vessels engaged in the surveillance of North Vietnam's coastal defenses. The U.S. response to these attacks was immediate and severe. Congress overwhelmingly passed the Southeast Asian Resolution or "Gulf of Tonkin Resolution," authorizing the president to use "all means necessary to protect American forces and to provide for the defense of the nation's allies in Southeast Asia." Considered by some in the administration as a loose declaration of war, this broad grant of authority encouraged Johnson to expand American military efforts within South Vietnam against North Vietnam and Southeast Asia.

TOP: The destroyer the USS *Turner Joy* which, with the *Maddox,* was conducting the De Soto operations off of the coast of North Vietnam when North Vietnamese torpedo boats attacked them in international waters, thus prompting the Tonkin Gulf Resolution of August 2, 1964. **BOTTOM:** A view of one of three North Vietnamese patrol boats, photographed from the USS *Maddox* during the attack on August 4, 1964. These actions prompted President Johnson's adimistration to commit ground troops to Vietnam.

1965

America Goes to War

In August 1964, the Gulf of Tonkin crisis precipitated more forceful and overt American involvement in Vietnam. The Viet Cong had stepped up its infiltration into the south and threatened the stability of the Saigon regime. Aided extensively by the North Vietnamese, and by the political instability in Saigon, the war in the countryside threatened to spill into the streets of the capital itself.

Sensing victory, the VC began to direct its attacks away from the Army of the Republic of Vietnam (ARVN) toward American targets, which included the large number of U.S. military advisers and installations. President Lyndon B. Johnson then ordered retaliatory air strikes against North Vietnam. On February 22, 1965, General William C. Westmoreland, Commander, U.S. Military Assistance Command, Vietnam (ComUSMACV), requested two marine battalions to guard the key U.S. air base facility at Da Nang. On March 8, 1965 the 9th Marine Expeditionary Brigade (MEB), with two of its three battalions, landed at Da Nang from the ships of the U.S. Navy's 7th Fleet and moved across Red Beach, while another battalion arrived from the island of Okinawa aboard U.S. Air Force C-130 transport aircraft. The 9th MEB then rapidly assumed operational control of the marine helicopter unit operating at Da Nang so that by the end of March 1965, nearly 5,000 U.S. Marines were installed in South Vietnam.

Even with the arrival of the 9th MEB, U.S. intervention in Vietnam was limited, principally by a directive from the Joint Chiefs of Staff stating that, "The U.S. Marine Force will not, repeat, will not, engage in day-to-day actions against the Viet Cong." The marines' sole responsibility was to defend the Da Nang air base, while overall defensive responsibility remained with the Army of the Republic of Vietnam (ARVN). This situation changed as attacks by the Viet Cong increased, and the ARVN proved unable to prevent further attacks on U.S. military personnel and facilities. These factors prompted a drastic change in the U.S. mission, from a role of static defense to one of active defense that included carrying the war to the Viet Cong.

In a series of high level conferences in Washington and Honolulu during April, U.S. defense and military authorities sought to prevent a further weakening of both the ARVN and the government of South Vietnam. Finally, the Joint Chiefs, along with Defense Secretary Robert McNamara permitted the marines to engage in offensive operations. By early May 1965, the marines had established two additional enclaves in South Vietnam, one at Chu Lai, 57 miles (92 km) south and another at Phu Bai, 30 miles (48 km) north of Da Nang. By this time the III Marine

---

ABOVE: Garlanded with flowers, Brigadier General F.J. Karch talks with local Vietnamese girls following the landing of U.S. Marines at Da Nang on March 8, 1965. Their mission was to guard the air base at Da Nang and so free the South Vietnamese troops of the garrison to conduct operations against the Viet Cong.

RIGHT: One of 19 Vietnamese civilian dead lies amongst the burning cars outside the U.S. Embassy in Saigon following an attack by the Viet Cong on March 30, 1965.

ABOVE RIGHT: On March 8, 1965 the USS *Henrico*, *Union* and *Vancouver* carrying the 9th Marine Expeditionary Brigade took up station 13,123 ft. (4,000 m) off Red Beach Two, north of Da Nang. First ashore was Battalion Landing Team (BLT) 3/9 which arrived on the beach at 9.18 a.m. Wearing full equipment and carrying their M14s, but also encumbered with life jackets, the Marines were met by sightseers, photographers, Vietnamese girls, and South Vietnamese Army officers. To General William Westmoreland's reported disgust, four U.S. Army soldiers who were attached to the South Vietnamese Army could not resist standing on the beach with a large sign saying "Welcome Gallant Marines." Western media, particularly the French, also found the rather contrived landing a source of amusement. Following the amphibious landing the rest of BLT 1/3 landed two hours later more conventionally at Da Nang Air Base. A day later, the first U.S. armor to be deployed in Vietnam, an M48A3 tank of the 3rd Marine Tank Battalion, landed. It would be followed a few days later by more tanks.

BELOW RIGHT: The naval and air base of Da Nang, the headquarters of the South Vietnamese Army's I Corps and 3rd Division. The Japanese used Da Nang during World War II when they occupied French Indochina. During the Vietnam War, the Americans would develop the port and build jet capable airfields. At various dates, it was the HQ of the U.S. III Marine Amphibious Force, the U.S. 1st and 3rd Marine Divisions, and later the U.S. Army's XXIV Corps. Following the fall of South Vietnam, in April 1975 Soviet ships and aircraft used the facilities.

Amphibious Force (III MAF) included headquarters and major elements of both the 3d Marine Division and the 1st Marine Air Wing. Further negotiations between MACV and Washington resulted in the deployment of additional marine and army forces to Vietnam. By the mid-summer of 1965, the marines at Da Nang had moved outside the confines of the airbase and had expanded their tactical area of responsibility (TAOR) to include the area south of the base. In August of 1965, the 7th Marine Regiment, the lead regiment of the 1st Marine Division, arrived in South Vietnam.

Even as the marines of the 9th MEB were landing at Da Nang, the U.S. Air Force had launched a series of punitive raids against the VC's main supply routes and facilities in North Vietnam. These raids, part of a campaign that became known collectively as "Rolling Thunder," had been designed to put maximum pressure on the North Vietnamese to end support for the Viet Cong. President Johnson also authorized the army to deploy 20,000 logistical troops to Southeast Asia. In order to protect U.S. advisers and bases in and around Saigon, the first major army combat unit, the 173rd

RIGHT: In a photograph which is framed by the barrel of an M14 rifle, U.S. Marines man an observation post (OP) in the mountains inland of Da Nang. The picture, taken on November 1, 1965, reflects the still surprisingly relaxed attitude that many troops had to the theater in the early stages of the Vietnam war. The men are either bareheaded or, like the radio operator, in a white T-shirt, and neither of them are wearing their web equipment. As the Viet Cong and North Vietnamese began to probe and the Marines began to patrol out from the perimeter, there were the first contacts and casualties, and attitudes changed from that point onward. A day after the picture was taken, Norman Morrison, a 32-year-old Quaker from Baltimore, immolated himself in front of the Pentagon. The public protests by civilians and veterans against U.S. involvement would increase year by year, and would see more fatalities in U.S. streets.

ABOVE: Holding his map, an officer of the South Vietnamese Army gets on the "horn" (the radio handset), and sends out a situation report as his patrol pauses next to a battered hut in a country village. The radio operator has his set concealed in a back pack, a move that makes him a less obvious target for snipers.

LEFT: Headed by a South Vietnamese Marine who is armed with a M1 Thompson sub machine-gun, a U.S. Adviser wades through flooded paddy fields in the Mekong Delta province of Dinh Tuong. The adviser, armed with an M1 Carbine, wears the carefully shaped but nonetheless slightly impractical green beret of the SVMC as a gesture of solidarity with the South Vietnamese Marines.

ROLLING THUNDER
The Thunder Rolls

Rolling Thunder was aptly named. Pity any nation that endures 800 tons of bombs whistling down onto them every single day for three years – one million tons of bombs in total. On February 13, 1965, President Johnson authorized the sustained bombing of North Vietnam as an attempt to bring Ho's nation to its knees, stop military supplies flowing south and allow the South to recover the military initiative. Actual bombing began on March 2. F-4 Phantoms, F-105 Thunderchiefs, and F-100 Super Sabres began systematically punching out road bridges, oil depots, military installations, and power stations. Resisting them were the MiGs of the North Vietnamese air force and one of the most sophisticated networks of SAM batteries – courtesy of China and the Soviet Union – the world had ever seen.

On October 31, 1968, Johnson stopped Rolling Thunder. Despite an annual increase in sorties – 304,000 in total – Rolling Thunder cost the U.S. $10 for every $1 of damage inflicted on the North. The Viet Cong and NVA were still as active – the North simply scattered its war efforts away into the countryside where the U.S. bombers couldn't pry. The terrorist situation in the South was getting worse, not better. Furthermore, the televised images of the world's greatest superpower pouring bombs into what amounted to a third world infrastructure caused national and international condemnation. So Rolling Thunder was stopped and negotiations opened. The world had learned a valuable lesson about the limits of military technology.

Airborne Brigade (Separate), was sent to South Vietnam. After fitting out on Okinawa, the paratroopers deployed in early May 1965, and moved quickly to secure the Bien Hoa Air Base, north of Saigon. With the arrival of the paratroopers, U.S. combat strength in Vietnam had risen to 50,000 soldiers, airmen, marines, and sailors. Even with the presence of an increasing number of American troops in Vietnam, U.S. forces had yet to engage the Viet Cong in full-scale combat.

General Westmoreland simply had to decide how to use the large numbers of American troops at his disposal. General Harold K. Johnson, the army Chief of Staff (and Westmoreland's boss) had wanted U.S. and South Vietnamese forces to blockade the Laotian panhandle to stop enemy infiltration from the north or counter a growing enemy threat in the central and northern provinces. This question of strategy remained unresolved as summer turned to fall in 1965. Some

BELOW: His helmet festooned with vegetation, a soldier of the 173rd Airborne Brigade carries the tripod for an M60 machine gun, ammunition box, and belted ammunition. The 173rd was the first major U.S. Army formation to be deployed in Vietnam, arriving for "temporary duty" in May 1965 and finally departing in August 1971. By the close of the war, the winged bayonet would have been replaced by a winged opium pipe in informal brigade insignia and 173rd Airborne Brigade would come to be known as "The Herd."

American military planners, most importantly Admiral Ulysses S.G. Sharp, Commander in Chief Pacific (CinCPac), and marine Lieutenant General Victor H. Krulak, told Westmoreland that population security and pacification would halt the deteriorating situation. Admiral Sharp and Lieutenant General Krulak both advocated a concentration of effort in coastal enclaves and around key urban centers and bases, such as Da Nang, Hue, and Saigon. U.S. forces would provide a security shield behind which the ARVN could expand its pacification zones and take the offensive against the Viet Cong. Supporting ARVN forces from their enclaves, American forces could then act as a mobile reactionary force.

It was this strategy that General Westmoreland followed during the initial months. He believed, however, that a "good defense is a good offense," and thus advocated the use of superior American firepower and the mobility of his forces in the remote, sparsely populated regions of South Vietnam to seek out and engage main force enemy units as they infiltrated into South Vietnam from the north; from bases in neutral Laos and Cambodia; and from secret bases in the south. Westmoreland and other senior U.S. military officials believed that unless U.S. ground forces were introduced into the fighting, the Saigon government would collapse.

The situation continued to deteriorate, however. While U.S. forces still required secure coastal logistical enclaves and base camps, the bulk of the military effort remained focused on the destruction of main force enemy units. Furthermore, MACV believed U.S. forces could act as an indirect shield for the pacification activities in the more heavily populated lowlands and Delta region. General Johnson continued to advocate an offensive across the Laotian panhandle to prevent enemy infiltration into South Vietnam. He believed that such an offensive-oriented strategy was a more direct and effective way to stop infiltration than the use of air power which had so far failed to stop the flow of enemy supplies and men heading south. While Johnson's plan contained many political and military problems, the idea was nonetheless resurrected periodically by General Westmoreland and others, although politicians repeatedly rejected it, believing it would widen rather than end the war. Thus, the military strategy pursued by the United States in Vietnam was essentially a compromise between the destruction of enemy main units and support of pacification in the countryside. Only in May 1970, with the intervention into neighboring Cambodia did the U.S. Army achieve, albeit temporarily, what it had long sought: the denial of sanctuaries to the enemy.

The American buildup continued into late 1965. Allied intelligence estimates of the total enemy strength in South Vietnam had risen

LEFT: Men of the 173rd Airborne Brigade armed with the new M16 rifle during a sweep north of Saigon near the town of Ben Cat in Binh Duong Province on September 28, 1965. The brigade based at Bien Hoa from May 1965 to October 1967 was commanded by Brigadier General Ellis W. Williamson. When committed to combat, it was the sole U.S. Pacific Command (USAPACOM) quick-reaction reserve.

BELOW: An empty 0.3 in. (7.62mm) cartridge case spins away ejected from an M14 rifle as a U.S. Marine engages a distant target. The man on the left has been spotting the target with binoculars. Both appear to be manning an observation post. The M14's weight – 11.2 lb. (5.1 kg) loaded – made it a poor weapon for the jungles of Vietnam.

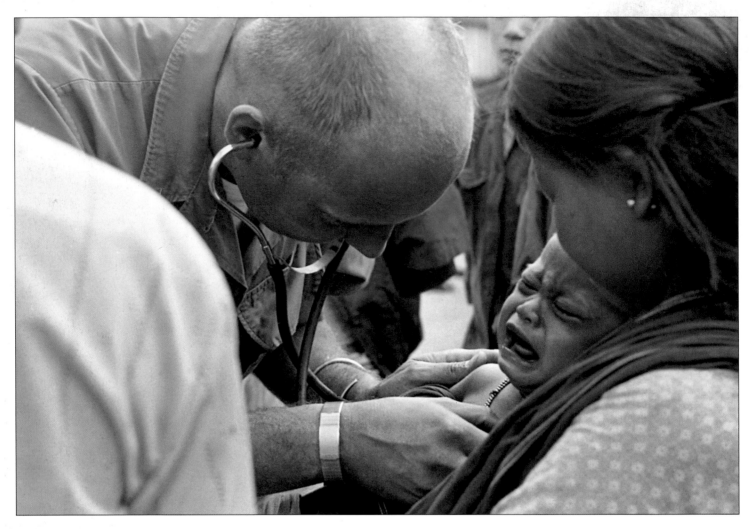

ABOVE: A U.S. Army doctor listens on his stethoscope to the lungs of a Vietnamese child during a Civic Aid Program (CAP). Adopting a concept from the British antiterrorist campaign in Malaya in the 1950s, assistance to the local community that included health care, sanitation, well construction, and agricultural aid hoped to win "the hearts and minds" of the rural population and wean them away from Communism.

RIGHT: A weary U.S. Marine glances up at the photographer on a hillside in Vietnam. Besides his helmet and fragmentation vest, the Marine has a heavily loaded jungle rucksack and a M18A1 Claymore antipersonnel mine in its green cotton bag slung around his neck.

from a possible 138,000 in March 1965 to over 226,000 by the end of the year. Intelligence reports from General Westmoreland's headquarters in Saigon estimated that there were more than 110,000 guerrillas, 39,000 political cadre, 18,000 combat support troops, and approximately 70,000 men organized into regular formations, including 19 regiments ranging from 2,000 to 2,500 men in strength. Seven included regular North Vietnamese Army (NVA) troops. Along with the establishment of a complex though unified command structure, General Westmoreland improved his logistical and support infrastructure for what was becoming a major American commitment.

On July 28, 1965, President Johnson announced plans to deploy additional combat units and to increase American military strength in South Vietnam to 175,000 by the end of the year. The newly activated 1st Cavalry (Air Mobile) Division, the 1st Brigade, 101st Airborne Division, and all

three brigades of the 1st Infantry Division constituted the first phase of the massive buildup that occurred during the summer and fall of 1965. The army found itself drawing on its strategic reserve in order to provide Vietnam-bound units with additional manpower.

Exacerbating the manpower problems was the adoption of the controversial one-year tour of duty (13 months) for soldiers in Vietnam. A large number of men were needed to sustain the rotational system, which often meant that combat soldiers returned to Vietnam after a very short break from duty, and this sapped morale. The one-year tour of duty also deprived units in South Vietnam of experienced leadership. Over time, the infusion of inexperienced NCOs and officers contributed to a host of morale problems that afflicted some army units.

In order to boost its combat strength, the army organized three additional infantry brigades, and reactivated the 9th Division. In the meantime, the 4th and 25th Infantry

BELOW: Seated on an inflatable raft, Cpl James Malone scans the banks of the Song Yen river as, along with members of a U.S. Marine reconnaissance patrol, he floats downstream near Da Nang. After the dank, green darkness of the jungle and life in trenches, the men have taken the opportunity to catch the sun. The problems of immersion foot from wet paddy fields and swamps as well as a huge variety of tropical diseases would beset U.S. servicemen during their tours in Vietnam.

Divisions were alerted for deployment to South Vietnam. With the exception of a brigade of the 25th, all of the combat units activated and alerted during the second half of 1965 deployed to South Vietnam during 1966 and 1967. In fact, by the end of 1965, U.S. military strength in South Vietnam had reached 184,000; a year later it stood at 385,000; and by the end of 1967, it approached 490,000. Army personnel accounted for nearly two-thirds of the total. Of the army's 18 divisions, seven were serving in South Vietnam at the end of 1967.

General Westmoreland planned to use his forces to blunt the enemy's spring-summer offensive. As new units arrived "in country," Westmoreland moved them into a defensive arc around Saigon and secured bases for the arrival of subsequent units. His initial aim was purely defensive – to prevent a further deterioration of the military situation, and to build up an infrastructure that could support the transition to an offensive, mobile campaign. As additional troops poured into Vietnam, including forces from Korea, Australia, and New Zealand, Westmoreland planned to seek out and defeat the enemy's core forces. This would give the ARVN time to re-train, re-fit, and re-equip. In a third and final stage, as enemy main forces were in the process of being driven

from their secret base camps, Westmoreland hoped to achieve victory by destroying those sanctuaries and shifting the weight of the military effort to pacification, thereby subduing the Viet Cong (and NVA) and driving them from throughout South Vietnam's countryside.

An ambitious plan, it was possible only if some political stability could be brought to South Vietnam. A final coup, which overthrew Ngo Dinh Diem in November 1963 and installed Lieutenant General Nguyen Van Thieu as president of South Vietnam, achieved as much stability as the country was ever to see.

Outside the political realm, Westmoreland's success also depended upon the Air Force's campaign against the North to reduce the infiltration of men and material. Westmoreland had hoped that the air campaign could dampen the intensity of combat in the South and force the VC and NVA troops to alter their strategic objectives. Without an effective air campaign, Westmoreland could not hope to stem the tide of the North's invasion.

Each phase of Westmoreland's plan depended on the other to succeed.

With Saigon as its center, General Westmoreland implemented his strategic concept starting in III and IV Corps area in the summer of 1965. His "concept of operations in the III Corps area had a clarity of design and purpose that was not always apparent elsewhere in Vietnam." Two years would pass before U.S. forces could maintain a security belt around the capital and at the same time attack the enemy's bases. But almost as soon as Westmoreland implemented this strategy in the summer and fall of 1965, U.S. soldiers encountered the frustrations in their day-to-day combat operations that were to characterize the war in Vietnam.

In June 1965, the 173rd Airborne Brigade and Australian infantrymen began combat operations in War Zone D, a longtime enemy base camp north of Saigon. Though diverted several times to other tasks, the brigade gained experience in conducting heliborne assaults and accustomed itself to the rigors of jungle

ABOVE: Watched by a "Butter Bar" – a U.S. Marine Corps 1st Lieutenant identifiable by his single gold rank bar – a South Vietnamese interrogator addresses an audience of Marines as he questions two Viet Cong suspects. It may have been a training exercise since the Marines appear relaxed and the "prisoners," who seem curious rather than cowed, are correctly tagged with the capture labels stating who they are and where and when they were taken. The interrogator holds a Chicom stick grenade, presumably found in their village, which had a TNT filling, weighed 2.75 lb. (1.25 kg), and had a four-second delay. Interrogations in rural areas could be far less humane than that shown here.

BELOW: Bowed under their bulging duffelbags, U.S. Army reinforcements from the 18th Infantry plod ashore past a welcoming honor guard early in the Vietnam War. As the war progressed, men arriving in theater would be flown via Hawaii and might be met by outgoing troops who had finished their 365-day tour. Young and nervous, their confidence would not be increased by ironic and sometimes cruel jokes from men happy to have survived to the "Wake Up" from the bad dream of Vietnam and their return to "the World."

operations. It also established a pattern of operations that became familiar to U.S. troops: airmobile assaults, often conducted in the wake of "arc lights" or B-52 bomber air strikes against tactical targets; extensive patroling, episodic contacts with the Viet Cong such as sniping and skirmishes; and withdrawal after a few days' stay in the enemy's territory. In early November, the airborne soldiers uncovered evidence of the enemy's recent and hasty departure from the area.

On November 8, moving deeper into War Zone D, the 173rd Airborne Brigade came across its first significant and sustained resistance. A multi-battalion Viet Cong force attacked at close quarters and forced the Americans into a tight defensive perimeter. Hand-to-hand combat ensued as the enemy tried to "hug" American soldiers in order to

prevent the GIs from using their supporting air and artillery fire. Unable to prepare a landing zone to receive reinforcements or to evacuate casualties, the beleaguered Americans withstood repeated enemy assaults. At nightfall, the Viet Cong withdrew under the cover of darkness.

Like the 173rd Airborne Brigade, the 1st Infantry Division initially divided its efforts. In addition to securing its base camps north of Saigon, the division helped South Vietnamese forces to clear an area west of the capital in the vicinity of Cu Chi in Hau Nghia Province. Reacting to reports of enemy troop concentrations, units of the division launched a series of operations in the fall of 1965 and early 1966 that entailed forays into the Ho Bo and Boi Loi woods, the Michelin Rubber Plantation, and the Rung Sat swamps in Tay Ninh Province.

ABOVE: With the point man armed with a 0.35 in. (9mm) Owen sub machine-gun, a patrol of B Company, 1st Battalion, Royal Australian Regiment (RAR) moves through jungle in War Zone D on December 7, 1965. Australian conscripts served a one-year tour in Vietnam, but within a battalion that was rotated as a formed unit after 365 days.

LEFT: Candidates for the South Vietnamese Army Airborne School at camp Hoang Hoa Tham near Tan Son Nhut Air Base, Saigon practise in a mock up of a C-47. Vietnamese paratroopers had served in the French Colonial forces and jumped at Die Bien Phu. The South Vietnamese Airborne rose from Brigade strength in the mid-1960s to a Division in the mid-1970s.

ABOVE: A McDonnell Douglas A-4 Skyhawk on the carrier USS *Enterprise* is prepared for takeoff. The deployment of the world's first nuclear powered aircraft carrier to the South China Sea, costing over $450 million to construct, was seen by some people as the commitment of the United States to winning the war. By others, the use of the huge 92,200 ton carrier that could sustain 12 days of intensive air activities before it required any replenishment was a gross overkill. When the *Enterprise* docked at the naval base at Sasebo in Japan in 1968, there were both antiwar and anti nuclear protests.

For most of 1965, the focus of Westmoreland's "search and destroy" strategy centered upon I and II Corps in the Central Highlands. Spearheaded by at least three NVA regiments, Communist forces mounted a strong offensive in South Vietnam's Central Highlands during the summer of 1965, overrunning border camps and besieging several district towns, threatening to cut the nation in two. To meet the danger, General Westmoreland introduced the newly organized army airmobile division, the 1st Cavalry Division, with its large contingent of helicopters, directly into the Highlands. Some of his superiors in Hawaii and Washington opposed this direct strategy, preferring to secure the coastal enclaves instead. Despite Westmoreland's repeated contention that this

enclave strategy "made poor use of U.S. mobility and firepower," he was unable to overcome the fear of an American Dien Bien Phu if a unit in the Central Highlands should be isolated and cut off from the sea.

General Westmoreland addressed two enemy threats in the Central Highlands. Local insurgents menaced populated areas along the coastal plain, while enemy main force units continued to push forward in the Western Highlands. Between the two regions stretched the piedmont, a transitional area in whose valleys and defiles the VC had established an elaborate complex of interlocking bunkers, logistical, and training facilities. Extension of the Ho Chi Minh Trail ran from the Highlands through the piedmont to the coast, enabling enemy units and supplies to move from

ABOVE: U.S. Navy armorers check 750 lb. (340 kg) bombs below deck aboard a carrier. The U.S. Navy and Air Force deployed a huge range or ordnance, including high drag Snakeye bombs that were designed for low-level delivery. Cluster munitions were used against surface to air missile (SAM) and antiaircraft (AA) gun sites as well as specialist anti-radiation missiles.

LEFT: Smoke and dust rises from a strike by McDonnell Douglas F-4 Phantom IIs. The Phantom carried various bomb loads, including 18 750 lb. (340 kg) bombs, 11 150 U.S. gallon napalm bombs, and four Bullpup missiles and 15 rockets.

province to province. To be effective, allied operations on the coast had to uproot local units living among the population and eradicate the enemy base areas along the coast.

Despite the fact that the Central Highlands were sparsely populated and had limited economic value, they held a strategic importance that was equal to, and perhaps greater than, the coastal enclaves established by the marines. Around the key Highland towns – Pleiku, Kontum, Ban Me Thuot, and Da Lat – South Vietnamese and U.S. forces had created enclaves. Allied forces, protected by the few roads that traversed the Highlands, screened the border and reinforced outposts and Montagnard settlements from which the indigenous South Vietnamese forces and U.S. Army Special Forces or "Green Berets" sought to detect enemy cross-border movements and to strengthen tribal resistance to the Communists. Such border posts and tribal camps, rather than major towns, were often the object of enemy attacks. Combined with road interdiction, these attacks enabled the Communists to disperse the limited number of defenders and to discourage the maintenance of outposts. Such actions served a larger strategic objective. The enemy planned to develop the Highlands into a major base area

ABOVE: Men of the U.S. 1st Infantry Division "Big Red One" hunch against the rotor blast from UH-1B helicopters as they come in to land on a road at Lai Khi on November 19, 1965. The man in the foreground carries the tins of a C Ration pack in a sock tied to his webbing harness.
RIGHT: The thunderous destruction of a B-52 "Arc Light" bombing run. Using the Combat Skyspot radar guidance system, the bombers could be directed onto a target and attack it from above cloud cover.
FAR RIGHT: A U.S. Marine M60 machine gun crew take aim. The M60 and the M16 rifle were unpopular weapons when introduced, both being prone to some malfunctions.

to mount or support operations in other areas and where Communist forces could mass. A Communist-dominated Highlands would enable the VC and NVA to shift the weight of his operations to any part of South Vietnam. Challenging American forces had become the principal objective of the leadership in Hanoi, who saw their plans to undermine Saigon's military resistance thwarted by U.S. intervention. Any victory, large or small, against American forces they believed might prevent a major build-up of U.S. forces and weaken Washington's resolve to continue the war.

With its 435 helicopters the 1st Air Cavalry Division (Airmobile) moved into this hornet's nest in September and established its main base at An Khe, an ARVN stronghold that straddled Route 19, halfway between the port of Qui Nhon and the highland city of Pleiku. At An Khe, the 1st Cavalry could help keep open the vital east-west road from the coast to the Highlands and could pivot between the Highlands and the coastal districts, where the Viet Cong had made deep inroads. Meanwhile, the 1st Brigade, 101st Airborne Division, had begun operations in the rugged Song Con Valley, approximately 18 miles (29 km) from An Khe. Here, on September 18, one battalion of the 101st

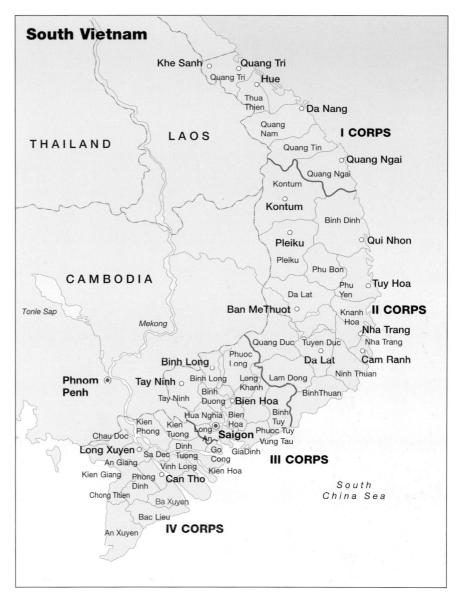

PREVIOUS PAGE: A South Vietnamese grandmother with her daughter and three grandchildren as they attempt to escape across a river near Qui Nhon on September 7, 1965 during an air strike called in on their village by U.S. Marines. The Japanese photographer, Kyoichi Sawada, won the 1966 Pulitzer Prize for this picture, but was killed in Laos in October 1970.

LEFT: A machine gunner cradles his M60 as a U.S. Army formation move through a burning village after a "search and destroy" mission. U.S. forces would move into Viet Cong controlled areas to seek combat with them and destroy buildings and food stocks. While fine as a theory, it made for some disturbing photographs and became a potential recruiting program for unpoliticized men and women who saw their homes and livelihoods destroyed.

BELOW LEFT: Sgt Arnold Jaudon of the 172nd Missile Bn hands psychological warfare leaflets to 1st Lt James Paris which were dropped from a UH-1B helicopter over Binh Duong Province in support of a sweep by the 173rd Airborne Brigade. Leaflets might be safe passes for Viet Cong wishing to surrender, or intended to persuade villagers to turn in the Viet Cong's political and military leaders to the Saigon government.

RIGHT: A "Tunnel Rat" from the 1st Infantry Division squeezes into a suspected Viet Cong tunnel system near Kanh Van during operations on October 2, 1965. "Tunnel Rats" were small soldiers who, armed with a pistol and a flashlight, entered the narrow tunnels dug in the hard, laterite clay and searched them for prisoners and documents. This man wears a respirator since CS gas has been pumped into the tunnel.

GENERAL WESTMORELAND
"Westy"

He seemed to be what was needed: a tough man who had seen combat in World War II and Korea, a man who liked to think big, root 'em out, and destroy 'em. General William Westmoreland took over as commander of Military Assistance Command Vietnam on June 20, 1946 and brought with him a new vision of how the war should be conducted: by attrition. The tactic was simple. Impose such heavy losses on the enemy's men and materiel that they can no longer sustain the war effort. Pass the 'break-even point' as he called it, and the North would collapse.

By 1967, he believed he had reached that point. He told a meeting of the National Press Club: "I am absolutely certain that, whereas in 1965 the enemy was winning, today he is certainly losing. The enemy's hopes are bankrupt."

The Tet Offensive proved him wrong. The major invasion of the South by the North in January 1968 showed an enemy still strong and prepared to take bold initiatives. Tet was massively defeated by the U.S. forces and the Viet Cong almost entirely destroyed, but U.S. public opinion found it hard to believe that it occurred at all after three years of Westmoreland's attritional warfare. Johnson was in a presidential election year, and had to be seen to act. Westmoreland was brought home and on July 3, 1968, General Creighton Abrams took over the MACV.

Westmoreland has since argued that the military were fettered by Washington politics, and that they could have won if they had gone on the offensive. Perhaps he is right. Yet his adversaries were fighting a war that thrived on U.S. political turbulence, and the world would not have tolerated the total crushing of North Vietnam by the U.S.

Airborne Division ran into heavy fire from an enemy force in a tree line around its landing zone. Four helicopters were lost and three company commanders killed; while reinforcements could not be landed due to the heavy enemy fire. As the VC once again employed their "hugging tactics," the Americans could not use close air support, artillery fire, or helicopter gunships without endangering its own troops. Nonetheless, that is exactly what occurred as U.S. commanders called in fire support from B-52s, artillery, helicopter gunships, and other supporting fire almost on top of the two forces. The cause of this heavy resistance was evident the next morning as the Americans discovered that they had landed in the midst of a heavily bunkered enemy base.

LEFT: Accompanied by a South Vietnamese Army interpreter, a U.S. Army patrol wades a river in the foothills of the Annamite mountain chain that ran most the length of North and South Vietnam. The mountains provided a secure and remote location for the Viet Cong and later the North Vietnamese Regulars.
ABOVE: A 19-year-old Viet Cong woman, Ho Thi Bay, waits to be taken to an interrogation center after being captured by the 101st Airborne in the Central Highlands on 22 September.

This fight had many of the hallmarks of the Highland battles that were to come. The Americans had only limited intelligence on the constantly shifting VC and, despite their overwhelming firepower, lacked an effective means to tackle the VC's close-quarter hugging tactics. Nor could they cope with the VC's habit of simply disappearing into the jungle when hard-pressed; for all their technical superiority, American troops could not fight an invisible enemy. For their part, the VC underestimated the accuracy and intensity of the supporting fire and the willingness of U.S. commanders to call it down on their own positions, which resulted in high Communist casualties. However, the VC realized that their hugging tactics were effective, but at Song Con Valley the Americans demonstrated that they would exploit their overwhelming advantage in firepower despite the risk to their own troops.

Within a month of the battle of Song Con, the 1st Cavalry received its baptism of fire in one of the most controversial battles of the Vietnam War. After elements of the NVA attacked a Special Forces camp at Plei Mei,

ABOVE: Smoke rises from a Landing Zone (LZ) near Bien Hoa in August 1965 as it is "prepped" – prepared by rocket machine gun fire from Huey Gunships prior to an insertion (landing) – by men of the 173rd Airborne Brigade so that the operation at the LZ does not become a "hot insertion." The tactics of Airmobile operations also included making dummy landings to draw off Viet Cong forces.

RIGHT: Johnny Cooper, a Special Forces Sergeant, instructs a group of Montagnard tribesmen in how to operate the 2.36 in. (60mm) Mortar M19. Cooper is shown flanked by two interpreters, one translating the instructions into Vietnamese, the other from Vietnamese into one of the dialects of the Montagnard mountain tribes.

General Westmoreland decided to initiate an offensive aimed at destroying the enemy regiments in the vicinity of the camp. In the battle of the Ia Drang Valley, named for a small river that flowed through the area of operations, the 1st Cavalry Division pursued and fought the 32d, 33d, and 66th North Vietnamese regiments for 35 days, until the enemy retreated into Cambodia.

The 1st Brigade established company bases from which patrols searched for enemy forces. For several days neither the ground patrols nor aerial reconnaissance found any trace of the enemy. On November 4, 1965 air observers discovered a regimental aid station several miles west of the Plei Mei base camp. Reacting quickly to catch the enemy off guard, General Westmoreland ordered his sky soldiers into action. Several heliborne infantry platoons converged on the site. Hovering above the area in their UH-1B "Huey" gun-

ships, the American soldiers came under heavy enemy machinegun and rocket fire from a battalion of NVA regulars. Despite the fact that they were operating beyond the effective range of artillery support, the American infantrymen engaged the enemy in what became a furious firefight.

Instead of withdrawing as in the past, the 1st Cavalry maintained the pressure on the enemy, concentrating their efforts in the vicinity of the Chu Pong Massif, a mountain near the Cambodian border that was an enemy base. Viet Cong and NVA forces were given little respite as the sky soldiers harried and ambushed them. The enemy responded in kind, as they conducted a nighttime attack on an American patrol at Landing Zone (LZ) Mary.

This proved to be only a prelude, however, as the heaviest fighting was yet to occur. As the division began the second stage of its search and destroy mission, enemy forces

BELOW: Soaked by rain in a monsoon downpour, a U.S. Marine Corps M60 machine gunner opens fire while his companion shouts to the men who are following. The Marines favored fragmentation vests (Flak vests) on operations, and while the Army helicopter pilots and AFV (Armoured Fighting Vehicle) crews wore fragmentation vests, they were less common with infantry in the field. The M1955 Armor-Body Fragmentation Protective was bulky and hot, hence the machine gunner's T-shirt, but it was effective in saving lives. In order to reduce the pressure from the load on his back, the M60 gunner in this photograph has padded out the back of his pack with a thick sheet of foam rubber.

LEFT: After making an amphibious landing, U.S. Marines lie awaiting orders for the next phase of an operation. Servicemen and women the world over have suffered from the stop-and-start character of operations, coining the ironic phrase "Hurry up and wait."

RIGHT: Smoke billows away from a U.S. Army M101A1 105mm (4.1 in.) Howitzer in action in its sand-bagged weapons pit. An experienced crew of eight could fire eight rounds in 10 minutes and 100 rounds in the course of an hour. The gun weighed 4,900 lb. (2,222 kg) and could be lifted into remote locations by the CH-47 helicopter and emplaced in three minutes. During the Vietnam War, artillery was used in a variety of roles, including "H and I" (Harassment and Interdiction missions), where shells were fired in a random pattern against tracks and axes in Viet Cong controlled areas during the night, intended to disrupt the movement of men and supplies in hostile areas. Determined North Vietnamese Army attacks forced American and Australian gunners to fire XM-546 "Beehive" shells, as the attacks threatened to overwhelm the gun pits.

BELOW RIGHT: Using his Zippo lighter, a U.S. soldier sets fire to the thatch of a hut during a sweep through a Viet Cong controlled area. The destruction of structures in "Search and Destroy" missions might make military sense, but on TV in the U.S. and elsewhere, looked like vandalism when undertaken by men on the ground, rather than remotely from the air.

FOLLOWING PAGE: A U.S. Marine Corps M60 machine gun crew with the weapon set up on its sustained fire tripod. The mount allowed the crew to engage targets out to 3,970 ft. (1,800 m).

began to withdraw from their positions in the Chu Pong. Using heavy CH-47 helicopters, the air cavalrymen airlifted 105mm howitzers into position and created a series of interlocking fire support bases and LZs at the base of the Chu Pong Mountain. Landing Zone X-Ray was at the center of a vicious battle on November 14, 1965 between three U.S. battalions and elements of two NVA regiments. Having withstood repeated enemy mortar and infantry attacks, the Americans called on all available firepower, leaving 600 NVA and VC dead and

79 Americans. One out of every three soldiers of the 2nd Battalion, 7th Cavalry had been killed. However, the enemy had been forced to retire from the battlefield, beaten back by the overwhelming weight of fire.

The fighting during the Ia Drang campaign "previewed the tactics of U.S. ground forces in the war." Helicopters were used in large numbers for the first time, a factor that enabled the 1st Cavalry to wage a relentless campaign over difficult terrain that consisted primarily of jungles and steep ridge lines and

LBJ

It was Vietnam that brought down the 36th President of the United States. None could have possibly imagined that the Lyndon Baines Johnson born into a poor family in south Texas in 1908, would eventually become a figure that inspired such conflicting emotions in his countrymen.

Johnson succeeded to the presidency with the assassination – in Texas – of John F. Kennedy in 1963: not the most auspicious circumstances in which to assume power. Yet in the midst of national mourning, Johnson was seen as a safe pair of hands. Early civil rights, welfare and tax legislation won him general approval from the populace, and consequently in 1964 an enormous 15 million US votes kept him in the White House. He continued in a reformist mood, hoping to create the 'Great Society' within the US borders. Yet the civil legislation he passed – including dramatic anti-racism laws and Medicare provision – began to disappear in the shadows of the looming Vietnam War.

Kennedy had led the US into Vietnam during his term of office, but Johnson led them into a war. In 1964, following dubious reports of North Vietnamese attacks on US Navy ships, he signed the Gulf of Tonkin resolution which committed the US to armed protection of South Vietnam and its own forces. Johnson later acknowledged his despair at this step, noting that he "was bound to be crucified either way I moved." Johnson recalled how, if he went to war, his program of domestic reform would be in tatters. Yet if he stayed away from the war, and let South Vietnam fall to the communists, he would be perceived as a 'coward.' Painfully conscious of the popularity of Kennedy's anti-communist ghost, Johnson fatefully chose the former path. By the end of 1964 there were 23,000 US troops in Vietnam. 1965 took the number to 60,000, 1966 to 268,000. By 1967, no less than 500,000 U.S. troops were in Vietnam and the escalation seemed never-ending. Rising death tolls and a lack of convincing victories started to suck the popularity out of Johnson's presidency with a vengeance. Students and civil rights leaders turned against him, and the enormous expense of maintaining the U.S. war machine so far from home crippled the administration.

By 1968 Johnson had had enough of what he called "this bitch of a war." He shocked the U.S. public by appearing live on television and announcing that he would be seeking peace talks with the North Vietnamese, as well as reducing the bombing of North Vietnam. On a personal

note, he added that he would not be seeking nor would he accept the Democratic party's candidacy in the 1968 presidential election.

Thus Lyndon Johnson left the White House, and passed the conduct of the war into the hands of Richard Nixon. Entanglement in the war he had been so loath to embark on had shattered his dream of fundamentally reforming American society, and taken a tremendous personal toll on the President himself. He returned home to peaceful Texas a man broken by the stresses of attempting the impossible task of winning an unwinnable war. He died of a heart attack less than a week before an agreement was signed that took the U.S. out of the Vietnam War. The loss of what Johnson might have achieved without the drain of Vietnam may be one of war's greatest tragedies.

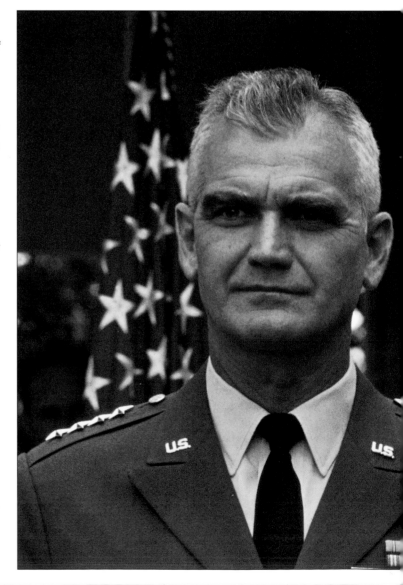

TOP LEFT: Vice President Lyndon Johnson listens as the youthful President John Kennedy is in the process of addressing Congress from the podium. Lyndon Johnson succeeded Kennedy as President following the young man's assassination on November 22, 1963. It remains one of the great imponderables of the history of the Vietnam War whether or not Kennedy – who had committed relatively small numbers of troops to the theater – would have escalated the conflict and increased the numbers of troops he was prepared to commit, had he not been assassinated. After the assassination, Johnson retained many of Kennedy's advisers and adopted the policy of "flexible response" to North Vietnam which they recommended in the U.S. military and diplomatic operations in Southeast Asia. The Americans were haunted by the "Domino Theory" that stated that if South Vietnam became Communist, it would follow that Laos, Cambodia, Thailand, and eventually Malaysia and Indonesia would fall like dominoes to Communist aggression. This fear was proved correct in the case of Vietnam, Laos, and Cambodia. It is part of the tragedy of Johnson's legacy that his commitment to social change in the United States and the creation of the "Great Society" – which has changed both the status and conditions of African Americans forever – has been overshadowed by the Vietnam War and the divisive effect it was to have on the country.

BELOW LEFT: The General and the President: Lyndon Johnson, in conversation with General William "Westy" Westmoreland. A veteran of World War II and Korea, Westmoreland assumed command of the Military Assistance Command Vietnam (MACVC) on June 20, 1964. Westmoreland had defeated the Viet Cong, by their own admission, by the time he handed command over to General Abrams in 1968. However, the war in Vietnam was by then no longer an insurgency, but a cross border invasion of the country by the North.

ABOVE: U.S. soldiers watch a UH-1B "Huey" as it lifts off from a jungle Landing Zone (LZ). The helicopter which, with the distinctive sound of the beat of its twin rotor blades that epitomized the Vietnam War, was a remarkable workhorse in the theater. It carried troops to combat, lifted casualties almost from the front line and, with rockets and machine guns, became flying artillery. The sliding doors on each side of the fuselage ensured that troops could exit and enter quickly. Veterans recalled that when bullets flew horizontally when leaving a hot LZ, it was more bearable than when they came through the floor of the helicopter.
LEFT: A distinctly slack U.S. Army patrol moves through thick nipa palm jungle. The men are bunched up, an easy target, and one man is smoking a cigarette. The alien smell of the tobacco smoke would be very distinctive in the jungle.

mountains. The 1st Cavalry Division's victory in the Ia Drang likewise confirmed General Westmoreland's decision to pursue a war of attrition as opposed to the marines' insistence on pacification. In fact, U.S. commanders in Vietnam later sought to "repeat the victory in the Ia Drang" with their emphasis on bringing massive amounts of firepower to bear on the enemy.

The North Vietnamese leaders drew a different conclusion. Generals such as General Vo Nguyen Giap called for an increased emphasis on guerrilla tactics. Other North Vietnamese field commanders, led by General Nguyen Chi Thanh, saw the battles in the Ia Drang Valley as a confirmation of the value of the "belt clinging" operations as a means of minimizing the effectiveness of American firepower.

The 1st Cavalry's victory in the Ia Drang Valley confirmed that the NVA and VC could be defeated in battle if detected. Moreover, the American soldier proved to be just as adept at fighting in the jungle as his NVA counterpart. Interestingly U.S. and NVA military officials drew the same conclusions from the fighting in the Ia Drang: that it would be in the conventional sphere that victory in the Vietnam War would be decided, and not in the pacification campaign being waged by the marines and other U.S. Army elements in I Corps.

By the summer of 1965, over 25,000 marines were deployed in Vietnam under the command of Lieutenant General Lewis W. Walt. Initially they were limited to defending Da Nang and other air facilities, but on July 30, 1965 General Westmoreland informed Lieutenant General Walt that he had a "free hand" in the conduct of military operations in the I Corps Tactical Zone (ICTZ). Westmoreland emphasized that he was to "undertake larger offensive operations at greater distances from base areas" in conjunction with ARVN and South Vietnamese marine units.

The first was Operation Starlite (August 18–24, 1965), the first multi-battalion, regimental-sized operation to be conducted by American forces since the Korean War.

Marines and ARVN troops conducted a classic amphibious assault on the beaches southeast of the Van Tuong Peninsula which were occupied by the 1st Viet Cong Regiment. In a devastating battle, allied troops decimated the VC regiment and prevented an attack on the Chu Lai air facility. It was proof of allied superiority in conventional battle born out of tactical and operational flexibility.

Despite the severity of Operations Starlite and the follow-up, Operation Piranha, the Viet

ABOVE: A 105mm (4.1 in.) M101A1 howitzer which has been underslung below a Boeing-Vertol CH47 Chinook is transported to a fire base deep in the jungle. The versatile Chinook, which was first deployed in Vietnam in September 1968, could carry up to 28,000 lb. (12,700 kg) on its external cargo hook, and was an ideal transporter for heavy weapons.

ABOVE: U.S. Marine Corporal R.G. Grice of Raleigh, North Carolina, writes a defiant and ironic message to the Viet Cong on the side of a 1102 lb. (500 kg) bomb with a stick of chalk. Though images such as this one were something of a visual cliché from the world of warfare, photographers were always keen to take photographs of armorers in the process of "personalizing" their bombs, which was a common practice that dated back to World War II, and would reappear in the Gulf War five decades later in 1991.

RIGHT: A soldier of the First Cavalry Division carries a trussed and blindfolded Viet Cong prisoner over his shoulder through the long grass of a hillside and to captivity. The First Cavalry – which had become an airmobile force and was designated Air Cavalry – took part in the Battle of Ia Drang in November 1965, the first major encounter with Regular North Vietnamese Army troops. As the war progressed, the division would eventually fight in all the four corps zones in Vietnam.

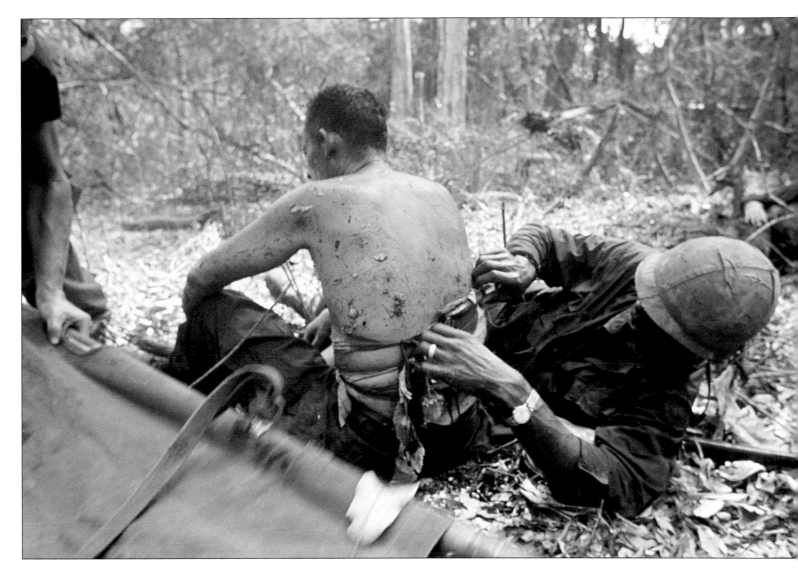

Cong did not remain idle. They mounted two small-scale – but deadly – raids on U.S. installations on October 27, managing to destroy or damage over 50 aircraft, and prompting a retaliatory amphibious operation by the marines.

In conjunction with the South Vietnamese marines, General Walt initiated Operation Blue Marlin, a two-phase amphibious plan. A combined force of American and South Vietnamese marines then landed at Tam Ky, 18 miles (29 km) north of Chu Lai and swept inland across Highway One, the main north-south artery mounted in tanks and armored personnel carriers. Phase II of Operation Blue Marlin began almost immediately. On November 16, another marine force landed south of Hoi An, 25 miles (40 km) south of Da Nang, and in a three-day operation, successfully engaged the enemy and killed 25 Viet Cong while capturing 15 of them.

Despite the onset of the monsoon in November 1965, the Viet Cong continued to launch spoiling raids against what enemy commanders considered "rewarding targets," intending to wear down the ARVN and the marines rather than seize territory. They concluded that they could not match the firepower and mobility of the Americans, but determined to strike at U.S. forces wherever possible.

At the battle for Thach Tru on November 22–23, it became clear that regular North Vietnamese troops had entered the fighting. Robert McNamara and General Westmoreland realized that with the introduction of an estimated nine regiments of regular PAVN troops (People's Army of Vietnam, or NVA), the emphasis should be on the destruction of such enemy units, although General Walt still asserted that the real war still lay in separating the villagers from the influence of the Viet Cong.

ABOVE: An Army Corpsman checks a field dressing on a man wounded by fragments before he is placed on a stretcher prior to evacuation. For surgeons, the men who arrived in theater might be suffering from terrible traumatic injuries but, though often exhausted and dehydrated, they were fit. If surgery could save them, they had a good chance of recovery. **FOLLOWING PAGE:** A South Vietnamese Army machine gunner shoulders the 23 lb. (10.48 kg) of an M60 before moving out on patrol. Initially the United States had equipped South Vietnam with weapons surplus from World War II, but by the mid-1960s, were sending modern weapons like the M61 fragmentation grenade and the 66mm (2.6 in.) Light Antitank Weapon.

LEFT: John Seltz of Berkley, California waves a red flag in front of a locomotive in an attempt to prevent the troop train leaving the station in August 24, 1965. The troops on the train interviewed subsequently by a TV crew expressed incomprehension at the protest; opposition to the war was still a minority activity. The locomotive driver was not deterred by the protestors who jumped clear as he rolled forward.

BELOW: Marine Sergeant William McCauley uses a M2A1-7 flame thrower to burn off vegetation on the perimeter of Da Nang airbase so that the Viet Cong could not find cover there. This flame thrower held 4 U.S. gallons (15 litres) of fuel and loaded weighed between 65 lb. (29.4 kg) and 51 lb. (23.2 kg). It had a range of 131–164 ft. (40–50 m) with thickened fuel and was able to fire a continuous burst for ten seconds.

ABOVE: U.S. Marines move toward their Sikorsky H-34D Seahorse helicopters. The USMC retained the H-34 long after the U.S. Army had adopted the UH-1B and almost made a perverse virtue out of the fact that as Marines, they had to wage war with 1950s technology in a 1960s war.

RIGHT: Empty cases are ejected as a U.S. Marine Corps M60 machine gunner opens fire during Operation Starlite. While firing a fully automatic 0.3 in. (7.62mm) caliber machine gun from the shoulder might not be very accurate, prone in the grass, the gunner would be unable to see his target.

NEXT PAGE: U.S. Marines urge Viet Cong prisoners up a hill near Da Nang. The prisoners were stripped in the search for hidden weapons and their hands were tied. The picture did little to help the international image of the U.S. armed forces in Vietnam.

In fact, even as the marines and soldiers carried out major conventional operations against the Viet Cong and North Vietnamese, the leathernecks of III MAF conducted a massive pacification program. This program soon began to show immediate results. From September 1 until mid-October 1965, certain elements of the 9th Marines conducted the first part of Operation Golden Fleece. They were charged with the responsibility of patrolling villages in order to prevent the VC from benefiting from the rice harvest.

Another aspect of the emphasis on counterinsurgency operations by the marines was the introduction of the combined action platoons (otherwise known as CAPs). These were platoons which had been intensively trained in counterinsurgency techniques and Vietnamese customs. A squad of 12 15 marines assigned to one of five Popular Force platoons lived in a village, training the inhabitants in tactics and communications, and winning over the "hearts and minds" of the South Vietnamese villagers.

By the end of 1965, just nine months after landing in Vietnam, U.S. troops had scored impressive results against a determined and ruthless adversary. Despite the fact that, at almost every turn, U.S. forces had defeated the VC and their NVA supporters in battle, the war was far from won. While General Westmoreland favored "search and destroy" operations, the marines, particularly Lieutenant General Walt and his superiors in Honolulu (Admiral Sharp and Lieutenant General Victor H. Krulak), continued to press for a larger effort devoted toward pacification of the countryside. While Walt agreed that this approach meant slower results, he argued that by separating the VC from the people in the countryside, the government in Saigon would be able to gain enough time to rebuild, reorganize, and shoulder the main burden of the war.

In the end, the Joint Chiefs of Staff sided with General Westmoreland and provided him with more manpower for an even larger conventional effort, in the meantime continuing to pay lip service to their pacification efforts.

ROBERT McNAMARA
The Statistics Man

Robert Strange McNamara always seemed destined for great things. A graduate of Berkeley and Harvard, President of the Ford Motor Company, and then Secretary of Defense under both Kennedy and Johnson, he was dynamic, persuasive, and energetic, as well as defiant and someone who did not suffer fools gladly. In Kennedy's words he was "the most dangerous man in the Cabinet."

Though one of the most influential advisers during the Vietnam War because of his organizational talents, his flaw was to subscribe to Vietnam as a numbers game. His calculation was, if we have X military capability and the enemy has Y, then if X is the greater force, we will win. This gained him the name 'the statistics man.' During the early years of the Vietnam conflict, he was one of the most passionate advocates of escalation. As early as 1963 he was proclaiming the war won. But the war took its toll on many people's beliefs, not least McNamara. By late 1967 he recommended to Johnson that the JCS (Joint Chiefs of Staff) plans for further expansion of the war be rejected. In its place, he sought negotiations and U.S. troops withdrawals. With these recommendations, he moved into the post of President of the World Bank. Later, McNamara accepted that he and his advisers had been blind to the realities of fighting the Vietnam War.

ABOVE: Aboard a carrier U.S. Navy and Marine Corps pilots discuss a contact with North Vietnamese fighters. As North Vietnamese fighters in their MiG-17, MiG-19, and MiG-21s often lacked experience, many of these encounters were one sided.

RIGHT: U.S. Marines watch as village women in South Vietnam husk their maize crop. Life in rural Vietnam was a mixture of subsistence farming with cash crops, like rice, sold to the cities.

FAR RIGHT: Sailors aboard the USS *Ticonderoga* dance with an artist from the Bob Hope Christmas show. The shows, organized by the Hollywood actor and comedian Bob Hope, had entertained serviceman far from home, both in World War II and Korea.

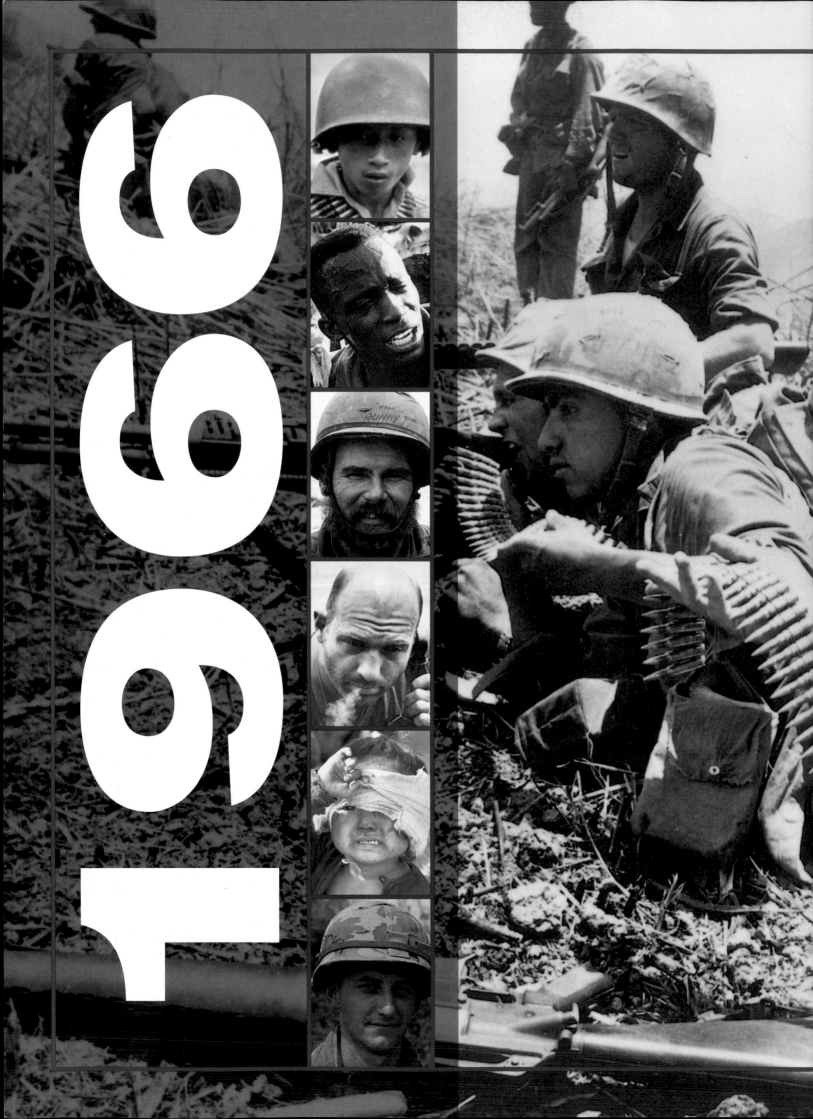

1969

A Year of Hard Fighting

As 1965 ended, the U.S. buildup in South Vietnam continued with little sign of any significant gains against the Viet Cong and North Vietnamese Army's infrastructure. By the end of 1965, General Westmoreland had achieved all of the objectives established in Phase I of his three-phased strategy for winning the war in Vietnam: the establishment of coastal enclaves as well as fire support bases, with U.S. troops acting as a reserve and rapid reaction force to secure the population and countryside from further exploitation by the VC; and to halt the successes enjoyed until then by the VC and the NVA. As U.S. and ARVN forces met and defeated the enemy forces in the field, MACV concentrated on improving its support and logistical base to allow a further buildup of U.S. combat forces.

After the fighting in the Ia Drang Valley, Westmoreland believed that the enemy might attempt to re-enter South Vietnam as the 1st Cavalry re-fitted after its first major combat with VC and NVA forces. With Phase I of his strategy firmly in place, General Westmoreland sought to implement Phase II, which called for more combat troops to seek out and destroy the VC and NVA in the field. As the Johnson administration promised more troops from the United States, Westmoreland hoped to vigorously pursue the enemy forces and separate them from the populace, while allowing the ARVN to assume a more active role in the pacification campaign. One part of General Westmoreland's strategy included capitalizing on the gains made in the Ia Drang and at Pleiku. Nevertheless MACV continued to husband its resources until all of the means were at hand to defeat the enemy.

As discussions with the Joint Chiefs of Staff continued, Westmoreland asked to deploy the army's elite 25th Infantry Division, "Tropic Lightning," to "fill in the gap in his combat power for the fighting that loomed ahead." In Hawaii as the Pacific Command's contingency force, the 25th Infantry Division had trained for years in jungle warfare and counter-guerrilla tactics. When the 3rd Brigade arrived in Vietnam, General Westmoreland sent it immediately to the Central Highlands, and within a month it had joined elements of the 1st Cavalry Division preparing to screen the border with Cambodia against further enemy infiltration. The 25th's 2nd Brigade was sent to Cu Chi, northwest of Saigon, to act as a blocking force against the enemy's attempt at seizing the capital. Finally, in April 1966, the 1st Brigade was sent to join its sister unit at Cu Chi, increasing the maneuver elements of Major General Frederick C. Weyand, the commanding general of the division, to six maneuver battalions and three cavalry troops (two armored and one airmobile).

ABOVE: At the close of a patrol, men of the 1st Air Cavalry walk away from their UH-1B helicopter. The yellow badge of the "1st Air Cav" can clearly be seen on the nose.
RIGHT: The intense concentration shows on the face of a U.S. Marine during a patrol in heavy secondary jungle near Tam Ky on August 22, 1966 during Operation Colorado.

ABOVE: A Catholic Padre from the U.S. Army in the process of celebrating Mass in the field. He has adapted well to the limitations of his environment by using the bonnet of an M151 as his altar. As in all wars, some men found spiritual solace and support from religion; for many others, the trauma of the death which was happening all around them and fear of their own deaths only served to destroy their faith. For many young Americans, conscription, the tour in Vietnam, and rejection by many of their peers when they returned to the United States remained a bitter, lasting memory that no amount of religious faith could prepare them for or protect them against.

While the U.S. Army positioned itself for renewed fighting in the Highlands, the VC and NVA continued to hit U.S. and ARVN forces in the region. In fact, despite the calm that followed the Ia Drang fighting, the North Vietnamese left their opponents in no doubt of their intention to infiltrate and challenge American forces along the borders of the Central Highlands. Throughout January and into early February 1966, NVA and VC forces conducted a series of hit-and-run operations near Cu Chi, in the Central Highlands, and in the A Shau Valley, where they overran a Special Forces camp in the remote northwest corner of I Corps. This gave them an excellent base from which to stage further attacks on U.S. forces and a logistical base to support troops filtering further down into the Mekong Delta region south of Saigon, as well as the coastal enclaves of Chu Lai and Da Nang.

Taking advantage of the availability of its large fleet of helicopters, army commanders in II Corps, for instance, sought to engage the enemy as close to the Cambodian border as possible, and were quick to respond to threats to Special Forces camps in the Highlands. Operations near the border were essential to Westmoreland's efforts to keep main force enemy units as far away as possible from heavily populated areas.

For Hanoi's strategists, however, there was a link between strategic and operational objectives in the Highlands and along the coastal regions. Here, as in the Delta and coastal areas, the VC and NVA remained a constant military threat as they sought to divert allied forces from efforts at pacification. Like the chronic shifting of units from the areas surrounding Saigon to the war zone in III Corps, the frequent movement of American troops between the coastal enclaves and border in II Corps reflected the Communist desire to remove allied military pressure from its guerrilla and local forces. In short, Hanoi's strategy to cope with U.S. forces was the same as that employed by the Vietminh against the French and by the Communist forces in 1964 and 1965 against the South Vietnamese Army.

For the next two years (1966–67) the 1st Cavalry Division, with the infantrymen of the 25th Division, would spend the bulk of their efforts fighting the Viet Cong and NVA units in the coastal plains and in the piedmont valleys of Binh Dinh Province. Here, the enemy had established an elaborate infrastructure of logistical and support facilities, and for the most part, the 1st Cavalry Division operated in the Bong Son plain and adjacent hills, from where enemy units reinforced the village guerrillas who gathered in taxes, food, and recruits. As in the Central Highlands area, the 1st Cavalry exploited its air mobility, using helicopters to establish positions in the upper reaches of the valleys. They flushed out the enemy from his hiding places and drove him toward the coast, where American, South Vietnamese, and South Korean forces held blocking positions.

When trapped, the enemy was pulverized from the ground and the air in classic "hammer and anvil" operations practiced on a large scale, with the natural barrier of the coastal plain and the South China Sea forming the killing zone. This operation became known as the Binh Dinh Pacification campaign.

For 42 days elements of the 1st Cavalry Airmobile Division searched the An Lao and Kim Son valleys, pursuing enemy units that had been surprised and routed from the Bong Son plain. Meanwhile, marine forces in neighboring Quang Ngai Province in southern I Corps barred the enemy's escape routes to the north. Both the VC and NVA units evaded the Americans, while the peasants, free from intimidation and exploitation by the VC, fled to safe areas established by ARVN and Civil Affairs administrators. This exodus significantly weakened the Viet Cong's infrastructure and directed a heavy blow at their prestige.

LEFT: A CH-47 Chinook helicopter delivers a cargo net load of ammunition to a heavily sandbagged fire base. Below it, a soldier from the 105mm (4.1 in.) Howitzer battery signals to the crew of the hovering helicopter how far the load is off the ground.

BELOW: During a training exercise, a soldier of the 25th Infantry Division "Tropic Lightning" falls into a pit dug on a specially prepared jungle trail. In reality, the bottom of the hole would have been covered with bamboo stakes sharpened to a fine point and hardened in a fire. Some would penetrate the soldier's foot; others would be positioned so that they trapped his leg. Panji stakes were coated with human or animal excrement to ensure an infection in the wound.

LEFT: Slung with a bandolier of M-16 magazines, a U.S. Marine from Force Recon confers with comrades on the edge of a grassy LZ. The man with his back to the camera has the USMC M61 first aid kit attached to his belt.

BELOW: Men of the U.S. Army Special Forces team, or "Green Berets," pose outside a fortified camp on the South Vietnam/ Cambodia border covering the infiltration routes along the Ho Chi Minh Trail. The arrival of the Fifth Special Forces Group in South Vietnam in October 1964 accelerated their construction. They expanded to 42,000 CIDG and Regional Force/Popular Force – "Ruffpuffs" – controlled by the Special Forces.

The air cavalrymen, having failed to locate the fleeing enemy in the An Lao valley, assaulted another enemy base area, a group of valleys and ridges southwest of the Bong Son plain known as the "Crow's Foot" or "Eagle Claw." Here, some army units tried to dislodge the enemy from upland bases, while other units established blocking positions at the "toe" of each valley, where it found an outlet to the surrounding plain. In a six-week campaign, U.S. and ARVN units killed over 1,300 VC and NVA soldiers. Once again, as in the Ia Drang, enemy forces in northern Binh Dinh Province were temporarily thrown off balance. Beyond this, however, the long term effects of the U.S. operation remained unclear. The 1st Cavalry did not stay in one area long enough to exploit its success. Whether the Saigon government could muster its forces decisively and utilize them effectively to provide local security while re-asserting (or in some cases merely establishing) its authority remained unclear.

General Westmoreland gave the enemy no respite. He ordered another attack without the extensive preparatory reconnaissance that often alerted the enemy to the start of an offensive. Once again, U.S. forces attacked a surprised enemy in the Bong Son area, but soon lost contact. The 1st Cavalry then attacked a VC and NVA build up near the Vinh Thanh Special Forces Camp, where the Green Berets had been monitoring the "Oregon Trail", an enemy infiltration corridor that passed through the Vinh Thanh valley from the Highlands to the coast.

After a brief diversion to forestall an enemy attack in the Central Highlands, the 1st Cavalry returned to Binh Dinh Province in September 1966 where the situation remained virtually unchanged since its brief departure

BELOW: An elderly South Vietnamese and his wife wait nervously outside their home as it is searched by U.S. soldiers. The kneeling soldier, who has a 66mm LAW slung across his back, guards the house armed with a 40mm M79 grenade launcher, known to soldiers as a "Blooper" because of the distinctive sound it made when it was fired. The M79 was first issued to the U.S. Army in 1961 and when production ceased ten years later, some 350,000 had been manufactured by the pistol company, Colt. The M79 weighed 6.5 lb. (2.95 kg) loaded and could fire nearly 20 different types of ammunition, including smoke, HE, illumination, and even airburst.

OPERATION MARKET TIME

The Communist war effort in the South needed constant feeding from the North. Apart from the Ho Chi Minh Trail, or across the DMZ, supplies were often sent by trawler down the Vietnamese coastline before slipping into the winding waterways of the Mekong Delta. On February 16, 1965, Task Force 71 was established to stop this.

Task Force 71 was a special anti-infiltration unit. Using shallow-draft fast patrol boats laden with firepower, their job was to stop and search all the boats moving down the coastline, and interdict VC shipping. In August of the same year, the Task Force 71 was relabeled as Task Force 115, and made part of Operation Market Time, one of the most successful naval interdiction operations in recent history. Over 600 boats were used, enough to scour the seas from the Gulf of Tonkin to the Gulf of Thailand, all backed by U.S. Navy surveillance aircraft such as the P-2 Neptune and P-3 Orion. The net was tight and few could slip through. Suspect ships were stopped and boarded. If all was in order, they were sent on their way. Yet if VC supplies were on board, either the ship surrendered or would face cannon, grenade launchers, machine guns, and rockets hammering into its structure. The result? Between 1965 and 1972, 48 out of 50 North Vietnamese trawlers trying to reach the South with supplies were either captured or destroyed.

earlier in the summer. In the absence of the American soldiers, the Viet Cong had successfully reestablished themselves in the area. For the remainder of 1966 and into 1967, the 1st Cavalry devoted most of its efforts at pacification and sealing off the border to the north of Binh Dinh Province. As the marines of the III MAF found themselves fighting along the DMZ, army units were increasingly sent to southern I Corps during 1967, replacing marine units in operations similar to those carried out in Binh Dinh Province.

In addition to the offensive operations carried out by the 1st Cavalry against the enemy's main forces, U.S. Army units in Binh Dinh Province worked in close coordination with South Vietnamese police, Regional (RF) and Popular Forces (PF), and ARVN to help Saigon gain an ideological foothold in the villages that the Viet Cong once dominated and exploited. Like the marines in I Corps, the 1st Cavalry Division adopted a number of techniques in support of their pacification efforts. Army units participated in cordon and search operations whereby airmobile forces seized positions around a hamlet or village at dawn to prevent the escape of local forces or cadres, while South Vietnamese authorities undertook a methodical house-to-house search. Specially trained pacification cadres also established the rudiments of a functioning basic government as well providing medical and other such services. Other units conducted checkpoints along highways, participated in "snatch" operations or established surprise roadblocks along major roadways and highways.

Despite having been mauled by the American and allied forces during Operation Irving, the VC and NVA sought to demonstrate that it was far from conquered. They wanted a military victory that would demonstrate to the local populace their presence and power. One such attack was aimed at Landing Zone Bird, an artillery base on the Bong Son plain. Taking advantage of the Christmas truce of 1966, enemy units moved into position and mounted a ferocious attack as soon as the truce ended. Despite the fact that the VC and NVA managed to overrun portions of the base,

LEFT: Blindfolded with adhesive tape, and still wearing his webbing, a captured Viet Cong soldier is dragged away from the bunker he was responsible for defending. His captors are two soldiers of the U.S. 1st Cavalry Division. The man was taken prisoner on January 29 near LZ 4 in the agressively named Operation Masher, which took place during a sweep to the north of Bong Son. The Viet Cong prisoner wears the black "uniform" of the Viet Cong – in reality these are rural working clothes – while his ChiCom chest pouch webbing has the smaller pouches designed to carry SKS rifle rounds. Upon capture, these prisoners were invariably blindfolded. This was done to prevent them from seeing anything which could later be of intelligence value, and also to make their escape even harder. As the result of political pressure, operation codenames were gradually changed during the Vietnam War, and they went from less obviously belligerent names like "Masher" to neutral, even harmless sounding ones with mythical resonance, like "Pegasus."

the attack floundered when the artillerymen leveled their guns at point blank range loaded with "Beehive" antipersonnel rounds.

In spite of the war of maneuver that took place in the region of the I Field Force, the allies could not concentrate their efforts every-where as they had at Binh Dinh during Operation Irving. Throughout 1966 and into 1967, the Americans engaged in a constant search for tactical concepts and techniques, not only to maximize their firepower and mobility, but also to compensate for the constraints in

ABOVE: Mountain tribesman taken during a sweep wait under guard. They will either be flown out of the area or, if their identities can be established over the radio, released. Though identity cards were issued by the South Vietnamese government, they might be lost or destroyed by the Viet Cong. Without formal identification a young male, particularly if he did not have callused peasant's hands, was immediately suspect.

LEFT: A Douglas A-1 Skyraider prepares for takeoff aboard the USS *Oriskany* in September 1966. The Skyraider had a maximum speed of 318 mph. (512 kmh). However, it was its low speed and ability to carry up to 7,936 lb. (3,600 kg) of external ordnance and deliver it accurately which made it a popular choice in the war.

time, distance, difficult terrain, and problems with the inviolable border. Here the war was fought primarily to prevent regular NVA units entering South Vietnam and to erode their combat strength once contact was made. In fact, it could be said that both the VC and NVA pursued a strategy that closely resembled Westmoreland's objective of military confrontation, seeking to weaken the fighting forces and sap the will of their opponent through a war of attrition. Both sides sought a military victory in order to convince the other

of the futility of continuing the war. For the North Vietnamese, however, the war in the Highlands had the additional purpose of diverting allied troops from other areas where pacification threatened to weaken their hold on the rural population. Thus, of all the factors influencing operations in the Highlands, the most significant may well have been the strength and success of the pacification efforts throughout South Vietnam.

For the Americans, the most difficult problem was to locate the enemy. During this period,

ABOVE: While he cools off, a U.S. Army radio operator listens out on the handset of his AN/PRC-25 radio known to soldiers as the "Prick 25." The headset of the radio is clipped onto the soldier's helmet. The soldier wears a colored bandana and has a tiger claw attached to the bead chain of his identity tags ("Dog Tags.") U.S. servicemen in the field sported an increasingly casual style as the war progressed.

LEFT: Dust and grass is kicked up as a UH-1B lifts off as South Vietnamese and U.S. Army soldiers take cover after being inserted into a hot LZ on February 11 during Operation Eagle's Claw in Thu Xuan. The men wear their basic M1956/67 web gear with a poncho strapped to the bottom of the combat pack "Butt Pack," suggesting this is a short patrol or small scale operation within the larger Eagle's Claw operation.
RIGHT: With his head swathed in a field dressing, a Vietnamese child wounded during operations near Dong Tre on June 22 gazes up at a frightening and hostile world. He was injured during Operation Nathan Hale when U.S. forces attacked Viet Cong positions 230 miles (370 km) northeast of Saigon.

ABOVE: Vietnamese suspects are questioned by gun-toting U.S. troops. This picture clearly shows the difference in physical stature between the well-fed Americans and the under-nourished Vietnamese, whether Viet Cong or ordinary civilians.

both VC and NVA units menaced Special Forces camps, trying to lure "allied forces into situations where he [the VC] held the military advantage." Army operations during 1966 in the Highlands were characterized by wide-ranging, often futile searches, punctuated by sporadic but intense battles fought usually at the enemy's initiative.

During the first few months of 1966, the enemy forces maintained a low profile in the Highlands. In May, however, a significant concentration appeared in Pleiku and Kontum Provinces. In response to this buildup, MACV rushed the 1st Brigade of the 101st Airborne Division, (the reserve element of the I Field Force) first to Pleiku and later to Dak To, a Civilian Irregular Defense Group (CIDG) camp in northern Kontum Province in order to assist a beleaguered ARVN force at the nearby government outpost at Toumorong. Although the 24th North Vietnamese Regiment had surrounded Toumorong, American and ARVN troops secured the road to Dak To, and succeeded in evacuating the ARVN troops trapped there. One battalion of the 101st Airborne remained inside the camp while another company of the same outfit occupied an exposed defensive position in the jungle a short distance beyond. On the night of June 6, 1966 a large NVA forces launched repeated assaults on this isolated company. Facing imminent disaster, the commander called in air strikes on his own position to stop the enemy's human wave attacks. Reinforcements arrived the next

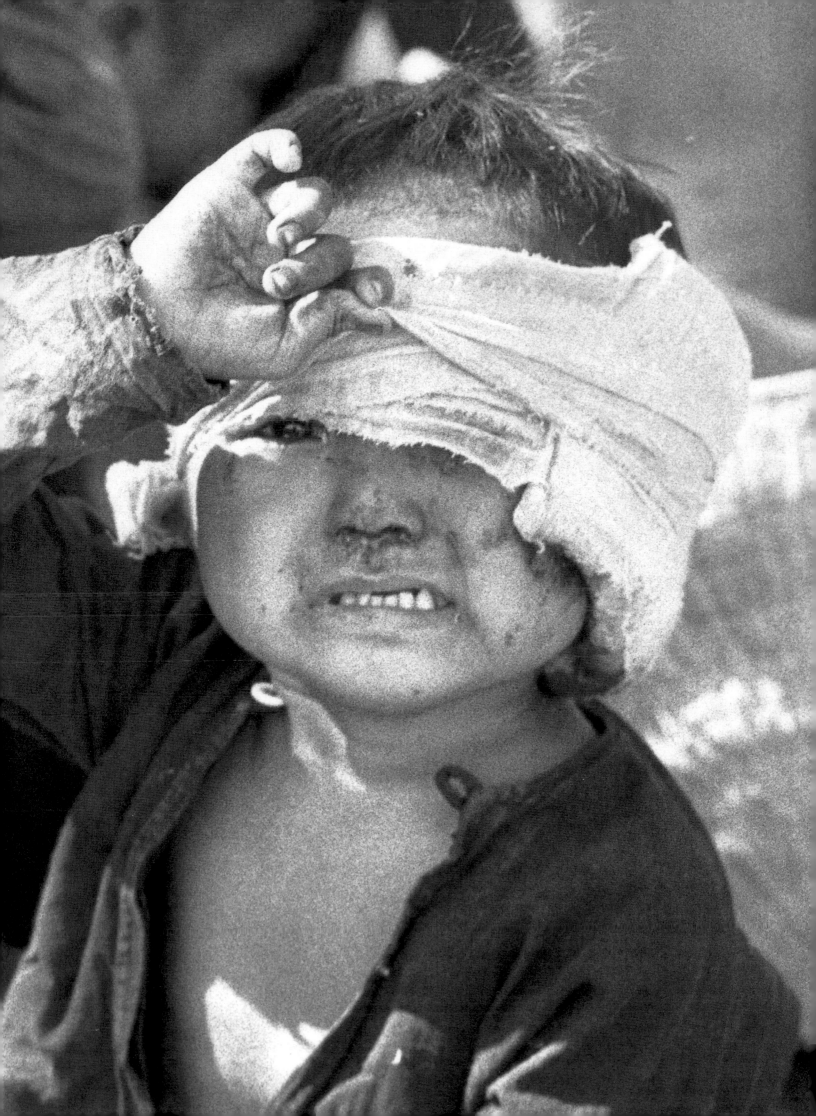

ABOVE : Teenage rebels during the Buddhist insurrection in Panang with machine gun ammunition and an M26A1 fragmentation grenade and a smoke grenade. The religion of Vietnam was a nominally 70 percent Buddhist but, reflecting its colonial past, the Catholics held many positions of power within the state. When Prime Minister Nguyen Cao Ky failed to hold elections and dismissed General Nguyen Chanh Thi, an ally of the Buddhist leader Thich Tri Quang, revolts took place in Hue and Da Nang.

ABOVE RIGHT: A South Vietnamese soldier observes a road in Hue. Ky's attempt to crush the revolt by force ended in failure and he was forced to negotiate with the Buddhists, hindering the "nation building" championed by the U.S.

morning as additional elements of the brigade were choppered to the battlefield to pursue and trap the North Vietnamese. As the American soldiers fought to close off the escape routes of the retreating enemy, Air Force B-52 bombers launched several arc light strikes while F-105 Thunderchiefs, F-100 Super Sabres, and F-4 Phantoms flew repeated sorties against enemy positions. By June 20, enemy resistance had ended, and the NVA regiments hurriedly left the battlefield, leaving behind them many dead as they fled into neighboring Laos.

Despite the fact that the Viet Cong and NVA's offensive into Kontum Province was halted, the siege at Toumorong was only one phase of the enemy's summer offensive in the Highlands. Suspecting that NVA forces meant to return to the Ia Drang, General Westmoreland dispatched the 3rd Brigade, 25th Infantry Division into the Ia Drang Valley in May 1966. Employing the French-inspired "ink blot" approach, MACV divided the area

ABOVE: Prime Minister Ky with Lieutenant General Le Nguyen Khang, Commandant of the Vietnam Marine Corps, talking to Catholic priests and government officials. Ky survived the Buddhist revolt partly because of the loss of support for the Buddhists by dissident elements of the military. He continued as Prime Minister until 1967, then became Vice-President of South Vietnam. Born at Son Tay near Hanoi, he fought in the French Vietnamese National Army raised to fight against the Vietminh. He served as an infantry officer and later as a pilot training in France and Algeria, marked out by his flamboyant style.
LEFT: A young Vietnamese boy glances back nervously as he paints an anti-government slogan on a wall in Saigon during the Buddhist revolt.

"Tunnel Rats" at Cu Chi

You needed to have strong nerves and a subdued imagination to be a "Tunnel Rat" in Cu Chi district. Armed with only a pistol and a flashlight, U.S. troops would go on their own into vast networks of Viet Cong underground tunnels – most little wider than a human body – and try to kill the enemy. Cu Chi was particularly notorious. It was an area 25 miles (40 km) from Saigon. Beneath this district snaked over 100 miles (160 km) of Viet Cong tunnels, used for storage, hiding troops and guerrillas, ambushes, and travelling in safety between villages. U.S. patrols would suddenly find an ambush bursting upon them as if from nowhere, and then puzzle over the disappearance of the attackers seemingly into thin air. Don't think of simple dirt tunnels. Here were ventilation shafts and storage bunkers, underwater entrances for the ultimate concealed access, space enough to hide, feed, and sleep thousands of men. Even the communist Central Office for South Vietnam had its residence in these tunnels for a time. The entrances and approaches were protected by poisoned spikes and booby traps, and the hapless tunnel rat could find himself shot in the groin by a waiting VC as he lowered himself into the hole (the VC would often not kill the soldier as the U.S. rescue attempt would allow the VC to make his escape). If he did make it into the bunker, he would have to crawl on hands and knees, sweat dripping from his face, pistol held out ready in front of him, and prepare for violent, claustrophobic action at every swing of his torch beam.

In an attempt to destroy Cu Chi, B-52 bombers pounded the area with high explosive. Yet they had little effect on the tunnel system so deep underground – after all, they were designed for the specific purpose of resisting air raids and the thick, laterite soil simply soaked up the concussions. So the Viet Cong used the tunnels to good effect. In 1968, they launched huge strikes on Saigon from beneath the ground in tandem with the Tet offensive. As a last resort, the U.S. almost wiped the Cu Chi area from the face of the earth. Bulldozers mashed down the foliage and ploughed over the earth to collapse the tunnels and imprison or crush those inside. This had a positive military result but a negative social result: Vietnamese people had to watch the U.S. destroy hundreds of square miles of their habitat. Such actions brought new recruits into the communist cause and built resentment against the U.S. presence. This was the story of the war.

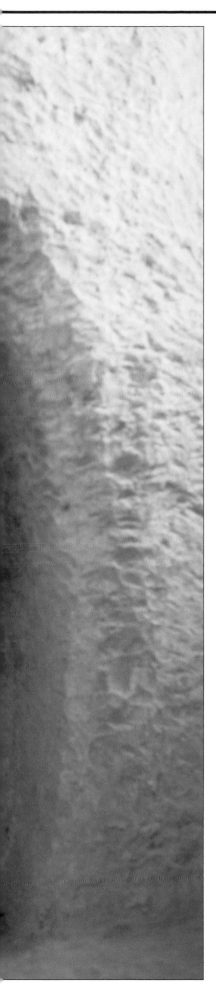

ABOVE: Dressed in T-Shirt and combat trousers, a sweating "Tunnel Rat" emerges from a complex. Since the tunnels were dug to accommodate the smaller physique of a Vietnamese, only small and courageous U.S. soldiers could investigate them. The only weapon that a Tunnel Rat could effectively use was a hand gun like a Colt .45. Fire fights were very noisy and at very short ranges.
LEFT: A Vietnamese inside a chamber within a tunnel complex. Underground, the Viet Cong constructed field hospitals, munitions factories, shelters, and headquarters. They also built into the tunnels traps, dead ends, and obstacles to stop or slow down any Tunnel Rat who might be bold enough to enter.
RIGHT: U.S. Army Engineers of the 73rd Engineer Company lower C4 Plastic Explosives into a tunnel. The charges are in old M18A1 Claymore Mine bags, each fitted with a short length of detonating cord, and will be linked up underground to make up a larger charge emplaced along the length of the tunnels. However, despite these explosive attacks, many tunnel complexes proved very difficult to destroy, let alone locate.

ABOVE U.S. Marine Lt Colonel Victor Ohanesian, a Chinese linguist, listens to a Viet Cong (VC) radio net during Operation Allegheny near Da Nang in September. The VC operators who were co-ordinating a sniper attack were speaking in Chinese for extra security. When they switched back to Vietnamese, Lt Droung Due Dhuy, the South Vietnamese Army interpreter attached to the Marines, took over. Using captured U.S. Army radios, the North Vietnamese and VC were able to monitor U.S. operations and sometimes evade sweeps against their positions.

into "checkerboard" squares with the brigade methodically searching each square. Small units of American infantry set out on long patrols and conducted ambushes for several days at a time without resupply by helicopter. Westmoreland wanted to avoid revealing the location of where the soldiers of the 25th Division would strike. After soldiers patrolled their sector of the "checkerboard," they then "leapfrogged" by helicopter into another sector. Though the GIs encountered sporadic contact, they nonetheless killed a large number of enemy soldiers. One of the more significant firefights occurred at the base of the Chu Pong Massif, scene of the earlier Ia Drang fighting. In May, soldiers of the 25th engaged in a protracted, running battle with both VC and NVA

units. Hoping to prevent the enemy from escaping into Cambodia, General Westmoreland appealed to Washington for permission to pursue the fleeing enemy across the border. Unfortunately, the Johnson administration, fearing intervention by China and the wrath of world and domestic opinion for widening the war, refused to grant MACV permission to cross the border areas.

The fighting along the Chu Pong had confirmed what American intelligence had been telling Westmoreland: that a sizable enemy force had returned to South Vietnam and, as during 1965, threatened the outposts at Plei Me and Duc Co. To meet the renewed threat, I Field Force sent additional army units to Pleiku, and launched a new operation under the 1st Cavalry's operational direction. The action followed the familiar pattern of extensive helicopter lifts, establishment of patrol bases, and intermittent contact with an enemy who usually avoided American forces. When the Communists elected to fight, they preferred to occupy the high ground. Many times, the soldiers of the I Field Force found it difficult to dislodge the enemy from their hilltop bunkers. Nonetheless, tactical air and artillery support proved the difference and by the end of the campaign that fall, the Americans counted 500 enemy dead.

Border battles continued, however, some of them very sharp. When the enemy forces appeared in strength around the CIDG camp at Plei Djering in October, elements of the 4th Infantry and 1st Cavalry Division rapidly reinforced the camps, clashing with the enemy in firefights during the entire month into November of 1966. As North Vietnamese forces withdrew through the Plei Trap Valley, the 1st Brigade, 101st Airborne ("Screaming

RIGHT: Soaked and thoroughly exhausted, a young Viet Cong soldier captured by U.S. Marines during an operation in Long An Province south of Saigon. The original caption said that he had attempted to escape by plunging into a river; however, he might have attempted to evade capture by hiding underwater against a riverbank and breathing through his mouth by using a hollow reed.

BELOW: A U.S. Army radio operator holds a Chinese Type 56 assault rifle as its former owner is escorted to a prisoner of war pen during a search and clear operation. It was uncommon to capture an unwounded VC with a weapon. The Type 56, like the weapon it was copied from, the Russian AK47, was a much prized, rugged and reliable capture.

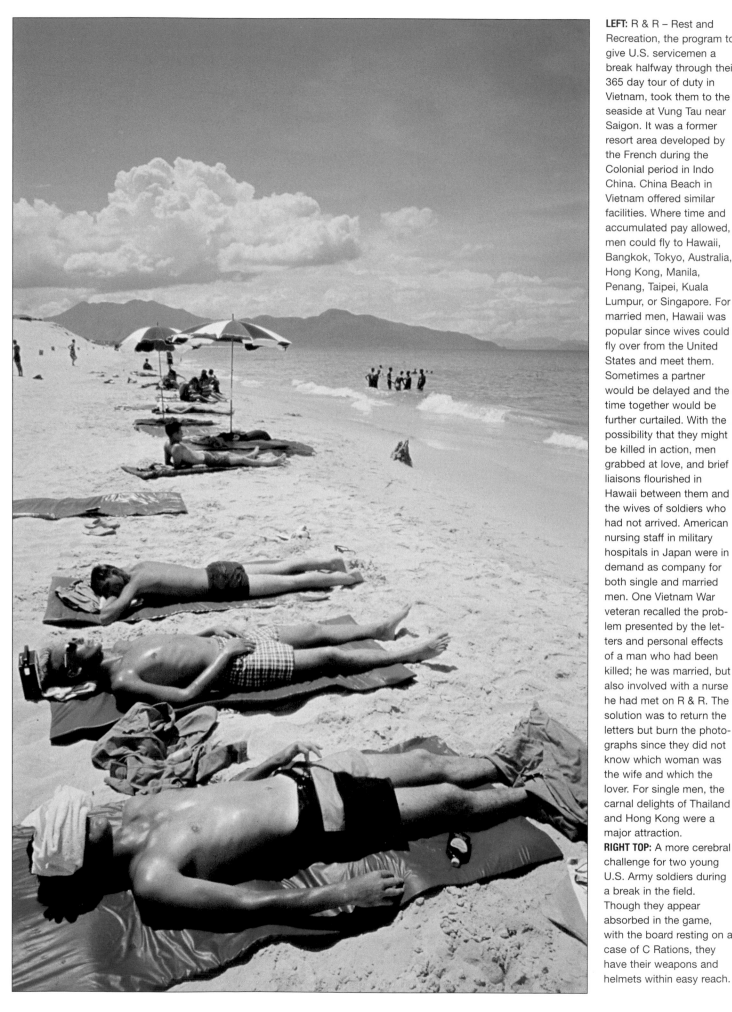

LEFT: R & R – Rest and Recreation, the program to give U.S. servicemen a break halfway through their 365 day tour of duty in Vietnam, took them to the seaside at Vung Tau near Saigon. It was a former resort area developed by the French during the Colonial period in Indo China. China Beach in Vietnam offered similar facilities. Where time and accumulated pay allowed, men could fly to Hawaii, Bangkok, Tokyo, Australia, Hong Kong, Manila, Penang, Taipei, Kuala Lumpur, or Singapore. For married men, Hawaii was popular since wives could fly over from the United States and meet them. Sometimes a partner would be delayed and the time together would be further curtailed. With the possibility that they might be killed in action, men grabbed at love, and brief liaisons flourished in Hawaii between them and the wives of soldiers who had not arrived. American nursing staff in military hospitals in Japan were in demand as company for both single and married men. One Vietnam War veteran recalled the problem presented by the letters and personal effects of a man who had been killed; he was married, but also involved with a nurse he had met on R & R. The solution was to return the letters but burn the photographs since they did not know which woman was the wife and which the lover. For single men, the carnal delights of Thailand and Hong Kong were a major attraction.

RIGHT TOP: A more cerebral challenge for two young U.S. Army soldiers during a break in the field. Though they appear absorbed in the game, with the board resting on a case of C Rations, they have their weapons and helmets within easy reach.

LEFT: The exhausted driver of a U.S. Marine Corps M-50 ONTOS armored vehicle lies for a minute on the front deck of his vehicle. Fatigue could build up over a period of days, and with disturbed nights, hard physical work, and intense concentration, men would take advantage of a lull in the fighting and try to rest or sleep at any opportunity possible. Even on the sharp angles of the deck of the ONTOS, this man has fallen asleep. The ONTOS – Greek for "Thing" – which he controlled was a unique antitank vehicle that mounted six M-40A1C 106mm Recoilless Rifles on a fully tracked chassis. It was often relegated to fighting as perimeter defense, but proved a valuable asset during the fighting in Hue in 1968.

LEFT: A U.S. Marine ruefully indicates the ricochet that glanced off his steel helmet. The M1 steel helmet would not stop a direct hit by a high velocity round but would protect the wearer from injury from shrapnel and rounds fired from some sub machine-guns and pistols. The adjustable liner could be removed and the helmet became an effective wash basin in the field.

BELOW: A U.S. Marine fires into the shadows at the back of a suspect structure during a patrol. It was understandable that men who had one year to survive in Vietnam would not take unnecessary risks. The "shoot first, ask questions afterward" approach might save soldiers' lives, but there was an inevitable price in civilian casualties. The hardest problem was that family bunkers in villages might contain innocent civilians, or Viet Cong planning a last stand.

Eagles") Division was airlifted from Phu Yen to northern Kontum in order to block their escape. However, the elusive enemy succeeded in slipping through the trap laid by the Screaming Eagles.

To intensify his operations in the Highlands, General Westmoreland deployed the 4th Infantry Division, where after three months' of intensive fighting, the "grunts" killed over 700 enemy soldiers. In addition, the soldiers of the 4th and 25th Divisions built a new road that ran between Pleiku and the highland outpost at Plei Djering, as well as resettling thousands of displaced Montagnard tribesmen in secure camps.

After the visit by Secretary of Defense Robert S. McNamara to South Vietnam, and a series of high-level conferences held at C-in-C Pac (Commander-in-Chief Pacific, under Admiral Sharp), it had been decided to introduce the entire 1st Marine Division into Vietnam. Infiltration of the enemy continued unabated, and pacification efforts required more manpower, so in March 1966, two-thirds of the 1st Marine Division was based in Chu

ABOVE: An officer if the 1st Infantry Division "Big Red One" speaks on the "horn" while his radio operator listens on the headset of the AN/PRC-25. The 1st Infantry deployed to Vietnam in October 1965 and returned to the U.S. in April 1970. During this period it suffered 20,770 killed and wounded, more than the 20,659 casualties in World War II, and almost as many as the 22,320 in World War I. During its time in Vietnam, 11 soldiers from the 1st Infantry Division were awarded the Medal of Honor, the United States' highest award for gallantry.

RIGHT: in an echo of an earlier war, bomb craters straddle the runway at Dien Bien Phu that had been repaired by the North Vietnamese during a 37-day lull in air strikes at the beginning of 1966. The airstrip that had originally been built by the French using PSP – Pierced Steel Planks – was repaired after 1954 and covered with concrete. The first strike against it in the Second Indo Chinese War was by F-105 Thunderchiefs "Thuds" and A-4 Skyhawks on July 2, 1965 exactly 11 years, one month, and 26 days after the French surrender. The aircraft expended 29 tons of 750 lb. (340 kg) HE bombs, 2.75 rockets, and Bullpup missiles against the target. The attack which took place in February 1966 hit the runway, adjacent parking area, and roads adjoining the site. The North Vietnamese were very efficient at repairing bomb damage, getting to work almost as soon as attacks were over, and in this way, they managed to keep supplies moving. Realizing that the U.S. targeters had placed domestic housing and cultural sites off limits, the North often moved vehicles and antiaircraft sites to within these protected areas.

Lai and assigned, along with the 2nd ARVN Division, to the southern two provinces of I Corps – Quang Tin and Quang Ngai.

Like the 1st Cavalry and 101st Airborne Divisions in the Highlands, the marines conducted an extensive pacification program. Before civic action could take place, marines and ARVN launched what they called a "County Fair," an elaborate cordon and search effort involving both U.S. and ARVN regulars.

These missions were intended to break down the infrastructure of the Viet Cong, a local cell of five to ten guerrillas who, when the main force left or were driven out of an area, remained behind and continued to exploit the hamlet populace. An area could not be considered "pacified," or ready for a civic affairs group, until hamlets were cleared.

During the dark of night, marines, sometimes with ARVN, would surround a hamlet in

Flat-top firebases

Nothing came close to the destructive force a carrier could wield. From the moment the USS *Kitty Hawk* steamed into the Gulf of Tonkin in April 1964, there began a deployment of the greatest ship-borne firepower the world had ever seen.

U.S. carriers were at the forefront of the U.S. campaigns from the start. The USS *Enterprise* alone carried some 24 F-4 Phantoms, 24 A-7 Corsairs, 10 A-6 Intruders, and over 40 other assorted aircraft. There were two main carrier stations: Yankee Station about 86 miles (139 km) off the coast of North Vietnam, and Dixie Station off the south coast, about 90 miles (145 km) southeast of Can Ranh Bay. Together they blanketed Vietnam with firepower. Yankee Station aircraft hammered North Vietnam during Rolling Thunder and bombed around the DMZ and Central Highlands, Dixie Station punished the Viet Cong in the southern provinces and attacked over into Laos and Cambodia.

The carriers fought until the last minute, sharing the bombing during the 1972 Linebacker raids and helping in the evacuations in 1975. 2,600 U.S. Navy personnel died, many of them pilots shot down over North Vietnam. Others were crewman killed during terrible carrier accidents, when missiles, men, and ammunition littered the decks. But the carriers proved themselves as one of the greatest tools in the U.S. arsenal, and the lesson has remained.

ABOVE: CA-4 Skyhawks from the USS *Enterprise* operating as part of Task Force 77 (TF 77), the carrier striking force en route for North Vietnam. The Skyhawk was such a compact design that, unlike most carrierborne aircraft, it did not need to have folding wings. On the night of August 13/14, 1965, two U.S. Navy A-4Es became the first aircraft to be shot down by surface to air missiles near Hanoi. One crashed but the other, badly damaged, limped back to the USS *Midway*.
RIGHT: A poster urging heroic opposition to U.S. aggression hangs forlornly from a telephone post amongst the rubble of an air attack. Though the United States did not wage an air campaign against civilians, inevitably bombs overshot or dropped short.
FAR RIGHT: A fireman listens for signs of life from a small girl rescued from a building in Hanoi's Gia Lam district following an air attack on December 13, 1966.

order to stop guerrillas from escaping and to prevent them from being reinforced. At dawn, using loudspeakers and leaflets dropped from the air, the marines asked the people to vacate the village until it was deemed "safe" to return home. After assembly at a general staging area, naval corpsmen would set up temporary medical dispensaries to treat the villagers. The

marines would distribute soda pop and candy to the children, while a musical combo entertained the villagers in a classic "hearts and minds" operation. Meanwhile, marines and ARVN soldiers would comb through the abandoned village, usually uncovering secret caches of arms, enemy tunnels, or VC themselves. If the Viet Cong refused to surrender

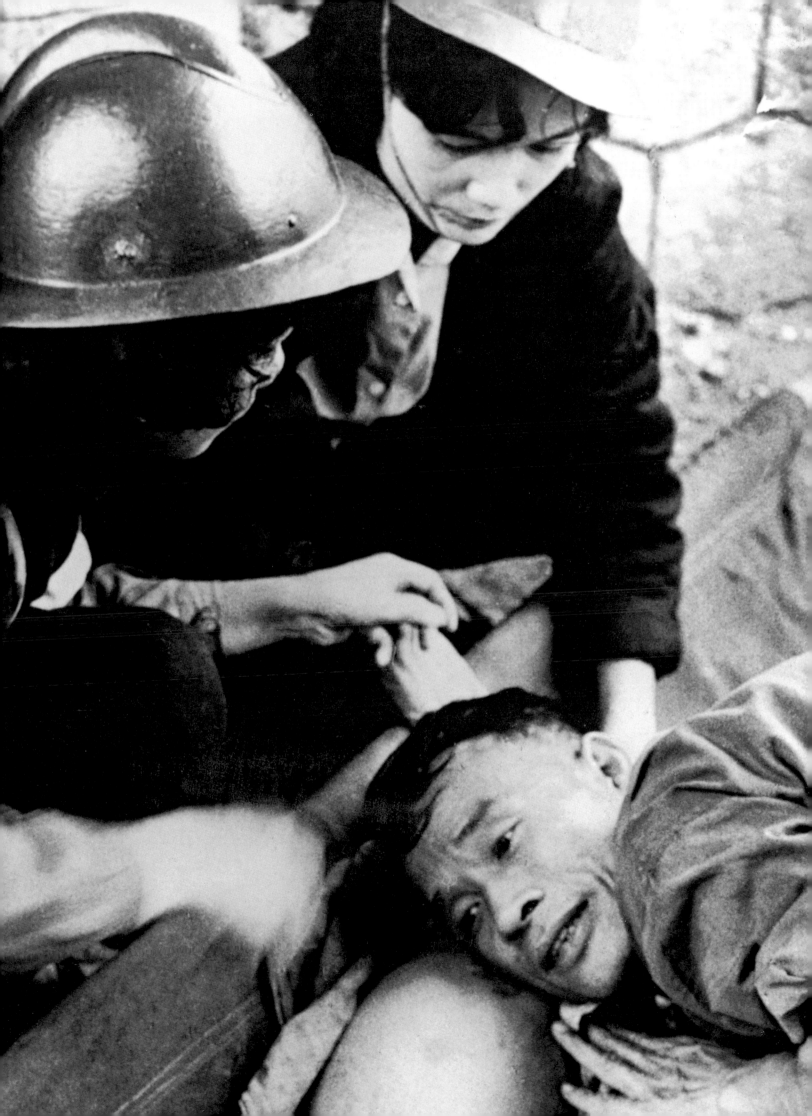

ABOVE: Fear distorts the face of a South Vietnamese soldier. The war in Vietnam had been harsh and cruel before the Americans arrived in strength. Prisoners were brutally interrogated, used to clear potentially mined or booby trapped areas, and then often executed. American firepower made the pain and destruction more impersonal.

LEFT: A South Vietnamese soldier carrying a Browning Automatic Rifle (BAR) grins as he follows a cigarette smoking comrade armed with an M1 Carbine. The men are bunched and distinctly casual for men on patrol. American advisers found the tactics and conduct of some troops they directed frustrating, often looking at the Viet Cong and asking "Why can't our Vietnamese be like their Vietnamese?"

they had to take their chances with the cordons and road blocks manned by the marines.

In February and March 1966, there were a series of extremely hard-fought, violent engagements between the marines, Viet Cong, and for the first time, NVA regulars. By the summer, even as General Kyle's 3rd Marine Division fought the elusive Viet Cong in Da Nang, a larger, and potentially more violent action was being fought during the first week of July in the north along the DMZ. III MAF intelligence had reported that the NVA's 324th Division, had moved across the DMZ into northern Quang Tri Province. What followed involved some 8,000 marines and 3,000 ARVN troops in what was the largest and possibly most savage battle of the Vietnam War up to that time.

Task Force Delta, commanded now by Brigadier General Lowell E. English, launched what became known as Operation Hastings on July 15, 1966. Using the airstrip at Dong Ha as its staging area, the three-battalion marine task force set out toward Cam Lo, accompanied by five ARVN battalions and for the first time fought the well-equipped, well-motivated North Vietnamese soldier.

The marines found fighting the NVA far tougher than the peasant guerrillas. As the Marine Corps's Official History stated, the marines had a "savage satisfaction" in meeting an enemy who stood and fought, instead of melting away and refusing to engage. Unlike their southern cousins in the Viet Cong, the NVA gave the marines. First, the NVA were attempting to locate a new, shorter route to the south as opposed to the longer, and more dangerous trek through Laos. Second, and perhaps more plausible is the fact that the NVA were attempting to take some of the pressure off the Viet Cong, which had sustained a high degree of casualties since the Americans

arrived in Vietnam. Whatever the reason for the NVA's sudden intervention into the fighting along the DMZ, both sides girded for what was now a conventional war of attrition.

At the conclusion of Hastings, three Marine battalions remained in the north along the demilitarized zone in order to prevent another attempt by NVA forces to re-enter Vietnam. Operation Hastings lasted well into January 1967. By the time it ended on January 31, seven Marine battalions and three ARVN battalions had killed over 1,397 NVA soldiers. In his end-of-year statement General Walt summed up the marine position: "Our most important job is eliminating the guerrilla ... The ultimate solution lies in pacification ... I believe in all my heart that we are on the right track ... but there are no dramatic changes in this war. It is slow because you are changing minds. That takes time."

BELOW: South Vietnamese soldiers move across a rice paddy. Before war wrecked the Vietnamese economy and agriculture, the country was an exporter of rice from the fertile Mekong delta area. Eventually many of the population were living on rice grown in the United States. The packs carried by the soldiers in the photograph suggest that they are going to be in the field for some days. Like so many operations in Vietnam, time and effort could be wasted if not based on good intelligence. Troops could sweep through areas and conduct searches to find nothing but women, children, and old people.

LEFT: Robert A. Talmanson a 19 year old American, burns his draft card outside the Federal Building at Winthrop, Massachusetts on November 4, 1966. He explained that he was burning the card as a protest against the conviction of 21 year old David A. Reed of Voluntown, Connecticut for failing to report for induction into the Army. During the Vietnam era, just over 26 million American males were of draft age. Of these, 8,720,000 enlisted voluntarily, 2,215,000 were drafted and 15,980,000 never served. Of those who did not serve, including Bill Clinton, the future President of the United States, some 15,410,000 were deferred, exempted, or disqualified. Apparent draft dodgers numbered some 570,000, of whom 209,517 were actually accused of dodging by the government. The draft had been introduced in World War I and II where it was a great success and reinstated in 1948, continuing through the Korean and Vietnam wars. The Vietnam era draft was a national disgrace, because those who benefited from American society – the affluent, the well educated – were the least likely to serve. College deferment, which did not end until December 1971, was a major loophole. A high school graduate was twice as likely to serve in the military as a college graduate. Although conscience played a role in some students' efforts to avoid the war, antiwar activity fell off dramatically as soon as the draft was ended.

In the meantime, the U.S. 7th Air Force provided air support to Operation Hastings in the Highlands in 1966. On July 20, 1966 they began an aerial interdiction campaign labeled "Tally Ho." While the marines and soldiers drove the enemy back across the DMZ, Air Force F-105 Thunderchiefs, F-100 Super Sabres, and F-4 Phantoms pounded the enemy from the air by striking logistical and ordnance depots, as well as lines of communications. B-52 bombers conducted numerous arc light strikes which "multiplied the firepower of the fighter-bombers," in mid-September 1966. During November, the U.S. 7th Air Force shifted its focus toward support of the U.S. Army in II Corps north of Saigon as it carried out Operation Attleboro. Operation Attleboro

had as its main goal the destruction of the enemy's fortified military facilities located in War Zones C, D, and some 40 miles (64 km) north of the city. Despite prolonged bombardment during 1965, both the NVA and VC held on tenaciously to these facilities, but this changed in 1966 as the Air Force and Army combined their efforts. In a series of offensives ("Silver City" in March; "Birmingham" in April; "El Paso II" in June) they succeeded in penetrating enemy strongpoints and managed to clear some out. Each time the army succeeded in taking these positions, the NVA and VC returned in strength to rebuild its bunkers, communications, and headquarters facilities. On November 1, 1966, two U.S. Army divisions entered these zones and, with the assistance of

ABOVE: RTOs – radio operators – of a headquarters group of the 173rd Airborne Brigade wait for orders. The man in the center has wrapped the hand set "horn" of his AN/PRC-25 in a polythene bag and taped it up so that moisture cannot penetrate. The FM radio used at platoon and company level had 920 channels and replaced the bigger AN/PRC-10.

LEFT: In the background of this photograph, one villager pleads not to be arrested, as in the front of the group, a man looks back at a South Vietnamese soldier who is running towards a hut. A village pig, probably the property of one of the prisoners, but destined to be the soldiers' lunch, wanders alongside with the group.

Find 'em, fix 'em, kill 'em

Search and Destroy was the cornerstone of U.S. tactics during the 1960s. Its principle was straightforward – kill enough of the enemy, wreck enough of their equipment, and there will come a point at which they can no longer function. It was to be a war of attrition, pure and simple.

History, however, has done a disservice to Search and Destroy. It was not a thoughtless strategy, a knee-jerk reaction from Westmoreland to the ineffective enclave strategy the U.S. had been previously pursuing. Instead, it was a considered tactical idea that came from Westmoreland but was also advocated by the JCS, Robert McNamara and Dean Rusk in February 1965. The aim of S&D was to take the NVA and Viet Cong to what Westmoreland called the "crossover point" – the point at which they could no longer make good their losses. What the U.S. had was confidence. Enormous resources of weaponry lay at its disposal – operations in mid-1967 alone saw 2,500,000 lb. (1,300,000 kg) of

explosive dropped from aircraft alone. It was confidently envisaged that the Communist forces could be brought to their knees within the year.

It didn't happen, but for many months it seemed like it might. S&D operations varied in size from small-unit attacks on VC-held villages, to massive battles between set forces. The battle for Ia Drang, for instance, lasted from October 23 to November 20 ,1965 and killed some 3,500 VC. Everywhere the U.S. boys went, the battle was won and the Communists took an enormous hammering, with fatality ratios usually in the region of 50:1 in favor of U.S. troops.

Yet there were problems. The emphasis of body counts led to some units inflating their kill scores through shooting civilians – "if it's dead, it's VC"was a common phrase. This created enormous bad politics, and the U.S. strategists started to lose the PR war at home: the U.S. was meant to field the good guys. Furthermore, U.S. troops were undeni-

ably winning, but they were also dying. Day by day, men were cut down by booby traps or a burst from a concealed AK47. Troops were led off planes in the U.S. missing limbs, the visible reminder of the cost of S&D. Every day the TV flashed up the new death tolls.

By 1967, both sides thought they were winning. Westmoreland believed that the VC had reached their "crossover point." Ho Chi Minh's strategy was to draw the U.S. forces away from the population centers for his 1968 invasion and he had succeeded. What ultimately demolished S&D was the Tet offensive. Why, people asked, had three years of attrition not stopped the Communists from being able to mount this massive invasion? After Tet, S&D was dramatically scaled down, but it lasted on a small-unit scale until it was finally wrapped up in 1972.

ABOVE: The air fills with the thudding roar of helicopter rotor blades as UH-1D slicks approach a landing zone which is situated in the Kim Son Valley. The helicopters were arriving to lift soldiers of the 1st Cavalry during the Eagle's Claw phase of Operation Masher/White Wing on February 16. Operation Masher was ultimately deemed by the military command of the allied forces to be a success after it had ended, since during the operation, the Cavalry had destroyed the 3rd Division of the North Vietnamese Army and had also killed 1,342 enemy, with an estimated 1,700 further casualties. In contrast to this, the 1st Cavalry had suffered only 228 killed and some 788 wounded.

LEFT: The "Mad Minute" U.S. soldiers fire their M16s and M60s on automatic into the surrounding jungle before they move on into the terrain in order to establish a base there. This rather crude tactic was intended to kill or wound any North Vietnamese or Viet Cong that might be hidden near the perimeter and so deter attacks during the night. Allies like the Australians and New Zealanders – who favored stealth – were horrified by the Americans' "Mad Minute," believing that it would give away the positions of any allied forces to the enemy immediately, therefore making them even more vulnerable to the stealth tactics employed by the NVA and Viet Cong.

LEFT: Wearing U.S. Marine Corps M1955 body armor and a Paratrooper's helmet with its distinctive chin strap, a bearded American grins at the photographer. The age, beard, and mix of clothing suggest that he is a journalist who is covering Vietnam. Correspondents who wished to go into the field could be dressed and equipped by the USMC or Army, but many found it quicker and easier to visit the black market in Saigon and buy items that had been stolen by the Vietnamese from consignments delivered at the docks.
RIGHT: U.S. Marines wearing their Utility Caps – known like all headwear in the Corps as a "cover" – and armed with M14s on patrol in assault boats. The need to patrol the rivers and waterways of the Mekong delta produced specialist Riverine forces drawn from the Navy, USMC, Army, and Coast Guard, affectionately known as the "Brown Water Navy."

LEFT: A U.S. Marine armed with a 3.5 in. (88.9 mm) M20 Rocket Launcher runs up the beach following a landing in rough weather. The launcher weighed only 12 lb. (5.5 kg) and could be folded into two sections for easier transport. The maximum effective anti-tank range was 360 ft. (110 m). The major drawback was a large flame which was projected behind the launcher when a rocket was fired.

B-52 bombers and fighter-bombers that flew over 1,700 sorties and 225 arc light strikes, the enemy was driven into neutral Cambodia.

As the ground war intensified, so too did the war in the air over the skies of North and South Vietnam, as well as along Vietnam's long coastline. While Rolling Thunder began as a campaign of strategic persuasion, it quickly switched to a tactical mission of interdiction. Throughout the three years and nine months of concerted bombing, the Air Force's objective was primarily to prevent supplies

reaching the battlefields in the south along the infamous Ho Chi Minh Trail. This switch in tactics and targets was associated with the larger decision to employ American ground forces in a more active role in South Vietnam.

From the very start, the air campaign over North and South Vietnam was controversial. Despite resistance from Air Force officials, who wanted to end the war in the South by bringing the North to its knees, the bombing concentrated on slowing the flow of men and supplies moving down the panhandle of North

FOLLOWING PAGE: A young U.S. Marine Corps sniper takes aim with the bolt action Model 700 Remington rifle that was introduced into service in April 1966 as the Rifle 7.02mm, Sniper M40. It is fitted with a Redfield Accu-Range 3x-9x variable power scope. USMC snipers worked as a two-man team, with one man spotting targets with 7 x 50 binoculars.

LEFT: U.S. Marines of the command post of the 1st Bn 7th Marines rush to assist two AN/PRC-10 radio operators who were hit by Viet Cong sniper fire near the An Hoa village complex during Operation Rio Blanco west of Quang Ngai in November 1966. As an important communications link, operators were an obvious target and so many attempted to conceal the radios inside packs.

BELOW: A U.S. Marine suffering from a head wound is evacuated aboard a Sikorsky H-34 during the course of fighting near the Demilitarized Zone with the North Vietnamese Army 324B Division in September. The Marine has a label on which a medically trained Marine has written details of his wound and his morphine treatment.

Vietnam. Almost simultaneously, a special national intelligence estimate concluded that extending air attacks to military targets in Hanoi and Haiphong Harbor would "neither injure the Viet Cong nor persuade the Hanoi government that the price of persisting was unacceptably high." Thus although the debate would continue for the next year, the bombing of North Vietnam became subordinated to the ground war in the South.

This was demonstrated in the targets selected for the early Rolling Thunder missions. During the first mission launched again North Vietnam, 100 Air Force F-105 Thunderchiefs and F-100 Super Sabre jets attacked the Xom Bang ammunition depot 35 miles (56 km) north of the DMZ. Two weeks later, on March 14, 1965, Republic of Vietnam Air Force (RVNAF) jets hit a North Vietnamese radar installation on Tiger Island, a few miles south of Xom Bang. Following up this mission the next day nearly 100 Air Force and Navy jets flying off aircraft carriers in the South China Sea pounded an ammunition depot 100 miles (160 km) southwest of Hanoi.

After a conference in Honolulu which included Secretary of Defense McNamara,

ABOVE: Headed by a Captain, a remarkably slack group of U.S. Marines cross a river in Vietnam. The men are bunched up and the one who is carrying a carton of C Rations is smoking a corncob pipe. These men would be an easy target for an ambush and would suffer casualties if they came under mortar or artillery fire. Morale, training, and leadership affected the performance of military formations of all sizes during the Vietnam war.

GOING NATIVE
The CIDGs

Theirs was a difficult role in an unusual war. The CIDGs – Civilian Irregular Defense Groups – were created by U.S. 5th Special Forces personnel as far back as 1961. Their mission: assist the South Vietnamese government in their anti-insurgency efforts and liaise with minority civilian communities to stop them becoming pro-VC. This latter role took the Green Berets deep into the Vietnamese jungles and high up its mountains. There they met with the Rhade and Montagnard tribes, became familiar with their cultures, and trained civilian units in military tactics and weaponry as active CIDGs. The CIDGs, thus trained, shouldered responsibility for their own village protection, including defensive perimeters, fighting patrols, and even their own intelligence networks. By 1962 alone, the Special Forces had brought over 1,000 people into CIDGs. By the late 1960s this number had risen to 48,000, with the 5SPG operating out of 84 camps spread throughout Vietnam.

Vietnam was full of ideas, good and bad. The CIDGs seemed one that worked. The SF troops become truly involved with their communities, fostering good relations and effective fighting skills. Only the process of Vietnamization undid the program. By 1971 all the SF troops had (officially) withdrawn and the CIDGs went into the hands of South Vietnamese officials. With the South disintegrating, the CIDGs collapsed with it.

General Westmoreland, Admiral Sharp, and Ambassador Maxwell Taylor, as well as other Johnson administration officials and military officers, the bombing campaign picked up in both intensity and scope. Sorties climbed from 3,600 in April to 4,000 in May 1966 and 4,800 in June. General John P. McConnell, Chief of Staff of the Air Force, urged McNamara to permit Air Force pilots to "Strike all targets on the list of 94," since he felt that an "intensified application" of air power against key industrial and military targets in North Vietnam would achieve the withdrawal of North Vietnamese support for the war in the South.

After the leader of North Vietnam, Ho Chi Minh, refused President Johnson's offer for a Mekong River Development program in April 1966, the administration ordered an increase in the number of sorties, but maintained the self-imposed restrictions forbidding the bombing of Haiphong Harbor or Hanoi. In fact, the Air Force and Navy were on an even tighter leash as strike days were specified with the number

FOLLOWING PAGE: A cheerful group of U.S. Air Force McDonnell Douglas F-4 Phantom pilots give the victory or peace sign at the close of a mission. On the air intake cover of the aircraft behind them, the bomb symbols show that this Phantom has flown 21 missions. By March 1966, seven F-4C Phantom squadron were engaged in combat, and in two years of serial fighting between 1965 and 1966, 54 F-4Cs were lost in combat. A pod mounted M-6A1 20mm gun was installed in U.S. Air Force Phantoms for air-to-air combat with North Vietnamese MiGs. Some F-4Cs were modified for the USAF Wild Weasel program, fitted with Electronic Counter Measures (ECM) warning sensors, vectoring equipment, jamming pods, chaff dispensers, and anti-radiation missiles to identify and neutralize North Vietnamese radar sites that controlled AA guns and surface to air missiles.

LEFT: President Lyndon Johnson, the Commander in Chief of U.S. Armed Forces, talks to a U.S. soldier in Vietnam. Throughout the war, Johnson feared that a dramatic escalation might draw China or the USSR directly into the conflict. His advisers failed to appreciate that to achieve their aim of conquering the South, North Vietnam was prepared and did take huge casualties. The U.S. government thought that military pressure and the offer to negotiate would bring a favorable end to the war.

BELOW: Drums of napalm stacked in a vast depot in the U.S. Napalm was an acronym derived from napththenic and palmitic acids, the salts of which were used in the jellied fuel in flame throwers and bombs, which could kill either by burning, or by suffocation.

CAUTION
DANGER
WARNING
CAUTION
U.S. AIR FORCE F-4C-22-MC
A. F. SERIAL 64-0693A
U.S.
CAUTION

ABOVE: As a wounded U.S. Airborne soldier awaits evacuation during fighting at Chu Pong in Vietnam, his comrade struggles to control the bleeding from his bandaged head wound. Body armor and helmets protected the top of the troops' head and the torso; however, limbs and feet were vulnerable, as were faces. Many of the men who were killed or were wounded in Vietnam suffered from blast and fragmentation injuries from the effects of booby traps and mines that managed to hit these vulnerable areas.

of sorties and targets. Attacks were normally limited to primary targets, with one or two designated alternatives. If bad weather prevented the bombing of alternative targets, pilots dumped their unused bombs into the South China Sea.

During the operation Rolling Thunder, there were two types of targets: numbered and unnumbered. Fixed targets, like the Than Hoa Bridge and the Thai Nguyen iron and steel complex, had designated target numbers. Unnumbered targets of opportunity included trucks, trains, and boats. From the beginning, the unnumbered targets – those struck in armed reconnaissance missions – received

more than 75 percent of the effort, in part because the system through which the numbered targets were selected was both complicated and in the end proved unwieldy.

During 1965 and into 1966, bombers were forbidden within 30 nautical miles (55 nautical km) of Hanoi and within 10 nautical miles (18 nautical km) of Haiphong Harbor. Targets near the Chinese border were likewise forbidden, as were factories (few as they were), power plants, and airfields. Haiphong Harbor was downplayed as a primary target, since the Johnson administration feared that one misplaced bomb might sink a Russian ship which was at that time sitting in the harbor. From its

very start, Rolling Thunder and the strategy of the entire air campaign against North Vietnam remained a source of controversy between the administration, the Pentagon, and the State Department. It was not until President Richard Nixon's massive bombing campaigns and the mining of Haiphong Harbor that the bombing campaign had any real effect on North Vietnam's will to continue the war.

In retrospect, it can be said that both the controversial Linebacker I and II bombings which were later initiated for only months under the Nixon administration had far more effect on the morale and capacity of the enemy than the two years of Rolling Thunder.

In conclusion, the fighting during 1966 reflected the unconventional nature of the Vietnam War, and was a strong indicator of the tasks facing U.S. and ARVN forces in the year ahead. While soldiers in I, II, III, and IV Corps fought the elusive North Vietnamese and Viet Cong field forces, the marines continued to insist that the pacification of the countryside was the key to eventual victory in defeating the Communist-inspired insurgency Nonetheless, the fighting in 1967, the "year before Tet," proved even more challenging as the U.S. troops shifted their operations from villages and hamlets to the demilitarized zone; here the war took on a conventional appearance.

ABOVE: U.S. Marines return fire in a coastal area in Vietnam. Because many white Americans were able to evade the draft through various schemes, including college deferment or volunteering for National Guard, many soldiers and Marines were either African American or from minority groups in the U.S. Eventually this imbalance would produce racial tensions that would almost destroy the forces' cohesion. One three-tour veteran remarked that "We had to get out of Vietnam before it destroyed the Army."

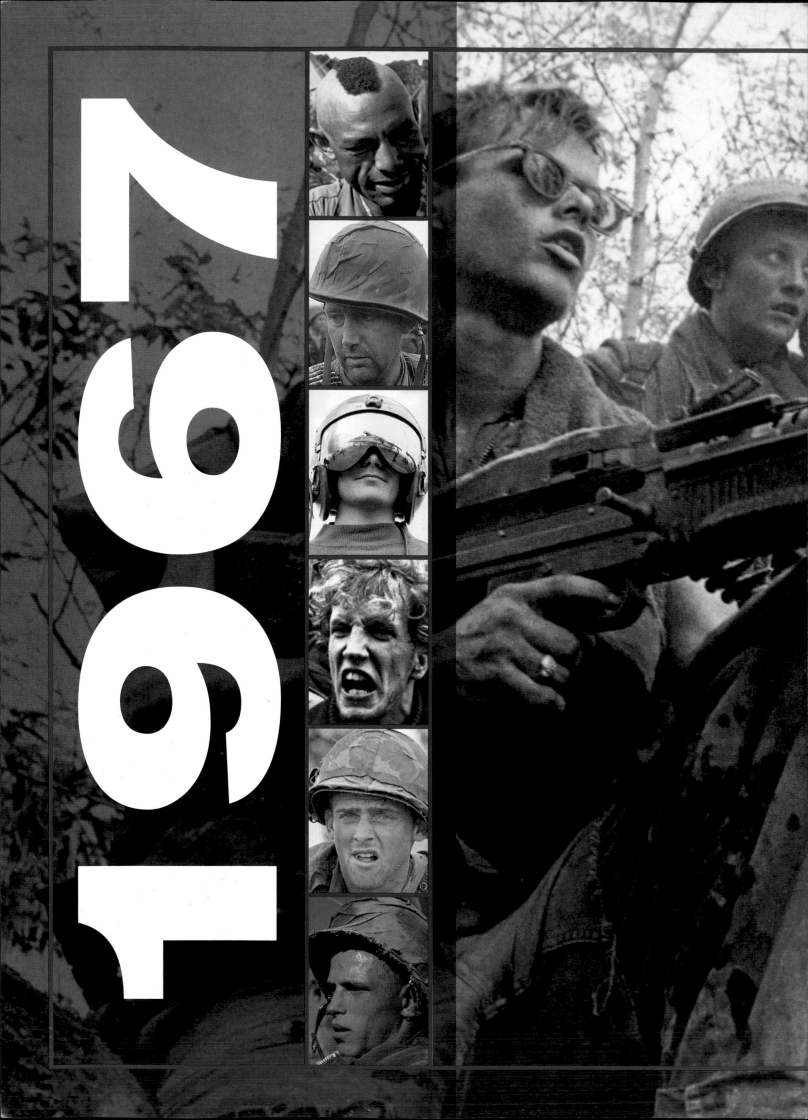

1991

Fighting the North Vietnamese

The fighting that raged in the highlands and along the Demilitarized Zone continued on into 1967. During the last few months of 1966 the first U.S. Army units, mainly batteries of 105mm and 175mm self-propelled howitzers, had arrived in I Corps. These guns could provide long range fire support for operations along the demilitarized zone, and bombardment and harassment of enemy positions in and across the DMZ. Westmoreland and his field commanders concluded that more troops would be required to permanently close the enemy's infiltration routes. Intelligence had estimated that the North Vietnamese had over 52 battalions operating in I Corps. While the Marines had held their own in the previous year's fighting, General Walt had no illusions that his forces "were stretched to the limit."

At the start of 1967, III MAF had 18 battalions operating throughout I Corps from the DMZ to the border of Binh Dinh Province and II Corps. The 3rd Marine Division was positioned north of the Hai Van Mountains. Four battalions were located in Quang Tri Province along the DMZ; three were positioned in Thua Thien Province, while the Division HQ was at Phu Bai, outside the old imperial capital of Hue.

To the south was 1st Marine Division around Da Nang, consisting of seven infantry battalions located in the Quang Nam Province. Based at Chu Lai, Task

Force X-ray consisted of a brigade-sized unit in Quang Tin Province and two in Quang Ngai Province along with the 2nd Korean Marine Corps "Blue Dragon" Brigade. Supporting the Marines of III MAF was the 1st Marine Air Wing (1st MAW), based at five principal airfields in I Corps – Phu Bai, Marble Mountain, Ky Ha, Da Nang, and Chu Lai. By the beginning of 1967, General Walt had under his command a total of 70,738 Marines and naval personnel.

The 1st ARVN Division had been re-organized and re-equipped after its involvement in the Buddhist revolt and factional struggles of 1966. The 51st Regiment of the ARVN was responsible for pacification in Quang Nam province south of Da Nang. The southern two provinces of I Corps, Quang Tin and Quang Ngai, had been placed under the operational control of the 2nd ARVN Division with its headquarters in Quang Ngai city. With Regular units – these including South Vietnamese Marines and three ARVN Ranger battalions – and the Regional Forces, ARVN's strength equaled that of General Walt's forces at around 75,000 soldiers.

For the leathernecks and ARVN forces in northern Quang Tri Province, the beginning of 1967 was little different from 1966. At the height of Operation Prairie, a continuation of Operation Hastings begun in

---

ABOVE: General William C. Westmoreland, veteran of World War II and Korea and, from June 20 1964 to July 1968, commander of Military Assistance Command Vietnam. Using mobility and firepower to defeat the Communist insurgency, his tactics worked, but he lost the support of U.S. public opinion.

RIGHT: Smoking two cigarettes, a soldier from the 1st Infantry Division – slung with a Claymore Mine haversack and carrying an early version of the M203 grenade launcher fitted beneath the barrel of his M16 – advances during Operation Junction City II near the Cambodian border.

July 1966, there were as many as six Marine battalions engaging both main force North Vietnamese units and irregular Viet Cong forces. By January 1967, with manpower stretched throughout I Corps, there were only four U.S. Marine battalions operating from Dong Ha in the east along Route 9 to the Khe Sahn fire base. In a month-long operation, the Marines killed a total of 1,397 NVA and VC and took 27 prisoners, while suffering 225 killed in action and 1,159 wounded. To maintain the pressure, Prairie II began on February 1, 1967 over the same ground. When it became apparent that the NVA had fled across the border, the leathernecks and ARVN conducted a

massive search and destroy operation in the area. The securing of the area helped deter further infiltration across the DMZ, suppressed VC activity in northern Quang Tri Province, and assisted 1st ARVN Division in its civic affairs programs.

The first significant operation of 1967 was actually a continuation of Operation Chinook begun on December 19, 1966 and still being fought out by elements of the 1st and 2nd Battalions, 26th Marines. The marines were to act as a blocking force preventing NVA forces infiltrating from the mountains towards Hue City. This would deny communist access to the "rice bowl" of the coastal area. On the last day

BELOW LEFT: A U.S. Marine rifleman from the 7th Marine Regiment, Task Force X-ray, 1st Marine Division races for the cover of a rice paddy dike as sniper fire cracks across the open ground. The text-book reaction when faced with enemy fire is to continue to advance until it becomes "effective" and your own troops take casualties, or would take them if they continued moving forward. However, during the war in Vietnam, lack of battle experience and a natural and powerful desire for self-preservation would often prompt many men to take cover prematurely when faced by enemy fire. The 7th Marine Regiment were part of Operation DeSoto, which was launched on January 26 in an area 25 miles (40 km) south of Quang Ngai. One veteran of these big sweeps against Viet Cong – and later North Vietnamese Army – positions would recall them as days of backbreaking movement on foot, punctuated by brief moments of terror and even moments of exhilaration. Some men surmised that the last emotion a man felt as a fatal burst of fire hit him was a sense of relief, as he knew that he would no longer have to "hump his ruck," that is, carry a laden rucksack across terrain that could be cruelly inhospitable. Adding to this load were the steel helmet and body armor. It is little wonder, then, that the men of the Long Range Reconnaissance Patrols (LRRPs) favored lighter clothing and equipment, and also that instead of the helmet, they wore the "Boony Hat," the name given to the soft jungle hat. In effect, they adopted a similar range of clothing as worn at that time by their enemies the North Vietnamese Army, as well as the Viet Cong.

LEFT: In a mock hut of the Fort Polk training area in the Louisiana outback, U.S. soldiers practice search techniques. Men from the 3rd Training Battalion have discovered a tunnel system or hide within the hut. To enhance realism, training complexes had "villagers" dressed in black, Vietnamese-style clothing. Soldiers learned about booby traps and enemy weapons, but there was still more that they could have been taught before going to Vietnam.

BELOW: Driving a half ton M274 Mechanical Mule, a Marine from "G" Company, 2nd Battalion, 9th Marine Regiment disembarks from a raft that has transported across a river 15 miles (24 km) northwest of Hue as part of an operation in mid-May, 1967.

of 1966 a 1,000-man enemy force was sighted moving into the Con Bi Than Tan Valley northwest of Hue and, despite the New Year truce, was engaged by U.S. Marine artillery and air power. The enemy force did escape, but only after suffering heavy losses. 2nd Battalion, 26th Marines remained in contact with the enemy throughout January 1967, engaging in firefights and ambushes. By the time Operation Chinook ended on February 6, 1967, the Marines had accounted for 159 NVA and VC soldiers killed in action, with another five taken prisoner. The Marines suffered four dead and 73 wounded.

In general, however, January saw relatively little enemy activity, although 1st Marine Division around Da Nang and Task Force X-ray in Quang Ngai accounted for a total of 190 enemy killed, and captured a number of prisoners and weapons. In Operation Desoto, which began on January 26, 1967, 25 miles (40 km) southeast of Quang Ngai, two battalions from 1st Marine Division conducted a massive search and secure operation aimed at clearing the coastal area from Mo Duc south to the border of Binh Dinh province of VC.

In the Mekong Delta region, previously not the responsibility of the marines, the Special Landing Force, 1st Battalion, 9th Marines landed 62 miles (100 km) south of Saigon in order to secure the mouths of the Mekong River against infiltrators. Dubbed "Deckhouse V," this was the first use of U.S. combat troops in the Mekong Delta and, despite poor intelligence, the SLF, with South Vietnamese Marines, inflicted substantial losses on local communist forces by the year's end.

In Quang Nam Province during Operation Independence and after, during the Tet truce, marines of 9th Division clashed regularly with NVA forces attempting to harass the Marines' positions, while Colonel Mallory's 1st Marines attempted to secure the area south of Da Nang, which continued to give problems.

Even as Marine activity spread throughout I Corps, North Vietnamese and Viet Cong

forces continued to harass U.S. facilities with rocket and mortar fire. The mortars, normally long-range Soviet-made 120mm mortar, could hit targets over 3 miles (5 km) away. They could be set up quickly and were hard to detect. The Communists also used 140mm rockets to strike the Da Nang airbase and pro-government villages in the region.

It was not only U.S. forces caught up in the fighting in early 1967. In the pre-dawn hours of February 14/15, 1967, the 1st Viet Cong Regiment, as well as elements of the 21st NVA Regiment, slammed into the positions of the 11th Company, 2nd Korean Marine Brigade southwest of Chu Lai. However, the Korean Marines held their positions and two ARVN airborne battalions airlifted in to help blocked the Communist escape route along the Tra Khuc River. With the VC and NVA forces unable to punch their way through the ARVN paratroopers, the 2nd Korean Brigade launched an all-out attack alongside a battalion of 5th U.S. Marines. The enemy units were decimated

and the 7th ARVN Battalion received the U.S. Presidential Unit Citation for their part in repulsing the attack.

Throughout the remainder of Operation Prairie II, the Marines continued to search out and engage the elusive enemy forces. When this phase of the "Prairie" operation came to an end on March 20, 1967, the Marines had killed 693 NVA and VC, taken 20 prisoners of war, and captured 137 weapons. The price was 93 Marines killed and 483 wounded, with one missing in action. During Prairie III, as Generals Walt and Westmoreland sought to maintain the pressure, marine forces operating from the DMZ to the southern provinces of I Corps killed more than 750 enemy soldiers.

On April 9, the first of the Army brigades, the 196th Light Infantry, arrived in southern I Corps with four battalions. Within a matter of days, they were in action along the borders of Quang Ngai and Quang Tin provinces as part of Operation Lawrence. On April 22, 1967, the 196th was joined by units of 25th Infantry and

BELOW: With heavily laden jungle rucksacks, a U.S. Army patrol moves slowly out during Operation Thayer II on January 17. The rucksack pictured here had an aluminium frame and a three pocket pack that most soldiers repositioned at the top of the frame. It had originally been designed for operations in the Arctic, but was to prove incredibly effective in Vietnam. Operation Thayer II, which was undertaken in Binh Dinh Province, had begun on October 25 and was a relatively long operation, since it lasted almost four months. At its close, MACV claimed it was a success and that 1,744 Viet Cong had been killed. At this point, body counts were seen as a reliable way of measuring success, but became increasingly discredited as the Vietnam war progressed.

LEFT: A soldier of the 101st Airborne Division looks untroubled by the fact that the engineer he is guarding, who is equipped with an AN/PRS 3 metallic mine detector, has found a mine and is prodding the road surface. In the background is an M48A3 tank waiting to advance once the road has been swept for mines.

BELOW: An M728 Combat Engineer vehicle uses its beam and winch to remove the barrel from an M107 175mm gun at a workshop in Vietnam. The M728 was equipped with a 165mm demolition gun with an indirect range of 15,977 ft. (4,870 m), a winch with a 27,558 lb. (12,500 kg) capacity, and beam and winch capable of hoisting 18,298 lb. (8,300 kg).

101st Airborne Division. Organized with supporting marine units into Task Force Oregon, they took over responsibility for the Chu Lai area on April 26, 1967.

As the fighting intensified throughout South Vietnam, senior U.S. military commanders sought to increase the number of troops committed to the region. General Wallace M. Greene, Jr., Commandant of the Marine Corps, testified before Congress that 40,000 Marines were needed in Vietnam alone to carry the fighting to the North Vietnamese. General William C. Westmoreland told the press that he remained committed to his strategy of defeating the enemy in the field. He told the reporters that "We'll just go on bleeding them until Hanoi wakes up to the fact that they have bled their country to the point of national disaster for generations. Then they will have to

THE KOREANS
Tigers and Horses

Vietnam was not just a U.S. war: far from it. Included in a myriad of contributing nations were some 47,000 soldiers from the Republic of Korea, lending a hand to the South Vietnamese with their own brutal approach to warfare. They were sent mainly to II Corps Tactical Zone, a coastal area which stretched down from Cam Ranh to Qui Nhon in Bin Dinh province. There they established a reign of terror among the VC.

The South Korean troops were avid haters of communism. Units such as the elite Capital (Tiger) Division and the 9th (White Horse) Division took search and destroy into the VC heartlands with a passion few other units in Vietnam could match. If VC were trapped, they would be killed without mercy. If captured, torture and violent death usually awaited them, often through the use of martial arts blows (all RoK troops were, and are, trained as martial arts experts.) Prisoner killings attracted international outrage, but the Korean troops also showed balance. Their relations with civilians were very good, and many RoK troops learnt Vietnamese so that they could converse better with the locals. Yet the fear they inspired amongst the VC meant that Binh Dinh province became one of the best controlled areas in the whole of Vietnam, and the contribution of these tough men should not be underestimated.

BELOW: Men of B Company, 2nd Battalion, Royal Australian Regiment (2 RAR) patrol a perimeter concertina barbed wire fence, armed with the L1A1 7.62 mm Self Loading Rifle (SLR). This weapon had a 20 round magazine and weighed 11.1 lb. (5.06 kg) when loaded. Later, Australian forces adopted the lighter and more compact M16 rifle and the M60 machine-gun. The Australians first deployed 1 RAR in 1965 and, after rotating regiments through the theater, would eventually withdraw from Vietnam in 1971. During this time, the men of the Australian Task Force – which reached a peak number of 7,672 in 1969 – won admiration from their allies. Their total losses in manpower amounted to 386 killed and 2,193 wounded.

reassess their position." With the arrival of the troops from the 196th Light Infantry and 25th Infantry Division, the 7th Marines were moved north from Chu Lai to Da Nang in order to counter the NVA threat to the airfield and the facilities around it. As the Marines battled the VC and NVA in I Corps, 1st Brigade, 101st Airborne sought an elusive enemy in II and III Corps. In the central highlands, frequent and violent clashes continued along the border with Laos and Cambodia. Although the action was erratic and unpredictable, troops of 4th Infantry Division killed over 700 enemy soldiers over a three month period.

As additional units reached Vietnam, U.S. commanders at last had the numbers to launch major operations which would carry the war to the enemy in the strongholds they had always thought impenetrable. One such stronghold was the "Iron Triangle," an area of roughly 40 square miles (104 square kilometers) of thick jungle northwest of Saigon. It had been a

Vietminh base during the struggle against the French and contained a vast complex of tunnels, which sweeps in 1965 had left virtually untouched. As such, it remained an important VC and NVA base area.

In Operation "Cedar Falls" in January 1967, the 1st and 25th Infantry Divisions, 173rd Airborne Brigade and 11th Cavalry Regiment were given the task of clearing this area once and for all in the largest operation of the war so far. Preceded by B-52 strikes, on January 8 an entire infantry battalion in 60 helicopters descended on the village of Ben Suc, considered the key to Communist control of the Triangle. The unit, 1st Battalion, 26th Infantry, commanded by Lieutenant-Colonel Alexander M. Haig, cleared the population and burned the village to the ground in what was supposed to be the beginning of a classic "hammer and anvil" operation. On January 5, 2nd Infantry Brigade and 196th Light Infantry Brigade, supported by ARVN units, had taken

LEFT: Australian soldiers ride on the upper deck on the outside of an M113 APC, which was common practice; if they detonated an antitank mine, troops inside ran a greater risk from blast and concussion injuries.

BELOW: An Australian Army captain listens out on the radio. The performance of Australian troops was greatly respected by U.S. forces, particularly the tough action at Long Tan over August 17–18, 1966, when 108 men of D Company, 6 RAR fought 1,000 VC and NVA, suffering 17 dead and 21 wounded, and drove the enemy back, leaving 245 dead on the battlefield.

LEFT: Men of 2nd Battalion, 7th Regiment, 1st Cavalry Division (Airmobile) assemble their equipment before boarding a vehicle for movement to An Khe Airfield at the start of a major Operation. During the Vietnam war, the 1st Cavalry of "First Team" won 25 Medals of Honor and, following the battle of the Ia Drang Valley in 1965, received a Presidential Unit Citation

BELOW: The 4th Battalion, 503rd Infantry, 173rd Airborne Brigade wait at an LZ prior to being lifted by UH-1D helicopters to the brigade's forward base in Xuan Loc Province. Though the 173rd used helicopters for battlefield mobility, it conducted a combat parachute jump in February 1967 in War Zone C.

RIGHT: A Ben Suc villager during the 18-day Operation Cedar Falls. Ben Suc was leveled after 6,000 inhabitants and suspected VC sympathizers were resettled 25 miles (40 km) south. With a total of 30,000 U.S. and ARVN troops, Operation Cedar Falls saw 750 enemy killed and 488 captured.

up blocking positions along the Saigon River. At dawn on January 9, 3rd Infantry Brigade swept through the Than Dien forest to the north east in a massive airmobile operation. At the same time the 173rd Airborne and 11th Armored Cavalry pushed into the Triangle from Ben Cat to the east, while 1st Battalion 503rd Infantry and 35th Ranger Battalion took up blocking positions along the Triangle's southeastern edge.

With nowhere to run, the VC would have no choice but to stand and fight, giving the U.S. troops the opportunity to inflict devastating losses and smash the Communist infrastructure in this area. That was the theory at least. To the immense frustration of the U.S. field commanders, and despite the fact that Cedar Falls had been planned amid such tight security that the South Vietnamese general

commanding III Corps was not informed until two days before the Operation began, the Viet Cong got wind of the impending assault. In classic guerrilla fashion, they simply withdrew from the area. For the next 19 days, the U.S. and ARVN forces "beat the bush" seeking to flush out units which simply were not there. Occasional snipers or small formations were encountered, but they rarely stood and fought, instead melting back into the forests. Evidence of the recent presence of the VC was found everywhere, but despite the numbers of men employed, not a single large scale action was fought throughout "Cedar Falls." The VC had managed to dodge the knock-out punch.

Although unable to engage the Communists in battle, the U.S. troops set about denying them the future use of the area. Massive bulldozers and M48 tankdozers went

ABOVE: A U.S. soldier squats in a communications trench and looks into the entrance of a VC bunker. The MACV patch on his jacket and the fragmentation grenades tucked in a contrived way into the top pockets suggest he is from the rear echelons; their obscene nickname was reduced to the initials "REMF." Staff officers and echelon troops could fly from their desks to an ongoing operation and return in time for an evening meal. For men filthy and tired from days of patrolling, these "REMF"s reinforced the feeling that a small group was doing the fighting and a far larger one was enjoying a comfortable "war."

on to flatten the jungle and tear up the trees. This clearance revealed the entrances to the massive network of tunnels which honeycombed the area. The "Tunnel Rats" of 1st Infantry's 242nd Chemical Detachment were given the job of exploring this network, while engineers prepared to demolish them. The "Rats" crawled through more than 12 miles (19 km) of tunnels during "Cedar Falls" and on January 18 made what the commander of II Field Force Vietnam, Lieutenant-Colonel J. Seaman, called "the biggest intelligence breakthrough of the war." In a tunnel complex west of the Saigon River they stumbled on the Viet Cong's Cu Chi district headquarters. Amongst the documents found were plans of future attacks and lists of communist sympathizers.

For three weeks the engineers worked, clearing the jungle and destroying tunnels. When the operation ended on January 26 more than 2,700 acres of jungle had been cleared, 6,000 civilians had been relocated, 500 tunnels and 1,100 bunkers destroyed, and 60,000 rounds of small arms ammunition, 7,500 uniforms, and an immense 3,700 tons of rice had been captured. Enemy casualties had only amounted to around 750 but it seemed reasonable to assume that the infamous "Iron Triangle" had been cleared. Even General Seaman concluded the Triangle was now "a military desert." In an attempt to ensure it remained that way, the area was declared a Free Fire Zone, which meant that anything that moved in the area could be attacked.

In reality, "Cedar Falls" had only scratched the surface. The tunnel complexes were too massive to be destroyed and at best the entrances had been sealed. Beneath the village of Ben Suc, which had to all appearances been obliterated, around 1,850 yds. (1,691 m) of tunnel remained untouched. Within days, there was evidence of renewed VC activity in the area, and as the jungle gradually returned to the Iron Triangle, so did the guerrillas. By the time of the Tet Offensive a year later, the Iron Triangle was once again a dagger pointed at the heart of Saigon.

The following month a yet larger attempt was made to inflict critical damage on the

Communist network in the south. Involving the only combat parachute assault of the Vietnam war and the first tactical use of B-52 strikes, Operation "Junction City" aimed at nothing less ambitious than penetrating the notorious communist-dominated War Zone C in Tay Ninh province, engaging and annihilating the Viet Cong 9th Division and destroying COSVN (Central Office for South Vietnam) the Viet Cong's high command in South Vietnam.

This time General Westmoreland was determined that the VC would not be allowed to slip away across the border into the safety of

BELOW: Holding a flashlight and a Colt service revolver, 23-year-old Cpl Charles Patchin of the 173rd Airborne Brigade works his way through a Viet Cong tunnel complex that his unit discovered on January 19 during Operation Cedar Falls in the Iron Triangle 20 miles (32 km) northwest of Saigon. Although it was heavily forested and sparsely populated, below the 40 square mile (104 sq km) area was a complex of tunnels and fortifications which were virtually bombproof.

THE IRON TRIANGLE

The Iron Triangle was known as by U.S. troops as 'Injun Country,' a 60 square mile (150 square kilometer) area dominated by the VC since 1965. North of Saigon, the triangle was bounded by the villages of Ben Suc and Ben Cat and the junction of the Saigon and Thi Tinh rivers. The area had been pounded by B-52s for two years, but the VC stayed put. So by 1967 the U.S. forces launched a major search and destroy operation – "Cedar Falls" to clear them out once and for all.

Operation Cedar Falls took place between January 8 and 26. The strategy to be applied was classic 'hammer-and-anvil,' the 2nd Infantry Brigade and the 196th Light Infantry Brigade acting as the anvil south of the Saigon river, while the hammer would be various cavalry, airborne, and armored divisions pushing down from the north. The operation began witha massive helicopter assault on the village of Ben Suc, but the anticipated confrontation with the Viet Cong never materialized. Apart from breif encounters with small units and scouts the U.S. troops and their ARVN allies found that their adversaries had simply slipped away, many of them across the border into Cambodia. Bulldozers and tankdozers were called in to destroy the bunkers and tunnel complexes in an attempt to prevent the VC from returning. The success was short lived however, within a matter of weeks the Viet Cong had moved back in reclaiming the Triangle once again.

Cambodia. Armored units were to provide the hammer, including the 11th Armored Cavalry regiment and the 5th Cavalry, the "Black Knights." The core of the force committed to "Junction City" was the 25th Infantry Division, the 1st Infantry Division, 173rd Airborne Brigade and 2nd Battalion, 503rd Airborne. In total, 22 U.S. and four ARVN battalions would be involved, a force of more than 25,000 men.

Behind the disguise of Operations Gadsden and Tucson, units from the 25th and 1st Divisions were maneuvered into blocking positions. On February 22 the operation swung into action as a horseshoe shaped cordon was established, into which pushed 2nd Brigade,

LEFT: With an M113 Armored Personnel Carrier in the rear, U.S. soldiers comb through the bomb-blasted jungle of the Iron Triangle. The area had been a Vietminh stronghold during the 1950s when Vietnam was still a French colony, and Cedar Falls was the first time it had been penetrated.
RIGHT: Dressed in foul-weather clothing, a U.S. Marine covers a bunker into which a smoke bomb has been thrown in order to flush out anyone who might be hiding in it. Smoke could also be used to establish the layout of a tunnel system; pumped in using a portable Mighty Mite pump, it would come up through the escape shafts and show up in the jungle. However, though explosives were used to destroy tunnels, they were often found to be largely ineffective. One option was to "seed" them with CS crystals. This tactic, it was hoped, would make them uninhabitable, since in the hot confines of the tunnel, the vapors given off by the CS crystals would severely irritate the mucus membranes of the nose and eyes of anyone hidden below who was not wearing a respirator.

25th Infantry Division and the 11th Armored Cavalry. At first, enemy contact was minimal. As the operation entered its second phase, however, American forces entering the eastern portions of War Zone C encountered bitter resistance. It was here that several large battles erupted as Viet Cong units attempted to cut off isolated pockets of U.S. soldiers, as their comrades escaped into neighboring Cambodia. On March 19, a mechanized unit of the 9th Infantry Division was attacked and nearly overrun along Route 13 near the destroyed village of Bau Bang. The combined firepower of the armored cavalry, supporting artillery, and close air support eventually forced the enemy to break contact. A few days later, at Fire

Support Base Gold in the vicinity of Soui Tre, an infantry and artillery battalion from the 25th Infantry Division engaged the 272nd Viet Cong Regiment. Behind an intense, walking barrage, VC forces managed to breach the perimeter and rushed into the inner portions of the base. Bitter hand-to-hand fighting ensued. The enemy's attack was eventually repelled when the artillerymen fired "Beehive" anti-personnel rounds directly into the enemy at point-blank range. The last major battle of Junction City occurred at the end of March when the 271st and 70th Viet Cong Regiments attacked a lone U.S. Army battalion of the 1st Infantry Division in a night defensive position in War Zone C, near the Cambodian border.

NEXT PAGE: Empty cases spin from the M16 of Pfc Michael J. Mendoza of Company A, 2nd Battalion, 502nd Infantry, 101st Airborne Brigade as he "recons by fire" the perimeter from where a sniper had fired on the U.S. soldiers. "Recon by fire," like the "Mad Minute," entailed firing with infantry weapons on automatic at enemy positions. At the time of this photograph, Pfc Mendoza was participating in Operation Cook in Quang Ngai Province 397 miles (640 km) northeast of Saigon.

BELOW: An officer with Company A, 1st Battalion, 16th Infantry, 1st Infantry Division – and veteran of an earlier tour in Vietnam – uses an AN/PRC-25 radio to talk down a helicopter to a jungle LZ. The picture was taken in March near the close of Junction City during a break 18.6 miles (30 km) northwest of Suoi Da. Helicopter pilots could find troops in the remotest locations. Where the jungle canopy was too thick for landing, or the troops were moving, pilots would hover and lower a special "Jungle Penetrator," a folding seat onto which a casualty could be secured and winched up.

The soldiers had the area bracketed for artillery and mortar, and slaughtered the Viet Cong. In one of the most lopsided battles of the Vietnam War, the soldiers of the 1st Infantry Division managed to kill over 600 enemy while losing only 10 of their own troops.

"Junction City" continued until May 14 and in all, five major actions were fought against Viet Cong units. In addition to the arc lights strikes by massive B-52s, Air Force F-105s, F-100s, F-4s, F-5s, and B-57 bombers flew an estimated 5,000 sorties. Alongside the fire support offered the American troops, Air Force C-130 and C-123s flew 2,000 supply sorties in order to support the attacking U.S. infantrymen. Junction City resulted in 2,728 Viet Cong killed and 34 captured. Six hundred

ABOVE: In the first major U.S. airborne combat assault since the Korean War, 900 men of the 173rd Airborne Brigade dropped over War Zone C to open Operation Junction City. Bordering Cambodia on the west – which gave the Viet Cong access to North Vietnamese supply base areas in Cambodia – War Zone C included the northern half of Tay Ninh Province, the western half of Binh Long Province, and the northwestern half of Binh Duong Province in III Corps.
RIGHT: The crew of an M48A3 tank watch as smoke rises from a treeline after air strikes. Junction City was a hard-fought operation, and on March 11, the U.S. 1st Infantry Division killed 210 NVA soldiers. By the end of the month, losing 10 dead and 64 wounded, U.S. forces had killed 591 Viet Cong.

weapons, 500,000 pages of documents, and 810 tons of rice were also taken. Significantly, however, all the actions were initiated by the Viet Cong, and although the VC 9th Division was hit hard, it was not destroyed and succeeded in slipping away. Nor was COSVN found; if it existed, it had slipped across the border into Cambodia, in spite of all the efforts of the U.S. troops. More significantly, as with countless previous operations, it proved impossible – with the exception of Special Forces – to maintain any long term military presence in the area, as had been the intention. In reality, the massive expenditure of effort and materiel had achieved little of value. The Viet Cong would soon return to War Zone C.

In an attempt to prevent the VC shelling of Saigon, General Westmoreland ordered the 1st Infantry Division to carry out operations into both the Ong Dong jungle and Vin Loi woods. Other operations swept the jungles and villages of Bien Hoa Province and sought to support pacification efforts in Hau Nghia Province. When elements of the 9th Infantry arrived in Vietnam, General Westmoreland immediately ordered them onto the offensive. Operation Fairfax, a year long operation in conjunction with South Vietnamese Rangers, attempted to uproot the local Viet Cong infra-structure. Typical operations included ambushes, cordon and search operations in villages and hamlets – often conducted with the assistance of the South Vietnamese police – psychological and civic operations, surprise road blocks, and searches for contraband and Viet Cong suspects. In addition, efforts were made to train the Regional and Popular Forces (Ruff Puffs), as well as local self-defense forces.

One of the most innovative initiatives of the Vietnam War was the development of the Mobile Riverine Force. A joint Army-Navy task force controlled by the ground commander, it allowed the U.S. and ARVN to dominate South Vietnam's inland waterways, and Westmoreland hoped to use it to prevent the Viet Cong from using southern Vietnam's extensive network of rivers as an avenue of movement and supply. Troops were moved by landing craft with fire support provided by

Nam in the Living Room

Sometimes it was only the cameras or the spiral-bound notebooks that set the media apart. They wore the same camouflages, hung about in military bunkers, smoked joints, and went head-first into the war zones. But most importantly, they projected the reality of the Vietnam War straight into the world's living rooms. Once it was there, opinions started to change.

Vietnam became the mecca for journalists, TV camera-men, and press photographers during the 1960s and 1970s. It was the place to make your mark, to make people stand up and take notice. By 1968, over 600 journalists were in Vietnam, not counting the other types of media personnel. At first the Press was quite pro-involvement – not surprising, since their accreditation often came from Diem and his regime, and any criticism of policy might lead to expulsion from the country. Yet following figures such as David Halberstam of the *New York Times* and Malcolm Browne of the Associated Press, the media started to become increasingly hostile to both the southern regime and the U.S. war effort.

There are many reasons why the media became so problematic for the U.S. administration during the Vietnam War. One of these was the nature and immediacy of the images televized or photographed. Though all journalists had to be accredited by the Joint United States Public Affairs Operation (JUSPAO), there was effectively no form of censorship apart from the caution of an officer's tongue. This allowed journalists to penetrate deep into operational settings and produce material which shocked and challenged. This was particularly true of photojournalism. Photographers such as Larry Burrows, Sean Flynn, Dana Stone, and Dicky Chapelle sent back picture-spreads which revealed the brutality of combat in ways never before seen. Their photographs sucked the glamor out of war, and also showed that U.S. troops could behave with a brutality to match that of the enemy. But perhaps the most persuasive form of media in Vietnam was television. One world-famous episode illustrates the power that this achieved – the summary execution of a Viet Cong suspect in Saigon by Police Director Loan. This incident of casual execution, caught from beginning to end on film, stunned the public. Never before had killing been seen so close up, and the public was revolted by what started to appear as a seedy, visceral war.

The result of this disturbing footage, however, was that television networks sought out more violence to feed an increasing public appetite. Transmission from the field to U.S. and European homes was quick: by the early 1970s footage could be transmitted by satellite from Japan to the U.S. only hours after it was taken. In 1972 a camera was present when the village of Tram Bang was napalmed by a U.S. jet. A badly burnt girl came running up the road and again focused the war into a single, famous, harrowing image. But that was in fact the problem with media coverage of the war: single images became representative, and

many today say that the press lost sight of the true picture. The man executed in Saigon had committed atrocities of his own, but somehow the camera seemed to portray him as an innocent.

Neil Archer, the Director of News at ABC, has remarked that during Vietnam "A good firefight is going to get in over a good pacification story." This tendency escalated until the public had no strategic overview. Thus an image of U.S. troops dragging wounded out of the jungle meant that they were losing the battle, whereas the opposite could in fact be true.

The crowning example of this was Tet. The media presented the invasion as a massive defeat for U.S. strategy, but somehow failed to present it as one of the greatest defeats for the North in living memory.

The partiality of the Vietnam media created giant political shockwaves. Antiwar movements effectively mobilized images of horror to generate support for their cause. Some have argued that the media lost the war in Vietnam. The issue is debatable. Yet it is true that since Vietnam, armies and governments have reinstated a tough control over what images the public receive back from their wars.

LEFT: A CBS television crew grab an interview with an M113 crew. The commentary for television footage, which was sometimes shot at considerable personal risk by camera crews, was often added in studios in the United States. Such was the rush to fly the film back to the States that there was often only a simple description on the filmcan, giving a date, unit, and location. The news editors at home added their own version of what was on screen. TV channels competed for dramatic news footage, and so explosions and fire was much more likely to be seen on TVs in America than more peaceful scenes from the war. In the field, while many correspondents had a wealth of experience, few had the real military knowledge to allow them to assess and pass valid comment on operations and actions. Some later admitted that the willing assistance of the U.S. Armed forces in equipping, accommodating, and flying journalists around Vietnam actually served to generate bad publicity for them. The men and women covering the war felt that the assistance they were being given should in no way be allowed to cloud their editorial impartiality or "buy" their good opinion. As a result, they often found themselves overcompensating by producing "knocking" stories, reports that were overtly critical of the U.S. Armed forces and their Vietnam operations.

specially built monitors, gunboats, and armed helicopters, as well as howitzers and mortars mounted on purpose-made floating platforms. Assigned to this Mobile Riverine Force was 2nd Brigade, 9th Infantry Division, which began operations against the Cam Son Secret Zone, ten miles (16 km) west of Dong Tam in May 1967.

Even as General Westmoreland shifted American, ARVN, and South Korean forces from II Corps to I Corps, fighting intensified in the highlands. After several engagements with enemy forces in May and June, Westmoreland ordered the 173rd Airborne Brigade from III Corps to II Corps in order to

serve as the I Field Force's strategic reserve. Even as the 173rd Brigade redeployed, the enemy struck several CIDG camps at Dak To, Dak Seang, and Dak Pek in northern Kontum Province. Under the control of the 4th Infantry Division, operations continued throughout the summer until the enemy threat waned. Within a few months, however, patrols in the vicinity of Dak To again detected a rapid buildup of enemy forces. Believing Dak To was threatened by a full regiment of NVA, 4th Infantry Division reinforced the garrison there. In order to deal with this renewed enemy threat, the 173rd Airborne Brigade also returned to ground they knew well, arriving at Dak To on

November 2, 1967.

Between November 3 and 15, an estimated 12,000 enemy troops probed, harassed, and attacked American and ARVN positions on the ridges and hills surrounding the fire bases manned by the 173rd Airborne Brigade. Instead of their usual hit-and-run tactics, the NVA and VC maintained contact with the Americans and ARVN forces, requiring General Westmoreland to reinforce the paratroopers with two battalions from the 1st Air Cavalry Division and six ARVN battalions.

Despite daily air and artillery bombardments of their positions, the North Vietnamese launched two attacks against Dak To on November 15, destroying two C-130 aircraft and severely damaging the camp's ammunition dump. Allied forces struggled to dislodge the NVA from their fortified positions on the surrounding hills. The center of enemy resistance was Hill 875; here two battalions of the 173rd Airborne Brigade made a slow and painful ascent against determined resistance, fighting for every foot of ground. Enemy fire was so intense and accurate that, at times, the Americans were unable to bring in reinforcements by helicopter or to provide fire support. In fighting that resembled the hill battles of the final stages of the Korean War, U.S. commanders on Hill 875 were forced to call in

BELOW: The driver of an M48A3 tank supporting the 25th "Tropic Lightning" Division peers out under his Combat Vehicle Crewman Helmet at the British photographer Tim Page on the Tay Ninh road. One of the youngest journalists to cover Vietnam, Page arrived at 18 and remained for five years. His work appeared in *Time-Life*, *Paris Match* and with AP and UPI. He suffered severe wounds and head injuries from "friendly fire" when U.S. aircraft strafed the sampan on which he was relaxing offshore.

RIGHT: The gutted interior of a U.S. Army M113 APC following an internal explosion. In addition to fuel, the vehicle would have been full of ammunition that would added to the destruction. If the roof and rear hatches had been closed and the explosion therefore contained, its effect would have been greater. It was the thought of the ghastly death inside an APC that prompted many soldiers to ride on top, even though they might be vulnerable to sniper fire.

LEFT: Lt Elmer J. Gilder-Sleeve, the Assistant Catapult Officer on board the USS *Oriskany*, prepares to launch an RF-8G Crusader photo-reconnaissance aircraft in August 1967. By 1967, the *Oriskany* part of Task Force 77 in the U.S. Navy 7th Fleet had already seen two deployments in operations off Vietnam. The U.S. Navy's photo-reconnaissance squadrons suffered three times the loss rate of other squadrons because the aircraft were forced to fly straight on a constant course to get the best imagery, thus making them vulnerable to antiaircraft fire. Twenty RF-8Gs were lost in the Vietnam War, nearly a quarter of Crusader losses. During the bombing pause between 1968 and 1971, such photo-reconnaissance sorties represented the majority of U.S. flights over North Vietnam.

BOTTOM RIGHT: During a lull in the fighting, Pfc James A.Tims of the 1st Infantry Division checks the condition of a wounded comrade who is lying in an overgrown rubber plantation situated in Tay Ninh, 7.4 miles (12 km) from the Cambodian border in War Zone C. The 1st Infantry Division had been in action against a North Vietnamese Army Regiment in April during Operation Junction City.

artillery and air strikes, including B-52 arc light strikes, at perilously close range to their own positions. On November 24, American forces finally gained control of Hill 875.

The battle of Dak To was, up to that time, the longest and most violent in the highlands since the battle of the Ia Drang two years before. Enemy casualties numbered in the thousands, including 1,400 dead. The Americans also paid a heavy price, since approximately one in five men of the 173rd Airborne Brigade became casualties. Senior U.S. Army officials concluded later that "If the battle of the Ia Drang exemplified air mobility in all of its versatility, the battle of Dak To, with the arduous ascent of Hill 875, epitomized infantry combat at its most basic and crushing levels."

Dak To was only one of several border battles fought in the last months of 1967 in the highlands. At Song Be and Loc Ninh in III

Corps, and all along the northern border of I Corps, the North Vietnamese Army and Viet Cong had been forced to reveal their positions in order to confront U.S. forces in heavy fighting. However, the Communists had forced Westmoreland to disperse his troops throughout the country in an increasingly difficult attempt to contain or channel them to specific regions where they could be destroyed in set-piece battles.

As Army and Marine historians now concede, the battles in the highlands and along the DMZ in 1967 were the opening actions of what would culminate in the 1968 "Tet" offensive. Furthermore, as U.S. forces dispersed throughout the countryside in an attempt to defeat the enemy, the vacuum created allowed the VC to re-occupy supposedly "pacified" areas, gather new recruits to fill their depleted ranks, and re-assert their control over the rural populace.

OPPOSITE: A U.S. Marine pulls a blindfolded Viet Cong prisoner to his feet after the man has tripped and fallen on May 27 during Operation Union 2, 20 miles (32 km) south of Da Nang. Blindfolding was a Standard Operating Procedure (SOP) since it made escape harder for the prisoners and also prevented them from seeing anything of intelligence value. However, it made for emotive images.

BELOW: O Battery, 2nd Battalion, 19th Artillery, 1st Cavalry Division prepare to fire their M102 105 mm light towed howitzers in the Vinh Thanh Valley in support of the 1st Battalion, 5th Cavalry during Operation Crazy Horse. At 3,196 lb. (1,450 kg), M102 howitzers could be lifted by Chinook helicopter.

LEFT: An ammunition dump at Dak To hit by NVA mortar fire in November. The fighting in the Central Highlands about 348 miles (560 km) north of Saigon was between four NVA regiments – about 6,000 troops – and men of the U.S. 4th Division and the 173rd Airborne Brigade.

BELOW: In the chaos of smashed trees, men of the 173rd Airborne Brigade take cover during the battle for Hill 875, one of the toughest actions during the fighting at Dak To.

RIGHT: A River Patrol Boat Mk II moves at a steady speed through a Mekong Delta backwater. Known as PBR, these 29 ft. 6 in. (9 m) fiberglass craft were armed with twin .5 caliber machine guns in the bow, a .3 in. caliber machine gun aft, and a rapid firing 40mm grenade launcher, and had a top speed of 29 knots.

Despite the change in tactics by the Viet Cong and North Vietnamese, the U.S. Forces continued to inflict defeats on the battlefield and the ARVN showed encouraging signs of improvement. However, NVA had shown its determination to match the American buildup, division by division. Even though the NVA could not match the firepower or resources possessed by the Americans, they maintained the tactical initiative, but they had failed to win a major battlefield victory over the Americans or, more importantly, ARVN, and the looked for revolutionary uprising in the countryside had not materialized. If anything, ARVN had held its own in the field, and was showing signs of developing into an effective fighting machine. North Vietnamese leaders

concluded that the "strategy of military confrontation had failed to stop the American military pressure on the North."

Even as these battles were being fought in the northernmost limits of I Corps, MACV began construction of what would become known as the "McNamara Line." Work first began in April 1967 on what was planned to be a 25 mile (40 km) long physical barrier laced with sophisticated electronic sensors and punctuated by carefully selected fortified positions. Designed to counter the massive infiltration of North Vietnamese troops across the DMZ, and alternatively known as the "Electric Fence," it

was the brain-child of a Harvard Law School professor and was championed by U.S. Secretary of Defense, Robert McNamara, who hoped to reduce the need for costly and continuous troop deployments in areas constantly subjected to enemy mortar and artillery fire. This anti-infiltration system had as its key feature electronically activated sensors that would be sown along key avenues of approach from the north.. All enemy movement, whether by foot or vehicle, could be measured. The U.S. Marines hoped to use the "Line" to detect enemy incursions and movements at great ranges.

NEXT PAGE: An M60 machine gunner of the 173rd Airborne Brigade, which suffered losses of 158 men, 30 of which were from a U.S. airstrike that landed short of its target during the fighting for Hill 875. In the 19 days of action around Dak To, the NVA fatalities were an estimated 1,455, while 285 U.S. servicemen were killed, 985 wounded, and 18 missing. The Brigade was later awarded a Presidential Unit Citation for bravery in action.

LEFT: Casualties are carried away from a U.S. Marine Corps Boeing-Vertol CH-46 Sea Knight. For casualty evacuation, the CH-46 – which had a crew of three – could carry 15 litters and two attendants. When used as a troop transport, it could lift between 17 and 25 Marines.

BELOW: Caught in a moment of intense concentration, Pullitzer Prize winning UPI photographer Kyoichi Sawada watches the action on Hill 875. Born in 1936 in Japan, Kyoichi Sawada was orphaned as a child. After World War II he was a picture editor for UPI in Tokyo before using his vacation to cover the Vietnam war. UPI assigned him to Vietnam and his work won first and second place in the 1966 World Press Photo Contest.

Work did begin in April but proved painfully slow. Constant harassment from enemy artillery, mortar, and rocket fire slowed down construction of the strongpoints and obstacles. Although it was never completed, certain sections of the line did go into operation. The results at places like Khe Sanh demonstrated that the system was more a tactical rather than strategic tool. The sensors did provide excellent information on enemy troop movements, which allowed them to be targeted by air power and artillery.

The McNamara Line had its critics, particularly after the full-scale construction of the line was abandoned, but the U.S. Senate hearings in 1970 which examined the effectiveness of the anti-infiltration system concluded that the system saved many lives by giving ground troops early warning of attacks. The sensors were likewise credited with increasing enemy losses in personnel and equipment, and also

with providing both the Army and Marines with a credible surveillance system that worked by day or night. Troop commanders explicitly praised the effectiveness of this anti-infiltration system in allowing them to find and track the enemy.

As spring turned into summer, the Marines continued to battle enemy forces both around the coastal enclaves and along the DMZ. In southern I Corps, a series of search and destroy missions were conducted against the elusive Viet Cong. While the VC continued its hit-and-run raids and ambushes, units from 1st and 5th Marines launched Operation Union southward from Da Nang along Route 1. In a classic heliborne operation, the Marines and ARVN Rangers attacked southwest of Thang Binh, attempting to force the VC into battle, resulting in a series of sharp clashes on April 25. Operation Beaver Cage, carried out in parallel with Union by Special Landing Force (1st

BELOW: Hunching down low, men of the 173rd Airborne Brigade race toward the summit of Hill 875 – carrying ammunition for machinegun crews – only a day before the feature was finally captured on November 24. On the same day in the Pentagon during an upbeat briefing, General William Westmoreland stated that Dak To was "the beginning of a great defeat for the enemy." He explained to his audience that captured documents – taken from the body of a dead North Vietnamese soldier – showed that the Dak To battle was intended by Hanoi to have been the beginning of a North Vietnamese Army winter/spring offensive by the B-3 Front in central Vietnam.

The Ho Chi Minh Trail

To understand the Ho Chi Minh Trail is perhaps to understand why the South fell to the communists. Over nearly 20 years, the trail was shelled, devastated by awesome B52 strikes, and invaded by U.S./ARVN troops, but each time North Vietnamese men, women, and children patched up the damage by hand, and the supplies kept rolling south. There are few better testaments to the Communist resolve.

The Ho Chi Minh Trail started small in 1959, nothing more than the widening of a few tribal trails down through Laos. North Vietnamese supply troops – then known as Group 559 – would head down the trail on foot, mule, or bicycle to supply the Viet Cong in the South with weapons, ammunition and explosives. But this north-south communication route just kept growing. Gangs of teenagers, known as Special Youth Shock Groups, showed enormous dedication to the widening of the route, expanding it to a size which allowed trucks to shift supplies down south in greater bulk. The trail became a place of incredible industry.

Supply depots, medical facilities, and rest stations sprung up along the way, feeding, caring, and providing for the thousands of men now pouring down the trail.

By 1964, the trail was reaching maximum development. What had started as a narrow system of tracks was now a buzzing network of supply routes. The next year the Soviet Union and China gave the North Vietnamese road-building machines, and this pushed development even further. The figures speak for themselves. In terms of human infiltration alone, in 1964 it was estimated that 10,000 NVA troops had infiltrated into South Vietnam from the trail, cutting into South Vietnam across the Laotian and Cambodian border. By 1968 the estimates rise to 100,000 troops and many thousands of tons of supplies.

Of course, the U.S. made every effort to take out the trail. Laos became one of the most bombed countries in history as B-52s pounded the trail day and night with 70,000 lb. (31,751 kg) payloads. Yet the trail was dug deep –

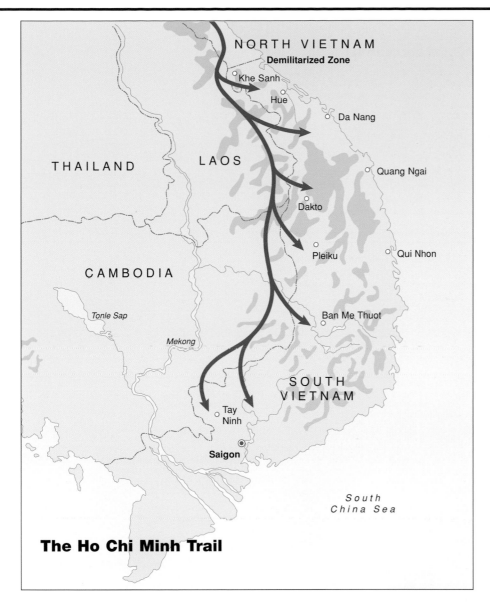

The Ho Chi Minh Trail

NORTH VIETNAM
Demilitarized Zone
Khe Sanh
Hue
Da Nang
Quang Ngai
THAILAND
LAOS
Dakto
CAMBODIA
Pleiku
Qui Nhon
Tonle Sap
Ban Me Thuot
Mekong
SOUTH VIETNAM
Tay Ninh
Saigon
South China Sea

FAR LEFT: A North Vietnamese Army crew man a Soviet M-1939 37mm Light antiaircraft gun on the Ho Chi Minh Trail. The gun, weighing 4,409 lb. (2,000 kg) in its firing position could fire 80 rounds a minute. Its maximum horizontal range was 26,246 ft. (8,000 m) and its vertical 19,685 ft. (6,000 m). Its armor-piercing ammunition could penetrate 46mm armor at 1,640 ft. (500 m). USAF and USN veterans of attacks on the Ho Ch Minh Trail were amused by the "tales of daring" of pilots who flew over South Vietnam under fire from 12.7mm machine guns. World War II veterans said that antiaircraft fire along Ho Chi Minh Trail was as effective as the German Flak situated in the Ruhr.

BELOW: On the Ho Chi Minh Trail, there were also 30,000 men and women in construction and repair units tasked with filling craters following air attacks. Theirs was a tough life, living on rations in tropical rainforest camps. The 12,430 mile (20,000 km) long trail was a complex spread of tracks and roads; though more than 10,000 trucks were used, porters and modified bicycles moved down narrower tracks. The North Vietnamese also laid 3,107 miles (5,000 km) of pipeline through deep river valleys and over peaks of 3,048 ft. (1,000 m). The trail was supplemented by shipments from the Cambodian port Sihanoukville (Kompong Som). From there, supplies could be transported by truck through Cambodia to bases along the border with South Vietnam. This route was interdicted by B-52 strikes in Operation Menu and closed when General Lon Nol assumed control in 1970. In February 1971, with U.S. air support, the ARVN launched operation Lam Son 719, attempting to cut the trail, but the NVA reacted violently and the South was forced to withdraw.

and was not one big route but hundreds of little ones – and always shrouded with jungle foliage. Those moving down the trail, make no doubt, suffered terribly. Yet the trail was easily repaired and nothing seemed to stop the incessant flow from the North. The trail soldiers moved only at night; in the day everything that could be spotted from the air was thrown under camouflage.

The closest moment the trail came to being cut was in 1971, when South Vietnamese forces launched Operation Lam Son 719. The fall of the pro-Communist government in Cambodia had limited the use of the Cambodian section of the trail. Consequently, large NVA concentrations built up in the Laotian pan-handle, and the South knew it had to act. Lam Son 719, a massive incursion into Laos, began as a successful strike deep into the country, but as the momentum slowed, it turned into a horrifying retreat under NVA artillery and ambush. It was the last time the trail was truly threatened, and it continued to pump supplies into South Vietnam until the country fell to the Communists in 1975.

Battalion, 3rd Marines), was a search and destroy mission 10 miles (16 km) northwest of Tam Ky. By the end of April, the two operations had resulted in 282 confirmed and 290 probable kills, and 34 prisoners captured. The South Vietnamese Rangers killed an additional 15 Viet Cong in a third operation dubbed Operation Lien Ket 102.

As Union ended, the struggle for another line of hills began at Hill 110. Here, Marine and Army artillery, as well as Marine aircraft bombed and strafed enemy positions as elements of 3rd and 5th Marines attempted to seize the hill itself. In a two-day battle against small groups of the enemy, the leathernecks killed more than 130 Viet Cong, suffering 12 dead and 59 wounded in the process.

In the northwest corner of I Corps, 9th Marines were embroiled in an even tougher fight which one official Marine history labeled "the First Battle of Khe Sanh." From September 1966 a rifle company of Marines had been stationed in and around Khe Sanh, and in April 1967 the Marines occupied a series of combat bases along Route 9 including – in addition to Khe Sanh – the Rockpile, Camp Carroll, and Dong Ha. These were specifically designed to impede NVA infiltration through the DMZ, and this line became the focus for most of the fighting in northern I Corps during 1967.

On the morning of April 24, 1967, 2nd Platoon, Company B, 1st Battalion, 9th Marines encountered an enemy force which at first attempted to avoid the Marines. When the 1st Platoon came to relieve their fellow Marines a furious firefight commenced. In what is now seen as the prelude to the battle for Khe Sanh, the outnumbered Marines suffered 30 casualties, but they had unknowingly

LEFT: A young soldier from the 173rd Airborne Brigade sits in the smashed trees atop Hill 875. On his helmet cover, he has written "Hill 875, The Smell of Death, Nov.20–21–22," in one of the few ways in which soldiers could express their attitudes or experiences with graffiti.
BELOW: The bodies of men from the 173rd Airborne Brigade lie in heaps of olive-green bodybags after being recovered from Hill 875. The bodybag, which was introduced in Vietnam, was both a practical and humane way of protecting the dead until their burial.

ABOVE: During Operation Baker 5 miles (8 km) north of Duc Pho, men of Company C, 2nd Battalion, 35th Infantry Regiment, 25th Infantry Division take a wounded comrade to a "dustoff." Some men craved wounds that were severe enough to take them out of action but did not cause long term damage.

upset the enemy plans, forcing him to attack prematurely and revealing his intention to assault the base in force.

Special Landing Force-Battalion Landing Team 2nd Battalion, 3rd Marines and Heavy Marine Helicopter Squadron were at this point involved in Operation Beacon Star, a search and destroy mission in and around the Quang Tri City area. The was to involve a beach

assault and a heliborne assault. While Beacon Star was underway, the Marines of the 3rd Bn., 3rd Marines clashed with strong enemy formations in the hills located west of Khe Sahn. Realizing that his force was too weak to meet this challenge alone, the 3rd Marine Division commander, Major General Bruno Hocmuth, ordered the SLF to break contact with the enemy and proceed to the Khe Sanh area.

THE McNAMARA LINE

The DMZ (Demilitarized Zone) was all that separated North from South Vietnam. Six miles (9.6 km) wide, carpeted in jungle, it provided the quickest route of infiltration for northern troops. By the mid-1960s, U.S. tacticians and engineers were looking for ways to halt this movement, and that's where McNamara stepped in.

The McNamara Line was not his idea, despite the name. In 1966, Professor Roger Fisher of the Harvard Law School proposed building a physical barrier across the entire length of the DMZ. He envisaged a barrier 160 miles (257 km) long and 10 miles (16 km) wide, full of electronic security equipment, military fireposts, electric and barbed wire fences, and minefields. The idea was taken seriously. In mid-1966 Robert McNamara gathered together a group of scientists and engineers to discuss the feasibility of the proposal. It was decided that the idea was workable, and in 1967 building of the "McNamara Line" began.

McNamara had huge plans for his line. New monitoring sensors were to be deployed – including fantastic devices such as seismic movement detectors disguised as dog dirt. Every motion detector and sensor was to be connected up to a firebase which would rain down shells should anything be disturbed. It was a plan which never happened. Only 10 miles (16 km) of line were built. NVA shelling ensured that the pace was painfully slow, and too many valuable combat troops found themselves grudgingly working as builders. Crucial, however, was the realization that the NVA could simply bypass the line through northern Laos. So millions of dollars later, McNamara's line was scrapped.

ABOVE: Jerry D. Coffin of Los Angeles burns his Draft Card in front of the historic Independence Hall in Philadelphia on October 16, as one of several young men who burned their cards in Philadelphia that day. Many men who served in Vietnam had no argument with those not prepared to serve in the Armed Forces, nor with those who burned their Draft Cards but were also prepared to go to jail; they had made a protest and accepted the consequences. However, Draft evaders who used college exemptions, contacts within the government, or who crossed the border and hid in Canada were regarded with contempt. The pardon and amnesty for men hidden in Canada particularly rankled with veterans.

On April 25, 1967, the 3rd Battalion, 3rd Marines, commanded by Lieutenant Colonel Gary Wilder, came into the Khe Sanh fire base from Dong Ha. By 6.30 p.m. that evening, one company was already heavily engaged with a suspected enemy battalion dug in along Hill 861. On the evening of April 28, both the 2nd and 3rd Battalion of the 3rd Marines began an offensive against the North Vietnamese and Viet Cong forces on and around Hills 861, 881 North, and 881 South. 2nd Battalion would seize Hill 881 North, while the 3rd Battalion secured Hill 881 South. Two rifle companies of the 3rd Battalion eventually reached the summit of Hill 881 South, but suffered heavy casualties in the process. To minimize casualties, Lieutenant Colonel Wilder decided to pound the objective with air strikes and artillery. The next day, May 1, the 1st Marine Air Wing flew over 150 missions in support of 3rd Battalion.

LEFT: 21-year-old Lance Corporal Perry M. Jolley, a machine gunner with 3rd Battalion, 11th Marine Regiment, 1st Marine Division wades a stream with his .45 Colt automatic pistol held out of its holster to keep it dry. The Marines were on an operation southwest of Da Nang in December.

RIGHT: During a break in Operation Big Spring near Bien Hoa, Sp5 Harris E. Wood shares out icecream to men of Company B, 2nd Battalion, 503rd Infantry, 173rd Airborne Brigade. In the 1960s and 1970s, the U.S. armed forces went to war with many luxuries that seemed extravagant to other nations. Ironically, in the Gulf War of 1990–91, the fresh food cooked by the British Army was a major attraction for U.S. soldiers who were obliged to eat Meals Ready to Eat (MREs), the combat rations that had replaced the C Rations of the Vietnam War.

FAR RIGHT: U.S. soldiers man a captured trench in secondary jungle. The fast-growing tropical vegetation in Vietnam made camouflage relatively easy for the Viet Cong and NVA once a position had been dug, since it would quickly take root in the freshly turned soil. U.S. and Allied tanks firing "Beehive" rounds – which were composed of thousands of small darts – would blast suspected areas, and this would expose bunkers and the prominent, dark shape of the weapon embrasure.

By mid-afternoon of May 2, Lt Col Wilder's battalion had seized Hill 881 South.

Heavy fighting likewise greeted the Marines from the 2nd Battalion as they battled their way through what intelligence later confirmed was a well-dug-in regiment of NVA regulars. After being hit by a heavy concentration of mortar fire, two companies of the 2nd Battalion advanced to the summit, engaging in heavy fighting as they advanced. 2nd Battalion finally reached the top of Hill 881 North on May 4.

Colonel Patrick Blessing, then a young company commander, recalled in a postwar interview that the key to the Marine's successes in "Indian territory," as Marines dubbed the area around Hills 881 North and South, was "the skillful and closely coordinated air-ground action." In fact, as the Marine Corps' official history stated, the heavy fighting in and around Khe Sanh "provided a classic example of integrated employment of modern, fixed-wing aviation in support of ground maneuver elements."

Blessing's account illustrates that on occasion aviation and supporting arms decided the outcome of the battle. The fighter-bombers normally waited on the tarmac at Chu Lai or Da Nang until a request for air support was received, at which point they scrambled. Once the aircraft reached the area, the target would be marked with a smoke grenade or flare. Sometimes, as in the case of the fighting on Hills 881 South and North, ground commanders would call in air support close to their own positions.

NEXT PAGE: Taken by UPI photographer Charles R. Eggleston – who would die in a rocket attack in the Tet Offensive of 1968 – this photo shows an M1 81mm Mortar crew of the 1st Infantry Division in action in War Zone C. The crew were supporting an attack near Quan Loi on the Cambodian border during Operation Junction City II.

LEFT: U.S. Marines cross rice paddies toward higher ground in the Da Nang region in December. The men are spaced about 90 ft. (30 m) apart, ensuring they would not suffer casualties from mortar fire or on entering the "killing ground" of an enemy ambush. UPI photographer Dana Stone – who went missing on April 6, 1970 on Route 1 in Cambodia – took the picture.

RIGHT: Wearing a locally produced camouflaged beret, an M60 machine gunner in a Long Range Reconnaissance Patrol (LRRP or "Lurp") scans the jungle for enemy movement. LRRPs penetrated deep into hostile territory for a variety of reasons, including to gather intelligence, capture prisoners, and assess bomb damage. Though later in the war these forces were to be formally established into four groups – Detachment B-52 Project DELTA, Detachment B-50 Project OMEGA, Detachment B-56 Project SIGMA, and the highly classified Detachment B-57 Project GAMMA – at the outset of the war, long range patrolling was less formally structured. In November 1967, OMEGA and SIGMA were absorbed into MACV-SOG. More commonly known as SOG, the Studies and Observation Group was an unconventional warfare task force. The men from this force were engaged in highly secret operations which ran throughout the Southeast Asian region.

Colonel Blessing recalled one such situation during the fight for Hill 881 North: "Artillery was slow that day [May 3, 1967], so I got on the international air net and began yelling 'Help!' Some pilot from VMFA (Marine Fighter-Attack Squadron) 323 came in and said, 'I don't have much fuel but if you could mark the target, I'll hit whatever is out there.' So I popped smoke [grenade] and the pilot came in and said, 'Isn't that too close [to your position]?' No, I said, just dump every-

thing you have on them [the NVA]. Flying single seat jets [A-4 Skyhawks], they did a splendid job!" Blessing commented after the war, "If you needed air, and Marine air was nearby, they helped, even, as in the case of this mission, if they were flying another mission, they came to lend assistance." In May 1967 alone, the 1st MAW flew a record 6,542 sorties in support of operations in and around the DMZ. They dropped over 9,350 tons of bombs and 1,502 tons of napalm, and fired 8,000 air-to-

BELOW: A plume of smoke drifts away from a smoke grenade. It has been thrown to give wind direction as a CH-47 Chinook brings in ammunition to a battery of M102 105mm light towed howitzers northwest of Tuy Hoa. The guns had been deployed to support search and destroy mission Operation Bolling in September. The CH-47 could carry 28,000 lb. (12,700 kg) externally.

RIGHT: The body of a NVA soldier is dumped into a common grave at LZ George at Ap Gu at the close of Operation Junction City II on the Cambodian border. After action at Long Tan in August 1966, Australian forces buried NVA soldiers in individual identifiable graves; when the South fell to the NVA in 1975, the North Vietnamese did not destroy the memorial with which the Australians commemorated their own dead.

BELOW: A South Vietnamese woman and child after a Viet Cong attack on their village near Da Nang. During it, VC forces captured 11 children aged between 11 and 16. Showing that Saigon could not protect rural communities had profound political and psychological value for the Viet Cong.

RIGHT: Followed by several riflemen, a headquarters group of the U.S. Marines moves through grassland in the highlands. The Marines shown here appear to be relaxed with a low-threat level, with one RTO even on the radio with his M16 rifle slung. The terrain in Vietnam was immensely varied, ranging from low-lying paddy fields, the swamps of the Mekong Delta, to the jungle highlands, where deeply entrenched rivers and streams and exposed grasslands were to be found. Combined with a hot, debilitating, and wet climate, any of these types of terrain could sap the strength of even the strongest soldier. For these men, their tactics would vary according to the terrain. While open grassland allowed long range, indirect fire weapons to be used, in the jungle, the engagement ranges could be down to several feet, calling for extremely fast reactions and reflexes. In the rural areas of paddy fields and small villages, U.S. soldiers would be haunted by the constant feeling that the peasants were hostile toward them, as if they were watching for an opportunity to inflict casualties on them either with booby traps, or with their other "homemade" devices. Whenever men were killed or wounded by these devices, the growing sense of anger and frustration among their comrades was – naturally – always acute.

ground rockets and 339,000 rounds of ammunition.

Fighting on and around Hills 881 South and North continued for the next few days. The area surrounding Hills 881 North and South deservedly became known as the "Badlands." In one action, the NVA ambushed a seven-man Marine reconnaissance as it was about to be extracted 5 miles (8 km) northwest of Hill 881 North. Enemy fire killed one Marine pilot and wounded a co-pilot and six crewmen. Of the original seven-man team inserted, four were killed and the remaining three wounded. They were finally evacuated

under the cover of darkness.

As U.S. forces took the fight to the enemy, General Westmoreland concentrated on effecting a qualitative and quantitative improvement in the ability of the South Vietnamese Army (ARVN) to allow it to eventually shoulder the burden of the fighting. In I Corps, the 1st ARVN Division expanded its area of responsibility even as its firepower was substantially increased. Starting in September 1967 MACV supplied the Division with 106mm Recoilless rifles, 60mm mortars, and M60 machine guns. Later in the year MACV began issuing ARVN M-16 rifles which replaced the heavier and bulkier M1 Garand and M1 Carbines, originally provided to the South Vietnamese government for its fledgling army. With this greatly

enhanced firepower, the morale of the 1st Division and their performance showed a marked improvement. One indication of the increased U.S. confidence in ARVN was the relief by a regiment of the 1st ARVN Division of U.S. Marines responsible for a sector of the DMZ. This steady improvement in ARVN equipment and performance continued into 1968.

For the remainder of 1967 MACV's attention focussed on the conventional war raging in I Corps around the infiltration routes that straddled the DMZ. On May 18, the Marines in northern I Corps began the ambitious task of ridding the southern half of the DMZ of enemy forces and installations in Operation Hickory. This would be the first major sortie

Antiwar Protests

Looking back at all the images of protest over the Vietnam War, it's easy to forget that when it started, most Americans were in approval. Communism was seen as a virus which had to be 'contained' to stop a global infection. Vietnam was a showdown between light and dark, good and evil. Yet it didn't take long for disillusion to set in. Policies seemed inefficient, and the Gulf of Tonkin resolution was vague about where the U.S. was going with the war. The South Vietnamese nation looked corrupt and unpredictable, rather than a fully democratic nation in need of saving. And all the time the death toll was steadily rising.

The 1960s in the U.S. were a time of protest, of revolutionary ideas. Civil rights was an explosive issue. A "flower power" generation was becoming increasing vocal with ideas of "Make Love, Not War". Vietnam consequently became the wrong war at the wrong time, its massive violence at odds with a world in which many sought other ways of living. The universities were initially the focal point of protest. Throughout the U.S., student groups formed large antiwar bodies, the most significant being the Students for a Democratic Society. Initially many saw these people as un-American extremists, a view reinforced when the anarchist group called the Weathermen bombed the Reserve Officer's Training Corps buildings.

Yet other issues evoked more popular ire. The draft process for Vietnam was constructed so that if you had

money or connections, you could bypass service – some 16 million Americans managed to evade their draft request. In October 1967, 100,000 people marched through Washington D.C. in protest at both the draft's unfairness and the fact it was happening at all. Violence resulted as some of the crowd attempted to invade the Pentagon.

The violence escalated. After Tet, many universities suffered aggressive protests harshly put down by the police in full view of the cameras. Following the assassination of Martin Luther King on April 4, 1968, 130 U.S. cities suffered rioting, with 46 people killed, whole neighborhoods burned to the ground, and 75,000 troops mobilized. The Democratic Party convention in August 1968 ended with 1,000 people injured by police teargas and batons. This last event axed America down the middle. Even after the election of Richard Nixon to the White House and Vietnamization started to take hold, protests continued to dog the administration – one million people held a nationwide day of peace in October 1969, and capital cities throughout the world felt the heat of protest.

By 1970 the U.S. people had had enough of war and unsettled lives. The final straw came when four students were shot dead by police at Kent State University in Ohio; they had been protesting the U.S. bombing of Cambodia. Two more students died at Jackson State University, Mississippi. The year 1970 proved to be a watershed. Nixon realized he had to get out of Vietnam, and he accelerated the withdrawal process. The people had defeated Vietnam.

BELOW OPPOSITE: Dr Benjamin Spock, the pediatrician whose writings had influenced many mothers in the U.S., had resigned from his practice to concentrate on the anti-Vietnam War protest and World Peace.

ABOVE OPPOSITE: Country Joe and the Fish, the American rock group whose catchy songs included lines like "One, two, three, what are we fighting for? Don't ask me I don't give a damn. Next stop is Vietnam" reflected the nihilistic attitude of sections of American youth to the foreign policy adopted by their parents' generation. Protest songs were a significant part of the antiwar movement; some like "Blowing in the Wind" haunting and questioning, while others were hostile. Joan Baez is usually associated with the protest song, but among the more unusual exemplars is Roy Orbison. In the mid-1960s, his song "There won't be many coming home" drew protests from the establishment who said that it was unpatriotic. At the opposite extreme, new words were put to an Irish folk tune to become "The Ballad of the Green Beret," a song about a member of the newly formed Special Forces.

LEFT: Women Concerned for Peace protest in a rally against the U.S. bombing policy in North Vietnam. Such protest groups eventually drew support from politicians, journalists, church groups, and other liberal organizations. The publication of the Pentagon Papers, smuggled out of the Pentagon by Daniel Ellsberg, showed how the United States had become drawn into the war and how the truth had been manipulated for policy ends. When it emerged that President Nixon had attempted to discredit Ellsberg by tasking the "Watergate Plumbers" – a team whose mission was to plug "leaks" – with stealing Ellsberg's medical records from his psychiatrist, it was one of the factors that doomed the Presidency. For the United States, the war in Vietnam appeared to offer no "light at the end of the tunnel" and, as drafted servicemen became mutinous and public opinion actively hostile, it became essential for the U.S. to withdraw from Southeast Asia.

ABOVE: "Dirty Fascist!" screams a student from the University of Wisconsin during an antiwar demonstration in December when police used truncheons and CS gas. The clash was also cultural, between the white-collared middle and the blue-collared working classes, a product of the police resentment of those destined for a better life than they had enjoyed.

by an entire Marine regiment into the demilitarized zone. Hickory was conducted in cooperation with 1st ARVN Division and a landing by the SLF, and benefited from the support of a joint Marine-Air Force operation. Two Marine battalions moved northward from the Con Thien fire support base, while another battalion moved into position northwest of the fire base close to the Ben Hai River. In some of the most sustained fighting yet, the Marines killed 61 NVA soldiers within the

first 48 hours. The 1st ARVN Division moved north from its bases at Gio Linh along Route 1 to just below "Freedom Bridge" from where it crossed the Ben Hai River in order to sweep southward. The Special Landing Force (1st Battalion, 3rd Marine), coordinating with the 9th Marines, made an assault using helicopters and Landing Craft into the northeastern portion of the DMZ. As the landing went in, Navy destroyers offshore pounded NVA positions.

RIGHT: British police confront demonstrators in Grosvenor Square, London at a demonstration in the fall of 1967. Among the student radicals who spoke in London are men and women who, nearly 35 years later, are respectable members of the "Establishment" in Britain in politics, journalism, or the arts. The United States found itself under attack from liberal and leftwing students, politicians, and writers throughout Europe. While some may have been – in Lenin's cool assessment of intellectuals at the time of the Bolshevik Revolution – "Useful Fools," many were people who felt strongly that U.S. involvement in Vietnam was unjust and the tactics criminal.

BELOW RIGHT: An African American student holds a placard with the catchy slogan "I Don't Give a Damn For Uncle Sam, I Ain't Going to Vietnam." The picture of the Argentine revolutionary and intellectual Ernesto "Che" Guevara on the poster reading "Crush the Draft" is an added provocation to the police and American middle classes. Guevara had just been killed in Bolivia while fomenting a revolution. A distinguishing feature of demonstrations were slogans that were easy to remember and chant, one of which, "Hey Hey, LBJ, How many kids did you kill today?" naturally rankled with Lyndon Baines Johnson, the U.S. President. Excoriated as the president who prosecuted the Vietnam war, Johnson's domestic achievements are often overlooked. He put several constitutional reforms promised by President John Kennedy through Congress, notably the 1964 Civil Rights Bill, and initiated community care and educational provisions, such as the Medicare program for older people.

Hickory proved one of the most effective operations of the Vietnam War with the Marines and ARVN conducting a classic "Hammer and Anvil" assault. A half dozen enemy battalions were caught off guard south of the DMZ, and Lieutenant Colonel Wendell C. Vest's 3rd Battalion, 4th Marines maneuvered itself behind several enemy units, annihilating many of them. By the time Hickory ended on May 28, 1967 the Marines had confirmed 445 NVA killed in action while ARVN counted an additional 370 dead NVA. The significance of Operation Hickory, in the words of the official Marine Corps history, was that "the enemy had been served notice that the southern half of the DMZ would no longer be inviolate to ground operations." The success enjoyed by the Marines and ARVN did not, however, result in the eradication of the NVA

ABOVE: With his .45 Colt M1918 automatic pistol drawn, a U.S. Marine officer moves carefully past his radio operator as the latter sends a "SitRep" – a Situation Report – about the course of fighting on Hill 881. The hill was one of three near Khe Sanh in Quang Tin Province close to the Demilitarized Zone (DMZ) which marked the border between North and South Vietnam, fought over between April 25 and May 5.
RIGHT AND FAR RIGHT: Two photographs taken by UPI photographer Frank B. Johnston show three Marines supporting a gravely wounded comrade off Hill 881. Once they had carried him to an LZ, his comrade cradled the head of the wounded man and waited for the "dust-off" casualty evacuation helicopter. During the fighting, the Marines lost 160 men killed and 746 wounded, half the combat strength of the two battalions of the 3rd Marine Regiment. The fighting at Khe Sanh reminded some historians of that at Dien Bien Phu prior to the final assault on the French position.

ABOVE: A U.S. Marine Corps patrol moves uphill through short elephant grass, armed with the M14 rifle. Following the fighting on Hill 881, there were criticisms of the M16 which, it was said, jammed, causing the death of several Marines. In August, the Defense Department acknowledged there had been a "serious increase in frequency of malfunctions in the M-16."

RIGHT: Viet Cong survey a U.S. Marine Corps LVTP5A1 amphibious assault vehicle south of the Ben Hai river in May in the Winter–Spring Offensive of 1966–67. The vehicle had a maximum speed on roads of 30 miles per hour (48.28 kph) and on water of 6.8 miles per hour (10.94 kph) and could carry 34 men. It was armed with a 7.62mm machine gun with 2,000 rounds of ammunition.

from the southern DMZ. Many of the enemy units had conducted a fighting retreat. Both Marine and ARVN commanders knew that the successes enjoyed during Hickory were temporary.

On May 29, 1967, during Prairie IV, 3rd Battalion, 4th Marines encountered heavy resistance near Con Thien and, after a prolonged fire fight, succeeded in driving the NVA from the area. As Prairie IV ended, Operation Cimarron began, which aimed to destroy the NVA forces that surrounded Con Thien. While Marine and ARVN forces annihilated the enemy on the ground, the joint Marine-Air Force task force pounded them from the air. In June of 1967 Air Force F-100 Super Sabres and B-52 bombers pounded NVA artillery emplacements that had been methodically shelling Con Thien. Meanwhile Skyhawks, Intruders, and Phantoms strafed, rocketed, and napalmed NVA troop concentrations along the DMZ.

In some of the heaviest fighting prior to the Tet offensive, Marines and ARVN units took on the elite 3rd and 21st North Vietnamese Regiments located in the Nui Loc Son Basin. 3rd Battalion, 5th Marines conducted a heliborne assault on elements of the 3rd North Vietnamese Regiment near Vinh Huy, triggering a prolonged engagement. Meanwhile elements of the 1st Battalion, 5th Marines took on 21st NVA Regiment dug-in along the rim of the Nui Loc Son Basin. Here the Marines of 1st Battalion, 5th Marines fought the NVA bunker-to-bunker as supporting air and artillery assisted in dislodging a stubborn enemy. The Marines managed to kill 540 NVA, losing 73 of their own, with a further 139 wounded in the process.

In Operation Adair, "Kilo" Company, 3rd Battalion, 5th Marines encountered two companies of NVA regulars near the railroad located at Thang Binh. Meanwhile, Marines from 2nd Battalion, 3rd Marines pushing toward the

ABOVE: U.S. Army gunners of a M101A1 105mm Howitzer battery prepare a firebase in a freshly cleared area of jungle. Sandbags are being used to construct ammunition storage bunkers while, to the rear of the gun, there is a small stack of ready use ammunition. It was available for a Final Protective Fire (FPF) mission on a predesignated target, either close to the firebase, or the position it was supporting.
NEXT PAGE: With faces drained by fatigue, two Marines of the 1st Battalion, 9th Marines sit in front of the altar of an An Hoa church after their unit had come under NVA mortar fire on May 16. The church was about 2.5 miles (4 km) south of the U.S. Marine base at Con Thien that had been besieged by the North Vietnamese Army.

BELOW: USMC LVTP5A1 assault vehicles on the run into the coast in South Vietnam. The Marines used their amphibious capability to launch "hammer and anvil" attacks from the sea, while a blocking force was positioned inland. In the water, the LVTP5A1 presented a small target with its low freeboard; out of the water it was a large, slabsided vehicle. A total of 1,124 LVTP5s were built, mostly APCs, but also Engineer, Recover, and Command Post variants, and a 105mm howitzer variant, the LVTH6.

Pagoda Valley ran into a company of Viet Cong soldiers and, in a well-coordinated assault that involved air and artillery support, the Marines forced the enemy to retreat minus the 50 VC killed in the fire fight. In early June through July, the majority of the fighting in and along the Demilitarized Zone in Quang Tri Province focused on the fire bases at Khe Sanh and Con Thien. 26th Marines fought a series of engagements with the NVA in and around Hills 881 North and South as the enemy launched probing attacks. Two other operations, Cimarron and Buffalo, attempted to relieve the pressure on Con Thien. In order to maintain the pressure on the enemy, 3rd

Marines launched Operation Hickory II. In conjunction with three ARVN battalions the Marines cleared the area called "Leatherneck Square" south of the DMZ. At the same time Operation Malheur involved Task Force Oregon in a series of company-sized actions, as the Army units, operating west of Route 1, drove northward as far as Mo Duc. In Malheur II, which began as Malheur ended, Army units cleared the entirety of Route 1 in I Corps.

Task Force Oregon's next operation, Hood River, in conjunction with the Korean Marine Brigade and 2nd ARVN Division, lasted a total of 11 days in a 25 mile (40 km) wide

RIGHT: Sweat runs down the face of a U.S. Marine during operations in Vietnam. The climate varied from tropical heat through monsoon rain to cool, dank weather in the highlands. For Europeans, and later North Americans, it was a debilitating climate in which to work; to fight in it was even harder. When casualties arrived at the forward hospitals, they were often dehydrated from loss of blood but also because of sweating as they carried packs, weapons, and ammunition through rugged terrain.

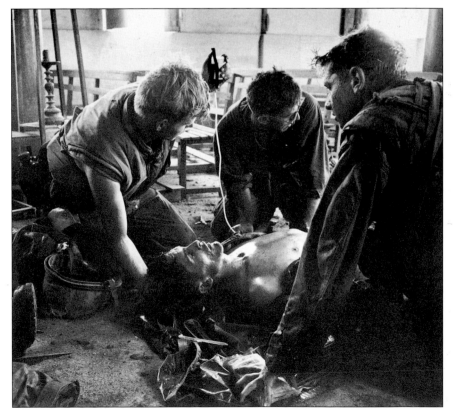

RIGHT: In an improvised aid post in a church near Con Thien, USMC corpsmen stabilize a wounded comrade. Plasma or saline has been administered to rehydrate the casualty. Speedy evacuation by helicopter of men wounded in battle and the sophisticated medical support – as well as the good health of U.S. servicemen – increased their chances of survival; many who would have died from blood poisoning, blood-loss, or shock in earlier wars survived Vietnam. Servicemen were taught four lifesaving steps - 1) stop the bleeding, 2) clear the airway, 3) protect the wound, and 4) treat or prevent shock. Malaria, immersions foot, snakebites, and leeches were additional hazards.

area. When these operations concluded on August 13, 1967, enemy losses stood at 78 killed, with seven taken prisoner. U.S. forces suffered three killed and 38 wounded.

Throughout the summer of 1967, Marine and ARVN efforts were concentrated on limiting infiltration of enemy forces into Quang Tri Province. At first there was very little contact with the enemy, but on July 28, elements of the 2nd Battalion, 9th Marines discovered an abandoned enemy base at Thon Cam Son, 5 miles (8 km) northwest of Con Thien. The Marines systematically destroyed around 150

concrete bunkers and pillboxes with M-48 tanks and amtracs. The next morning "Hotel" Company ran into heavy enemy resistance. They were reinforced by "Fox" and "Golf" companies as a company of 4th Marines moved against enemy's rear from the south. To avoid the trap, the NVA withdrew, leaving 48 dead behind but the Marine had also suffered heavily with 24 dead and 142 wounded, all of whom required evacuation by helicopter.

For the remainder of the summer and into early fall the Marines fought a series of small engagements with the NVA and VC. In one of the larger clashes on August 21, two companies from 3rd Marines caught a battalion of NVA soldiers attempting to set up an ambush north of Cu Lu. Trapped between the Marines, the NVA were annihilated as fighter-bombers and artillery shredded their ranks while the leathernecks on the ground poured on mortar and machine gun fire. In the aftermath the Marines counted 105 confirmed "kills" and another 305 "probables." History repeated itself on the same ground two weeks later on September 7 as the NVA ambushed a Marine convoy. Once again Marines closed in from two sides. After an eight-hour fire fight involving Marine air power and artillery, the Marines counted 92 confirmed enemy KIAs and 93 "probables." As the Marines and soldiers of Task Force Oregon were engaged in these actions, the enemy launched mortar and rocket attacks on the Da Nang Air Base, destroying two F-8E "Crusaders," two C-130 "Hercules" transports, and 6 F-4 C "Phantom" jet fighters.

On August 11, 5th Marines, 2nd ARVN Division and a force of ARVN Rangers engaged a sizable enemy force near Tam Ky, in Operation "Cochise." As 5th Marines engaged the VC, units from 1st Marines moved to block their escape. On this occasion the ARVN units recorded a higher bodycount than their U.S. comrades. This and the heavier casualties they suffered were perhaps an early indication of the ARVN shouldering more of the burden of the fighting.

While the Marines and ARVN battled the VC in during Cochise, the Army's Task Force

LEFT: In the noisy interior of a C130 Hercules, Marines are lost in thought or attempt to sleep as they are flown north on August 26. One man has spotted the photographer on the loading ramp at the rear of the aircraft. The four-engined Hercules C130A had a maximum cruising speed of 356 miles per hour (573 kph) and a maximum range of 1,830 miles (2,945 km).

BELOW: Men of the Republic of Korea Marine Corps (ROKMC) 2nd Brigade "The Blue Dragons." The South Korean Marines arrived in South Vietnam in 1965 and was assigned the Cam Linh Peninsula in the III Corps area as its tactical area of operations. By the time they withdrew, they had killed 1,500 VC or NVA.

LEFT: An RTO with the 1st Infantry Division throws a grenade during fighting in a rubber plantation. The fighting, less than 1.2 miles (2 km) from the U.S. Special Forces camp at Bu Dop, took place on December 5. The practice of throwing grenades in thick woodland presented the thrower with a potentially lethal hazard. This was because some grenades were prone to bouncing off the trunk of a tree and then ricochet back towards the thrower. The signaler shown here may have been using the grenade as a marker. In this case, it would be a colored smoke grenade which would show the position of forward troops to the aircraft which had been called in to give ground support. He would have transmitted a message to the pilots to the effect that friendly forces were south or west of the purple smoke.

RIGHT: In this picture, the photographer Kyoichi Sawada, who worked for UPI, has caught the shock and fatigue on the face of a soldier from the 1st Infantry Division mortar crew drinking his coffee. The photograph was taken on the morning of December 15 after a night-fire mission. The man in the picture has wrapped himself in a poncho liner, a light polyester batting blanket which proved to be an invaluable piece of kit during the Vietnam war, as it could be tied into a waterproof poncho to make an improvised sleeping bag. The liner had the advantage that it could be used as a sunshade if it was rigged above a position, and in wet weather, did not increase in weight. It had the insulation properties of a heavy wool blanket, but when dry weighed less than 2.2 lb. (1 kg).

DEFOLIATION
"Only you can prevent forests"

That was the motto of Operation Ranch Hand, perhaps the world's largest deliberate destruction of a natural environment for military purposes. Dense and dangerous, the jungle which coated South Vietnam provided a protective shield under which the VC could operate, a shield the U.S. wanted to remove. The instrument was Agent Orange, a dioxin-based defoliant so titled from the color of its storage canisters. The mission to deploy it was called Operation Hades, but became more commonly known as Operation Ranch Hand.

The operation began proper in 1962. C-123 aircraft swooped over the jungle, each aircraft carrying enough Agent Orange to reduce 300 acres of virgin forest to a desolate brown wasteland full of dead and decaying plants. The operation peaked in 1967 when 1.7 million acres of land were doused in the defoliant. Yet the military results were negligible, the VC were more adaptable than imagined. The political results, however, were treacherous for U.S. foreign policy. Not only did the deforestation of one seventh of the entire country seem vandalous to many, but sinister illnesses started to occur in those exposed to the chemical. Soldiers and civilians developed alarming cancers, and babies were born with hideous birth defects. As the source of these illnesses was confirmed in 1968 as Agent Orange, Ranch Hand was wound down, the final flight occurring in January 1971.

Oregon launched a brigade-level operation, Benton, on August 14. The helicopter assault on a suspected enemy base area resulted in numerous skirmishes as the enemy sought to avoid contact. In one of the first operations to use tanks extensively, the 3rd Battalion, 5th Marines led a combined air-ground assault to fight their way overland to relieve elements of 1st Battalion which had been fighting a day-long battle with the NVA near Hill 63 in the Nui Loc Son Basin. Thirty-six hours of fighting resulted in over 190 NVA soldiers killed and numerous weapons captured. Operation Swift, actually a continuation of the previous day's battle, saw a nighttime counterattack kill a further 150 enemy troops within a few hours.

Task Force Oregon and four battalions of the 101st Airborne Division began Operation Wheeler on September 10, 20 miles (32 km) west of Tam Ky. On September 22, MACV

LEFT: U.S. Marines offload ammunition boxes from a Boeing-Vertol CH-46 Sea Knight. The helicopter could carry 4,000 lb. (1,814 kg) of stores and would be invaluable in resupply operations at Con Thien and Khe Sanh.
BELOW LEFT: U.S. Marines carry a wounded comrade following a NVA artillery barrage against the base at Con Thien. On October 13 the NVA fired 364 rounds of artillery and recoilless rifle fire at the base and the following day, after a 130-round mortar barrage, launched a ground assault. They were thrown back after tough, hand-to-hand fighting.
RIGHT: A Marine adjusts the cross leveling on an 81mm M1 mortar at Con Thien. Firing HE M-43A1 ammunition, the mortar had a range of 9,895 ft. (3,016m), and could fire three types of HE, Illuminating, and two types of smoke ammunition. The picture is contrived since the crewman would not be so close to the muzzle if a bomb was about to be loaded; the blast would be considerable when the charge increments attached to the bomb detonated and projected it up and out.

designated the semi-permanent elements comprising Task Force Oregon as the 23rd Infantry – or American – Division. On December 19, the Army's 11th Infantry Brigade arrived at Duc Pho and was immediately added to the American Division. Shortly after relieving the 5th Marines at Chu Lai on October 4, Brigade, 1st Cavalry Division (Airmobile) launched Operation Wallowa in the heavily disputed area west of the Da Nang Air Base. By the end of December, a total of 3,188 NVA and VC had been killed and 126 prisoners taken as a result of both Wheeler and Wallowa.

Meanwhile fighting continued around the Con Thien fire support base. The NVA wanted to surround the base – occupied by a battalion of Marines and units of 105mm and 155mm artillery – and cut it off. In a series of spoiling attacks with tanks, artillery, machine guns, and mortars, 26th Marines broke up repeated enemy assaults. Having had one force attempting to probe the northeastern edge of the base driven off, the NVA launched a massive mortar and artillery bombardment of Con Thien. The assistant commander of 1st Marine Division told reporters that the NVA "were there in strength," and that "they would pay a heavy price" for assaulting Con Thien. Fearful of an American "Dien Bien Phu," General Westmoreland ordered B-52 bombers and artillery to beat back the NVA's offensive. By October 4, the siege had been broken, and "the enemy had suffered a crushing defeat."

The Hai Lang National Fortress was a major enemy command and logistics center and was, in addition, suspected of harboring the 5th and 6th Regiments of the North Vietnamese Army. On October 5, 1st Marines moved in to eradicate this nest of vipers in Operation Medina. In a parallel combined operation dubbed Bastion Hill, the Special Landing Force conducted a search and destroy mission to drive the enemy from his mountain haven. The SLF pushed on to Thua Thien Province, linking up with the 1st Marines and ARVN, and continuing to inflict casualties on the enemy. Medina and Bastion Hill marked the end of Operation Kingfisher, which in four months had accounted for over 1,117 NVA and VC soldiers killed, while the Marines had lost 340 KIAs and 3,086 wounded. In late December the Special Landing Force was once again in action as efforts were made to destroy enemy units operating along the southeastern coast of I Corps. While Marines were busily eradicating the NVA on the coast, the U.S. Army's 198th Light Infantry Brigade arrived in I Corps, adding three more battalions to III MAF's firepower.

ABOVE: An RTO of the 4th Infantry Division comforts a comrade who has collapsed from combat fatigue following heavy fighting 27 miles (43 km) west of Pleiku on May 28. For many men who fought in Vietnam, memories and flashbacks would haunt them long after they had returned to the U.S. The psychological injuries later identified as Post-Traumatic Stress Disorder were compounded by the fact that servicemen returned alone to a U.S. that did not wish to acknowledge them.
RIGHT: Marines of the 3rd Marine Division relax after a three-day action during Operation Kingfisher in northern Vietnam. The operation began on July 16 and ended on October 31. The Marines were to suffer 340 killed and 3,086 wounded.

Elsewhere units from the U.S. Army's 25th Infantry Division moved to seal off escape routes across the Cambodian border, while elements of the 1st Infantry resumed a massive sweep of Route 13 prior to its commitment to the seizure of Loc Ninh. On October 29, a VC assault on the CIDG camp successfully breached the outer defenses. Only an intense and sustained air and artillery bombardment drove the enemy off. On October 31, 1967, ten U.S. Army battalions stood poised to take Loc Ninh. As the buildup entered its final day, the Communists launched heavy attacks to drive the Americans away from the border. At the end of the two-day battle, U.S. forces had killed over 800 Viet Cong. As in Cedar Falls

and Junction City, air power was vital: the Air Force flew over 425 missions, conducted eight B-52 arc light strikes, and the artillery fired more than 30,000 rounds of artillery. But these actions continued to pull U.S. forces into the hinterlands of Vietnam and away from the populated areas. Westmoreland was happy, as the enemy now seemed to be fighting the kind of conventional war he had sought from the outset. The massive resources at the disposal of the U.S. and its allies would allow the enemy forces to be annihilated

Across Vietnam, U.S. troop levels had climbed to over 480,000 men, but 9,378 combat casualties had been suffered in 1967, nearly double that of the previous year. 1967 had

BELOW: A U.S. Marine captain glances away from the camera as his men assemble following the three-day action during Operation Kingfisher. Frontline soldiers and Marines resented some journalists and photographers, who could arrive by helicopter, collect facts and take photographs, and then depart.
NEXT PAGE: Sergeant First Class Emmanuel Bradford chats and compares Mohawk haircuts with his Platoon leader 1st Lt Alfred E. Lehman, Jr. during a break at Company base at Dac Pho in the Central Highlands.

ABOVE: A U.S. Navy McDonnell Douglas F-4 Phantom II is readied for takeoff. This versatile aircraft saw action as a bomber, reconnaissance aircraft, and fighter. In this latter role, scoring their first kill, downing a MiG-17 on July 10, 1965. By the end of the war, 362 Phantoms had been lost, the majority in combat. Only the F-105 suffered a higher attrition rate in Southeast Asia.

RIGHT: Smoke and dust rise from the Thanh Hoa bridge in North Vietnam following an attack by A-4 Skyhawks from the USS *Oriskany* in November 1967. The bridge survived.

OPPOSITE: A North American RA-5 Vigilante is reflected in the mirrored visor of a crewman on the flightdeck of the U.S.S *Saratoga*. The bomber's bomb bays were adapted for cameras, and it became a two-seat reconnaissance aircraft.

A Stay at the Hilton

In whole or in part, it had many nicknames. Camp One, Camp Unity, Heartbreak, Little Vegas, New Guy Village, West Court. Yet its most famous title was Hanoi Hilton, ironically named by U.S. POWs who spent tortuous years in this most brutal of prisons. The Hoa Lo prison was built by the French at the turn of the nineteenth century. Its name actually translates as 'portable earthen stove,' referring back to the type of goods manufactured on the site in the 1800s. Between August 11, 1964 to March 28, 1973, it became one of the most notorious destinations for U.S. POWs during the Vietnam War.

Its notoriety came from the utter brutality of its regime. Torture of the most hideous kind faced the inmates on a daily basis, and some inmates would be there for nearly eight years. Common tortures included being tied to a tiny three-legged stool and left there for about ten days – any movement would be rewarded by vicious beatings. The same type of exercise was also repeated with the inmate standing or kneeling on a concrete floor. Prisoners were electrocuted, repeatedly half-suffocated by soaking towels placed over their heads, given food which contained razor blades and bits of sharp wire. Even when returned to their cell, the torture continued. In summer the cells had internal temperatures of around 110 degrees Farenheit, in winter they were icy cold. The prisoner would often have to live amidst his own excrement, and swarms of mosquitoes would attack the already vulnerable and emaciated body; one captive remembers that he could put his fist between his thighs and not touch flesh.

The ostensible purpose of this torture was to extract confessions of war crimes. North Vietnam classed all U.S. military personnel as war criminals through its own amendment of the 1957 Geneva Convention, and they put them outside all conventions of humane treatment. In most cases, the U.S. troops relented – years of torture would break even the

LEFT: Bandaged, bloody, and dressed in the tattered remains of his flying overalls, Lt Col James Lindberg Hughes is escorted under guard through a public park in Hanoi to the International Club on May 6. Pilots recalled that though their politicized prison guards were brutal, sometimes ordinary people at the least were neutral or curious, and at the best offered refreshment.

BELOW: The original caption for this picture which was released through a studio in Berlin – then part of Communist East Germany – read "The eldest of a group of U.S. pilots who after his release wrote a book claiming he had been tortured." The reality was that during the Vietnam war, the North Vietnamese went to considerable efforts to break down the will of their prisoners to use them for propaganda. Many of them were permanently injured and some who attempted to escape were caught and killed.

strongest. Yet almost all put up incredible feats of resistance, and many died doing so.

The Hanoi Hilton was not exceptional. There were many prisons just as brutal in North Vietnam, such as Cu Loc and Son Tay, most being concentrated around Hanoi. The vast majority of the inmates were pilots – over 580 USAF pilots alone were captured or went missing between 1962 and 1973 and many others from the Navy and Marines. With pilots responsible for thousands of civilian deaths in North Vietnam, they were sometimes killed by the local population if they were shot down. Yet should they reach prison, they would need all their resources of training and mental will to survive. Some survived through their religious faith, others by performing lengthy mental tasks, such as building their dream house in their mind in real time. Many did make it through to survive and be released. Some carried with them physical deformities, others mental scars that would never heal. Yet most still retained a belief in why they were in Vietnam, some more so now that they had seen the nature of the regime they were fighting.

LEFT: A U.S. POW in Hanoi talks to a fellow prisoner in March 1973. Most images released by the North Vietnamese were carefully edited. When U.S. pilots were visited by Americans who were sympathetic to North Vietnam and tried to show their bruised and scarred arms, the visitors refused to "see" these injuries. Among them was the actress Jane Fonda. In 1992, this would produce the ribald bumper sticker "What's the difference between Fonda and Clinton? Fonda went to Vietnam."

proved to be a year of hard fighting for the U.S. and its allies. But on November 17, President Johnson told the nation on television that, "We are inflicting greater losses than we're taking. We are making progress." Later the same month, General Westmoreland told U.S. newsmen "I am absolutely certain that whereas in 1965 the enemy was winning, today he is certainly losing" and that there was "light at the end of the tunnel." Within three months, both the President and his senior commander in Vietnam would come to rue these words. In the numbers game the U.S. might be winning, but the enemy were playing a different game and were far from down and out. In fact, in a stunningly spectacular offensive, the Communists were about to transform the political landscape of the war.

OPPOSITE TOP: Assisted by an interpreter, an officer of the U.S. 1st Infantry Division questions a captured member of the Viet Cong. Language and culture – as well as the policy of the one-year tour for individual soldiers – meant that American troops found it hard to fully comprehend the motives of their enemy.

BELOW LEFT: A South Vietnamese soldier armed with an M16 rifle and fragmentation grenades stands guard outside a polling booth. The democratic political process was a constant target for the Viet Cong, who saw it as an example of the Saigon government extending its influence into the country. To Washington, it was part of the process of "nation building" that was to be encouraged wherever a country was under threat from Communism. Elections also helped to legitimize South Vietnamese leaders like President Thieu.

RIGHT: Highly decorated from three wars, polished, and confident, General Westmoreland explains the strategy and tactics of the Vietnam war to Washington audiences, having been ordered back to the U.S. to reassure Congress that the war was going well. His confidence of November 1967 that cordon and search operations and battles for highlands features were wearing down the Viet Cong and North Vietnamese made the Tet Offensive of 1968 come as a great shock.

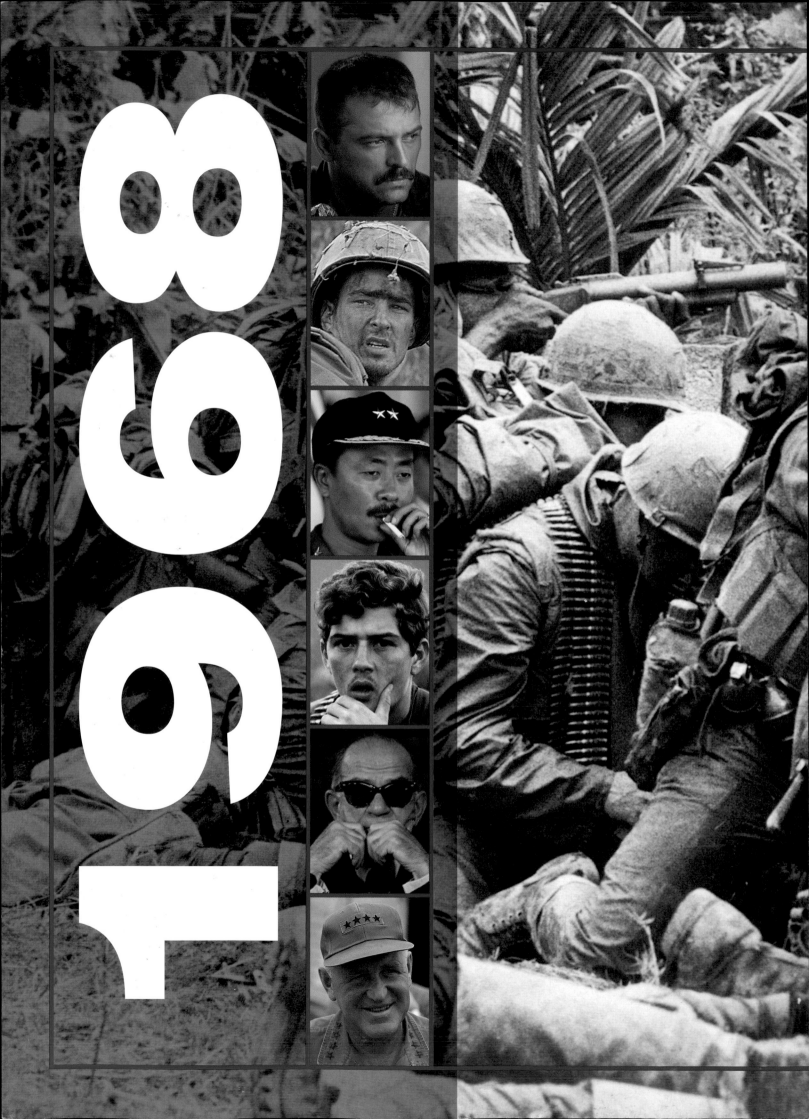

The Turning Point

On New Year's Day, 1968, Radio Hanoi broadcast a poem written by Ho Chi Minh which proclaimed the inevitability of a total victory for the Communist cause in the upcoming spring. In a similar spirit of optimism, Vo Nguyen Giap and other senior North Vietnamese Army (NVA) officers alluded to future triumphs that would bring the Americans and the

South Vietnamese to their knees. Communist actions around this time seemed to substantiate their rhetoric. For almost three months, NVA and Vietcong forces had been attacking Loc Ninh, Dak To, Con Thien, and other isolated American positions in the Central Highlands and near the Demilitarized Zone (DMZ) in the north.

Although they were regimental or even divisional in size, and equipped with new machine guns, flame-throwers, artillery and backpack radios, the NVA forces were repulsed and incurred heavy losses in the face of superior American firepower. However, American reconnaissance and intelligence services noticed increasing enemy troop and supply move-ments down the Ho Chi Minh Trail. Although General Westmoreland and other senior commanders anticipated that an offensive of some type would break out in 1968, and accordingly put their troops on alert, they were far from certain about when or where it would occur.

Westmoreland believed and hoped that the NVA would continue launching conventional attacks on the border regions, especially in the northern provinces. However, III Corps com-mander, General Frederick C. Weyand, suspected that these border actions were merely diversions and implored "Westy" to keep Saigon, Hue, and other heavily populated areas well-defended. Although Westmoreland eventually dispatched 15 battalions from border regions to places around Saigon, he left urban security in the hands of the ARVN. Unfortunately, his South Vietnamese allies did not take this responsibility seriously.. The South Vietnamese President, Nguyen Van Thieu, allowed many of this soldiers to go on leave for the upcoming Tet holiday, while he and his wife departed for the delta resort town of My Tho.

Westmoreland also guessed that the attack would occur in early to mid-January, before the new year Tet holiday. Every previous year during the American intervention in Vietnam, both sides had observed a Tet ceasefire; the Communists themselves had pro-claimed a truce for that day in 1968. A violation of this would alienate them from the South Vietnamese people. However, Westmoreland and others had not learned Vietnamese history. Had they done so, they would have made the discovery that Vietnamese

---

ABOVE: General William Westmoreland, in his last days as the Commander in Chief of U.S. and Allied Forces in South Vietnam, discusses a tactical problem with an officer of the 1st Royal Australian Regiment.
RIGHT: Khe Sanh looking west showing the main airstrip to the south apron, near the far end of which are the Control Tower, MATCU, Charlie Med (medical center), and Air Freight centers. In the foreground are the perimeter trenches of the 37th South Vietnamese Ranger Battalion protecting the main ammunition dump, and two batteries of 4.1 in. (105mm) guns.

ABOVE: A mortar crew from the United States Army prepares its weapon – a 3.2in. (81mm) mortar gun – in a forest clearing in order that they may give supporting fire. They have removed their shirts so that they can more easily complete the construction of their base. So intensely preoccupied are these men with the task in hand that every single one is totally oblivious to the wreckage of a Bell UH-1 "Huey" which is lying on its side just behind them. Purple smoke rises into the air from a grenade, which has been fired to act as a reference point for another UH-1, which can be seen in the distance approaching the small clearing, about to deliver its load to the troops on the brow of the hill.

folk heroes had launched battles and other violent actions many times during Tet, while their adversaries were lulled into a false sense of security. This misconception led Westmoreland to focus his attention on the Marine Corps base at Khe Sanh, 15 miles (24 km) south of the DMZ and near the Laotian border, when Communist forces advanced upon the area at the beginning of the year.

On January 5, Westmoreland and his senior commanders developed a contingency plan aimed at providing adequate air defense for Khe Sanh. Called Operation Niagara, the plan included two phases. Phase I began immediately and consisted of information-gathering activity that identified and located suitable enemy targets to hit. Phase II would begin once the Communists began their offensive on Khe Sanh and involved committing aircraft and artillery forces to fight against the attacking enemies. Like many other American air

campaigns, Niagara involved both B-52 sorties and air strikes from Navy, Marine Corps, and Air Force fighter-bombers, as well as 3,000 helicopters and propeller-driven South Vietnamese A-1 Skyraiders.

Westmoreland even wanted access to tactical nuclear weapons. Back in Washington, Joint Chiefs of Staff chairman General Earle G. Wheeler concurred with this view. But the White House balked and asked him not to raise the issue again in case the press heard about it and generated a public outcry. In vain, Westmoreland pressed his case, comparing the North Vietnamese offensive action in the South with the Japanese attack on Pearl Harbor, which had ultimately led to the bombings of Hiroshima. The comparison did not impress his superiors in Washington.

Thus, the Americans seemed well-prepared for the anticipated offensive on Khe Sanh and adjacent areas in Military Region 1 (MR 1).

ABOVE: A Douglas A-1 Skyraider readies for take-off from a U.S. Navy carrier. The Skyraider, known affectionately as the "Spad" after the World War I fighter, was a slow aircraft with a top speed of 318 mph (512 kmph); however, this was ideal for a ground attack bomber that carried up to 8,000 lb. (3,600 kg) of bombs, rockets, or napalm.

RIGHT: As a US Marine shovels loose soil from the bottom of a trench at Khe Sanh his comrades load an M2 .50 Browning heavy machine gun. The sand bagged bunker on which they have positioned the gun would have been hot during the day, and from this position they would have had a wide field of fire to the barbed wire perimeter.

BELOW: The crew of an M40-A1 4.2in. (106mm) recoilless rifle in action. The recoilless rifle is mounted on an M274 Mule light vehicle which belongs to the U.S. Marine 3rd Division. The vehicle is parked on Hill 881 South near Khe Sanh, and is seen here in the process of opening fire on a position held by the North Vietnamese 325th Division. The gun which was fitted on the Mule could also be dismounted and fitted to the standard M79 ground mount. The lightweight recoilless rifles gave the Marines the equivalent of artillery support on the battlefield without the need for heavy equipment to transport the guns.

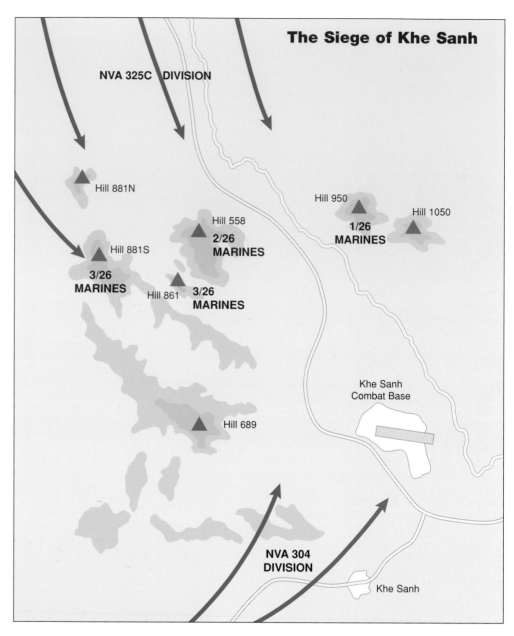

The Siege of Khe Sanh

NVA 325C DIVISION

Hill 881N

Hill 950

Hill 1050

Hill 558

1/26 MARINES

2/26 MARINES

Hill 881S

3/26 MARINES

Hill 861

3/26 MARINES

Khe Sanh Combat Base

Hill 689

NVA 304 DIVISION

Khe Sanh

An old Green Beret camp situated on Route 9, which ran from Laos to Quang Tri City and Hue, Khe Sanh was situated on a plateau and surrounded by several hills. The marines had maintained a substantial presence there since 1966 and expanded it the following year so that it might serve as a launching pad for a possible offensive against enemy sanctuaries in Laos. In 1967, the Marine Corps force occupying the base included the 1st and 3rd Battalions of the 26th Regiment. Throughout the spring and summer, these units fought several skirmishes with NVA forces in the area.

The following January, in response to NVA advances in the area, Westmoreland dispatched the 1st Battalion, 13th Regiment to Khe Sanh. The battalions each possessed seven batteries of 175mm guns, three batteries of

LEFT: Waving a PPSh sub machine gun high in the air, a leader of a North Vietnamese militia group in Phu Tho province looks toward the sky to the direction of the attacks which are raining down on his troops. These strikes are coming from the U.S. Air Force and Navy. Militias such as these pictured here were always quick to intercept U.S. pilots who had been unlucky enough to be downed, as well as the sabotage and intelli-gence-gathering teams which had been sent north by the Saigon government and the CIA.
BELOW: US Marines carry on their shoulders the weighty 249 lb. (113 kg) of an M40-A1 4.2in. (106mm) recoilless rifle, as it is in the process of being rede-ployed at Khe Sanh. The standard ground mount M79 added an extra 194 lb. (88 kg) of weight and the spotting rifle added 60 lb. (27 kg). The Marines also had at their disposal six M40-A1 barrels mount-ed on the M-50 Ontos, a tracked, armored antitank vehicle which was used in perimeter defense at the base.

105mm howitzers, one battery of 155mm how-itzers, and one battery of 4.2-in. mortars. Altogether, the marine garrison had 46 artillery pieces. Later in the month, other units would arrive to help defend the base, bringing its total manpower strength to about 6,000 men holding the base itself and the surrounding hills. Colonel David E. Lownds served as Khe Sanh's base commander.

In preparation for what seemed to be an inevitable offensive, the marines constructed bunkers, excavated trenches, and covered the perimeter of the base with triple coils of razor-sharp barbed wire, claymore mines, and trip flares. The company-size units from the 26th Marine Regiment charged with guarding the surrounding hills engaged in similar precau-tions. Thus protected, the marines atop these

Vo Nguyen Giap

Vo Nguyen Giap was a brilliant, ferocious man. While Ho Chi Minh took the focus during the Vietnam War, it was Giap who so often masterminded the tactics that defeated both the French and the U.S. over three decades of conflict. This self-taught strategist knew exactly how to tackle the bigger enemy, applying principles of revolutionary war with an insistent disregard of casualties.

From only 13 years old, Giap was classed as a dangerous revolutionary. As a youth he joined the Tan Viet Cach Menh Dang, the Revolutionary Party of Young Vietnam. Under the French, Giap's father and sister had died after anti-colonial protests in the 1880s, and the young Giap grew up with an eye towards revolutionary nationalism. This led him to join Ho's Indochinese Communist Party in 1937, where he became an avid student of military theory and practice. However, in 1939 the ICP was outlawed. Giap made an escape to China, but his sister-in-law was captured and went to the guillotine, and his wife of only a year, Minh Thai, was sentenced to life imprisonment and died

after only three years in captivity. The desire for vengeance became even greater in Giap.

In 1941, Giap's military knowledge found its application. Having made alliances with Ho Chi Minh and other Vietnamese guerrilla groups, he spent four tough years in the jungle slugging it out with the Japanese and commanding some 5000 insurgents. Giap proved himself a resourceful leader in action, and a cunning tactician. After four years of struggle, the Japanese surrendered and Giap marched with Ho into Hanoi in August 1945. For the short period before the French expelled the fledgling government, Giap became the commander-in-chief of the armed forces and commander of the police. Here he showed his ruthless side, executing political rivals and silencing opposition media. Yet with the French return, Giap once again stepped into the guerrilla's uniform.

By 1954, Giap's Viet Minh army had brought the might of France to the point of surrender. How? Giap was an eclectic tactician, borrowing from whatever theories he

RIGHT: General Vo Nguyen Giap, the victor of Dien Bien Phu who began his professional life as a history teacher. Though he was the mastermind behind the Tet Offensive, he admitted later that it had been a terribly costly operation that had virtually destroyed the Viet Cong infrastructure in South Vietnam. He had assumed that through the Tet Offensive, he would achieve a military victory, but he had not foreseen the complex political triumph that would result from the operation. As a military tactician, Giap borrowed from several sources. However, he was particularly drawn to the ideas of Mao Tse Tung, who believed in revolutionary war, that is, as many small counterinsurgency measures as it took, over a period of several years, to lead to all-out war.

LEFT: General Giap, of whom it was said he attempted to fight and win a second Dien Bien Phu at Tet and later in the offensive against South Vietnam of March 1972. Here he meets a group of young officers at a National Party Congress of the Vietnam Workers' Party. Like these officers, Giap's political involvement began at an early age; from only 13 years old, he was classed by the authorities as a dangerous revolutionary and, as a youth, joined the Tan Viet Cach Menh Dang, the Revolutionary Party of Young Vietnam. Under the French, Giap's father and sister had died after anti-colonial protests in the 1880s, and when his sister-in-law and his wife both died for their political beliefs, Giap's path to revolutionary socialism was set.

found useful. Yet like Ho, he took the long view of war. He was particularly influenced by Mao Tse Tung's ideas of revolutionary war. Revolutionary war was the conflict of slow buildup – moving patiently from small insurgency actions to outright conventional war over a period of years. Within this were two types of *dau tranh* (struggle): military and political. While the military *dau tranh* chipped away at the enemy's military strength, political *dau tranh* weakened his alliances and public image, making it harder for him to fight the war. Consequently, in Giap's words, the enemy 'has to drag out the war in order to win it and does not possess, on the other hand, the psychological and political means to fight a long, drawn-out war.'

Giap's rounded view of war-fighting served him well in the next Vietnam War, and enabled him to visit the same defeat upon the United States (though the U.S. had military successes far in excess of those of the French). As deputy prime minister, minister of defense, and commander in chief of the armed forces of North Vietnam, he oversaw with Ho a war in which public relations were handled with as much violence as the fighting in the field.

If Giap had one major failing, it was that he occasionally rushed into outright battles too impetuously, losing many thousands of men in the process. Yet, for Giap, it was the outcome of the struggle, and not the journey undertaken during it, which mattered.

TOP: Amongst a litter of C Ration cartons, U.S. Marines dive for cover as the distinctive sound of incoming artillery fire alerts them to imminent danger.
ABOVE: US Marines sit hunched against a heap of red laterite soil thrown up as field defenses were being dug. Though the Army and Marines patrolled and launched large-scale operations against suspected Viet Cong or North Vietnamese safe areas, in the field they did this from the security of fire-bases that were dug in and protected by barbed wire and mines.

ABOVE: Flames rise in the night sky as fighting in the suburbs of Saigon continues following the Tet offensive. The material damage to many of the cities in South Vietnam was caused less by the initial attacks than by the U.S. response, which involved the use of aircraft and helicopter gunships, as well as artillery.

LEFT: Napalm bursts on a Viet Cong or North Vietnamese Army position in the jungle in South Vietnam. Napalm, a jellied fuel that burned and stuck to its target, was an effective weapon, but the burns that it caused made it one of the targets for anti-war protests.
BOTTOM LEFT: U.S. Marines at Khe Sanh read a copy of the French magazine *Paris Match*. The cover features a story on Khe Sanh; the French were fascinated by the war.
RIGHT: U.S. Marines of G Company, 4th Marine Regiment pick a path up the smoking explosives-churned soil of a hillside.
NEXT PAGE: U.S. Marines under fire at Khe Sanh.

high positions prepared for the worst. Company K, 3rd Battalion reinforced to bring its total to about 300 men, occupied Hill 861. On Hill 950, north of the main base, the 2nd Platoon, Company A, 1st Battalion guarded a radio relay station. West of these positions, Company I (India), 3rd Battalion protected Hill 881 South (881S), reinforced with elements of Company M (Mike).

Early in the morning of January 20, members of India Company collided with an NVA battalion while patrolling Hill 881 North, about 5 miles (8 km) northwest of the Khe Sanh perimeter. The ensuing firefight killed 20 marines and provoked Lownds into putting the entire base on alert. The marines at the main base supported their comrades at Hill 881N with a bombardment of 155mm artillery rounds upon Communist positions, but lacked the ability to pinpoint enemy positions because the thick jungle canopy and heavy cloud cover hindered aerial reconnaissance. Moreover, the presence of NVA infantry in the surrounding countryside deterred forward artillery observers from moving out of the perimeter and radioing coordinates to the base.

By this time, a large NVA invasion force was in the area, consisting of four infantry divisions, two armored units, and two artillery

BELOW: Hunkered low in a trench, U.S. Army soldiers endeavor to locate a Viet Cong sniper hidden in the jungle near their position. Good camouflage and field craft made it extremely hard to see individual enemy soldiers, while a single shot that might kill or wound a U.S. soldier or Marine was hard to locate. Experiences like this served to sap morale in the troops and build up their frustration. The year 1968 was a turning point for many who had been forced to endure hours of this kind of tension.

regiments armed with 130mm and 152mm howitzers. The elite 304th Division (Hanoi Guards) swept in from the southwest, while Division 325C approached from the north. Division 324B entrenched itself near Dong Ha, and the 320th Division near Camp Carroll and the Rockpile Firebase. Altogether, anywhere from 20,000 to 40,000 Communist troops were in the area to threaten Khe Sanh. Meanwhile, the 2nd Battalion, 26th Marine Regiment had reached the main base on January 16. Colonel Lownds promptly dispatched companies from this battalion to occupy Hills 558 and 861A northwest of the main base.

On the same day as India Company's fight on Hill 881N, an NVA lieutenant named La Than Tonc approached the base with a white flag in an apparent attempt to desert his comrades. Once inside the perimeter, he warned his hosts that the Communists were going to bombard Khe Sanh with heavy ordnance just after midnight. Specifically, Lieutenant Tonc predicted that his former comrades would strike Hill 861first, then Hill 881S, then the main base. Presumably, the NVA planned to conquer the base and then take Route 9 straight to Quang Tri City and Hue. Impressed with the defector's story, Lownds ordered India Company to return to its garrison at Hill 881S and prepare for the worst.

As Lieutenant Tonc had predicted, an artillery salvo began on its appointed time, at 12:30 a.m. on January 21, and was directed against Hill 861, situated between Hill 881 and the main base. Thirty minutes later, 300 NVA ground troops attacked K Company's positions. Led by an elite detachment of combat engineers, they charged through artillery and machine gun fire and breached the perimeter wire with Bangalore torpedoes, satchel charges, and bamboo ladders. However, the marines eventually repelled the attackers in a

ABOVE: The ironic slogan on the Flak jacket of a Marine of the 3rd Battalion, 26th Marine Reglment that held the western perimeter of Khe Sanh and fought a particularly hard battle for the outlying position of Hill 861. Here 300 North Vietnamese soldiers attacked the hill at 01.00 a.m. on January 21 and fought hand-to-hand with the Marines.

LEFT: As a Boeing-Vertol CH-46 Sea Knight helicopter comes in to land, an M29 3.2in. (81mm) mortar crew of the 2nd Battalion, 9th Marine Regiment prepare to fire at Viet Cong mortar positions. An experienced crew could fire 18 rounds a minute. Under pressure, this could rise to 30 rounds a minute.

ABOVE: A U.S. Marine steps carefully over the body of a comrade killed on a hill near Khe Sanh as a CH-46 Sea Knight comes in to pick up the casualties. They had been killed when bombs from a ground attack aircraft fell short as it ran in to attack North Vietnamese positions close to the perimeter.

TOP RIGHT: A Fairchild C-123K Provider on the airstrip at Khe Sanh after being hit by North Vietnamese AA fire. Foam sprayed by fire fighting teams covers the foreground. The wreckage was used as a dramatic backdrop for TV reporters, but aircraft losses were not severe at Khe Sanh.

RIGHT: A U.S. Marine who has suffered horrific burn injuries walks down the main road in the Khe Sanh Combat Base.

vicious counterattack, thanks in part to supporting mortar fire provided from Hill 881S. Five hours later, the Communists struck the inner ring of Khe Sanh.

In the attack on the main base, NVA artillerists treated their adversaries to a fireworks display that included howitzer rounds, heavy mortar fire, and 122mm rockets. Almost immediately, one rocket hit a bunker on the eastern end of the base, detonating 1,500 tons of ammunition stored there. The ensuing explosion knocked over six helicopters, perforated several tents and buildings, and ignited aviation fuel, enhancing the destructive and terrifying effect of the Communist bombardment. This lucky shot also deprived the Americans of about 90 percent of their ammunition. Another round penetrated a tear gas cache, causing a noxious cloud to cover the entire base for several hours. The following morning, much of Khe Sanh was in ruins; and the NVA was just getting started. Now under a

US GUNSHIPS
Fire from the Sky

During the 1950s in Ecuador, the missionary Nate Saint discovered that he could put his aircraft in a continual circle with one wing low and create such a focused circle that supplies could actually be lowered to the ground on a 1000 ft. (3048 m) rope. A decade later and the U.S. Air Force was experimenting with combat applications of this so-called 'pylon turn' for delivering massive firepower against a single point, and the gunship was born. The first gunship was a conversion of the Douglas AC-47 Dakota. Fitted with three multi-barrel M133 or M134 7.62mm miniguns – each with a 6000 rpm rate-of-fire – they circled communist troop concentrations and slashed the jungle, men, and vehicles to pieces in a storm of firepower. Their notoriety grew, and became known a 'Puff-the-magic-dragon' or 'Spooky.' Yet Spooky was somewhat crude – the pilot aimed the fire through a side cockpit window. It was superseded by two improved, and truly lethal, aircraft: the AC-119G Shadow (a modification of the Fairchild flying Boxcar) and the AC-130 Spectre (a Lockheed Hercules). Both had awesome firepower. The Shadow had four miniguns, while a variant, the Stinger, even added two 20mm cannons. The AC-130, however, was the ultimate. It came in many configurations, but an AC-130H featured two miniguns, two 20mm cannons, one 40mm cannon, and even a 105mm howitzer on a movable mount. The lethality of the Stinger and Spectre was improved by having computer targeting systems which calculated everything from angle of turn to windage, and later models even featured laser targeting systems. The gunships were ferocious weapons. NVA troop movements at night down the Ho Chi Minh Trail were decimated by floods of cannon shells and machine gun bullets streaming down from the night sky. U.S. veterans recall the tracer stream as so dense that it looked like a searchlight – even then there was four other bullets going out to every tracer. They remain possibly the greatest expression of raw firepower ever seen in the air.

ABOVE: Standing on their M47 Patton tanks in sand bagged revetments, U.S. Marines watch smoke which is rising from air strikes close to the outer barbed wire of Khe Sanh. Though U.S. Air Force, Marine, and Navy pilots sometimes made mistakes with these "danger close" strikes, they generally enjoyed a good record for accuracy.

LEFT: Part of the 60,000 lb. (27,240 kg) bomb load of a B-52 bomber. During the battle for Khe Sanh, attacks by B-52s – code-named Arc Light – totaled 2,700, and the aircraft dropped 110,000 tons of ordnance. At the height of the fighting, a three-plane cell arrived every 90 minutes. The B-52 was still in service in the Gulf War of 1990–91, giving rise to the joke, "Fly the plane your father flew."

state of siege, the marines in Khe Sanh would endure many more days and evenings like this.

The marines at Khe Sanh realized that they needed to cling to their positions on the hills northwest of the inner ring if they wished to endure the siege. If the Communists seized these locations, they would be well-positioned to strike the main plateau with mortars, rockets, and howitzers. Thus, the companies occupying these highlands had to hold their ground at all cost. At Hill 881S, the 400 men from India Company and two platoons from Mike Company had formed defensive positions which included three 105mm howitzers, a section of 81mm mortars, and two 106mm recoilless rifles. India Company's Captain William H. Dabney and Mike Company's Captain Harry Jenkins commanded these units.

A steep hill that rose about 500 feet (152 m) from the surrounding terrain, 881S was the most remote of the highland positions and thus the most difficult to reinforce. The marines on this isolated hill were resupplied by air deliveries from CH-46 Sea Knight helicopters based at Dong Ha. Bloody fighting on Hill 881S during the previous year had rendered it barren in many places. It was also covered with craters and collapsed bunkers filled with the remains of slain NVA soldiers.

As instructed by Colonel Lownds, the marines had returned to Hill 881S after repelling an NVA ambush, employing a classic infantry charge to send their enemies down the slopes. Tactical aircraft then doused the surrounding area with napalm in order to roast the surviving Communists before they could regroup. Temporarily secure on their high ground, the men of India and Mike companies launched mortar barrages in support of another beleaguered garrison at Hill 861 to the east.

BELOW: U.S. Marines in Khe Sanh hug the ground to steel themselves against the blast of incoming North Vietnamese rocket or artillery fire which is exploding within the perimeter area. At the time of the siege of Khe Sanh, many international military pundits, both in Europe and the United States, compared the battle for the base with that for the French base at Dien Bien Phu in Vietnam, which took place in 1954. This did not bode at all well for the marines at Khe Sanh, since the French suffered heavy casualties and a disastrous defeat at Dien Bien Phu. It was a battle that brought to an end France's struggle to retain her colony and her withdrawal from Indochina.

ABOVE: The heavily sand bagged and protected Marine Air Traffic Control Unit (MATCU) at Khe Sanh. The message neatly inscribed on the red wooden boards of the unit can clearly be seen, and no doubt it was intended to parody the greetings which are displayed at commercial airports all over the world. Despite this ironic messsage, the efficient functioning of this unit was essential to the success of the operation, as well as to the survival of the marines who were trapped in the perimeter area, as low, overcast and bad weather made accurate information from the Marine Air Traffic Control Unit critical for the pilots who were coming in to land at Khe Sanh. The MATCU was positioned south of the control tower, in the center of the Marine base.

During this action, the marines urinated on the mortar tubes to keep them from overheating.

Frustrated by their failure to take Hill 881S with infantry assaults, NVA forces turned to their antiaircraft artillery to prevent American aircraft from aiding the marines. On January 22, the Communists destroyed a medevac helicopter that had just taken off from the hill with 20 wounded men. By February, NVA artillerists and snipers were inflicting more than a 50 percent casualty rate upon the Americans. Later in the month, improving weather conditions enabled Dabney and Jenkins to call in precise coordinates for artillery and tactical air support. In March, the Communists surrounding the hill became demoralized at the heavy losses that they were sustaining from these countermeasures and pressure on the marines of India and Mike companies abated.

During the early stages of the siege, Khe Sanh received the last of its ground-based

reinforcements. On January 22, the 1st Battalion, 9th Marine Regiment arrived and took up positions along a ridge situated southwest of the main base. Five days later, the 37th ARVN Ranger Battalion reached the base and occupied the eastern sector. Both units were airlifted into Khe Sanh and the defenders settled into a wretched existence.

While periodic artillery bombardments attacked their ears and eyes, nauseating odors from piles of garbage and excrement burning in oil drums filled their nostrils. Marines and ARVN rangers trying to sleep in their bunkers faced a second enemy. Rats infested the base, forcing men to wrap themselves tight in their ponchos during periods of rest. Those bitten by the rodents received hideous scars and suffered serious infections. Finally, the defenders of Khe Sanh had to live with the constant fear of facing a human-wave infantry invasion that might very well engulf the entire base, regardless of how well they fought. To keep their

ABOVE: A USAF C-130 Hercules flies down the dusty airstrip of Khe Sanh and delivers pallets of stores using Low Altitude Parachute Extraction – LAPES. This ensured that though the aircraft did not land – and so was a harder target for the North Vietnamese gunners – it also placed the stores accurately, from where they could be quickly retrieved.

LEFT: Marines relax by the wreckage of the Fairchild C-123K Provider which had been shot down March 6 with the loss of 48 passengers and crew. The photograph, which was taken in June at the close of the siege, shows men awaiting helicopters to lift them south of the base, where they will conduct a sweep against residual North Vietnamese forces.

LEFT: A U.S. Air Force M151 utility truck fitted with an M60 machine gun is parked near the burned out wreckage of a Douglas C-47. The versatile World War II-vintage transport aircraft, popularly known as the Dakota, had been hit by Viet Cong mortar fire. Smoke from the same attack rises in the background.

BELOW RIGHT: During a "Hearts and Minds" operation, a father and son Marine Corps team distribute clothes donated by residents of San Diego, California. Corporal D. Thrasher watches as Marine Sergeant Jimmy Thrasher tries a garment for size against a South Vietnamese youngster who sports the Marine NCO's cap. Other children crowd the window behind them.

BELOW LEFT: During a break in operations in the Hiep Doc valley, Private First Class Ronald Dalia of New Jersey, a 21-year-old M60 machine gunner, writes a note to his girlfriend. In the background, his assistant, 19-year-old Joseph Des Grandes, laden with belted ammunition, takes the opportunity to have a rest.

THE RIVER WAR
Brown Water Navy

War in the Mekong Delta required strong nerves. The delta was some 3,000 miles (4,800 km) of slow-flowing waterways running deep through Viet Cong territory and South Vietnam's most densely populated region. Initially, responsibility for patrolling them fell to the U.S. Navy's River Patrol Force (RPF). Formed in 1965, the RPF's most famous action was Operation Game Warden of 1966, during which River Patrol Boats (RPBs) – 25-knot fast-craft with machine guns, 20mm cannon and automatic grenade launchers – interdicted suspicious shipping at the mouth of the Mekong and on its inland waterways. Suspicious vessels were inspected for VC supplies and destroyed if any were found. In 1967, 400,000 vessels were inspected and 1,300 VC killed or captured.

Yet the delta was a huge, seemingly endless world. Operations had to be stepped up with the formation of the joint-arms unit, the Mobile Riverine Force (MRF), the amphibious version of search and destroy. Flame-throwers, 81mm mortars and 40mm grenades were bolted into large armored river craft called Monitors which provided fire-support for landings of army operations. Progress was inch by watery inch, and close-quarters violence waited in almost impenetrable shoreside foliage or bunker complexes sunk into rice paddies. Yet the 'brown water navy' had real impact. After Tet, when the SEALORDS (Southeast Asia Lake, Ocean, River, and Delta) strategy was implemented to cut off VC supplies from Cambodia, over 3,000 VC were killed and 500 tons of supplies seized. Having reached a strength of 258 boats and 3,700 ground troops, the RPF's firepower was potent. Like so many aspects of the U.S. war in Vietnam, successful regional operations were over-ruled by general political movements. By April 1971 the U.S. had turned over operations to the South Vietnamese.

sanity, they kept busy by playing cards and shooting rats for target practice. Some even smoked marijuana.

On some days, more than 1,000 rounds of artillery shells struck Khe Sanh. During one bombardment on February 8, 21 marines perished. Meanwhile, Communist snipers preyed upon any marine who strayed too far from his bunker. On February 23, a team of 29 marines ventured from the perimeter to locate a mortar position that was hitting the base with unusual precision. During a charge across open ground, the team suffered a withering discharge of rifle fire from the Communists. Only four men returned to the main base alive. Although the NVA divisions never did launch a serious, large-scale infantry assault on Khe Sanh, they

LEFT: Armed with a Colt Commando, the cut-down carbine version of the M16 rifle issued to regular forces, a Special Forces radio operator watches carefully from inside a building. During the Tet Offensive, small groups of U.S. Army advisers found themselves trapped in compounds and even single buildings as the fighting flowed around them. They remained in radio communications with support forces, and many were later able to be rescued after the Communist attacks had been beaten off.

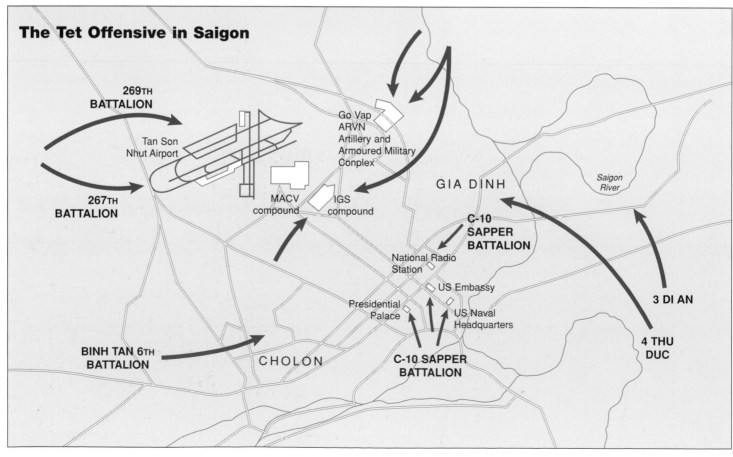

The Tet Offensive in Saigon

269TH BATTALION

267TH BATTALION

Tan Son Nhut Airport

Go Vap ARVN Artillery and Armoured Military Complex

MACV compound

IGS compound

GIA DINH

Saigon River

C-10 SAPPER BATTALION

National Radio Station

US Embassy

3 DI AN

Presidential Palace

US Naval Headquarters

BINH TAN 6TH BATTALION

CHOLON

C-10 SAPPER BATTALION

4 THU DUC

maintained a tight gauntlet around the base and harassed its occupants constantly with artillery strikes and skirmishes.

However, the Americans possessed more than enough firepower to make the NVA pay a heavy price for its actions against Khe Sanh. On the base itself, artillery and mortar batteries sometimes returned fire with great effect. To the northeast, the 16 175mm guns at nearby Camp Carroll and the Rockpile Firebase had enough range to reach NVA positions around Khe Sanh. And from the sky above, the 7th Air Force unleashed Operation Niagara, which spilled waterfalls of deadly explosives upon Communist soldiers in the area.

As commander of the 7th Air Force, General William Monmeyer assumed the

RIGHT: Two off-duty GIs in Saigon on November 2, listening to a broadcast on the Armed Forces Network of President Johnson's announcement that he would halt the bombing of the North and seek ways of finding a peace agreement. Most American servicemen knew that they would have to see out their 365-day tours.
BELOW: U.S. Army Military Police in the grounds of the U.S. Consulate in Saigon during the Viet Cong attack by 17 men from a force of 23 men of the elite C-10 Sapper Battalion. In the foreground lie the bodies of two U.S. soldiers killed in the attack.

LEFT: White phosphorous shells in an ammunition dump at Camp Holloway, Pleiku exploded all day after North Vietnamese mortar or rocket fire scored a lucky hit in the closing months of 1968. In the foreground the UH-1 "Huey" helicopter in its revetment looks almost abandoned as soldiers take cover from burning fragments and the risk of secondary explosions.

BELOW LEFT: Sergeant Eaton of the USAF takes cover with a comrade who has armed himself with an M16 and donned a Flak jacket as incoming rockets explode on the base at Da Nang. The huge size of military and airforce bases made them relatively easy targets for simple unguided weapons like the 4.2 in. (107 mm), 4.8 in. (122 mm) and 5.5 in. (140 mm) rockets fired by the Viet Cong and North Vietnamese.

responsibility of administering Operation
Niagara. Within 24 hours after the start of the
siege on Khe Sanh, he launched 49 B-52 sor
ties and over 600 tactical air strikes upon
enemy positions, destroying bunkers, trenches,
tunnel networks, and storage areas. Fighter-
bombers also attacked NVA ground forces that
had been located by reconnaissance services
during Phase I of the operation, inflicting
heavy losses. During the course of the Khe
Sanh siege, Operation Niagara would involve
2,700 B-52 sorties, 24,000 tactical air strikes
from about 350 fighter-bombers, and nightly
harassing actions by AC-47 gunships.

Within the operation, the B-52s served primarily as a deterrent for NVA reinforcements
attempting to reach the area and aid in the
siege. Each Stratofortress was able to carry up
to 54,000lb. (24500 kg) of bombs per mission.
The ability of these bombers to bomb such

vast areas led the Communists to refer to them
as the "whispering death" from above.
Altogether, in nine weeks, B-52s dropped
some 75,000 tons of explosives over NVA
positions near Khe Sanh.

On the eve of the Tet Offensive, General
Giap himself almost perished during a visit to
his troops just across the Laotian border, when
36 B-52s appeared and unloaded about 1,000
tons of bombs near his field headquarters.
American electronic surveillance services had
picked up information indicating the arrival of
a prominent Communist official from Hanoi,
thus leading Westmoreland to order the bomb
ing raid. Later in the day, nine more bombers
hit the same target. Although Giap survived
the raid, the Communist command and communication center in the Laotian panhandle
suffered considerable damage, enabling the
marines at Khe Sanh to enjoy a moment of

ABOVE: A Viet Cong soldier
is photographed here
armed with a 0.3in (7.62
mm) Degtyarev (РПD) light
machine gun. His function
in this operation is to give
supporting fire to his
comrades who, armed with
AK47 assault rifles, are in
the process of leaping out
to attack from cover. By
the close of the war in
Vietnam, the North
Vietnamese and Viet Cong
had modern, robust and
well-designed Soviet automatic weapons that gave
them formidable fire
power. The Viet Cong and
North Vietnamese would
come to depend heavily on
the technical innovations –
which came from the
Soviet Union and China –
for much of their arms and
artillery, as well as tanks.

LEFT: Wrapped in a poncho liner with a first field dressing over a head wound, a soldier of the U.S. Army 1st Cavalry, the "Air Cavalry," waits for "Dust Off," the medical evacuation helicopter. The cigarette is probably from the five packs that were part of the tinned C ration packs issued to individual soldiers.
BELOW: A U.S. Marine, as the point man, glances back awaiting the order to advance into scrub. A bayonet is fitted to his M16 rifle, suggesting that the enemy is close and the Marines expect to become involved in close combat. Bayonets rooted out hidden enemies from vegetation and scrub.

relative tranquility while the rest of Vietnam exploded in violence during the Tet holiday.

While the Stratofortresses carpet-bombed the Communists, tactical aircraft struck specific NVA targets at lower altitudes. Marine Corps and Air Force Forward Air Controllers (FACs) aboard light airplanes swooped into troubled areas, located enemy positions, and provided the fighter-bomber pilots with the necessary coordinates. Unlike the B-52s, these warplanes flew low enough to be hit by Communist antiaircraft weapons. During the course of the Khe Sanh siege, the Americans lost one A-4 Skyhawk, one F-4 Phantom, and 17 marine helicopters in such operations. In the early stages of the siege, heavy cloud cover often made tactical air strikes difficult to execute effectively.

While warplanes punished the NVA positions around Khe Sanh, pilots flying cargo aircraft did what they could to keep the base supplied during the siege. Unfortunately, part of the base runway had been destroyed on January 21, when a rocket had slammed into the ammunition dump situated in the eastern sector. Now only 2,000 yards (1,829 m) long, the airfield was too small to accommodate the four-engine C-130 Hercules transports, forcing the Americans to rely upon the much smaller C-123 Providers, which carried 5 tons of cargo, only a third of the supplies that the C-130s could hold. By the end of the month, the garrison succeeded in repairing enough of the runway to allow the larger transports to land.

Not surprisingly, landing operations for these cargo airplanes proved to be harrowing experiences. NVA ground troops were able to fire at the aircraft with precision, putting bullet holes into almost every airplane that descended upon Khe Sanh. To minimize the likelihood of being shot down, the crewmen employed a technique of delivery known as the Low Altitude Parachute Extraction System (LAPES). Pilots swooped into Khe Sanh at a level very close to the ground at 130 miles per hour (209 kmph), while a parachute pulled a large crate of supplies out of an open door on the back of the aircraft. The marines on the ground then extracted the supplies from the runway before the Communist artillery fixed on the packages and destroyed them. When LAPES worked effectively, the C-130s spent only a few minutes on the ground and left very quickly.

BELOW: With camouflaged packs, their faces alert and concentrated, a male and female soldier of the Viet Cong support their comrades. As they move stealthily by canoe across a deserted branch of the Mekong, they have their weapons at the ready. The woman in the stern is armed with a MAS Mle 1936 rifle, while her comrade carries a Chatellerault M1924/29 light machine gun. Neither of these weapons were made by the indigenous population of Vietnam, rather they would have been captured in the 1950s during the struggle with the French.

The Viet Cong – Charlie

The Viet Cong – a slang name for Vietnamese communist – were the most infamous guerrilla force in history. Armed with the simplest of weaponry and living off minimal nutrition in the jungle, the Viet Cong ate away at the lives of U.S. units through ambush, booby-traps, and bombs. Yet put the popular image to one side, and it is notable how little is really understood about this body of fighters.

The Viet Cong were the military arm of the National Liberation Front of South Vietnam, an organization formed on December 20, 1960. Many of the Viet Cong ranks were former Viet Minh fighters who had stayed on in the South after the division of Vietnam in 1954. Their aim: assist the North through military means in the reunification of Vietnam under communist rule. One of the greatest aids to the growth of the Viet Cong was the inept and partisan leadership coming from government. In 1959 the number of VC was about 5,000. After four years of Diem's blundering, numbers went up to about 40,000, not counting the thousands of sympathizers in the civilian population. This growth, especially in urban areas (the Vietcong were traditionally sited in rural districts), enabled the VC to suffer amazingly high casualties, yet still annually increase their number.

Organization was tight and managed by political overseers from the North. A typical VC battalion consisted of 300–600 men and women. Around 150 would form a front-line infantry company, and a similar number would be in charge of heavy weapons (mortars, recoilless rifles, anti-tank rockets, etc.) while the rest would be staff, engineers, reconnaissance, and signals units. They were the nimblest of fighters. Lethal booby traps would be created from simple sticks and twine. They would launch ambushes as if out of nowhere, hacking down patrols with AK bursts before letting the jungle soak them back up. U.S. units could take casualties for weeks from VC mines and booby traps, but not actually see a single VC soldier in the flesh. Masters of their environment, bolstered by a supportive populace, they were feared opponents who showed technology was no substitute for elusive tactics and a relentless will to fight.

Yet here we must separate the myth from the reality. The VC were not invulnerable; far from it. U.S./VC kill ratios in action always favored the U.S. Moreover, the VC were strong as long as they remained covert. So it was that the Tet offensive – a campaign which led many VC out into open war – effectively resulted in the VC's annihilation. 30,000 VC lost their lives during Tet. Units such as the elite 316 Company operating south of Saigon had their strength reduced from 300 to three. Some say this was intended by the North, who wanted to remove any potential opposition parties should reunification be achieved. Whatever the case, the losses suffered during Tet meant the VC never had the cohesion they previously possessed, and their ranks were instead filled out with NVA regulars. Such was the disillusion with the North that VC even started to defect in significant numbers. Tet took out the force from the Viet Cong, yet since the early 1960s they had been inflicting heavy casualties on enemies far stronger in manpower and technology than them, and they have given us one of the most enduring images of the Vietnam War.

RIGHT: Armed with B-40 rocket propelled grenade launchers these Main Force Viet Cong fighters pause on a jungle track. The B-40 with its shaped charge warhead could be used as an anti-tank weapon capable of penetrating seven inches of armour or with a fragmentation sleeve fitted in an anti-personnel role. Extra ammunition was carried in a light haversack. Although initially relying on "home made" or captured weaponry, by the time of the Tet Offensive many VC units were well equipped with modern small arms. Nevertheless, their strength was as a guerrilla force. Tet committed them to the kind of conventional battle for which they were unsuited. Tet was effectively the swan song of the Viet Cong. The devastating losses they suffered crippled them as a significant force and they were increasingly superceded by North Vietnamese regulars.

LEFT: Holding his AK47 assault rifle in one hand, a Viet Cong guerrilla named Dang Van Huong pulls the friction cord in the hollow handle of a Chicom hand grenade with his teeth. In the early days of the war in South Vietnam, weapons such as mines and hand grenades were manufactured in workshops hidden away deep within the jungle terrains. Later on in the conflict, they were shipped from the North down the Ho Chi Minh Trail.

RIGHT: Two U.S. Marines retrieve the weapons of one of the Embassy's slain assailants. The attack on the Embassy achieved total surprise but the death of the VC unit's commander early in the attack robbed the assault of much of its impetus. As U.S. reinforcements arrived the tide turned.

BELOW: U.S. Military Police and soldiers cluster around the U.S. Ambassador Ellsworth Bunker as he views the damage to the Embassy following the Viet Cong attack on January 31, 1968. The body of one of the attackers can be seen to the left. The attack, though unsuccessful, was a spectacular propaganda coup, attracting global media attention.

American pilots were also able to drop supplies on parachutes from the air and performed about 600 such missions during the course of the siege. However, this method was often inaccurate and even dangerous to the marines on the ground. On March 2, one marine died when a crate crashed through his bunker. The incident led the pilots to rely primarily upon LAPES to deliver cargo. During the siege, C-130 crews performed 273 landings, while C-123 crews accomplished 179 and C-7A Caribou pilots another eight. Miraculously, the Americans lost only two C-130s and three C-123s while performing these actions.

In the hills surrounding the main base, the marines received their supplies from helicopters. In 30-second actions known as "Super Gaggle" operations, 12 CH-46s each dropped about 3,000lb. (1,360 kg) of supplies on to

RIGHT: A photographer from the U.S. Army Public Information Office holds the Great Seal of the United States that had been hit by small arms fire and had come off the wall. Because the attack had been at night, the Military Police and soldiers of the 101st Airborne were unable to penetrate the building for six hours. Staff held out behind locked doors and fought off Viet Cong attacks.

BELOW: Traumatized civilian staff help carry out casualties from the Embassy compound. Although costly in terms of casualties, televison images of the Viet Cong attacks in the heart of Saigon and particularly on such a potent symbol of apparent American strength profoundly shocked a U.S. public that had been fed on a diet of positive messages about how the war was being won for over two years. If the enemy could wreak this sort of havoc, how could an end be in sight?

ABOVE: Flames rise behind a platoon of U.S. Marines during the process of a search and destroy operation. These operations, intended as they were to destroy food stocks and buildings that might be used by the North Vietnamese or Viet Cong, often resulted in the destruction of stocks that had been built up over time by poor villagers and consequently served to antagonize the indigenous population.

RIGHT: A young soldier, armed with an M16, looks nervously at the street below over the rear ramp of the M113 armoured personnel carrier in which he is riding. Stacked on the back of the APC are the bodies of three men who were killed when the buildings they were guarding near Tan Son Nhut – the commercial airport and USAF airbase at Saigon – were attacked by the 269th and 267th battalions of the North Vietnamese Army.

nets staked out by ground forces. The Sea Knight crews performed these operations three times a day under the protection of artillery, mortars, and A-4 Skyhawks. Altogether, the Communists managed to shoot down 17 helicopters during the offensive on Khe Sanh.

By itself, Khe Sanh was a significant battle in the Vietnam War. For years, the American public had been receiving reports from Westmoreland and other senior officers proclaiming the disintegration of the Communist war effort and the steady pacification of the South Vietnamese countryside. Suddenly, televised images of marines ducking for cover from artillery rounds revealed to citizens in the United States that the Vietnamese Communists still had plenty of fight left in them. Not surprisingly, Khe Sanh and other events in 1968 would provoke widespread disillusionment among Americans and embolden antiwar activists to become more vociferous in their opposition to the White House.

ABOVE RIGHT: In the comfort of his M151 light truck, a Major of the Danh-Du' To'-Quoc – the South Vietnamese Marines – consults his map as his troops move off without cover along the edge of a paddy field. Although some South Vietnamese officers were good leaders and cared for their troops, many of them were often regarded as lazy and corrupt by the Americans who fought alongside them as their allies.

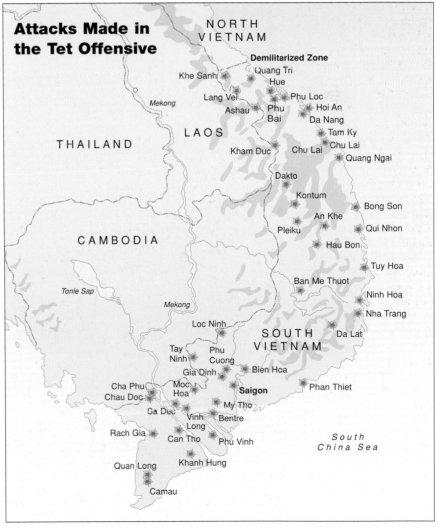

Attacks Made in the Tet Offensive

NORTH VIETNAM

Demilitarized Zone

Khe Sanh
Quang Tri
Hue
Mekong
Lang Vei
Phu Loc
Ashau
Phu Bai
Hoi An
Da Nang

LAOS
Tam Ky
Chu Lai
Kham Duc
Chu Lai
Quang Ngai

THAILAND

Dakto

Kontum
Bong Son
An Khe
Qui Nhon
Pleiku

CAMBODIA
Hau Bon

Tuy Hoa

Ban Me Thuot

Tonle Sap
Ninh Hoa

Mekong
Nha Trang

Loc Ninh
SOUTH
VIETNAM
Da Lat

Tay Ninh
Phu Cuong
Gia Dinh
Bien Hoa
Cha Phu
Chau Doc
Moc Hoa
Saigon
Phan Thiet

Sa Dec
My Tho
Vinh Long
Bentre
Rach Gia
Can Tho
Phu Vinh

South China Sea

Quan Long
Khanh Hung

Camau

ABOVE: A South Vietnamese Army Ranger, his camouflaged helmet painted with the distinctive insignia of a black panther face, clutches his weapon to him with a look of intense concentration as he doubles quickly along a road leading into Saigon. In the meantime, M113 armored personnel carriers belonging to the U.S. Army grind into the city on the road behind him. The South Vietnamese Army Rangers would have secured the houses in Saigon to withstand the regular ambushes during the battle for dominance in the city, which came either from the Viet Cong, or from further afield, in the shape of the North Vietnamese forces.

Khe Sanh also became an object of obsession both for Westmoreland and President Lyndon B. Johnson (LBJ). The president and some of his advisers saw the siege as a struggle similar to Dien Bien Phu in 1954, in which Vietminh artillerists had pounded a French garrison mercilessly until its occupants surrendered, thus liberating Vietnam from French control. Fearful of a similar result in Khe Sanh, LBJ had a model of the base placed in the basement of the White House and spent hours brooding over the miniature, demanding daily reports about the progress of the siege. He also extracted a solemn oath from the Joint Chiefs of Staff pledging to hold Khe Sanh at all costs.

Like LBJ, Wheeler and Westmoreland saw the offensive on Khe Sanh as an attempt by the Communists to score a victory similar to that of Dien Bien Phu. However, they welcomed the prospect of a conventional offensive in the area around the base as an opportunity for the Americans to smash their enemies in a climactic battle similar to those fought in Europe during World War II. Westmoreland also noted significant differences between Khe Sanh and Dien Bien Phu. The French garrison was situated in a valley, while Khe Sanh was atop a plateau. And unlike the French in 1954, the Americans at Khe Sanh commanded the surrounding high ground. Finally, the marines still had an airport and enjoyed massive air and artillery support that the French had lacked. This sense of optimism led "Westy" to divert forces to far-flung areas within MR 1, increasing the total American troop strength above Hue to about 40,000 men. He also brought French veterans of the Dien Bien Phu siege to Saigon to offer insight and advice based upon their experiences.

RIGHT: South Vietnamese Rangers watch impassively as, in the course of an interrogation, an intelligence officer beats a suspected Viet Cong prisoner. To the Rangers, the suspect's youth and physique as well as the condition of his hands would be indicators that he was not a peasant farmer. Brutality was not the preserve of any side during the war in Vietnam.

BELOW: Military police escort one of the surviving Viet Cong C-10 Sapper Battalion who launched the attack on the U.S. Embassy in Saigon. Rather optimistically, he holds the Chieu Hoi amnesty leaflet in his left hand, indicating that he wishes to surrender. After the huge losses in Tet, the Chieu Hoi - "Open Arms" – program produced over 45,000 Viet Cong wishing to surrender to their enemy.

Walter Cronkite and Tet

During the Vietnam War, the journalist and broadcaster Walter Cronkite became known as "the most trusted man in television." It was a time when the viewing public needed someone to trust. The government stories of progress being made in the Vietnam War seemed hollow when compared with the graphic images regularly broadcast into U.S. homes each night. Both the government and the military gave dry statistical accounts of the war and many felt they needed someone impartial to interpret what was going on.

For many, that person was Walter Cronkite. Cronkite had been in journalism since the mid-1930s. During 11 years with United Press, he reported direct from the front line in many key World War II battles, such as the Allied landings at North Africa and later at Normandy on D-Day, even flying inside B-17s during raids over Germany. In 1950 Cronkite joined CBS, quickly becoming a news anchorman

and a respected voice on domestic and international affairs. So it was natural that by the time America was immersed in the Vietnam War, he was a voice of authority for the nation and helped make CBS the most watched news network in the nation.

During the first years of the war, Cronkite's patriotism and belief in democratic principles led him to give support for the war, like many others in the U.S. Every night on CBS Evening News, he would lend his sanction to the U.S. boys such a long way away. Much of the public followed his opinions as gospel.

Yet everything changed with Tet. Like many, Cronkite had accepted that the might of the U.S. would win through in Vietnam, as it had done in earlier conflicts. What Tet seemed to demonstrate was that three years of promises of quick victory were nonsensical when the North was capable of mounting such a massive invasion. Revising his

view of the future, Cronkite now announced that the war in Vietnam was not heading for a U.S. victory, but rather a bloody stalemate. On February 27, 1968, with over nine million U.S. citizens watching him across the country, Cronkite made a shocking expression of his changed heart: "But it is increasingly clear to this reporter that the only rational way out then will be to negotiate, not as victors but as an honorable people who lived up to their pledge to defend democracy, and did the best they could. This is Walter Cronkite. Good night."

This renunciation of military action coalesced many people's dissatisfaction with the war. When such an establishment figure as Cronkite turned against U.S. policy, people knew something was profoundly wrong. Rejection of the war became as much a principle of the middle classes as the radical classes, and there was no way for the U.S. government's public-relations machine to rebuild confidence.

BOTTOM LEFT: In the late 1960s Walter Cronkite was one of the most respected T.V. journalists in the United States and the anchorman for the CBS news network. He was seen as the voice of middle America and was a former war correspondent himself. As such his opinions on the conflict in Southeast Asia carried huge weight. His public change of heart over the ability of the U.S. to achieve a military victory in Vietnam, represented a watershed in the gradual erosion of public support for the war.

BELOW: The media provides the view from the front line as a camera crew from an American TV station conducts an interview with a Major General during the Tet Offensive. Though "live" television via satellites was to be a thing of the future, in 1968 film could be flown back to the U.S. overnight. In editing suites across the U.S., it was inevitable that the most spectacular shots were used, and commentaries written in the printed media did little to dispel the impression that Tet was an American disaster.

RIGHT: Shock and bewilderment mark the faces of a South Vietnamese family of a mother and four children who have been caught up in a sweep which was being conducted through a village. The communities of rural areas in South Vietnam suffered from the depredations of both sides, the Army by day, and the Viet Cong by night. This created much hardship and, as a result, many were driven to look for work or security in the slum suburbs of the larger cities.

FAR RIGHT: A South Vietnamese soldier from Company A, 30th Ranger Battalion opens fire against a suspected enemy position as the Rangers patrol a village close to Saigon during the Tet Lunar New Year Holiday. Many South Vietnamese soldiers were on leave with their families enjoying the holiday when the Viet Cong and North Vietnamese attacked.

Some senior officers attempted to dissuade Westmoreland from focusing so much on the northern border, arguing that the NVA action against Khe Sanh was just a ruse to draw American forces away from Saigon and other population centers. Most notably, Major-General Lowell English, the top Marine Corps commander of MR 1, implored Westmoreland not to commit himself to hold Khe Sanh, arguing that the base was a remote, worthless piece of dirt that did not merit the costs and risks required to retain it. General Maxwell Taylor offered a similar view to LBJ back in Washington. This advice fell on deaf ears. In fact, Westmoreland took the opposite view, perceiving Communist attacks upon South Vietnamese cities as diversions aimed at discouraging him from sending reinforcements to

NEXT PAGE: A South Vietnamese officer indicates a target for a support weapon crew during the fighting for a defended village. The South Vietnamese Army was armed and equipped by the United States, but many of its officers kept the style – like a cavalier attitude to responsibility for troops under command – of their former Colonial masters, the French.
BELOW: A Vietnamese girl who has been wounded in a fire fight lies unconscious from loss of blood. This fire fight took place between the Viet Cong and soldiers of the 9th Division of the U.S. Army during the Mini Tet in 1968. Ricochets from bullets and shell and mortar fragments as well as mines and booby traps killed and wounded civilians in heavily populated areas.

Khe Sanh. He also identified the base as a "crucial anchor" which the Americans needed to retain to prevent Quang Tri City and Hue from falling to the NVA.

Subsequent events over the Tet holiday would substantiate the views of Major-General English and other critics of Westmoreland's strategy. Before dawn on January 30, NVA and Viet Cong fighters infiltrated several population centers throughout South Vietnam and fired mortar rounds, rockets, and other devices into government buildings and military installations. In MR 1, the Communists struck Hoi An and hurled ordnance into the American air base at Da Nang. Further south, 2,000 enemy soldiers attacked Ban Me Thuot after subjecting the area to a barrage of rocket and mortar fire. In the Central Highlands, five battalions assaulted Kon Tum, while rockets slammed into nearby Pleiku. On the coast, the Communists struck Qui Nhon and the headquarters of US I Field Force at Nha Trang, which was also the location of the Vietnamese Naval Training Center.

Within a day, the Allies killed or captured most of the assailants in these locations. At

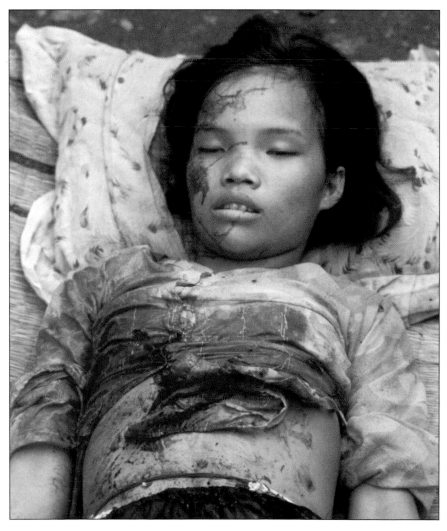

RIGHT: Local children watch as South Vietnamese soldiers conduct a sweep of their village. Death and suffering were everyday sights to many children during the Vietnam conflict.
FAR RIGHT: Part of the crew of a U.S. Army M48A3 Patton tank of the 5th Mechanised Division are seated outside, on top of their vehicle. They are positioned there to watch carefully, since the tank is in the process of fording an arm of the Ben Hai river, south of Con Thien. If the tank sank, the crew on the outside would be able to jump clear. However, it would be very different for the driver – to whom the commander is talking on the intercom – who would be trapped inside the vehicle. It was therefore important that difficult operations such as a river crossings were closely monitored.

Nha Trang, the Communists failed to make effective use of their mortars and delayed their ground assault long enough to enable ARVN forces to prepare. When the attack occurred, the South Vietnamese repulsed it, killing 377 enemy troops and capturing 78. In the Central Highlands, the Viet Cong H-15 Local Force Battalion had to assault Pleiku alone when the NVA 95B Regiment failed to reach the city. When the ensuing battle ended on February 3, the Viet Cong battalion had lost 632 men killed, with another 182 captured after a fruitless struggle with an ARVN armored unit.

Reacting to these attacks, Brigadier-General Phillip B. Davidson, chief of intelligence for Military Assistance Command,

Vietnam (MACV), predicted that another series of assaults throughout the country would occur within 24 hours. Westmoreland agreed with this assessment and placed all American personnel on full alert. However, he remained committed to keeping most of his forces in MR 1 because he believed that the Communists would concentrate the upcoming offensive in that area. He also urged President Nguyen Van Thieu to place the South Vietnamese armed forces on full alert and even cancel the Tet ceasefire altogether so that they might be prepared for aggressive actions around Saigon.

Thieu declined the second request, arguing that it would benefit Communist propagandists

RIGHT: A Vietnamese Marine armed with a 3.5 in. M20 Rocket Launcher. He is shown here in this photograph working his way carefully forward, the tail fins of a rocket projecting from his backpack. The 3.5 in. Rocket Launcher was designed as an antitank weapon, but with its 120 yds (110m) range, it was also useful as a bunker busting weapon. On the right of the photo, the presence of a following marine is indicated by the bayonet on the end of his gun barrel.

and undermine the morale of his troops. He did agree to shorten the holiday leave from 48 to 36 hours, but failed to ensure that his military officers would carry out this order in a timely manner. The allied success in repelling the January 30 attacks at Da Nang, Pleiku, and elsewhere had lulled Thieu and other South Vietnamese leaders into a false sense of security. In fact, the president himself continued his vacation in My Tho. Some ARVN officers did enforce the 12-hour reduction in time to the ceasefire by confining their troops to barracks and enacting security measures in their respective areas of command. However, too many other officers joined in the Tet festivities, satisfied that the enemy would never attack on a sacred holiday.

Meanwhile, the cities of South Vietnam became loud bastions of revelry for residents celebrating the Vietnamese New Year. Not surprisingly, the disorganized crowds swarming the streets provided excellent cover for infiltrating Communist commandos. In fact, the

ABOVE: A dead Viet Cong sprawls in a camouflaged trench in a rice paddy field. In the background, South Vietnamese Rangers can be seen in the process of escorting prisoners to a helicopter landing zone. Farmers in paddy fields soon learned to ignore helicopters and not to run away if they saw them since, to door gunners, running was seen as a sure sign that these civilians were in fact hostile.
RIGHT: With a belt of 0.3in. (7.62 mm) M60 machine gun ammunition draped over his shoulder, a young U.S. soldier – nicknamed a "Grunt" – prepares for yet another day of conflict in Vietnam. The hair was worn long by the standards of the U.S. Army in the late 1960s and, along with the vestigial moustache, was seen as a youth protest against military conformity as well as an objection to the fact that the conscript has been posted to Vietnam.

noise produced by firecrackers would even obscure the sounds of gunshots and explosions generated by Viet Cong assailants for a brief time. Amid this very favorable environment, the members of the C-10 Sapper Battalion prepared to strike important targets in Saigon which they reached by confiscating taxicabs and other vehicles to use as clandestine military transport.

At 3.00 a.m. on January 31, a truck and a taxicab approached the United States embassy on Thong Nhat Boulevard in Saigon. Nineteen Viet Cong sappers emerged from the vehicles and blasted their way through the outer walls of the building, to the horror of four nearby South Vietnamese policemen charged with providing security for the embassy. While the policemen fled the area, the sappers poured through the gaping hole they had created and fired their small arms in all directions, killing five American guards within minutes. While pinning down six more guards with suppressive fire, the sappers fired antitank rockets at the heavy front door of the embassy building. The supposedly worn-out Communists were now taking the war right into the heart of the American war machine in Vietnam.

The attack on the American embassy was only one of several battles fought throughout the country during what would be known as the Tet Offensive. Not counting the NVA divisions involved in the sieges of Khe Sanh and Loc Ninh, as many as 84,000 Communist troops struck almost every major base and population center in South Vietnam. Altogether, the NVA and Viet Cong armies brought violence to five out of the six autonomous cities within the country, 36 out of South Vietnam's 44 provincial capitals, and 72 out of 245 district capitals. In Saigon alone, 11 Viet Cong battalions had infiltrated the city limits during the embassy attack.

Apart from Saigon, the area most severely affected by the Tet Offensive was Military Region 1 in the northern part of South Vietnam. In this section, NVA and Viet Cong forces struck military bases at Phu Bai, Phu Loc, and Chu Lai, pinning American troops down with heavy ordnance while destroying

ABOVE: Wrapped in a poncho, a soldier of the 1st Air Cavalry moves down a trail in the Central Highlands in January during the winter monsoon. Veterans would later testify to the volume and weight of the rain that would fall during this period. The soldier is armed with a 12 gauge Winchester Trench Gun, a weapon that dated back to World War I and which could be fitted with an M1905 sword bayonet.

MAKE WAR
NOT LOVE

several aircraft on base runways. Communist forces also attacked the headquarters of the South Korean army. More important, they penetrated the cities of Quang Tri, Tam Ky, and Hue, along with every provincial capital in the region. At Quang Ngai City, the Communists liberated thousands of prisoners from a local jail. With most American forces committed to Khe Sanh and other far-flung positions, NVA and Viet Cong units were able to capture Hue and hold it for almost a month.

In Military Region 2, the Communists struck Phan Thiet, Hau Bon, Tuy Hoa, and the American bases at An Khe, Cam Ranh Bay, and Bong Son. Six battalions also attacked Da Lat, a popular resort town for South Vietnamese military officers and the location of ARVN's military academy. During the fight

LEFT: With a cheerful transposition of the Flower Power antiwar slogan of the United States "Make Love Not War" painted on his helmet cover, a young radio operator waits on the edge of a paddy field. The AN/PRC25 radio here is strapped to a pack frame.

BELOW: The victim of a "water torture" has a moment's respite. The South Vietnamese soldiers have pushed him head first into the pot of water until he is close to drowning; he has then been pulled out, revived, and questioned.

NGUYEN CAO KY

He seemed the ideal candidate for U.S. support in the early years of the Vietnam War. Nguyen Cao Ky was a fervent anti-communist, even fighting on the side of the French forces against Vietnamese nationalism during the first Indochinese war. Following the Geneva Accords and the division of Vietnam in 1954, Ky joined the South Vietnamese Air Force and during the 1960s Ky became close with U.S. advisers. Ky was a strident, bullish character, a personality which sat well with U.S. confidence at the time. His influence steadily snowballed. Following the overthrow and execution of Ngo Dinh Diem in 1963, Ky stepped into the position of commander of the air force and developed a personal army of 10,000 men.

Ky's ambitions were greater, however. In June 1965 he participated in a coup with Major General Nguyen Van Thieu and General Duong Van Minh, overthrowing Premier Phan Huy Quat and his shortlived government. Ky took the position of Premier and launched, like so many before him, into a disastrous exercise in government. Like Diem, Ky's regime was oppressive and exclusive, particularly alienating the Buddhist community. The situation reached such a perilous state that in May 1966 factional ARVN troops fought each other in Hue, Saigon, and Danang. South Vietnam was on the edge of civil war, and one-third of ARVN soldiers deserted.

Eventually in 1967 under external pressure Thieu took over as leader of Vietnam and Ky became vice-president. He held this position for four years, but was never happy playing second fiddle. After a failed attempt at presidential election in 1971, Ky returned to the air force, but had to flee the country when South Vietnam fell to the communists in 1975. Naturally he headed for the U.S. where he had a long career on the lecture circuit, more as a political curiosity than a political sage.

LEFT: A U.S. Marine Corps flame throwing M48 tank projects a stream of blazing fuel in a test or demonstration. While flame could be used in attacks on enemy bunkers and field defenses, it could also be employed to burn off vegetation along river banks and road sides in order to reduce the ever-present risk of ambushes.

BELOW: The aftermath of counter-attacks in the Cholon district of Saigon during "mini-Tet." Cholon, the Chinese area of Saigon, was a hotbed of communist sympathies and saw heavy fighting during Tet in January and mini-Tet in May. ARVN and U.S. troops had few qualms about calling in artillery and air strikes in the battle to clear communist forces from this area.

RIGHT: A life blighted by war almost before it has begun. A five year old South Vietnamese girl waits patiently for treatment in the Save The Children Fund clinic in Qui Nhon. For those disabled by the war, South Vietnam could be a harsh country and limbless soldiers begging on the streets of the major cities were a common sight. If life was difficult in South Vietnam, it became even worse when the North took over the whole country.

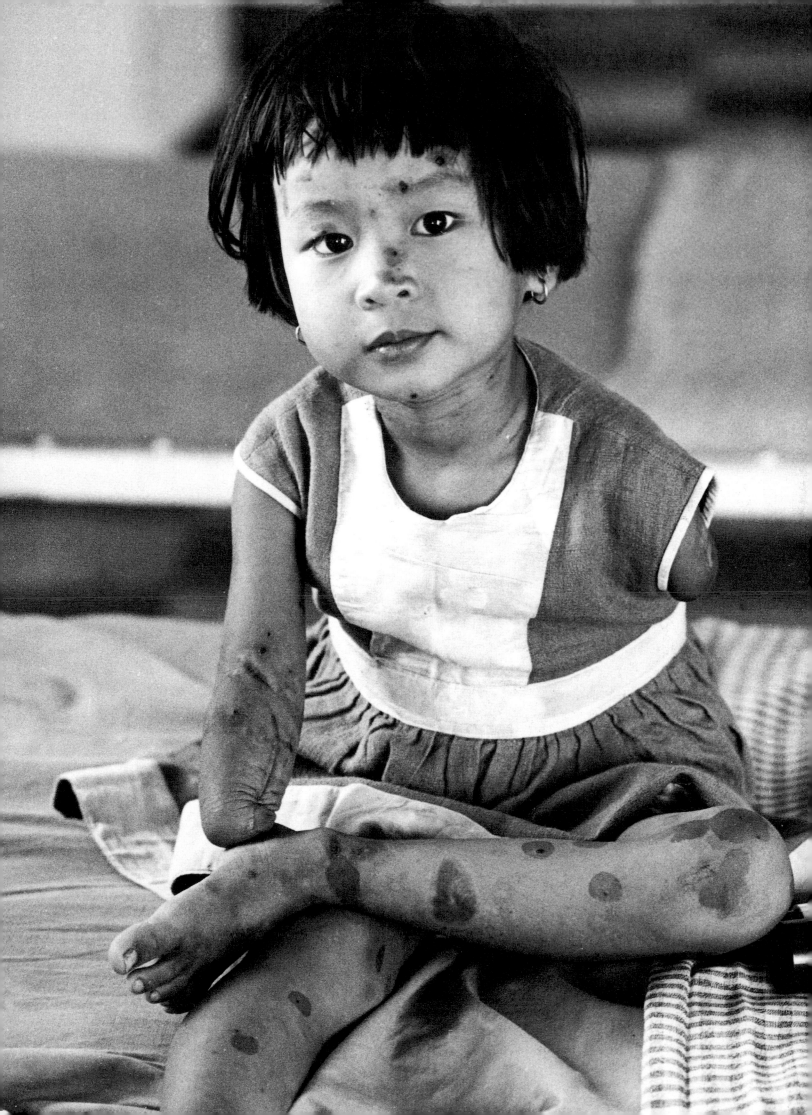

RIGHT: Rockets stream from the pods of a UH-1B armed helicopter. Known as "Gunships," this version of the versatile "Huey" was armed with four M60 machine guns, one in each door and two mounted coaxially with the rocket pods, and two pods containing a total of 48 2.75 in. unguided rockets. Other armament could include the 40mm automatic grenade launcher and M 22 guided missiles.

BELOW: The awesome pattern of tracer fire in the sky near Saigon as an AC-47 gunship fires at suspected enemy positions. Known both as "Puff the Magic Dragon" and "Spooky" this aircraft carried three 7.62 mm Miniguns. They could fire 18,000 rounds a minute into precisely defined areas and so were invaluable when patrols were trapped and surrounded.

for this town, a deputy province chief showed inspiring leadership when he assembled a defense force consisting of freshman cadets, two Regional Force (RF) companies, and some American soldiers who were enjoying themselves in a local brothel when the offensive began. In such instances when South Vietnamese leaders were competent and courageous, ARVN and other military and police units usually performed well against Communist attacks.

Far to the south, Viet Cong forces were just as aggressive in the Mekong Delta, where the Americans had served mostly in an advisory role to South Vietnamese troops. Within this region (MR 4), fighting broke out from Moc Hoa near Cambodia all the way down to Ca Mau, on the southern tip of South Vietnam. Viet Cong troops also attacked Soc Trang, Can Tho, Sa Dec, Rach Gia, Chau Phu, Phu Vinh, Ben Tre, and Vinh Long. They even struck My Tho, President Thieu's vacation resort. In many instances, Viet Cong forces occupied impoverished neighborhoods in the delta's provincial capitals and were very difficult for ARVN troops to extricate. At Can Tho, the top South Vietnamese commander of MR 4 barricaded himself in his headquarters and allowed his American advisers to direct operations against the Communists.

ABOVE: In a village which has been battered and blasted by the force of artillery fire, a mother has managed to save a few utensils as well as her bicycle, and rig a hammock for her daughter to sleep in. Many American soldiers were surprised and impressed by the resilience of the Vietnamese female population, as many women were able to recover and rebuild their lives, often after several catastrophes, and without any assistance from males.

ABOVE: The head of South Vietnam's National Police, Brigadier General Nguyen Ngoc Loan, executes a captured Viet Cong officer in a Saigon street. Loan had just learned that the Viet Cong had killed a fellow police officer and his complete family. Captured on film and in this photograph, this horrifying image shocked public opinion in the United States, bringing the atrocities of the war home to them to become a matter of public interest. This image, taken by AP photographer Eddie Adams, earned the photographer a Pulitzer Prize in 1969.

The meticulous planning by the Communists deep inside South Vietnamese territory revealed how unsuccessful the allied pacification campaign had been. Thirty miles (48 km) north of Saigon, Viet Cong operatives had prepared their assault on the capital in a rubber plantation that they were using as a secret headquarters. From there they shipped truckloads of arms and explosives hidden under piles of produce and even inside coffins to a safe-house within the city, easily evading the notoriously lax security system used by the South Vietnamese police. The Viet Cong insurgents kept most of their supplies in a repair garage owned by a former chauffeur for the American embassy, who was a known Communist sympathizer. For several weeks,

Viet Cong guerrillas entered Saigon unarmed and checked into hotel rooms while they waited and prepared. Not surprisingly, South Vietnamese police officials failed to notice the high number of strangers from the countryside who were occupying the city's hotels.

In addition to the American embassy, the Communists struck several areas across the capital and maintained control over entire neighborhoods. West of the city, the 267th and 269th Battalions attacked the Tan Son Nhut international airport. From the north, the 101st Viet Cong Regiment assaulted the Go Vap ARVN Artillery and Armored Military Complex. The 2nd Go Man Battalion joined this attack and moved further into the city to strike the ARVN Joint General Staff (JGS)

Compound near the main headquarters of MACV. In the southwest, the 6th Binh Tan Battalion occupied Cholon, the Chinese district of Saigon. Within a day, much of the southern and western parts of the city fell into Communist hands, at least temporarily.

East of these areas, the C-10 Sapper Battalion carried out raids on the high-profile targets within the capital. In addition to the American embassy, members of this group attacked the presidential palace, the headquarters of the American and South Vietnamese navies, the Korean and Filipino embassies, and the National Radio Station. When residents of the city first realized that firearms and explosives were being discharged during the Tet festivities, many initially believed that the cause of the disturbance was a coup being staged by Vice-President Nguyen Cao Ky to seize the reins of government from Thieu. Few of them considered the possibility of a Viet Cong seizure of power.

An imposing, six-story building that towered over central Saigon, the United States embassy symbolized American influence in South Vietnam. Until Tet 1968, the diplomatic staff and Marine Corps security detachment had felt secure in the fortress-like compound, away from the fighting that was taking place in remote rural areas. Now confronted with a small squad of sappers shooting and blasting their way into the embassy grounds, the American guards suddenly found themselves in a ferocious gunfight. However, the Communist assailants were in even greater peril when the surviving marine guards recovered from their initial shock and returned fire, killing the Viet Cong commando leaders.

Deprived of their commanders, the members of the raiding party failed to press the advantages they had gained with their surprise attack. While the marine defenders hunkered behind the heavy doors of the main chancery building, American reinforcements arrived to retake the compound. Although disorganized, the sappers fought tenaciously for over six hours before Americans marines, paratroopers, and military policemen killed all of them and re-established control over the embassy.

During this battle, television news crews provided live footage of the fighting. Although the carnage was taking place in the early hours of the morning in South Vietnam, back on the east coast of the United States, it was the middle of the afternoon. Citizens at home also saw the grisly images of dead Viet Cong commandos strewn across the embassy compound in various contorted positions, along with those of bleeding embassy staff and the noticeable damage done to the compound. Television footage also depicted the widespread feeling of shock that seemed to appear on the faces of American personnel caught in the violence of the offensive in Saigon and elsewhere. Almost overnight, the Vietnam War went from being a mundane news story ignored by many Americans, to a

BELOW: Tied at the elbows, unable to move their arms, captured Vietcong endure the unwanted attention from South Vietnamese soldiers in Saigon. Encircled by South Vietnamese, the section chief of the Viet Cong's 308 Battalion (second from the right) has been identified, and looks his enemy in the eye, at the same time knowing that he is about to become subject to a brutal interrogation. Later on, when his captors have learned all they require from him, his fate will be decided. His captors will make a choice for their prisoner between death, or an indefinite period in a prison camp.

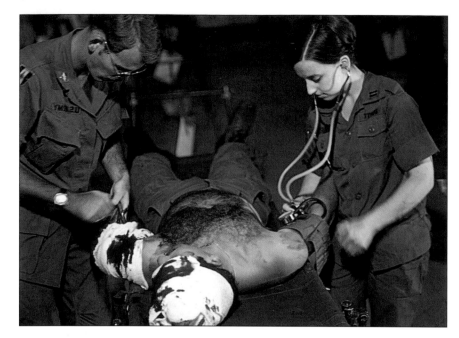

LEFT: At the U.S. field hospital, a doctor examines one of the wounds of a casualty, while a nurse checks the blood pressure. Medical resources were limited, so that if mass casualties arrived at a hospital, it was necessary to split the wounded into three categories: those that were likely to die, those that would survive with sustained care, and those that could be patched up before being forwarded along the casualty evacuation system. **RIGHT:** Bound and guarded captured North Vietnamese soldiers await an uncertain fate, one of them suffering a head wound which has been tended to by his captors. Above them hangs a tattered remnant of a Tet Lunar New Year decoration. The firecrackers which were normally set off at Tet to ward off the evil spirits for the new year provided a useful cover for the sound of small-arms fire during the initial assaults.

BELOW LEFT: A South Vietnamese soldier vents his frustration and anger on the body of a Viet Cong soldier by a roadside. In Tet, the South Vietnamese Army surprised the Americans as its forces fought hard; however, many men were defending their homes, and were imbued with a sense of urgency. In areas where the Viet Cong were able to seize control during the Tet Offensive, they carried out the execution of soldiers and government officials, as well as members of their families.

THE AUSTRALIANS
The "Diggers" in Vietnam

Australia's commitment to Vietnam in effect began in 1954 when it signed up to the Southeast Asia Treaty Organization (SEATO). SEATO was a body of eight nations, all pledging to protect the Southeast Asian region from communist expansion. The commitment of SEATO members to protecting South Vietnam was varied, but Australia took the lead of the U.S. with some of the earliest deployments of troops. On August 3, 1962, 30 soldiers designated the Australian Army Training Team (AATV) arrived in Vietnam. Like the U.S. Special Forces, their job was to train local forces in combat tactics, and some 1,000 such soldiers would serve in Vietnam between 1962 and 1972. Thirty-three would be killed and 122 wounded, and decorations included four Victoria Crosses and two Distinguished Service Orders.

Yet the AATV was only a slice of the Australian input. In 1965 the 1 Royal Australian Regiment was deployed as the third battalion of the U.S. 173rd Airborne Brigade, conducting heavy operations throughout III Corps Tactical Zone. Additional combat and logistical units from Australia and New Zealand followed, including artillery units. The configuration of the units changed each year, but what didn't change was the reputation of the Australian's for hard fighting. Having built a name on actions such as those at Gallipoli and in the Pacific campaigns of World War II, the Australian forces were known to be dogged, self-denying soldiers, showing themselves as resilient in the field and intelligent players in combat. Some 55,000 Australian personnel served in Vietnam, 413 troops were killed, and over 2,000 wounded. D Coy 6 RAR received a United States Presidential Unit Citation.

RIGHT: The men of 1st ARVN Division's elite Hac Bo (Black Panther) Recondo Company were the only unit standing between two battalions of NVA regulars and the 1st Divison's headquarters in the city of Hue.

BELOW: A North Vietnamese photograph purporting to show an assault on a US Marine Corps outpost at Khe Sanh. The terrain looks too gentle for the area and attacks were normally launched in darkness to nullify as far as possible the air power and artillery fire that could be brought to bear on the enemy as they formed up for assaults

traumatic upheaval that seized the attention of almost the entire country.

Television crews filmed many other disturbing incidents during the fight for Saigon, including the battle for the National Radio Station. Two hundred yards (182 m) from the facility, 15 Viet Cong commandos, under the command of a veteran revolutionary named Dang Xuan Teo, had occupied a villa that was stuffed with war matériel. As the squad assigned to spearhead the attack on the radio station, Teo's group was to seize the building and hold it for two hours until a larger Viet Cong force relieved him and his comrades. In the early morning of Tet, the raiding party loaded an automobile full of explosives and crashed it into the front gates of the station, overwhelming a surprised platoon of South

Vietnamese guards who had been sleeping when the attack began. Within ten minutes, Teo's raiding party crushed all resistance.

However, the operation soon went awry. Before the sappers could consolidate their control over the station, government technicians had severed the connection to its transmitter 14 miles (23 km) away, foiling any attempt to broadcast Communist propaganda. Moreover, the Viet Cong relief force failed to arrive on schedule, leaving the 15 sappers trapped in a useless building. By daylight, half of the raiding party had perished during an ARVN counterattack, and the other half was running out of ammunition. Teo slipped out of the station to find his superiors and bring a relief force to save his comrades, only to see the last of them kill themselves by detonating the building

while they were still inside. When the smoke cleared, the South Vietnamese soldiers descended upon the ruins, looting the corpses of their enemies and anything of value within the building not destroyed in the blast.

The failure of the raid on the National Radio Station was typical of many Communist attacks during the Tet Offensive. Their forces were spread too thinly. Viet Cong attacks generally began with suppressive mortar fire to pin down enemy forces while sapper units spearheaded an assault on a targeted position. If the sappers succeeded, they were to hold on to it at all costs until reinforcements arrived to consolidate control. However, the wide dispersion and frequency of offensive activity during Tet often kept reinforcements preoccupied, especially during the allied counterattacks,

BELOW: Machine gunner Pfc Dominick J. Carango of Company H of the 2nd Bn, 5th Marine Regiment rests his chin on his M60. His assistant squats beside him, swathed in belts of ammunition. Carango has written his girlfriend's name on his helmet cover. Decorating helmet covers was officially frowned on, but was universal.

NEXT PAGE: In the modern suburbs south of the Perfume River, a U.S. Marine M60 machine gunner of Task Force X-Ray stands up to engage a North Vietnamese position in Hue while some of his comrades observe or return fire. Kneeling, an RTO sends a situation report over the radio.

ABOVE: An M48A3 Patton tank noses its way past an immobilized M151 light truck with little room to spare on the southern, treelined road leading into Hue. In the foreground, the tragic detritus of the street fighting can clearly be seen: a dead Vietnamese girl lies amongst the fallen leaves beside a shattered, looted hand cart, while closer, an upturned stretcher testifies to an attempt at rescuing the wounded which has been abandoned in the sudden flight to safety.

thus leaving the small sapper units alone in their positions to sacrifice themselves like kamikaze pilots. When the Communists did succeed in reinforcing the areas they had taken, they became very difficult to dislodge without massive firepower that frequently destroyed entire neighborhoods.

To keep the Americans at least temporarily off balance during the offensive, the Communists also attacked American positions in suburban areas northeast of Saigon. An entire division moved on an ARVN corps headquarters at Bien Hoa, pinning down allied troops with considerable firepower. At General

Weyand's III Corps headquarters in Long Binh, rockets crashed into the area, destroying an ammunition dump in a spectacular explosion. Meanwhile, other Communist forces established blocking positions on the major roads into Saigon in an effort to delay the arrival of allied reinforcements. Within MR 3, the Viet Cong also struck Tay Ninh, Phu Cuong, Duc Hoa, Gia Dinh, and Phuoc Le.

When Communist forces occupied specific towns and neighborhoods within Saigon and other cities, they created a political climate similar to that of China during the Cultural Revolution which, at the time, was in its most violent phase. Armed with bullhorns, political cadres followed Viet Cong and NVA combat units into captured areas, bombarding local residents with revolutionary rhetoric. These commissars also brought blacklists filled with the names of residents known to be military or

civilian officers connected to the South Vietnamese government, and initiated house-to-house searches to seize these fugitives and try them in "people's courts" for being "enemies of the revolution." Not surprisingly, these exercises often led to summary executions. The cadres also required residents to attend "group criticism" sessions in which citizens received verbal abuse for failing to support the National Liberation Front (NLF). The purpose of these actions was to demonstrate to the people of South Vietnam the power of the NLF and to "encourage" them to support it.

At the beginning of the offensive, allied forces inside the capital were scarce. In addition to the United States Marine Corps Saigon Guard Detachment at the embassy, the American presence within the city limits included the Army's 716th Military Police Battalion. The South Vietnamese presence

consisted of the 5th ARVN Ranger Group and two airborne battalions that were supposed to be up in MR 1 but were fortuitously held back by transportation problems. During the early stages of the Saigon offensive, MACV officers established a makeshift unit of American personnel within the city called the "MACV Tigers" to protect key facilities from the Communist onslaught.

Within a day of the outbreak of the Tet Offensive, allied units organized defensive actions while reinforcements arrived to retake the parts of the capital that had fallen to the

ABOVE: A U.S. Marine armed with an M79 40 mm grenade launcher – known as a "Blooper" because of its distinctive sound when fired – sprints up a road on the south side of Hue. He is followed by two men armed with M16 rifles and loaded with bandoliers of ammunition.

ABOVE LEFT: A U.S. Marine pulls a wounded comrade to the welcome shelter of an M48 tank during the fighting which has broken out in the southern approaches to the city of Hue.

RIGHT: Medics from the U.S. Marines treat a severely wounded North Vietnamese soldier – who seems to be unconscious from his injuries – carefully attending to his wounds. Normally, the Viet Cong and North Vietnamese made great efforts to recover their dead and wounded from the battle-field, so this photograph captures a fairly rare sight during the conflict. However, assisting the wounded to recovery was not a completely altruistic act, bearing in mind the fact that a prisoner who had been treated humanely and brought back to health might well be a source of useful – even if low-level – intelligence for his enemy.

FAR RIGHT: Men of the 2nd Battalion, 5th Marine Regiment, wait for further action as they line the perimeter wall of the Quon Hoc High School in Hue. The Quon Hoc High School to the right was built by the French in the 1950s in the modern southern suburbs of the city. By being seated, the men are under cover and can rest a little, taking the weight off their feet; those in the foreground seem to be in the process of some kind of discussion. The experience of fighting with-in the close confines of the city was a horrific one for most, and especially for those soldiers who were used to combat in the shelter of Vietnamese jun-gle terrain. Periods of tense waiting would be fol-lowed by a sudden burst of life-threatening activity, and this was to create a great reduction in morale in U.S. troops, especially dur-ing the year of the Tet Offensive.

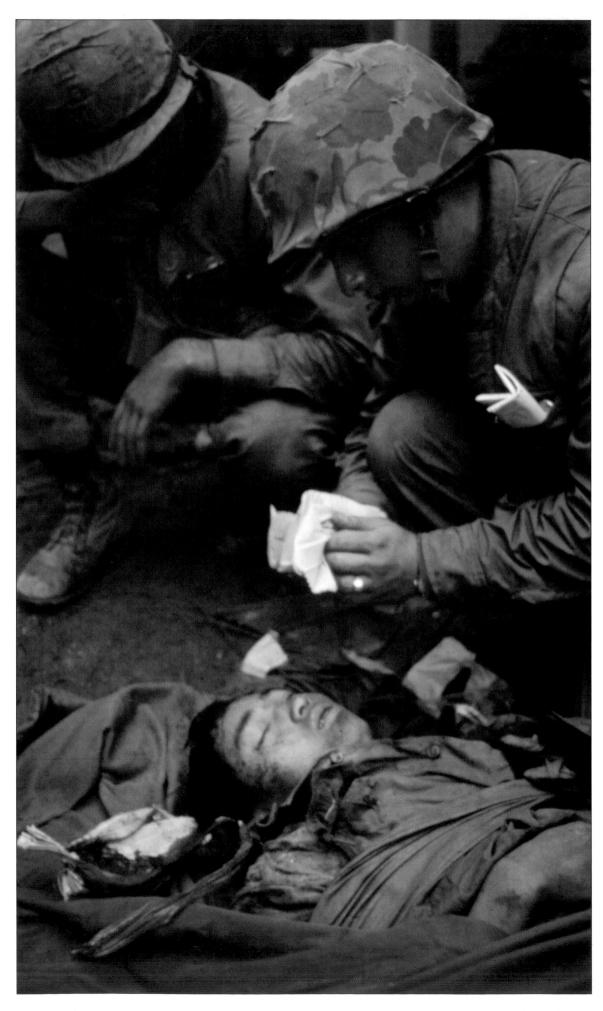

BELOW: U.S. Marines are shown in the process of recovering one of their dead in Hue. Both sides did their utmost to recover their dead from the battlefield. In this case a tarpaulin is being used as a temporary stretcher to carry the body back to base. The victim may have been shot by a Viet Cong sniper, a common way to die in the urban environment of Hue, which gave plenty of opportunities to snipers of both sides for concealment.

Viet Cong. Throughout Saigon, isolated American servicemen barricaded themselves in apartments and other buildings and fired at any stranger who seemed threatening. Sometimes, they even shot at the military policemen sent to retrieve them. By the evening of January 31, five American combat battalions reached the city. Four days later, another five ARVN battalions arrived and launched Operation Tran Hung Do, the South Vietnamese counteroffensive in Saigon.

The initial shock felt by many American and South Vietnamese servicemen at the start of the Tet Offensive soon gave way to feelings of vengeful bloodlust against their enemies. Not surprisingly, allied forces expressed this sentiment by unleashing destructive counterattacks against any Viet Cong units holed up in buildings and houses throughout Saigon and

other population centers. Near the presidential palace, television crews filmed American and ARVN troops leveling an apartment building occupied by 13 Communist sappers who had attempted to capture the executive residence. This method of clearing enemy forces out of residential neighborhoods and other sections of the city was not atypical.

After recoiling in horror at the damage inflicted by Viet Cong guerrillas, residents of the city now winced as jet fighters, helicopter gunships, and infantry squads armed with recoilless rifles destroyed many of their homes in order to root out enemy units. More preoccupied with preserving their own lives, American and ARVN troops did not seem to care about demolishing houses, apartments, or shops if such actions rid them of dangerous enemies. In many instances, the use of heavy

ABOVE: Men from Company A, 1st Battalion, 1st Marine Regiment watch from the window of a house in Hue during street fighting. They are armed with the 0.22 in. (5.56mm) M16, a rifle that initially had a bad reputation for malfunctions that prompted many Marines to favor the older, heavier 0.3 in. (7.62mm) M14 rifle.

LEFT: The hazards of street fighting are amply demonstrated in this photograph of a U.S. Marine 3.5 in. (89mm) Rocket Launcher crew as they make their way across an exposed patch of garden in Hue. One of their comrades can be seen in the background by the entrance to the garden providing cover on the street, while two men who are under cover in the garden watch their slow progress. In front of them lies the body of one of their comrades.

COMMUNIST ATROCITIES IN HUE
Slaughter at Hue

The battle for the ancient city of Hue was one of the most vicious of the Vietnam War, not least for what went on in the small Gia Hoi district of the ancient Citadel. Gia Hoi was the one part of Hue that the Communists managed to totally secure. Once they had it in their grasp, they started a dress rehearsal for revolutionary government. It would prove to be government down the barrel of a gun, and a reign of terror began on the streets of Hue.

The NVA political leaders in Hue had lists of those they considered political criminals – in short, those who had any sort of liaison with the U.S. All lists had been provided courtesy of informers, those prepared to sacrifice neighbors to align themselves with the Communists. NVA officers marched through the streets of Gia Hoi, reading out the names on the lists through loudspeakers. Those called were told to report to a local school. If they did as they were told, on arrival their hands were tied behind their backs and a single shot fired into the back of their skull. If they went into hiding, they were hunted relentlessly and when found, met the same fate. Only when Gia Hoi looked as if it would return to U.S./ARVN hands did the NVA change their method; they buried whole groups of people alive to speed up the process.

Some 3,000 Vietnamese civilians were massacred in Gia Hoi, although the impact of the Tet offensive overshadowed the slaughter in the media. It did affect U.S. policy, however. Withdrawal of U.S. troops was instigated after Tet, but Nixon slowed the pace through fear that quick withdrawal would lead to NVA massacres in all South Vietnam's regions. This action was warranted, and it was an ethical decision easily overlooked in the failed politics of the Vietnam War.

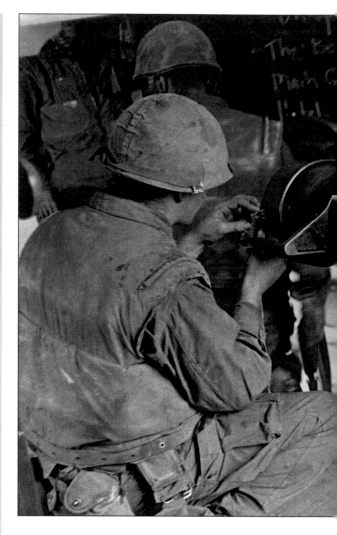

weapons burned entire rows of houses and other buildings to the ground. As the nerve center of the Viet Cong offensive within Saigon, the Cholon district was hit particularly hard. Predictably, these actions rendered thousands of civilians homeless refugees.

While allied troops devastated much of Saigon in their battles with Viet Cong guerrillas, South Vietnamese police officers launched swift reprisals against suspecting insurgents. Perhaps the most notorious incident caught on film occurred the morning after the outbreak of the offensive and involved General Nguyen Ngoc Loan, chief of the South Vietnamese national police. A surly authoritarian known for his suppression of political dissidents in earlier years, Loan was in an angry mood. Viet Cong assassins had slaughtered many of his men, including one officer shot with his family in their home.

While traversing Saigon in an effort to help coordinate defensive actions by government forces, General Loan encountered a

LEFT: The crew of a 4.1 in. (106mm) recoilless rifle prepare their weapon for use on temporary platform. The spotting rifle used for aiming rounds is clearly visible on top of the weapon's barrel. Using recoilless rifles indoors is not usually recommended due to their large back blast, but the stress of the situation shows on the nearest crewman's face.
BELOW: High on the roof of a building in the southern part of Hue, a U.S. Marine sniper takes aim through the x 3 - x 9 variable Redfield scope on his 0.3 in. (7.62mm) M40 bolt action rifle. He has rested the rifle on a sandbag for extra stability and, from this point up high, can command any movement on the boulevard below him. His comrades survey the streets from other angles, and more sand-bags are at the ready to be used for firing at various points from their rooftop station.

BELOW: Three children play in the bullet-scarred wall which runs the perimeter of Hue University. Miraculously, they appear to be physically unharmed by the fighting, but they almost certainly would carry emotional scars. The University was captured by the 804th Battalion of the 4th Regiment of the North Vietnamese Army, and was liberated by men of the 1st Battalion 1st Marine Regiment after some fierce fighting.

patrol of soldiers with a captured guerrilla in their custody. An American press photographer and a Vietnamese film cameraman employed by the National Broadcasting Company (NBC) were present recording the scene. Oblivious to these observers, Loan motioned the soldiers away from their prisoner, drew his revolver, and fired it into the captive's head. As the insurgent collapsed to the pavement, blood oozed from his head and covered much of the ground beneath him. Later that day, photographs of the execution appeared in newspapers throughout the world, while NBC broadcast its

exclusive film of the incident to the nation on the evening news.

As allied forces gradually wore down the pockets of Viet Cong resistance in Saigon and reassumed control over much of the city, the Thieu regime imposed a curfew within the capital. Meanwhile, American and South Vietnamese forces cordoned off sections still under Viet Cong control and proceeded to root out remaining enemy guerrillas. On February 2, while the allied counteroffensive was just getting started, LBJ publicly proclaimed the Tet Offensive a failure for the Communists. In

a similar spirit of optimism, allied troops and police squads described the street fight in Saigon as a "mopping-up" operation. Six days later, combat in the capital wound down when the United States 199th Light Brigade trapped and decimated the last of the Viet Cong attackers at the Phu Tho racetrack, where the Communists had established a makeshift field hospital. By February 10, the Viet Cong attack on Saigon was over and the Allies had retaken almost all of the areas that had fallen into enemy hands, except for the ancient capital of Hue.

The Communists launched their assault on Hue at roughly the same time as their attacks on Saigon and other population centers, in the early morning of January 31. The offensive began with rockets slamming into the Imperial Citadel on the north bank of the Perfume River. Then the 800th and 802nd Battalions of the 6th NVA Regiment swept into the Citadel

from the southwest and pushed aside scattered resistance guarding the ramparts surrounding the structure. These battalions next proceeded to the headquarters of the 1st ARVN Division, commanded by Brigadier-General Ngo Quang Truong, located on the northern tip of the Citadel. On the opposite end of the fortress, the 12th Sapper Battalion attacked the Imperial Palace of Peace.

Only the ARVN division's elite Hac Bo (Black Panther) Recondo Company stood in the way of the NVA battalions. The Black Panthers took a stand at the Tay Loc airport and repulsed the 800th Battalion, forcing the Communists to turn south and move into the residential section of the Citadel. The 802nd went further and actually penetrated the perimeter of the divisional headquarters before being turned back by the Black Panthers. Although the South Vietnamese company could not prevent the NVA from seizing most

ABOVE: Having moved up under cover, U.S. Marines of the 1st Battalion, 5th Marine Regiment decide on risky action. Taking their lives in their hands, they sprint past the rubble and debris of earlier fighting across a bridge. Although this bridge stretches only a short distance over a canal within the Citadel, it makes the men easy targets. To add to the discomfort of the fighting within the city, it would often rain, so men were not only loaded up with Flak jackets, weapons, and ammunition to protect them against their enemies, but also waterproof jackets and trousers to protect them against the elements.

of the city, they kept their headquarters out of Communist hands.

On the other side of the Perfume River, the 804th and K4B Battalions of the 4th NVA Regiment descended upon the New City. From the east, the 804th Battalion attacked the Hue headquarters of MACV, which was defended by only 200 hastily assembled Americans. After enduring rocket, mortar, and machine gun fire, the defenders repelled the Communist ground assault. Meanwhile, K4B Battalion attempted to block allied reinforcements arriving from the south on Route 1. Within hours, the Communists secured control over most of the Citadel, including the Imperial Palace, along with much of the south bank and the Gia Hoi section of Hue in the northeast. During their rampage through these areas, they struck over 200 targets, including police stations, the Thua Thien provincial headquarters, and houses owned by American and South Vietnamese officers.

Secure in Hue, the Communists initiated a reign of terror over the unfortunate residents in their captivity. Prior to the attack, NLF infiltrators in the city had compiled a list of "tyrants" and "reactionaries," which were all those who

ABOVE: His Flak jacket and equipment pink from dirt and brick dust, a U.S. Marine with his M16 rifle at the ready scans the roof tops in Hue. Visible by his respirator is a privately purchased revolver.

LEFT: A bizarre scene in Hue as an officer with his RTO, who carries an AN/PRC25 radio, watch from a window. In the foreground, a centerfold peels away from the wall; probably a piece of improvised interior decoration by a Marine.

RIGHT: U.S. Marine Pfc Danny Roth of Galena, Illinois, escapes from the violent reality of the street fighting in Hue into the fantasy violence of the Wild West with a thriller, *Call Me Hazard*. In his helmet band he has a bottle of weapon lubricant.

RIGHT: Two U.S. Marine RTOs from the 2nd Battalion, 5th Marine Regiment moving up behind their battalion check a wounded and unarmed Vietnamese near Quon Hoc High School. The Vietnamese man may have been a member of K48 battalion of the North Vietnamese Army, 4th Regiment that seized the area on January 31.

OPPOSITE: Keeping low in a drainage ditch, soldiers from the U.S. Army move cautiously towards the western edges of Hue. While the U.S. Marines and South Vietnamese Army Airborne battalions fought it out inside the Citadel with the North Vietnamese, the 1st Air Cavalry and 101st Airborne cut the supply and reinforcement route to the Citadel via the Western Gate on February 21.

NEXT PAGE: U.S. Marines from Company A, 1st Engineers fire at snipers from the North Vietnamese Army across the Perfume River from the cover of an ornate building in Hue. They are relatively safe from where they shoot, but they were not used to front line combat. However, their fighting was a necessity, as the Tet Offensive and other battles in Hue saw support troops – like Engineers – pitched into front line combat, since the persistence and stealth of the Viet Cong and North Vietnamese meant they were able to penetrate areas normally considered to be secure.

were known to be agents or supporters of the Saigon government. When NVA and Viet Cong forces marched into the city, political cadres followed, arresting people whose names appeared on this list, along with all foreigners trapped within the area of Communist control. For the most part, the arrests occurred without incident because the Communists persuaded their victims to surrender with assurances of humane treatment consisting of a quick "re-education" session that would turn the detainees into good revolutionaries. But when the detainees reported for rehabilitation, they were never seen alive again. On February 5, a Radio Hanoi announcer boasted about the

severe punishment that Communist officials were inflicting upon the "hooligan lackeys" and "cruel agents" within Hue.

Inside his headquarters on the edge of the Citadel, General Truong ordered all available units from his 1st Division to fall back on Hue and assist the Black Panthers. From a marine base at Phu Bai, 8 miles (13 km) southeast of the city, Brigadier-General Foster Lahue sent a small American relief force consisting of A Company, 1st Battalion, 1st Marine Regiment and four tanks to aid in the defense of the MACV headquarters. At the time, Phu Bai itself was under attack and protected by Task Force X-Ray, with only three understrength

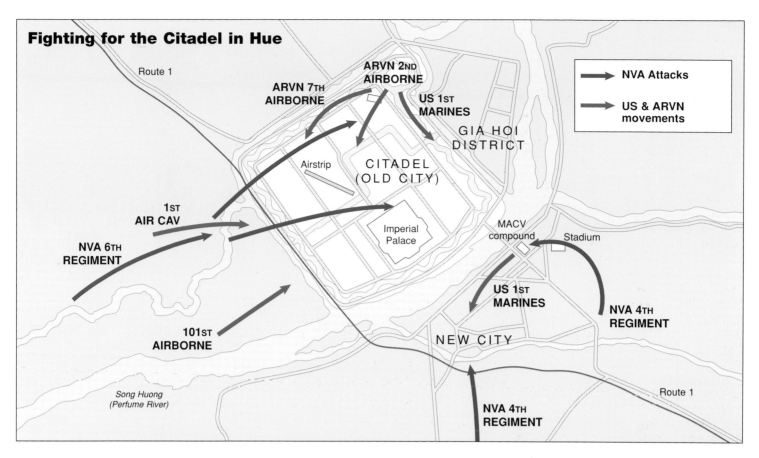

Fighting for the Citadel in Hue

Route 1

ARVN 2ND
AIRBORNE

ARVN 7TH
AIRBORNE

US 1ST
MARINES

GIA HOI
DISTRICT

Airstrip

CITADEL
(OLD CITY)

1ST
AIR CAV

Imperial
Palace

MACV
compound

Stadium

NVA 6TH
REGIMENT

US 1ST
MARINES

NVA 4TH
REGIMENT

101ST
AIRBORNE

NEW CITY

Song Huong
(Perfume River)

Route 1

NVA 4TH
REGIMENT

→ NVA Attacks

→ US & ARVN
movements

LEFT: Stretcher bearers race out to fetch a wounded man back to the first aid post for medical attention in Hue. They are crouching as low as possible while running for cover, which shows that fighting is still very much in progress in this area. Stretcher bearers and corpsmen faced as much, if not more, danger than the ordinary "Grunts" in the field.

BELOW: A U.S. Marine M60 machine gun crew stands guard on the morning of February 16 amidst the wreckage of buildings and shattered trees destroyed in the fighting in Hue. In the foreground, the blood-streaked bodies of two North Vietnamese soldiers who were responsible for defending the corrugated iron shacks lie partially covered, their blood running down the wall.

battalions, or 4,000 men collectively. Moreover, General Lahue did not yet realize the magnitude of the attack on Hue.

Halfway to Hue, A Company found itself pinned down by an enemy ambush while advancing along Route 1. This situation led Lahue to send the rest of the 1st Battalion up the highway, rescue the company, and proceed to the MACV building on the south bank of the Perfume River. Commanded by Lieutenant-Colonel Marcus Gravel, the relief column also included G Company, 2nd Battalion, 5th Regiment; a tank platoon, and an engineer contingent. Gravel's forces pushed through the NVA units blocking Route 1, retrieved A Company, and reached MACV headquarters, losing ten men killed and 30 wounded. Meanwhile, enough reinforcements from the

1st ARVN Division reached Truong's headquarters to secure it, at least temporarily.

From MACV HQ, Colonel Gravel attempted to lead his forces across the Perfume River to reach General Truong's headquarters, then mobilize an allied counterattack. At the Nguyen Hoang bridge, Gravel kept his armored units back because of their vulnerability to antitank weaponry in urban combat. The remainder of his relief column crossed the bridge but were soon hurled back by NVA forces enjoying overwhelming numerical superiority. By this time, the Communists were well-entrenched in the Citadel and receiving reinforcements from the west, eventually bringing their strength up to ten battalions.

Ultimately, the allied counterattack on Hue would involve six U.S. Army battalions, three

ABOVE: A Marines Corps sniper takes aim through the telescopic sight of his M40 rifle during fighting in Hue. The Redfield sight could be adjusted from x 3 magnification which allowed the sniper to scan the area and then be brought into x 9 focus when he sighted a target.
NEXT PAGE: In the wrecked side streets of Hue, U.S. Marines dressed in flak jackets and festooned with ammunition pouches and respirators hunch behind an M48A3 tank as it advances cautiously. While tanks were powerful mobile firepower, they also attracted enemy fire, including mortars and B40 rocket-propelled grenades.

ABOVE: The Nguyen Hoang Bridge in the southeast corner of the Citadel in Hue straddles the Perfume River. It was destroyed by the North Vietnamese on February 7. The Military Assistance Command Vietnam (MACV) compound is in the lower part of the photograph, while the Imperial Palace of Peace, set in its grounds, is in the top.

RIGHT: A U.S. Marine Corps Cessna 0-1 Bird Dog, an aircraft known to the North Vietnamese and Viet Cong as "The Little Old Lady," flies low along the northern bank of the Perfume River in Hue. The pilot and observer in this light aircraft are very vulnerable to small arms fire, but would be able to form a picture of the progress of the fighting as well as being able to use smoke rockets to mark targets for ground attack aircraft. The devastation wrought upon the city by the fighting can be clearly seen from this vantage point.

undermanned Marine Corps battalions, and 11 ARVN battalions. In their campaign to retake the Citadel, these forces had to dislodge adversaries that were in an extremely favorable defensive position. Constructed in 1802 during the reign of the Emperor Gia Long, the Citadel seemed to be an impenetrable fortress. Surrounded by a moat, it possessed a stone outer wall that was 30 feet (9.1 m) tall and 20 feet (6 m) thick, as well as a brick inner wall. Within these barriers, the NVA kept a central command post in the well-fortified Imperial Palace. Typical of an urban environment, it provided many favorable positions for snipers and other harassing elements to occupy.

In their preparation for a counterattack on Hue, the Allies divided the city into two tactical zones. The Americans were to focus their

ABOVE: Inside the battered walls of the citadel in Hue, a U.S. Marine radio operator presses the handset to his ear and struggles to hear orders over the radio. The fight for Hue, the ancient capital of Vietnam, was a long, drawn out battle with heavy casualties and massive damage to many ancient buildings.

Fighting for the Citadel

Apart from terrorist attacks in Saigon and other Vietnamese cities, the first years of the Vietnam War were overwhelmingly conducted away from the urban centers. This was all part of the North's plan. During 1967, Giap's strategy was to draw U.S. forces away from the main population centers in preparation for the Tet offensive of 1968. With the U.S. forces in the countryside, it was hoped that the urban populations would unite with city-based Viet Cong in an uprising against the southern government.

It nearly worked. When Tet was launched in January 1968, the NVA forces punched straight through to many key cities, none more important than Hue. An ancient and beautiful city,, Hue was once the imperial capital of Vietnam. The city is divided into two halves, split by the evocatively named Perfume River. To the south is the modern New City, while to the north is the ancient, densely populated Citadel.

The attack on Hue burst into violent life on January 31, 1968. Following a heavy smashing of the city by artillery, 8,000 NVA troops swarmed into its streets. Within a few hours, the Citadel and most of New City had fallen, such was the level of surprise and vigor in attack. At first, U.S. commanders could not believe the reports of disaster from Hue. U.S. Marines at Phu Bai sent less than two companies of troops to the city to investigate to be met by a storm of fire by over a division of NVA. When reality finally dawned, three Marine battalions and 11 ARVN battalions were committed. Their objective: reclaim Hue, whatever it takes.

For troops who had been immersed in jungle warfare for years, Hue was a disorientating experience. The violence was claustrophobic, dynamic. The NVA had dug in for a fight, and they contested every stairwell, room, and street corner. Fire could come from any angle, and casualties on both sides started to stack up. In the New City – the U.S. Marines' objective – only four blocks of advance were made in six days. Eventually the New City fell into U.S. hands, but to the north, the Citadel was proving obstinate. Because of the Citadel's ancient architectural heritage, the U.S. had initially resisted in the use of its heavy firepower. It became apparent that this policy could not be maintained. Thus U.S. ground-attack aircraft and artillery started to demolish the citadel street by street, and the Marines crossed the river into action.

It took until February 24 to re-capture the Citadel. Eight thousand soldiers were dead, 75 percent of the population was homeless, and thousands of civilians killed, caught between NVA ruthlessness and U.S. firepower.

LEFT: Dust is kicked up into the line of sight by the blast from the muzzle as a U.S. Marine fires his M16. The photograph was taken during the fighting on the east side of the Citadel at Hue. The M16 could be fired on full automatic which, though potentially inaccurate, was useful if a heavy volume of fire was required to suppress the enemy during an assault. The devastation of the city is visible in this photograph. At the beginning of the fighting in Hue, the U.S. resisted using heavy force because of the city's rich architectural heritage, but soon they realized that they could not sustain this policy, and so began their counterattack against the North Vietnamese artillery with a fierce and unrelenting determination. After the fighting was over, three-quarters of the population was homeless.

RIGHT: Festooned with bandoliers of ammunition, a U.S. Marine holds his M16 and surveys the interior of the citadel in Hue. The crossed steel girders behind him make an improvised Calvary, effective as a reference point, as well as an inspiration to the Marines who are dug in at its base. For soldiers who had spent years locked in combat in jungle terrain, fighting in a built-up city proved to be an immensely claustrophobic experience. The New City fell to the Americans, but the heavily fortified Citadel was not captured until three weeks after 8,000 NVA troops had invaded the city.

LEFT: A U.S. Marine, temporarily seen without rifle or helmet for protection, drags the body of a dead comrade down from the ruins of the Citadel gatehouse, visible in the background, where he died. Although technically an American victory, the recapture of Hue – and the thick-walled Citadel in particular – cost the lives of many Marines and ARVN troops. American film and television crews naturally focused on the U.S. casualties, and ignored the large number of NVA and Viet Cong killed, which gave the impression of a defeat.

RIGHT: A U.S. Navy A-4 Skyhawk ground attack fighter flies overhead as a headquarters group of the 1st Battalion 5th Marine Regiment huddles with a radio in the cover of the wall of Citadel in Hue, waiting for the napalm it has just dropped to do its task. Some of the men have ponchos and waterproofs strapped to their light packs, ready to be donned in the event of a tropical downpour. Although initially the weight of American firepower was not brought to bear on the NVA and Viet Cong due to the historical importance of Hue, it soon proved necessary to use whatever means the American and South Vietnamese troops had at their disposal.

BELOW: Napalm bursts into flame above the citadel in Hue as U.S. fighter ground attack aircraft pound the North Vietnamese positions. In the foreground, the bridge across the moat can be clearly seen. This bridge leads to Tran Hung Dao Street on the south side of the citadel. The battered, heavily fought-over gate house looms above the wall.

OPPOSITE PAGE: As one Viet Cong soldier fires his AK47 assault rifle, his comrade pulls the arming cord in the handle of a stick grenade by holding it in his teeth. If this was a real moment in a street battle, the photographer would have to be either very brave, or very foolish, since in order to take the picture, he appears to be standing out in the open, in the middle of a fire fight. It is more likely that this was a deliberately staged shot used for propaganda purposes.

LEFT: A night time shore bombardment by the 6-inch guns of guided missile light cruiser USS *Oklahoma City* gives fire support to American troops on the Vietnamese mainland. These "floating firebases" were able to operate virtually unhindered by the prospect of a night time Viet Cong attack, unlike their counterparts on land.

BELOW: A North Vietnamese crew open fire against U.S. aircraft with a 0.3 in. (7.62 mm) Goryunov M1943 machine gun. While one weapon might be effective, if hit by massed small arms fire, a low flying combat aircraft could be damaged and even shot down, so every armed man and woman in the North Vietnamese Army was encouraged to shoot at enemy aircraft whenever they appeared.

actions on the New City, while the South Vietnamese were to concentrate on the Citadel, although the Americans would join the South Vietnamese on the north bank of the Perfume River once the New City was secured. Six miles (9.6 km) west of the city, the 3rd Brigade, 1st Air Cavalry (Airmobile) Division descended upon a landing zone on February 2 in an effort to sever supply and reinforcement links between Laos and Hue. Within three days, the brigade's 2nd Battalion reached a hill 4 miles (6.4 km) west of the city and shelled Communist positions in a nearby valley.

Further west, the Airmobile's 5th Battalion, 7th Regiment, 3rd Brigade attempted to reach the 2nd Battalion and help it maintain control over the hill. However, NVA forces quickly maneuvered between the two American units and prevented the 5th Battalion from reaching the hill. Hopelessly outnumbered on their own, the members of the

2nd Battalion had to abandon their position and fight their way north to join their sister battalion in an attack on the village of Thong Bon Tri. With this task accomplished, the two battalions drove NVA units out of the village.

Two battalions from the 101st Airborne Divisions later arrived and helped the cavalry-men clear out Communist supply networks and establish blocking positions to prevent enemy reinforcements from entering the city. Altogether, the American presence west of Hue kept three NVA regiments out of the city. The paratroopers from the 101st and local ARVN forces then moved south to complete the encir-clement. Meanwhile, the cavalrymen from the Airmobile Division continued the pressure north and west of the city after being rein-forced to four battalions.

What then ensued was almost a month of vicious, house-to-house fighting. As usual, the Allies had access to massive air, naval, and

ABOVE: An F-4 Phantom from a U.S. carrier drops its load of "iron" bombs high over Vietnam. Though the bombs were unguided, each aircraft could carry up to 16,000 lb. (7257 kg) of ordance, which would severely disrupt any Viet Cong attack or knock out their positions. Pilots on board the U.S. carriers returned to familiar sur-roundings after each mis-sion, and suffered few of the hardships of their Army and Marine colleagues. However, if shot down, they faced capture and imprisonment by the North Vietnamese.

African Americans in Vietnam

The Vietnam War integrated African American and white troops like no other conflict before it. In the field in Vietnam, the boundaries dissolved because your life depended on trusting the man next to you, whatever color he was. African Americans and whites had to hack through the same jungle, fight the same firefights, share the same losses, and live the same fear. So mixed race units became a fact of life, and broke down much of the segregation that existed back in the States.

Yet there were still injustices built into the system, and Vietnam didn't offer a perfect model of racial harmony in action. Take the draft, for instance. During the 1960s, African Americans made up about 11 percent of the U.S. population. The draft figures seemed to reflect this. In Vietnam, about 12

percent of the Army was African American and about ten percent of the Air Force (the Navy figure was the exception, which ran at only five per cent). But out in the field where the combat was happening, a different composition prevailed. About 25 percent of front line combat troops in Vietnam were African American, and in units such as airborne troops, which were overtly involved in fighting duties, the figure could rise up to 60 percent. These numbers explain why as many as 23 percent of U.S. war dead between 1965 and 1967 were in fact African Americans.

The draft did not consciously discriminate against the African American population, but the injustices of the U.S. racial situation extended through to the Vietnam combat zones. African Americans in the U.S. were disadvantaged over whites when it came to access to education, which meant they were more likely to be sent to the front line as combatants rather than posted behind the lines as staff: hence the strong African American presence in Vietnam's firefights.

Yet while the Vietnam War undoubtedly brought African Americans and whites together during combat in the field, there often existed a kind of on-and-off segregation. African American veterans noted how they would fight side-by-side with a white man in the field, fighting for each other's lives, but once in the rear the two races would go their separate ways. Sometimes this was simply because of cultural factors, such as differences in musical taste or food, but often it was through racism and mistrust. Racist taunts, graffiti, and actual violence faced African Americans who wandered into white-dominated areas. In Saigon, bars and brothels, even entire districts became in effect separate African American or white zones, and the response toward those who were found to be crossing the invisible lines could be hostile, to say the least.

For this very reason, the Viet Cong often targeted the African American troops with their propaganda. They presented the war as a white man's affair in which the African Americans were doing a disproportionate amount of dying. Many back in the States agreed. Radical groups on both sides of the racial divide saw that heavy question marks hung over the death toll statistics.

Nevertheless, in the field African Americans fought side-by-side with their white counterparts, pushing the U.S. armed forces into a state of genuine race integration.

RIGHT: A U.S. Navy rating restocks the magazine of a gun turret on one of the vessels floating in the Gulf of Tonkin. Compared to those serving on land, his was a relatively easy life. Though required to work hard manhandling heavy shells, his chances of seeing out his tour of duty were much higher than those of an infantryman.

BELOW RIGHT: An exhausted U.S. Marine slumped against an ambulance in a vehicle park in Hue, trying to sleep off some of his tiredness. His helmet cover expresses many of the sentiments of resignation which were increasingly being adopted by men in Vietnam for their 365-day tour, especially in 1968. He states that he was "Born By Accident" and wishes "Gooks (North Vietnamese and Viet Cong) Go Home." Like the Marine pictured here, about 25 percent of front line troops in the U.S. forces were African American.

LEFT: A young African American M60 machine gunner purposefully makes his way up through a fire base which has been constructed by U.S. forces on high ground. There was a high African American presence in the fire fights of the Vietnam war, as African American soldiers were often directed to front-line fighting. The fire base shown here has been dug and was also constructed from sandbags and ammunition boxes which are weighted down with packed earth. Helicopters allowed a fire base to be set up speedily, flying in defense stores to remote locations which were often found to be inaccessible by road.

RIGHT: In regal splendor, a U.S. Marine sits triumphantly on the throne in the Imperial Palace of Peace which, though it was amongst the last of the areas to be liberated in the Citadel in Hue, managed to survive the conflict remarkably undamaged. The center of the city had been hit by artillery fire and bombs as well as napalm, as the Marines and South Vietnamese forces fought to liberate it.

BELOW: U.S. Marines storm the gate house of the citadel in Hue. With thick, brick walls angled to give good fields of fire, and surrounded by a deep moat, the citadel incorporated the defensive architecture of earlier centuries. This architecture, although beautiful, was just as effective in defense against artillery fire and bombs in 1968 as it had been during earlier centuries against the muskets and cannon.

artillery support for their ground forces storming the New City and the Citadel. However, senior allied officers were reluctant to employ such instruments of destruction because doing so would obliterate much of the historical architecture within Hue. Not surprisingly, the marines who had to fight their way into the Citadel resented this policy of attaching more value to a "gook" temple than to their lives. On February 5, when the intensity of Communist resistance in the Citadel indicated that ground troops could not take the area by themselves without heavy casualties, the allied high command relented, thus condemning Hue to suffer the same devastation as other South Vietnamese communities during the post-Tet counteroffensive.

The task of retaking the New City had fallen to the 1st Battalion, 1st Marine Regiment under Colonel Stanley Hughes, and the 2nd Battalion, 5th Marine Regiment under Lieutenant-Colonel Earnest C. Cheatham. The two units spent six days battling their way from the MACV compound to the provincial hospital four blocks to the southwest, suffering 150 casualties in the process. Most of the marines in this operation were young recruits possessing little, if any, experience of close-quarter urban combat. Learning quickly as they went along, they operated in 10- or 11-man squads, supported by mortars, machine guns, and recoilless rifles. Four men would guard the exits of a target building, while two others charged forward and tossed grenades into the structure. The rest of the squad covered the grenade-throwers with rifle fire.

By February 6, the marine battalions had recaptured the city's prison, hospital, and provincial headquarters. Four days later, the Americans declared the south bank secure. However, isolated Communist snipers continued to operate in the area and NVA artillerists were able to shell the New City from the other side of the river. Like many other population centers in South Vietnam, the area teemed with displaced refugees roaming the streets and sleeping in makeshift relief shelters.

Meanwhile, soldiers from the 1st ARVN Division defended their headquarters on the

northern tip of the Citadel and gradually pushed their enemies back from the northern half of the area. The forces charged with carrying out this counteroffensive included the 2nd, 7th, and 9th Airborne Battalions, along with the 3rd Infantry Regiment and units of South Vietnamese marines. With considerable effort, they retook the airport and most areas north of the Imperial Palace, except for a pocket of resistance on the western tip of the Citadel. However, Communist resistance stiffened in

ABOVE: Against the background of a wall pitted with bomb or shell fragments, U.S. Marines share a C Ration cigarette. Unaware of the potential harm of smoking, the U.S. Government contractors included a packet of five cigarettes in the accessory pack of each ration. Smoking calmed the front line soldiers' nerves and appeased their hunger.

BELOW: Corporal Lester A. Tully receives the Silver Star for bravery during the Vietnam War. The officer presenting the Silver Star to Corporal Tully is Lieutenant Colonel Cheatham of the 2nd Battalion, 5th Marine Regiment. Tully's feat of bravery had recently taken place when he had charged into combat across the Nguyen Hoang Bridge and had single handedly killed the five-man crew of a North Vietnamese Army machine gun who were responsible for just killing or wounding ten Marines who were in the process of attempting to cross the bridge.

the southern half of the fortress, repulsing all ARVN attacks on NVA positions. To complete the recapture of Hue, American forces would have to join the offensive on the Citadel.

On the night of February 11, the 1st Battalion, 5th Marine Regiment crossed the Perfume River under heavy fire and entered the Citadel. By this time, the Allies had gained permission from President Thieu to employ all artillery and aircraft at their disposal on any target within the fortress except the Imperial Palace. So, while ARVN and American ground forces continued the close-quarter fighting within the city, American F-4 Phantoms and South Vietnamese A-1 Skyraiders incinerated enemy positions with 250 lb. (113 kg) "snake-eye" bombs and 500 lb (227 kg) napalm canisters. Altogether, the Allies dropped some 290,000 lb. (131,370 kg) of explosives on Hue. In addition, allied artillery units shot over 18,000 rounds into the city, while American

warships fired 5,191 rounds from the Gulf of Tonkin during the course of the counterattack.

Despite this punishing bombardment, the NVA remained stubborn in their resistance to allied ground forces. The marines of the 1st Battalion sustained heavy losses during their slow advance on the palace, suffering one casualty for every yard captured. The Communists challenged their enemies effectively with mortars, heavy machine guns, anti-tank rockets, and captured armored vehicles. Without reinforcements available to relieve them in their protracted struggle for the Citadel, the marines became weary and demoralized. When not preoccupied with combat, they gazed sadly at images of a scenic and ancient city that was becoming an open grave of ruined buildings and rotting corpses.

The American assault took a turn for the better in mid-February, when two platoons and a tank from the 1st Battalion captured a tall

RIGHT: After pulling back from the heat of the city fighting in the claustrophobic conditions of Hue, U.S. Marines slump against a building on the southern outskirts of the city. While the men might appear to be dulled and deadened by fatigue, and are seen here lying on the ground, they are probably far from a rested state of mind. Showing that they anticipate having to resume action in a very short while, the Marines are still wearing their Flak jackets, and their weapons are readily to hand; one has not even bothered to remove his helmet. For many of these men, it was impossible to relax during lulls in battle, or after they had withdrawn from the immediate fighting, since the city was awash with troops – 8,000 of the NVA alone – and the sound of nearby fighting could always be heard in every area, loud and clear. The ornate buildings which many troops took shelter under in Hue – such as those pictured here in the background – were too fragile to offer any real protection against attack, and many of them were destroyed during the fight for the city, rendering thousands of Vietnamese civilians homeless.

LEFT: A South Vietnamese soldier holds his weapon down as he surveys the bodies of two South Vietnamese Marines lying in the heat of the sun at the edge of a highway, their packs strewn about near to them. These Marines have been dismembered by the blast from mortar fire which caught them as they were traveling down Highway One, one of the main roads running near Camp Evans, a base situated about 18 miles (29 km) from Hue. The dark scars which were left on the terrain by the explosion of these mortar bombs show that one burst on the road between the two Marines. The land around Highway One was flat and barren, making any troops – or indeed civilians – traveling along it an easy target for harsh attacks by enemy gunfire or shelling.

BELOW LEFT: Headed by an M60 machine gunner, who is festooned with ammunition bandoliers, a helmeted patrol of the U.S. 9th Division – who were given the nickname the "Old Reliables" – cautiously makes its way along the embankment of a rice paddy field close to the edge of the water. The rice paddy field, which is situated in the Tan An Delta, could be a source of hidden danger for these men. Concealed mines and booby traps like punji stake pits which had been buried by the enemy on obvious routes like this embankment were to cause many horrific casualties to both troops and civilians alike during the Vietnam War, and wary of this, the patrol are carefully scanning the land around them as they move forward.

tower on the east wall of the Citadel. This enabled the marines to target nearby artillery batteries on enemy positions with far greater precision. The Allies had also learned from intercepted radio transmissions that the commander of NVA forces in Hue had been killed and that his successor had unsuccessfully requested permission to withdraw from the city. This communication indicated that Communist morale in the Citadel was faltering, encouraging allied forces to tighten their encirclement around the fortress.

West of the city, the Airmobile Division intensified its pressure on the Communist logistical network, meeting fierce resistance from three NVA units: the 29th Regiment, Division 325C; the 24th Regiment, 304th Division; and the 99th Regiment, Division 324B. On February 21, the cavalrymen over-

came these forces and closed the NVA's last line of supply and communication from Laos to Hue. Within the Citadel, American marines and ARVN paratroopers penetrated the Imperial Palace that same day.

Three days later, the 2nd Battalion, 3rd Regiment, 1st ARVN Division pushed enemy units off the south wall and captured the Midway Gate of the palace. Members of the battalion then cut down the NLF flag and hoisted the South Vietnamese flag atop the gate. The rest of the division poured into the palace the following morning, February 25, only to discover that the Communists had slipped out of the city during the previous night. After 26 days of grueling combat, Hue was in allied hands once again.

Like many other battles in the Vietnam War, the fight for Hue had produced lopsided

ABOVE: A GI hitches a ride on "Wild One 4," the nickname which was given to an M48 tank belonging to the 1st Platoon, 919th Armored Engineer Company of the 11th Armored Cavalry. The tank shown here had just managed to detonate a mine which was buried in the dirt road, but despite this, shows little indication of any damage to its structure. However, perhaps most telling about the extent to which this tank's crew feel safe is that fact that most of them have taken up position perched outside the tank, and are ready to jump free if – or when – they detonate something bigger.

RIGHT: Four of the seven prisoners who were captured in a Viet Cong tunnel complex await their fate. Their faces show varying degrees of resignation and fear, while their captors stand in discussion behind them. These prisoners were taken by U.S. men of the 2nd Battalion, 503rd Airborne Infantry, 173rd Airborne Brigade while they were attempting to hide out in the Thanh Dien Forest. This Forest was situated in the Iron Triangle, an area 20 miles (32 km) northwest of Saigon in the III Corps area. The Iron Triangle was an immense 125 miles (200 km) of heavy, dense forests that provided excellent cover for North Vietnamese and Viet Cong forces, as it was sparsely populated and therefore served as a base for attacks on Saigon. Numbers of Viet Cong were hard to estimate at the time this photograph was taken, but the force had grown from 5,000 in 1959 to 40,000 by the early 1960s as, once traditionally based in rural areas, they began to find sympathizers in city populations. As the exponents of revolutionary war, their work was covert and stealthy, but the Tet Offensive brought many out into open war, and thus caused many more to be caught in incidents like this.

casualty rates. Total American losses included 142 marines killed and 857 wounded, along with army casualties of 74 killed and 507 wounded. For the bravery and tenacity that they had shown storming the Citadel, the 1st Marine Regiment received a presidential citation. The South Vietnamese suffered 384 troops killed and 1,830 wounded, while Communist casualties exceeded 5,000 killed, along with 89 captured. Among the civilians residing in Hue, at least 5,800 were either dead or missing by the time the battle ended. And with at least half of the city destroyed, about 116,000 people from a population totaling 140,000 were now homeless.

The recapture of Hue brought with it evidence of massacres perpetrated by Communist forces occupying the city. A Viet Cong document that had fallen into allied hands included a list of 1,892 South Vietnamese bureaucrats, 38 policemen, and 70 "tyrants" who had been killed. Over a period of 18 months, search parties recovered as many as 3,000 corpses buried in mass graves in riverbeds, jungle clearings, and coastal salt flats. The victims included soldiers, civil servants, merchants, clergymen, schoolteachers, intellectuals, and foreigners. In addition, the Communists killed witnesses who might have offered the Allies details about the massacres. Most of the victims had died from gunshot wounds or severe beatings. Some had been buried alive. Ironically, most American citizens took little notice when these mass graves were found because they were more interested in the revelations about the March 1968 My Lai massacre that came to light at about the same time.

Although the siege of Khe Sanh was not yet over, the recapture of Hue effectively ended the Tet Offensive of 1968. By March MACV officers estimated the total human cost of the campaign at 50,000 NVA and Viet Cong soldiers, 11,000 South Vietnamese troops, and 2,000 Americans killed. Most of the dead Communist soldiers were Viet Cong southerners. In addition, the offensive had killed about 14,000 civilians and injured at least 20,000. Another 500,000 civilians became refugees after seeing their homes obliterated. As in Hue,

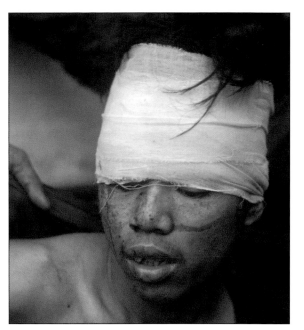

LEFT: His head swathed in a bandage, a Viet Cong prisoner, groggy from the wounds suffered in a fire-fight, awaits evacuation from the combat area. Prisoners taken by U.S. troops were handed over to the South Vietnamese authorities where they might be held in camps, or persuaded to fight for the Saigon government.
BELOW: A South Vietnamese Marine officer triumphantly straddles a pile of bolt action rifles captured during a sweep of a village. In the background, disconsolate villagers await their fate.

LEFT: A child clings to her grandmother as, soaked by monsoon rain, they watch U.S. troops conduct a sweep through of their village. The expression of resignation and fear on the old woman's face is a reflection of the hazardous and often dangerous life that perforce was endured by rural Vietnamese during the war.

BELOW LEFT: President Thieu and the American ambassador to South Vietnam, Ellsworth Bunker, at a reception. Although the ARVN troops performed well during the Tet Offensive, which bolstered Thieu's confidence, his regime was still far from popular. Despite pressure from his American allies, Thieu paid little but lip-service to the demands for economic and social reform until it was far too late. In any case, the political infrastructure of South Vietnam was far too full of self-interest and corruption to allow reform.

RIGHT: A chicken which has been looted by a South Vietnamese soldier during a patrol is strapped firmly under the flap of his rucksack. Poor pay and conditions for private soldiers as well as the obvious examples of corruption among the officers gave soldiers little incentive for observing the rules of war when they were forced to survive out in the field.

FAR RIGHT: Young Americans who have been drafted and passed the initial tests take the oath of allegiance administered by Captain Robert Gallagher, the Executive Officer at an Induction Office. Not all draftees were destined for Vietnam; some remained in the United States and others were posted to West Germany as part of NATO. Even those who went to Vietnam were not necessarily destined to be part of the combat arms.

many population centers were heavily damaged by artillery, air strikes, and the effects of urban combat. In the Mekong Delta, an American army major coined a memorable phrase when he explained the reason for the destruction of almost half of Ben Tre: "It became necessary to destroy the town in order to save it."

From a purely military point of view, Westmoreland and other American officers were justified in calling the Tet Offensive a major defeat for the Communists. Apart from Saigon and Hue, they failed to hold on to their captured areas for any great length of time. Moreover, the heavy losses suffered by the Viet Cong almost destroyed the insurgent organization as a viable combat force and effectively shifted the burden of continuing the Communist war effort to the NVA. After being intoxicated with promises of a decisive victory that would liberate their country from American imperialism, many NLF members became demoralized by the result of the offensive and the effects of the Phoenix Program and the Accelerated Pacification Campaign on their supply and infiltration network.

Finally, the failure of General Giap to realize the objectives he had identified in planning the Tet Offensive allowed the Allies to claim a significant victory in the Vietnam War. As the primary architect of the offensive, Giap professed little interest in the possibility of turning American public opinion against the war. Instead, he and other North Vietnamese strategists were more interested in using massive force to impress South Vietnamese public opinion. By striking every major population center and military target in the South, Giap had hoped that his divisions would apply enough pressure to turn the South Vietnamese people against the Thieu regime and cause that government and its armed forces to collapse like a house of cards. Confronted with this reality, the Americans would agree to any peace terms dictated by the Hanoi government.

This scenario failed to materialize because the South Vietnamese people were not as pro-Communist as Hanoi had presumed, and because ARVN soldiers proved to be better fighters than their reputation had indicated. Anti-American and anti-Thieu sentiment was

THE DRAFT AND DODGERS
Dodging the Draft

The draft undoubtedly plugged the U.S. manpower problem in the Vietnam War, yet it also proved divisive and preferential. For reasons which are now fairly easy to understand, many simply did not want to go. They had two options: consciously resist the draft call on grounds of principle, or take advantage of some of the loopholes draft law made available. Few took the first option, which amounted to a federal crime. However, draft rejectors often gathered together in focused protest groups. 'The Resistance,' for instance, collected over 1,100 cards of people who were refusing their draft demand. More famously, the boxer Muhammed Ali refused his draft call in 1967 and was sentenced to five years in prison, a sentence quashed while he was on bail by the U.S. Supreme Court on the grounds of conscientious objection.

Yet for those who did not want to flout the legal system there were several other options, provided you were rich enough or had influential friends. University or college students were exempt from military service, so the 1960s saw a massive explosion in higher-education attendance (hence the universities became the focus of much anti-war protest). Deferment could also be achieved by opting for service in the National Guard, famously a choice for many a would-be politician which could haunt him in later years. Anyone homosexual, physically infirm, or with dependent children was also exempt. Most controversially, there was a list of professions – generally well-paid white collar positions – which exempted from service. The overall result was that the poor or uneducated went to Vietnam, while many of the wealthier middle classes managed to avoid the draft. Sixteen million individuals slipped away from the draft call, and though it was made fairer in 1970 (based on a lottery of birthdates), it never regained its credibility.

RIGHT: A South Vietnamese Ranger patrol engage an enemy sniper while on patrol through streets full of rubble. Few units operating during the Tet attacks could avoid a photographer or television crew tagging along, and this patrol is clearly no exception. The Ranger units were generally regarded as being of a higher quality than regular ARVN forces, with some justification. All South Vietnamese units used the same equipment as their American colleagues, so this patrol is equipped with M16 assault rifles. The M16 is a 0.22 in. (5.56mm) caliber weapon, but the velocity of its lightweight bullet is so high that it can kill a person hit in a non-vital area of the body through trauma alone, and one bullet is powerful enough to remove limbs.

BELOW: An ARVN infantry unit battles to clear houses in a Saigon surburb during the counter-attacks in the aftermath of the Mini Tet offensive in May. A series of smaller outbreaks followed the January attacks, all of which increased the destruction and misery, particularly in Saigon itself. Although the house behind them appears to be largely undamaged, the Tet attacks brought the war into urban areas on a large scale for the first time. The ARVN soldier in the foreground holds his M60 in an aggressive manner, but if fired from the hip, the force of the gun's recoil would be likely to knock him backwards.

NEXT PAGE: The devastated 8th Division Headquarters in the Cholon area of Saigon following shelling in the Mini Tet offensive in February and March 1969. The attacks caused destruction and some panic, but were not on the scale of Tet 1968. Cholon was the market area of Saigon that was inhabited by a large, ethnic Chinese population.

widespread among the population, especially after allied aircraft and artillery had destroyed thousands of homes and neighborhoods during the post-Tet counteroffensive. However, many more South Vietnamese citizens were fearful of living in a Soviet-style dictatorship. As reports of Communist atrocities in Saigon, Hue, and other areas spread, this anxiety increased.

More significantly, ARVN soldiers shocked their Viet Cong and NVA adversaries with their tenacity in street battles during the Tet Offensive. Like cornered animals, many South Vietnamese troops fought ferociously against what they perceived to be a merciless enemy that would bury them in a riverbed or salt flat if they surrendered or tried to flee. This stubbornness greatly enhanced the ARVN's reputation among the general population and led to voluntary enlistment that swelled the ranks of the South Vietnamese armed forces. Popular expressions of confidence in the ARVN emboldened President

Thieu to introduce a conscription bill that the National Assembly would pass on June 19.

However, one of General Giap's objectives was achieved. The spectacular series of coordinated attacks across the country completely undermined General Westmoreland's oft-repeated claim of having the Communists on the brink of defeat. The scale of the offensive and images of the savage fighting which appeared on millions of TV screens across the United Sates suggested to the American public that the war was, at best, a stalemate which the Americans could not break without committing more men, equipment, and money. Giap and other strategists reasoned that the United States could not divert such resources to Vietnam because of commitments to so many other parts of the world. They also perceived

LEFT: A major peace protest march in Washington by 250,000 people comments on President Johnson's drive to integrate African Americans into the wider community of the United States.

BELOW LEFT: Dr Timothy Leary (center), an advocate of the drug LSD, joins Abbie Hoffman (left) urging a "flower guerrilla" attack on the Democratic Party Convention at Chicago. A popular slogan of the period was "Don't Trust Anyone Over 30."

OPPOSITE: In the White House, President Johnson studies a telex message stating North Vietnam's willingness to negotiate. The Tet offensive was a political victory for the Viet Cong and NVA, though they had suffered huge casualties and the U.S. had won a military victory.

that LBJ would not want to cut funding for his domestic programs in order to help finance a military escalation in Southeast Asia. Faced with an ongoing commitment and with no end in sight, the United States would have to abandon South Vietnam. In the aftermath of the Tet Offensive, many Americans shared a similar view.

Public opinion polls in the United States had indicated steady erosion of popular support for the conduct of the Vietnam War since 1966. The Tet Offensive seemed to turn this erosion into a landslide. When the offensive first erupted, most Americans rallied to the war effort in a temporary burst of patriotism. Later, television images of Viet Cong sappers storming the embassy in Saigon, marines struggling to retake Hue, and other memorable spectacles took their toll on any optimistic feelings about the result of the conflict. Despite suffering terrible losses during the offensive, the Communists had achieved a victory of sorts merely by showing up to fight in battles throughout South Vietnam, thus demonstrating that the war was far from over.

However, dissatisfaction with the conduct of the war did not necessarily mean that a peace

FBIS 75 (SEE 70)
*****
B U L L E T I N

DRV PROPOSAL

FOR YOUR INFORMATION

FOLLOWING IS AN OUT-OF-TURN QUOTATION FROM THE DRV STATEMENT
BROADCAST BY HANOI DOMESTIC SERVICE IN VIETNAMESE AT 1430 GMT ON
5 APRIL:

"IT IS CLEAR THAT THE U.S. GOVERNMENT HAS NOT CORRECTLY AND
FULLY RESPONDED TO THE JUST DEMAND OF THE DRV GOVERNMENT, OF U.S.
PROGRESSIVE OPINION, AND OF WORLD OPINION. IN ORDER TO PROVE ITS
THE DRV GOVERNMENT DECLARES ITS READINESS TO SEND ITS
REPRESENTATIVES TO MAKE CONTACT WITH U.S. REPRESENTATIVES TO DISCUSS
WITH THE U.S. SIDE THE UNCONDITIONAL CESSATION OF BOMBING AND
ALL OTHER WAR ACTS AGAINST THE DRV SO THAT TALKS COULD BEGIN."

5 APR 1457Z PAX/WP

RIGHT: Dean Rusk, the U.S. Secretary of State who shaped much of the policy on Vietnam adopted by the government of President Johnson. Following Tet when General Westmoreland requested an additional 200,000 troops, Rusk recommended that the President author- ize this increase in troop strengths. Rusk felt that the Paris Peace Talks were not in the best interests of the United States.

BELOW: The Senate Foreign Relations Committee which was critical of U.S. involve- ment in Vietnam in 1966, especially George Kennan and retired General James Gavin, who warned that China might be drawn into a wider conflict. Dean Rusk and General Maxwell Taylor insisted that Vietnam was a limited war that would halt Chinese expansionism.

sentiment prevailed among most Americans. In fact, some polls showed that many citizens actually wanted more rigorous military action in Vietnam, even if such threatened to ignite world war three. Widespread disillusionment with the conduct of the war coincided with waning faith in Great Society programs and wreaked havoc on LBJ's approval ratings. Having misled the people with rosy statements proclaiming an inevitable American victory in Vietnam, the United States government now became an object of distrust, especially among younger citizens confronted with the possibility of being drafted into the military and sent to fight in the war.

The president also saw many high-profile celebrities and former supporters abandon him over the war. After returning from a trip to South Vietnam, the popular news anchorman Walter Cronkite delivered an editorial on February 27, declaring the war unwinnable. LBJ saw Cronkite as the voice of Middle America and presumed that losing the support of the newsman meant that the president was losing the support of the American people.

Meanwhile, student agitation against the war gained momentum in college campuses across the country. Desperate for solutions, LBJ turned to his advisers for suggestions on what to do about the Vietnam quagmire.

Predictably, General Wheeler wanted to commit more men to Vietnam. In late February, he went to Saigon and persuaded General Westmoreland to join him in this effort. Consequently, Westmoreland requested 206,000 more troops from LBJ, although the general was aware that this a request seemed to contradict earlier public statements proclaiming Tet a great allied victory. Two weeks later, a Department of Defense official named Daniel Ellsberg leaked this troop solicitation to Senator Robert F. Kennedy, a presidential contender and political enemy of LBJ. The ensuing outcry within Congress and among the American public intimidated the president into backing away from Westmoreland's request. Ultimately, LBJ sent another 13,500 men to Vietnam, but admonished Westmoreland not to expect any more than that number. In the future, the president warned, the South

BELOW: Senator James W. Fulbright, who was a strident and a forthright critic of the U.S. policy of intervention in Vietnam. In February 1968 he held closed hearings in order to determine if the United States had provoked the Tonkin Gulf Incident, and charged that the U.S. Government had misled Congress over the attack by North Vietnamese PT boats against the destroyer the USS *Maddox* in August 1964. February 1968 was a bad month for President Johnson; student protests escalated and Walter Cronkite returned from reporting in Vietnam and announced that the war there was unwinnable for the United States.

MR. FULBRIGHT

ABOVE: An M60 machine gunner of the 1st Air Cavalry, part of the force for Operation Pegasus, the joint U.S. Army, Marine Corps, and ARVN attack that lifted the siege of Khe Sanh. The gunner is on Hill 471, one of the features captured on Highway 9 that dominated the route to the Marine Corps base.
LEFT: A U.S. Army radio operator turns his back to the dirt kicked up by the rotors of a "Huey" as it comes in to land. The men on board stand ready with feet on the skids to make a quick exit, while on the ground the man on the right signals the pilot how far he has to descend before they can jump off.
FAR RIGHT: U.S. soldiers look at a PT76 light amphibious tank, eleven of which overran the U.S. Army Special Forces camp at Lang Vei on February 6; only 14 Americans survived the attack.

Vietnamese government had to start holding its own as a military power.

By this time, congressional opposition to the conduct of the Vietnam War was becoming widespread and more vocal. In mid-March, William J. Fulbright presided over a hearing on the war in which the Senate Foreign Relations Committee grilled Secretary of State Dean Rusk in a televised interview. Meanwhile, Senator Eugene McCarthy shocked the Democratic Party establishment when he ran surprisingly well in the New Hampshire primary election in a bid to capture the party's nomination for the 1968 presidential election. In a challenge to LBJ's candidacy, McCarthy was running on a peace platform that many Democrats found appealing and had received only 300 fewer votes than the president out of 50,000 votes cast. The result of this primary encouraged the charismatic Senator Kennedy to enter the presidential election as a peace candidate.

Confronted with such strong antiwar sentiment within his party, LBJ fell under the sway of cabinet officials who advocated de-escalation and negotiations with the North Vietnamese. After replacing Robert S. McNamara early in the year as secretary of defense, Clark Clifford led this peace faction, arguing that the United States could never achieve a complete victory in Southeast Asia. In his view, LBJ needed to embrace a peace platform if the president wished to ensure a Democratic victory in the 1968 elections. In late March, Clifford assembled a group of prominent statesmen that included Henry Cabot Lodge, Dean Acheson, and General Omar Bradley. Known as the "wise men," this advisory panel concurred with Clifford's analysis and urged the president to disengage from Vietnam.

Swayed by these pressures, LBJ delivered a speech on March 31. Before television cameras, he announced an end to all bombings against North Vietnam above the 20th parallel and hinted that he might end air strikes completely if the Hanoi government indicated a willingness to act with restraint toward South Vietnam in the future. He also revealed his

LANG VEI

The Special Forces had some of the loneliest jobs in the Vietnam War, many of them based in isolated camps along South Vietnam's border with Laos and Cambodia and around the DMZ abutting North Vietnam. Lang Vei was situated five miles (8 km) from Khe Sanh. It was one of three bases in the area which were manned by Montagnard Vietnamese under the leadership of small Green Beret units, each base regularly sliding reconnaissance units across the border to spy on troop movements down the Ho Chi Minh Trail. The problem was that the NVA was also aware of their presence, and it was in their best interest to see these cross-border spy centers and firebases removed.

The siege of Lang Vei began in early February 1969. After a day of artillery bombardment, just after midnight on February 7, the NVA descended in swarms. What was so distinctive about the NVA assault was that they brought armor with them: five PT-76 light tanks, courtesy of the Soviet Union, which were an unusual sight in jungle warfare. With massed troops and tanks facing them, the prospects for the 25 U.S. soldiers and 500 Montagnard were poor, yet they put up a blistering resistance. One of the tanks was destroyed by anti-tank rockets, and scores of NVA were mown down by M60 machine guns and trained bursts from M16s. The odds, however, were unsustainable. Soon the camp was swarming with NVA, who blew up bunkers with satchel charges and thermite grenades. Some allied troops were rescued by helicopter, while others fled into the jungle for a painful and arduous march to safety. Lang Vei fell to the cost of 200 Montagnard fighters and seven U.S. soldiers.

BELOW: A 4.7 in. (120 mm) mortar in action against the Viet Cong. Like artillery units, mortars were often placed in defended firebases which dominated the local area. However the firebases gave the Viet Cong an obvious target to attack, and their very immobility made them vulnerable. That said, firebases were often placed close enough to each other to provide mutual support in case of an attack, but usually the Viet Cong attack began with little or no warning, and there was a risk of rounds falling on "friendlys."

intention to send Averell Harriman to Paris as the head of a negotiating team to develop with North Vietnamese representatives an equitable diplomatic resolution to the war. Finally, he surprised millions of American television viewers and even his own speechwriters when he declared that he would not seek re-election to the presidency. LBJ had contemplated this action for many months; his responsibilities had wearied him and debilitated his health, and the Tet Offensive certainly encouraged him in his decision to retire from politics.

While the president fielded criticism for his management of the war, American military commanders back in Vietnam pondered effective solutions for the siege of Khe Sanh. In early February, the marines received disturbing news. Southwest of the main base, two NVA infantry platoons with flamethrowers and a squadron of tanks overran a Special

Forces camp at Lang Vei, near the Laotian border. With support from Khe Sanh's artillery batteries, 24 Green Berets and 476 local irregulars disabled three tanks. However, two more tanks pushed through the perimeter, while sappers struck targets within the camp with grenades and satchel charges.

After several hours of fighting, the Communists overran the camp while surviving defenders slipped away and reached Khe Sanh the following morning. Allied casualties from the battle exceeded 50 percent. The brutal NVA ground assault on Lang Vei led many Americans to fear that Khe Sanh might suffer the same fate as the Green Beret camp. This prompted Westmoreland to authorize a relief operation for the beleaguered marines, Operation Pegasus.

While waiting for help, the marines in Khe Sanh planned a recovery operation to retrieve

the remains of comrades who had been killed in an ambush during a reconnaissance patrol in late February. At the end of March, the Americans struck NVA positions around the main base with artillery, mortar, and tactical air strikes. Then, on the morning of March 30, a company-size attack unit emerged from the perimeter and charged enemy bunkers with bayonets fixed. Although some of the marines fell to NVA mortar fire, most of them reached an enemy trench and incinerated its occupants with flamethrowers and grenades. After killing over 100 NVA troops, the marine company gathered their dead comrades and returned to the base.

On April 1 the 1st Cavalry Division began Operation Pegasus. Northeast of Khe Sanh, the relief expedition descended upon landing zones (LZs) near Route 9 and proceeded to the base in a leapfrogging movement from LZ to LZ. From the town of Ca Lu, the 2nd

Battalion, 1st Marine Regiment advanced with the cavalrymen down the highway, while the 2nd Battalion, 3rd Marine Regiment arrived from the south. Eventually, a company from the 3rd ARVN Airborne Division arrived, bringing the total strength of the relief force to 30,000 men. Although the Americans received periodic artillery and rocket fire en route to the base, they encountered little opposition on the ground and uncovered several caches of munitions. Meanwhile, army, navy, and marine engineers followed the relief column down Route 9, repairing 3 miles (4.8 km) of road and four bridges.

Within four days, the Americans reached the Khe Sanh valley. With little effort, the 1st Battalion, 9th Marine Regiment seized Hill 471. On April 5, the 66th NVA Regiment attempted to retake the hill in a pitched battle, only to be repulsed by air and artillery strikes. The following day, the Air Cavalry's 2nd

ABOVE: A U.S. Marine gives a wounded comrade a cigarette to calm his nerves as they wait for the "Dust Off", the name given to the casualty evacuation helicopter that will fly the wounded man to a field hospital. Helicopters became the staple mode of transport – both to and from the battlefield – for U.S. troops and sometimes their allies thoroughout the conflict. The speed that helicopters could move men from the front line to the operating theaters of field hospitals (a time which was often quoted as being only 40 minutes) saved many lives in the Vietnam War, as speedy evacuation and medical attention reduced the chances of death from shock or from loss of blood.

RIGHT: Several U.S. Navy armorers aboard a carrier work hard to maneuver bombs – which are unfuzed – in order to position them on the ship. They are being placed on the carrier to prepare for their subsequent loading onto USAF aircraft. One of the most frequently employed aircraft was the Vought A-7 Corsair II, an example of which can be seen in the background of this picture. The Corsair theoretically enjoyed an external bomb load of up to 4115 lb. (9072 kg), and the aircraft first saw action in 1967. It was adopted for use by the USAF and it flew the last combat strike of the Southeast Asian war, when Captain Lonnie O. Ratley hit targets which were in Cambodia on August 15, 1973.

BELOW RIGHT: Swathed in steam – which is coming from the catapult launcher – a U.S. Navy aircraft waits, ready for take off, on the flight deck of a carrier. The aircraft in this case is the McDonnell Douglas A4 Skyhawk, which was known all over the world to be a versatile and reliable plane – so reliable, in fact, that it was still in active service 14 years later when, flown by the Argentine Navy, it saw action off of the Falkland Islands against Royal Navy warships from the UK. Its delta wing configuration not only gave it stability and lift, but the ability to carry large amounts of ordnance on ground attack missions. The probe at the front of the aircraft is for in-flight refueling.

Battalion, 5th Regiment, 3rd Brigade occupied a strategic position south of Khe Sanh after a bloody fight. Further south, ARVN paratroopers maintained their ground in the face of punishing enemy attacks on April 8. Halfway between the village of Khe Sanh and the base, NVA remnants took a stand in an old French fort. With both overwhelming numbers and firepower, the cavalrymen smashed enemy resistance. Operation Pegasus reached a successful conclusion when the Airmobile Division reached the base and most Communist forces withdrew from the area, ending the siege by mid-April.

The relief of Khe Sanh brought little consolation, either for the local inhabitants or the American public back home. Once an area known for its beauty and lush vegetation, the

ABOVE: Pilots on the carrier USS *Intrepid* walk away from their McDonnell Douglas A-4 Skyhawks, following a mission over North Vietnam. The Skyhawk, known as "The Scooter," was among the first aircraft to see action over North Vietnam in the summer of 1964.

RIGHT: In a munitions factory in a cave in northern North Vietnam, liquid high explosives are poured into a mine designed for use in the rivers and inland waterways of the Mekong. When artillery or aircraft ordnance failed to explode, the explosive contents of the shell or bomb were extracted, melted down, and turned into mines.

RIGHT: After their first solo flight in 1968 in a T-2A Buckeye trainer, three pilots pose to have their photograph taken, still wearing their flight gloves. The smiling aviator on the right was Ensign Randall H. Cunningham of the U.S. Navy, a man who would, four years later – flying an F-4 Phantom – become a Navy ace. To achieve this accolade, he was responsible for shooting down four VPAF MiG-17s as well as a MiG-21. When this photograph was taken, at this point in the war, U.S. aircraft from both the Air Force and the Navy had already been conducting air attacks on enemy positions for four years.

surrounding countryside was now a desolate, crater-riddled wasteland. Like many other parts of South Vietnam after Tet, the village of Khe Sanh was in ruins, as were nearby coffee plantations. After expending so much manpower and matériel to hold the base, MACV determined that it was an unnecessary position and ordered an evacuation. On June 17, the marines destroyed their bunkers, dismantled their fortifications, took their ammunition with them, and departed. The casual abandonment of Khe Sanh caused many Americans to wonder why Westmoreland and LBJ had been so committed to the base when its occupants could have been better deployed elsewhere before and during the Tet Offensive.

For many antiwar activists in the United States, the siege at Khe Sanh served as a symbol of the war's futility. Other critics argued that Westmoreland's concentration of forces in the area had enabled the NVA to march into Hue almost unopposed. But "Westy" and his defenders stuck to their earlier assessments,

arguing that allowing Khe Sanh to fall would have enabled three NVA divisions to move unopposed throughout Military Region 1 and send many more reinforcements to Hue when the city was under Communist occupation. Thus, Westmoreland continued to assert that the Tet attacks on Saigon and other populous areas were the diversions and that Khe Sanh was the real objective, not vice versa. He also contended that the siege had provided the Americans with a great opportunity to use artillery and air power to inflict heavy losses on the NVA while suffering relatively few casualties. Anchored in static positions around the base, the Communists had lost at least 10,000 soldiers during the attack.

In addition, Westmoreland and other senior officers believed that the high casualties suffered by the Communists during the Tet Offensive presented the Allies with a chance to launch punishing counteroffensives that might inflict more injury upon the Viet Cong and bring the war to a favorable conclusion. In

BELOW: Mikoyan-Gurevich MiG-21 fighters of the 2nd Squadron of the Vietnam People's Air Force (VPAF). The pilots developed tactics that in 1968 accounted for 18 American aircraft for a loss of five MiG-21s. After an attack, the North Vietnamese pilots had the significant advantage that they could evade interception by seeking refuge in China. The North Koreans had adopted similar tactics in the Korean War, where they would escape over the Yalu River, which marked the Korean–Chinese border.

RIGHT: Exhausted and soaked, a peasant dressed in the simple black work clothes of Vietnam stands surrounded by South Vietnamese soldiers. While some men might be members of the Viet Cong and would therefore attempt to avoid capture, others might be innocent but fear they would be tortured or killed. By hiding, however, they would appear guilty to South Vietnamese troops if they were discovered.

BELOW: M113 Armored Personnel Carriers (APCs) of 1st Battalion, 50th Infantry, 173rd Airborne Brigade, move through farmland in May. Part of a blocking force during a search of Phu Loc village, where North Vietnamese soldiers and two nurses were believed to be hiding, troops ride on the top to reduce the risk of injury from mine blasts.

areas near Saigon, the Allies tried to achieve exactly this result against three enemy divisions that seemed poised to strike the capital. On March 11, 33 American and ARVN battalions launched Operation Quyet Thang (Resolve to Win). Altogether, about 50,000 allied troops organized into seven formations moved through six provinces in a month-long campaign that killed more than 2,600 Communists. Although the operation knocked the enemy divisions off balance and prevented them from attacking the capital, it never produced the decisive battle that Westmoreland was seeking to land a knockout blow on the Communist war effort.

A month later, the Allies launched an even larger operation called Toan Thang (Complete Victory) in Gia Dinh province south of Saigon. During this campaign, 77 battalions, numbering about 100,000 troops collectively, sent patrols through the area. From April 8 until May 31, they launched search missions in the daytime and ambushes at night. When

Operation Toan Thang ended, its participants had killed about 7,600 Communist soldiers.

Allied forces also struck Viet Cong positions in the Mekong Delta. Flying above the U Minh Forest, American tactical aircraft pilots dropped white-phosphorus rockets and napalm in an effort to spread a dry-weather fire throughout the vast jungle, which was a favorite hideout for NLF forces. Meanwhile, American cruisers in the Gulf of Thailand pummeled suspected Viet Cong bases with hundreds of rockets. Attempts by the Communist guerrillas within the base to dig firebreaks proved futile as the conflagration swept through their camps and detonated their fuel and munitions. By April 20, over 80 percent of U Minh Forest became a charred wasteland that would be inhospitable to NLF cells for at least a year.

Far to the north of these areas, American and South Vietnamese forces launched a massive raid in the A Shau Valley near the Laotian border. Since 1966, the valley had served as a

BELOW: The crewman of an UH-1 helicopter belonging to the U.S. Army 82nd Medical Detachment is faced with a difficult prospect. He has somehow to load a badly wounded man from the South Vietnamese Army Rangers onto a helicopter, and this aircraft is already overcrowded with several wounded troops. The South Vietnamese Army Rangers had suffered 50 casualties during the fighting with forces of the Viet Cong in the Mekong delta. The nearby U.S. Army 82nd Medical Detachment was based at Soc Trang, and the wounded had to be lifted to safety before they suffered from shock or profuse bleeding, or the helicopter was attacked.

RIGHT: Men of the 101st Airborne Division hunch under the down draught of a Bell UH-1 "Huey" as it lifts off from a landing zone blasted from the jungle northwest of Dak To on June 4. Along with the 1st Cavalry (Air Cavalry), the 101st Airborne pioneered the tactics of airmobility.

BELOW: With belts of ammunition wrapped around his M60 machine gun, an American soldier advances through knee-high grass in the A Shau valley. The towel across his shoulders helps pad out the 4.75 lb. (10.48 kg) of gun. The valley, close to the Laotian border, was a Viet Cong and North Vietnamese Army staging area and became the site of heavy fighting in 1968 and 1969.

NEXT PAGE: Blindfolded on the floor of a UH-1 "Huey" helicopter, three suspect Viet Cong or North Vietnamese are evacuated by men of the 101st Airborne after a heavy period of combat in the A Shau valley. The men were captured during a night operation.

large base area and supply depot for the NVA. Protected by antiaircraft batteries and at least 5,000 troops, the region also provided the Communists with a launching point for campaigns in the South, such as the Tet Offensive. In early April, Lieutenant-General William B. Rosson developed a plan that would send troops from the 1st Air Cavalry into the valley aboard helicopter transports. From their LZs, these soldiers would then drive the NVA garrison out of the area and seize its supplies.

Called both Operation Delaware and Lam Son 216, the attack was preceded by bombing sorties that were supposed to neutralize enemy antiaircraft units so that the helicopters could land troops safely. Although B-52s had hammered NVA positions throughout the valley, antiaircraft batteries hidden in the surrounding hills remained undisturbed and wreaked havoc upon American helicopters when the operation

GENERAL CREIGHTON ABRAMS

With Westmoreland's return home after Tet, a new commander was needed for the Military Assistance Command Vietnam. This man would be General Creighton Abrams. Facing a very different set of circumstances than his predecessor, his was to prove a difficult job. Whereas Westmoreland presided over military escalation, Abrams task was to preside over Vietnamization and withdrawal, and yet he nevertheless had to be seen to be acting positively.

Search and destroy did continue under Abrams, but with a very different emphasis. Instead of the massive sweep operations conducted under Westmoreland, Abrams used S&D in small-unit fighting patrols which aimed at protecting civilian areas from VC penetration. These small-unit actions by U.S. troops still meant that blood was being spilt in significant quantities. Indeed, the casualties from booby traps and mines actually went up, while gunshot-wound casualty figures decreased because there were less open firefights involved. Yet Abrams' overall strategy was much more focused on the transfer of responsibility – assist Vietnamization by protecting the villages and enabling the South Vietnamese to defend themselves – in short, 'Pacification.' To back this up, several other programs were initiated to further hamper VC efficiency. The Chieu Hoi ('Open Arms') program was developed to encourage defection by VC soldiers, with the promise of an amnesty and rehabilitation into society, even the ARVN. The Phoenix program, begun under Westmoreland, was an intelligence-gathering operation that resulted in over 22,000 assassinations, many under dubious circumstances or identification. Although pacification was of questionable success, Abrams does seem to have grasped the complexities of mixing his military position with the political sensitivities of the time.

began on April 19. On that day, the Communists shot down ten helicopters. In addition, heavy cloud cover and occasional thunderstorms made air travel difficult and time consuming.

Landing at the northern end of the A Shau Valley, the 1st Air Cavalry Division established LZs Tiger and Vicki and occupied an old French airfield at A Luoi, which would serve as a location for C-123 Providers to deliver supplies. The cavalrymen also formed a blocking position on Route 548 and proceeded south on the highway. Meanwhile, two battalions from the 101st Airborne Division advanced along Route 547 toward the central part of the valley. On April 22, the skies cleared, enabling CH-47 Chinook helicopters to bring howitzers to American positions within the valley. A week later, the cavalrymen established a landing zone at Ta Bai. The 3rd

BELOW: Viet Cong prisoners are rounded up by South Vietnamese troops and marched into captivity during a sweep through a village. Although most sweeps yielded nothing, sometimes arms or food caches were found. The Viet Cong became adept at hiding materiel in innocuous or inconspicuous places, such as under a cooking fire or down a well. It would require an extremely diligent patrol to find such hiding places. Occasionally prisoners were taken, but most Viet Cong took care to avoid contact with patrols during the day, unless conducting an ambush.

ARVN Regiment then arrived at this location and launched assaults along the Rao Lao River.

During Operation Delaware/Lam Son 216, the greatest danger for the Allies was in the air. Before the campaign ended on May 13, the NVA succeeded in shooting down or damaging at least 60 helicopters and one C-130 airplane. On the ground, the operation was almost anticlimactic. Instead of fighting for their base area, the Communists withdrew into the hills and harassed allied patrols with artillery barrages. Altogether, the Americans lost 139 troops killed. Communist losses amounted to 850 fatalities, along with massive quantities of weapons, ammunition, explosives, fuel, rations, and vehicles that the retreating NVA forces had left behind.

While the A Shau valley operation was winding down, the Communists launched a "mini-Tet" offensive against Saigon and 118 other cities, towns, and military bases on May 5. In most places, the attackers merely launched rockets and mortar rounds. This time, the allies were ready for the offensive, thanks to an NVA colonel who had defected and warned his hosts of the upcoming trouble. This information enabled the Allies to intercept and repel most of the Communist forces approaching the capital. However, at least nine battalions managed to push through the city limits and bring the war into Saigon once again. For over a week, the city saw bloody street battles in Cholon, Tan Son Nhut airport, and several other locations.

Intense combat also occurred up in Quang Tri province at Dong Ha, where 5,000 American marines and South Vietnamese troops repelled 8,000 soldiers from the 320th NVA Division after three days of fighting. The battle killed 68 Americans and 856 Communists. In the Central Highlands, the

2nd NVA Division encircled 1,800 allied troops at a Green Beret camp at Kham Duc when a group of helicopters and C-130s arrived to evacuate the camp. Although the flight crews of these aircraft successfully extracted most members of the garrison, the Communists managed to shoot down five helicopters, two C-130s, and an A-1 Skyraider.

On May 25, fighting broke out in Saigon yet again when two NVA regiments swept into the northern suburbs and converted several buildings into fortified bases. Meanwhile, local Viet Cong units re-entered Cholon and occupied a post office. After yet another week of combat within the city, ARVN brigades retook these areas with the help of helicopter gunships that devastated occupied buildings. Despite being ejected from the city limits, the Communists continued to terrorize the capital for another 38 days by firing 122mm rockets

into it from the nearby countryside. Not surprisingly, thcsc May "mini-Tct" actions killcd or wounded thousands of civilians and left many more homeless.

For the next two months, clashes between Communist and allied forces gradually subsided while peace negotiations between American and North Vietnamese diplomats proceeded in Paris. During this lull in the fighting, General Westmoreland stepped down as Commander, U.S. Military Assistance Command, Vietnam (COMUSMACV) and became the Army Chief of Staff back in Washington. His replacement, General Creighton W. Abrams, took a different approach in executing the war in Vietnam. Unlike Westmoreland, Abrams was more of a realist who perceived the likelihood of American disengagement from Southeast Asia and thus an end to the lavish amounts of men,

ABOVE: Flames burn in the aftermath of an explosion in a Vietnamese street, which has gained the attention of a patrol searching nearby houses for Viet Cong suspects and arms caches. The Viet Cong were expert in melting into the background in the confusion that reigned after an explosion. Attacks like these demoralized the civilians and military alike, for if a suspect was not caught, he would be likely to strike again without warning.

RIGHT: Her face contorted by fear, a woman hurries away from a loose cordon of South Vietnamese soldiers. Behind her, a child appears to be looking back toward the soldiers, but is actually holding his hand out, urging another child to catch up with him. For many Vietnamese people, war had been the only experience they had known since French Indo China had been invaded by the Japanese in World War II. French Colonial, and later American, soldiers had little knowledge of Vietnamese culture, nor often indeed any liking for it, with the result that they failed to treat the civilian Vietnamese people with much respect.

LEFT: A U.S. Marine M60 machine gunner stands guard over a Vietnamese street while his colleagues check the buildings for the Viet Cong or signs of enemy activity. Known unaffectionately as the "Pig", the M60 was not well liked by its users. It was both unreliable and extremely heavy for its size.

RIGHT: South Vietnamese youngsters reach out as a U.S. soldier distributes comic books in a village near Saigon in August 1968. Many children and villagers learned a rudimentary and often crude form of spoken English from soldiers. It was sufficient to trade and make simple transactions; however, the obscenities that were also picked up were a surprise to men new in theater.

money, and matériel sent from the United States to Saigon. This reality meant that American officials in Vietnam needed to strengthen their client state and pacify the countryside.

Abrams implemented a significant change in allied strategy. Instead of launching large-scale military campaigns against elusive enemy forces that were adept at melting into the countryside, he ordered company and battalion-size maneuvers that would surprise Communist units with ambushes and raids to seize munitions caches. He also stressed the importance of protecting population centers from artillery and ground assaults, and redeployed his divisions to deter such mishaps. The 4th Infantry Division occupied positions along the Laotian and Cambodian borders,

while the 3rd Marine Division protected areas near the DMZ. Most of the remaining American forces, which totaled about eight divisions in strength, defended areas around Saigon and other urban areas.

General Abrams and the CIA officer William Colby also sought to undermine Viet Cong influence in the hamlets by strengthening the reservist Regional and Popular Forces. President Thieu cooperated with this effort by allowing draft-age men to join these units rather than the ARVN. The Allies also established a volunteer village militia force called the People's Self-Defense Force (PSDF), which had open membership for all ages and both sexes. Later in the year, Colby initiated the Accelerated Pacification Campaign (APC), an expansion of the Phoenix Program

RIGHT: Women of the South Vietnamese People's Self-Defense Force parade with their weapons. This organization was intended to help combat the influence of the Communists in the villages of South Vietnam, and they were a mixed success. Under the Accelerated Pacification Campaign, an extension of the Phoenix Program, these local forces were deployed in hamlets and villages throughout South Vietnam. The establishment of these and other local forces was the beginning of the "Vietnamization" program which would gather impetus over the following years as pressure at home in the United States forced the newly-elected President Nixon to begin a policy of withdrawing American servicemen from Vietnam.

which deployed these local forces in hamlets to hinder NLF infiltration. These new policies effectively constituted the beginning of a strategy that would be known as "Vietnamization."

Abrams received his first serious test in mid-August, when the Communists launched a "third Tet offensive" on Saigon and other areas. As in May, the Allies were prepared. In fact, Abrams had ordered preemptive raids and air strikes against enemy positions and cache sites that prevented enemy forces from hitting their targets as hard as they wanted. Twenty miles (32 km) north of Saigon, allied units captured a base area that possessed a hospital with 4,000 beds and refrigerators with blood supplies, as well as several concrete bunkers. Thanks to these aggressive countermeasures, the "third Tet" was little more than a harassment action with artillery, rockets, and mortars against allied positions in Vietnam.

Back in the United States, a war among the American people was escalating. A growing disillusionment over the Vietnam War coincided with racial conflict that exploded

ABOVE: With the powerful support of an M47 tank, men of Company C, 206th Infantry, 101st Airborne Division relax and talk during a house to house search for Viet Cong snipers. It was often impossible for these men to make an effective search of the buildings of an entire village, where pressure of time prevented a detailed examination of all the many and diverse hiding places which might house the Viet Cong enemy.

RIGHT: Head down in a camouflaged hiding place a US Army soldier pulls out documents which are examined by Lt Dave Lewis. Tunnels and "spider holes" were used for concealment and also protection against artillery and air attack. The laterite soil in which the tunnels were dug could become as hard as concrete in some circumstances.

Airmobility

Vietnam was a helicopter war. By the end of the conflict in 1975, U.S. helicopters had flown an utterly astonishing 36,125,000 sorties. Whether winching an injured man out of a jungle clearing in a medevac operation, or rocketing VC positions from a gunship, the helicopter became a ubiquitous symbol of the war.

U.S. helicopter operations first began in 1961 when various helicopter types were provided to the South Vietnamese forces to assist in supply and reconnaissance missions. It was the introduction of U.S. ground troops into the war, however, that escalated helicopter deployment. Some 5,000 Bell UH-1s moved in in the first years of the war, ferrying soldiers to landing zones (LZs), performing medevac duties, and transporting weaponry. But they were just the tip of the iceberg. Once helicopters started proving their worth, in flooded machines which added a whole new dimension to airmobility. In reconnaissance roles came the

Hughes OH-6. The OH-58A Kiowa gave patrol and target acquisition capabilities. Downed aircrew were lifted to safety by rescue teams in Sikorsky HH-3E. Assault teams were flown in in Hueys or in the massive dual-rotor CH-47 Chinook. The Chinook also acted in logistical duties alongside the powerful CH-54 Tarhe Skycrane. And in combat, Huey and Cobra gunships blasted VC positions with ferocious firepower.

The U.S. war effort in Vietnam became completely reliant upon helicopters. Vietnam is a mountainous and inaccessible country, and for many U.S. bases – particularly artillery firebases and special forces camps – helicopter was the only way in which they could receive supplies and reinforcements. But more than that, entire units were soon becoming fully airmobile in a combat capacity. The 1st Cavalry (Airmobile) Division could be lifted in its entirety by an enormous flight of helicopters, and it takes the accolade of being the first division which could achieve this feat. With this capability, search and destroy missions could be pushed into action with lightning speed and flexibility.

For the soldiers fighting on the ground, perhaps the most comforting feature of the helicopter presence was as Medical Evacuation (medevac). Soldiers could be injured many miles from base, but a simple radio call for medevac would bring a helicopter right to the injured man's position within minutes. An Australian Brigade in Phuoc Tuy province claimed that from the moment of injury their medevac teams would have the wounded soldier on the operating table within 40 minutes. Yet medevac operations were acutely dangerous for helicopter crews. The Viet Cong used to intentionally wound U.S. soldiers to draw out a medevac attempt. A close-range hovering helicopter was easy prey for small-arms fire – just one bullet in the right place could cause the helicopter to drop like a brick. Some of this danger was alleviated by bringing along a gunship for support, but even they were vulnerable. In 1972, the NVA acquired new SAM-7 shoulder-launched anti-aircraft missiles. These missiles were effective against slow-moving low-level aircraft, and so helicopters became perilously exposed to their fire. For this reason. ARVN helicopter operations in the last years of the war diminished markedly over those conducted by the U.S, but until the end of the war, Vietnam was a place which continually rang with the sounds of rotor blades chopping the air.

LEFT: An American heavy lift helicopter moves a metal platform into place. Although Korea had seen the first widespread use of helicopters on the battlefield, by the time of the conflict in Vietnam engine power and efficiency had greatly improved, and they had become almost ubiquitous.

ABOVE: A squad disembarks from a hovering UH-1 "Huey." Helicopters operating in areas where the enemy was known or suspected to be active were reluctant to land, as it took some time for the helicopter's engines to spool up to full power to take off, leaving it vulnerable to attack.

RIGHT: Artillery shells packed in wooden crates are loaded into a Bell UH-1 "Huey" helicopter of the type made famous by the Hollywood movie "Apocalypse Now". The "Hueys" were the workhorse of the American presence in Vietnam, being used for everything, from transport helicopter to casevac (casualty evacuation) to gunships. It is no exaggeration to say that the entire American effort in Vietnam depended heavily on the Bell helicopter.

RIGHT: Dr Martin Luther King, the 39-year-old Baptist preacher and civil rights activist, speaks at a rally. His assassination on April 4 in Memphis prompted an outcry in the United States, and led to widespread rioting. He was buried on April 9 after a nationally televised funeral march through Atlanta, Georgia. His speech the day before he died seemed to suggest that he had a suspicion that he might soon be killed.

BELOW RIGHT: Two African Americans are silhouetted against a huge cloud of smoke coming from a blazing building. The men, engaged in discussion, are picking their way through the debris of a glass-littered street in Washington, DC, in the aftermath of street riots. Following the assassination of Dr Martin Luther King, these riots swept through at least 20 cities throughout the U.S. In Washington, President Johnson was forced to make the decision to order Federal troops into the city after Police so that law and order could be maintained.

into urban riots when Martin Luther King, Jr. fell to an assassin's bullet on April 4. For a brief period, the prospects of national reconciliation seemed possible when Robert F. Kennedy emerged as the front-running presidential candidate for the Democratic Party. A charismatic leader who enjoyed wide appeal among diverse racial and economic groups, Kennedy appeared to be the knight in shining armor that would end the war, resolve the country's domestic problems, and bring a sense of unity to all Americans. This promise came to a violent end on June 5, when he too was assassinated in a Los Angeles hotel while celebrating his victory in the California election primary.

The following month, Richard M. Nixon won the Republican nomination for the presidential election on August 8, with Spiro T.

Agnew as his running mate. In their campaign for the White House, Nixon offered voters a vague "secret plan" for bringing a satisfactory end to the Vietnam War. A little over two weeks later, the Democrats held their nominating convention at the Conrad Hilton Hotel in Chicago. In the wake of Kennedy's death, Vice-President Hubert H. Humphrey emerged as the favored candidate among the party establishment. However, his efforts to walk a centrist tightrope between southern conservatives and northern antiwar liberals satisfied neither faction. Violent clashes between student protesters and city policemen outside the hotel only added to the atmosphere of tension that prevailed within the faction-ridden party.

After an acrimonious debate, most delegates in the convention voted for a resolution that essentially endorsed LBJ's policy of cau-

ABOVE: A National Guardsman patrols a deserted and burned out street in a U.S. city, determination etched on his face. Several U.S. city centers were damaged in August 1968 following riots triggered by the killing of Dr Martin Luther King, and whole urban areas took on the air of the war-torn cities which were being fought over by U.S. troops and Viet Cong many miles away. Dr King's peaceful but persistent approach to improving the lot of African Americans had won him support with liberal White Americans, and his untimely death would radicalize the opinions of African Americans for decades to come.

RIGHT: Moments before he lost consciousness, Senator Robert "Bobby" looks up as aids rush to assist him after he was shot by 24-year-old Jordanian-born Sirhan Sirhan. Kennedy, a critic of the war in Vietnam, had offered his candidacy for the 1968 presidential race and was celebrating after his victory in the Californian primary. His killing was claimed to be a protest against the U.S. support for Israel.

BELOW RIGHT: During the "Stop the Draft Week" protests in December, construction workers on a building site with two young men raise the Stars and Stripes into the air and make their protests heard as part of an Anti-Anti-War demonstration. President Nixon favored these kinds of actions and would later claim that the war was popular with most Americans, refering to people like these construction workers – and their less demonstrative friends and relatives – as "the silent majority."

OPPOSITE: A draft-age anti-war protestor stands near the Lincoln Memorial in Washington, holding up a placard which states that he would go to Vietnam when "Lynda Bird" – President Johnson's wife – went. Although there were many people of draft age dodging the draft using various means, such as bad health, sexual orientation, and university attendance, there was a short period when public opinion had rallied behind the war, especially during the Tet Offensive, when the lives of many U.S. troops were seriously placed at risk by the fighting in Vietnam.

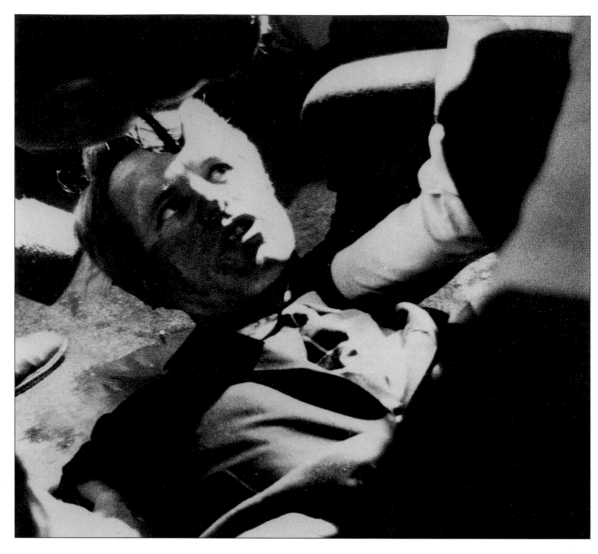

tious de-escalation and nominated Humphrey as the Democratic candidate. That still left a large, disaffected antiwar minority, who protested loudly and hinted at the possibility of a mass-defection to a third-party peace candidate. However, the real third-party threat ultimately came from the right. Like many other southerners, Governor George Wallace of Alabama had grown weary of what he considered to be a liberal domination over the Democratic organization. Thus he ran as presidential candidate for the American Party with General Curtis LeMay as his running mate. Both men were very "hawkish" in their stand on the war.

To shore up support within members of his own party, Humphrey distanced himself from LBJ and proposed a detailed peace plan . This peace plan called for a complete bilateral withdrawal from South Vietnam and a cease-fire which was to be supervised by the United Nations. In October, his campaign steadily

I'LL GO WHEN LYNDA BIRD GOES

SELF-
ETERMINATION
FOR
CK AMERICA
D VIETNAM

HE WA

END
THE DRAFT—
SUPPORT
THE MEN
WHO SAY NO

WE KILL

LOSE

ABOVE: Richard Nixon, the Republican Presidential Candidate, with his Vice President Spiro Agnew in the 1968 campaign. Nixon became the 37th President of the United States and the only one of his era to understand that the war with North Vietnam was a war of wills. He used air power to bludgeon the North to the negotiating table, but by then, America was disenchanted with what seemed a war with no obvious end in sight.

LEFT: Outside the Hilton Hotel, the Democratic Convention headquarters in Chicago, police break up antiwar demonstrations. The clash between largely middle-class protestors and police who had been recruited from a working class background was a clash of cultures, and the violence it engendered shocked America.

LEFT: At the Democratic National Convention, several delegates are shown displaying protest banners and shouting their objections to the war. They have chosen to take this disruptive action during the votes to adopt President Lyndon Johnson and Vice President Hubert Humphrey for another term in office. Antiwar protests such as these were now not only the preserve of the young and radical, but also of the establishment. There were many mothers and fathers of Middle America who had seen too many of their sons killed and wounded by fighting taking place miles away in Vietnam.

gained momentum, especially when LBJ announced that negotiators had reached a compromise and had agreed a temporary ceasefire, as well as a complete halt to the bombings on North Vietnam.

In a two-way contest, Humphrey might have beaten Nixon. However, Wallace siphoned just enough votes from the southern states as well as from blue-collar northerners to thwart Humphrey's campaign and tip the election to Nixon. On November 5, Nixon won the election with a narrow majority and prepared to assume the burden of solving the Vietnam problem.

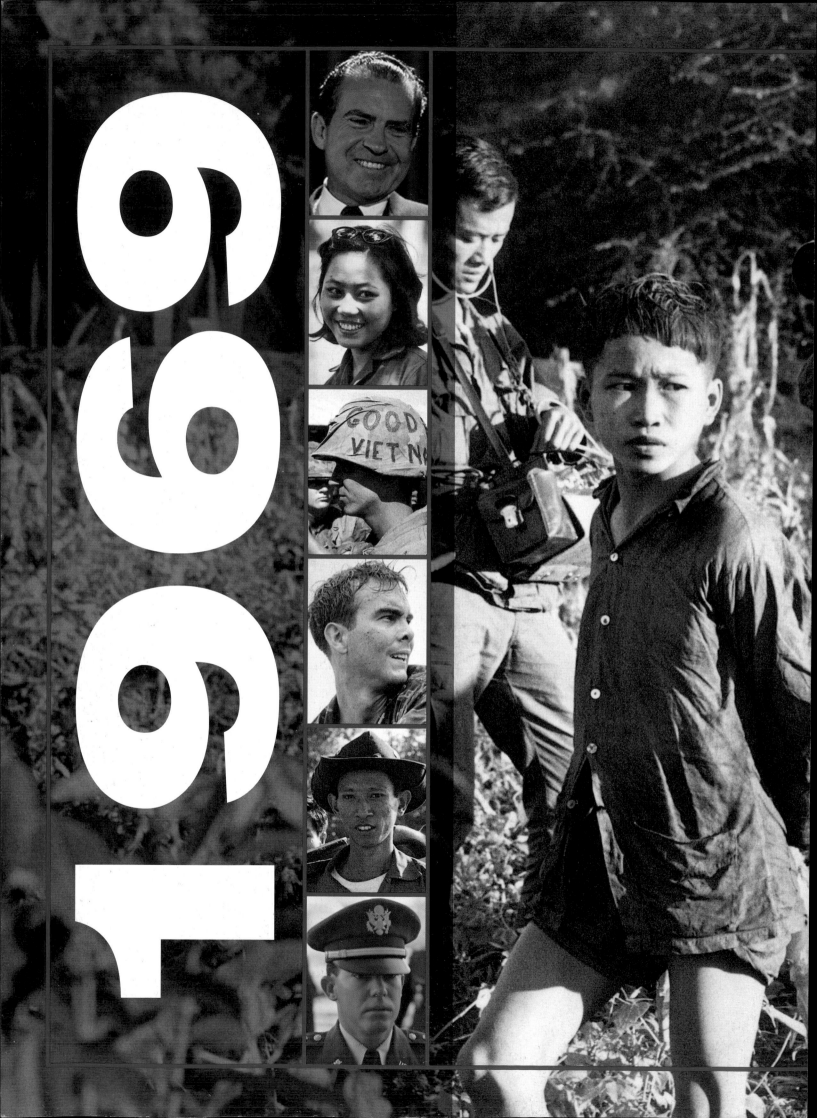

1969

Mr Nixon's War

Richard Milhous Nixon assumed the Presidency on January 20, 1969, elected to office with a "secret plan" for ending the Vietnam War. However, some voters who had supported him because of this promise quickly became apprehensive during his inaugural address, in which he cautioned that peace could only be achieved after several years of "patient and prolonged diplomacy." The relevant members of his cabinet charged with working on this project included his Secretary of Defense Melvin Laird, Secretary of State William Rogers, Undersecretary of State Elliot Richardson, and Ellsworth Bunker, the Ambassador to Saigon. Among these officers, Laird achieved some significance by coining the term "Vietnamization" as the policy of the Nixon administration in which the U.S. incrementally shifted the burden of fighting the war to its ally in Saigon. However, the most important foreign-policy figure within the Nixon administration was the National Security Council adviser, Henry Kissinger.

While at Harvard University, Henry Kissinger had written his Ph.D. dissertation on the 1815 Congress of Vienna. In this study, he came to the conclusion that bureaucratic inertia was the greatest hindrance to effective diplomacy. Organized for the purpose of executing, rather than conceiving, initiatives, civil servants working in diplomatic offices would often

exceed their authority at the expense of the statesmen who were supposed to enjoy the exclusive prerogative of controlling a nation's foreign policy. Thus, Kissinger believed that effective diplomats needed to act as free agents who were working independently of government bureaucracies. Within the Nixon administration, Kissinger would follow this principle scrupulously in Vietnam and other parts of the world as the President's foreign policy tsar. In his post as National Security Council adviser, he was answerable only to Nixon.

Nixon and Kissinger developed a two-pronged approach to the problem of disengaging the United States from Vietnam without suffering a defeat in the war. First, the United States would strengthen South Vietnam into a viable country which was capable of defending itself from the Communists. Second, Kissinger would negotiate an amicable armistice with Hanoi, but only after the United States and its client achieved a satisfactory military situation to command an advantageous bargaining position at the peace talks. During their first year in the White House, Nixon and Kissinger determined that this situation had not yet been achieved sufficiently to permit open, official negotiations with North Vietnam, although Kissinger did meet secretly with a North Vietnamese representative at Paris in August.

ABOVE: The new President, Richard Milhous Nixon, confers with Admiral John S. McCain in the White House. In January 1969, Nixon took office claiming to have a secret plan for ending the Vietnam War, although he never explained exactly what this scheme was.
RIGHT: West of Saigon, an airport policeman stands guard at Tan Son Nhut airbase. Although the facility had been an important target for Communist attacks during the 1968 Tet Offensive, little action took place in the area in the following year.

ABOVE: An experienced river patrolman from the American forces assists a South Vietnamese trainee during an operation along the Mekong Rive; in later years, South Vietnamese forces would also inherit modern U.S. craft. Here, the American points out notable features in the surroundings, while the Stars and Stripes flag hangs from the flagpole identifying the rivercraft as an allied vessel. By 1969, the American forces had managed to clear most of the Viet Cong elements out of this delta, and were able to turn their attentions to other troublesome areas, refocusing their efforts upriver and closer to Cambodia.

Although the two men seemed to be of one mind in their effort to arrive at an acceptable conclusion to the American involvement in Southeast Asia, they did have one important contradiction. Kissinger's top priority was to pull the United States out of the region in an honorable way in order to maintain its prestige in a world still divided by the Cold War. The permanent existence of South Vietnam as a self-sufficient nation was only a secondary concern. For Nixon, these two priorities were reversed. During the later years of his administration, this difference would become more noticeable.

Nixon and Kissinger believed that the belligerents in the war could achieve peace by drawing up an agreement that covered only military issues such as rates of American troop withdrawals and the release of prisoners of war. In their expressed view, political issues were internal Vietnamese problems that need not involve the United States. However, neither Hanoi nor Saigon accepted this rationale and affirmed irreconcilable demands which effectively precluded any armistice in the near future. In Saigon, President Nguyen Van Thieu proclaimed three requirements for peace. First, the National Liberation Front (NLF) had to renounce Communism. Second, the North Vietnamese Army (NVA) had to leave South Vietnamese soil. Finally, Thieu proclaimed that he would never allow any coalition government that included Communists. In Hanoi, the Democratic Republic of Vietnam announced that there would be no NVA pullout from the South and no negotiations with Saigon as long as Thieu was in power.

These disagreements became especially manifest to American and Vietnamese observers on May 14, when Nixon issued an eight-point peace plan. Points one to four covered the terms and rates of American troop withdrawals. Point five called for an international body of peacekeepers to supervise the implementation of an armistice and disarmament of the NLF/Viet Cong. Point six demanded the release of all war prisoners. Point seven urged the observation of the 1954 and 1962 Geneva Accords. Finally, point eight served as the only political component in Nixon's peace plan, calling for internationally supervised elections in South Vietnam. Not surprisingly, the North Vietnamese government balked at these terms, seeing them as an effort to render the Viet Cong helpless in the presence of Saigon's well-armed military machine, the Army of the Republic of Vietnam (ARVN). What shocked and dismayed Nixon much more was Thieu's unexpected rejection of the peace plan. The South Vietnamese President interpreted the eighth point as an open door to political participation for the NLF.

While the Nixon administration set out to find an acceptable resolution to the war, American ground forces in Vietnam explored new tactics to subdue their elusive enemies. The top commander in the country, General Creighton Abrams, and the commander of the 3rd Marine Division, Major General Raymond A. Davis, decided to disperse battalion-size Army and Marine bases into more numerous company-size positions that were better able to send mobile units through the countryside. In earlier years, entire battalions would hunker into fixed positions and prepare for enemy attacks or large-scale campaigns directed at guerilla forces capable of melting into the jungle before being hit by advancing Americans. In 1969 and succeeding years, American officers would order less ambitious operations. Instead of flailing clumsily at elusive guerilla forces, soldiers and marines would employ smaller units to disrupt enemy logistics and undermine the Communist presence in the villages.

Within his own sphere, Major General Davis set about to increase the mobility of his division, which was stationed along the Demilitarized Zone (DMZ). He established 60 four-man reconnaissance teams who were to snake through mountains and rainforest and report all enemy activity that they could see. At least 20 of these teams would be operating

RICHARD MILHOUS NIXON
"Tricky Dicky"

Today, it is the name Watergate that defines the reputation of Richard M. Nixon; it was a scandal which took him from political supremacy to outright ignominy in the space of five years in office. Yet like Johnson before him, his administration during the Vietnam war forms a backdrop to his fall.

The "Nixon Doctrine" (as it was known) in Vietnam was one of "Vietnamization." The Tet Offensive had occurred the year prior to Nixon's taking office, and he correctly judged the U.S. desire for withdrawal from Vietnam. Heavy military supplies to South Vietnam were maintained, but Nixon began withdrawing large numbers of U.S. troops and warned that ground commanders should avoid dangerous combat encounters in order to reduce casualties. Yet this is not the full picture. Alongside restraint and withdrawal was expansion and involvement elsewhere. Nixon allowed the war to spill over into neighboring Cambodia and Laos. During 1969–70, Nixon sanctioned secret bombing strikes into Cambodia and Laos against Communist targets. Then he went even further, allowing U.S. and ARVN troops to cross the Cambodian border in ground assaults. To the U.S. public it looked like the start of a widening war in Southeast Asia, and they told Nixon so with protests.

Despite this, Nixon still won his second term in office in 1972 with a landslide victory. The very next year, the U.S. concluded its involvement in Vietnam after negotiations by Nixon's national security adviser, Henry Kissinger. Nixon had fulfilled his goal of bringing the U.S. out of the war. His position should have been unassailable, but the secret bombings of three years before came to light, including DoD falsification of documents. Nixon's final downfall, however, began when five men broke into the Democratic Party HQ on June 17, 1972. With an already questionable reputation, Nixon was drawn into the Watergate scandal. On August 8, 1974, he resigned.

RIGHT: An American serviceman hunches down on a jungle patrol, his weapon resting on his forearm for stability. Patches of sunlight streaming through the trees onto the jungle floor belie a hostile environment. Although he has removed his helmet, around his torso the serviceman is wearing a bandolier of bullets all of which – providing he manages to stay alive – he will later give to one of his colleagues operating an M-60 machine gun. In most instances during the Vietnam war, each infantry squad of the U.S. forces was fortified by at least one man who was armed with such a weapon. For ease of movement several members in the unit would drape ammunition belts on their bodies rather than carry them in their hands through the difficult terrains in which they were fighting. After long periods of inactivity firefights could break out with no warning at all, requiring the troops to have their weapons at the ready at all times.

in the countryside at a time, under strict orders not to engage any enemy forces, but only report the location of the enemy presence to the home base. Thus informed, the companies operating in the area could surround the enemy location with Fire Support Bases (FSBs), bombard it with artillery shots, and send infantry companies in to neutralize it. Davis also emulated the Army's air cavalry by making greater use of Huey helicopters to transport marine units into areas of trouble with greater speed.

The 3rd Marine Division had the opportunity to carry out at least some of these new tactics on the day of Nixon's inauguration at a place called Dewey Canyon. North of the A Shau Valley and near the Laotian border, a reconnaissance team located a large NVA supply depot that would be known as Base Area 611. With about a thousand trucks moving through it per day, the base area contained two infantry regiments, an artillery regiment, and an engineering unit. About three-fourths of the base was on the Laotian side of the border.

Suspecting that this activity was in preparation for another Tet offensive to be launched on Hue, Da Nang, and other lowland cities in northern South Vietnam, Davis ordered the commander of the division's 9th Regiment, Colonel Robert H. Barrow, to raid Area 611 and destroy its supplies.

Confronted with rugged jungle terrain, the enemy's proximity to Laos, and poor weather that prevented air strikes and reconnaissance flights, the 9th Regiment proceeded to Area 611 in a three-phase operation. The first phase involved the occupation and establishment of Fire Support Bases (FSBs) north of the target. On January 20, the regiment rode helicopters to FSBs Shiloh, Henderson, and Tun Tavern along the Da Kong River. Two days later, Company H from the regiment's 2nd Battalion headed south and established FSB Razor, which would be occupied by 1,500 marines and a battery of 105mm howitzers within 48 hours. On January 24, the 3rd Battalion completed Phase I by constructing FSB

ABOVE: Between Highway 13 and the town of Dau Tieng, members of the 1st Cavalry Division attack a Viet Cong base within a rubber plantation. Dissatisfied with the quality of the two ARVN divisions protecting Saigon, in 1969 General Creighton Abrams deployed this organization near to the capital, but the troops began to suffer from morale problems, caused by a growing sense of futility toward the war effort.

NEXT PAGE: A disabled casualty of the war makes his way through the crowds. As the conflict escalated, the streets of South Vietnamese cities teemed with many such unfortunate veterans, as well as war widows and orphans. By 1969, many South Vietnamese veterans were as frustrated about the war as some Americans.

ABOVE: In the Mekong Delta, a South Vietnamese soldier consumes a meal in front of a hungry child. Before the implementation of a land reform policy in 1970, the Saigon government made little effort to compete with the Viet Cong for the loyalty of impoverished villagers in the countryside.

RIGHT: Looking like something that would be more at home on a Paris catwalk, the appearance of this ARVN officer contrasts starkly with the ordinary soldiers behind him.

battalions marched from these positions closer to Area 611 in three columns spaced 1.2–1.8 miles (2–3 km) apart.

On February 2, amid a period of foul weather that continued to keep American aircraft from the area of operations, the NVA lashed out at its adversaries. From Laos, its 65th Artillery Regiment fired 122mm artillery rounds into FSB Cunningham, killing five marines with a direct hit on the base's fire direction center. Although Cunningham and Razor were well-supplied with bullets and rations, they were running out of artillery shells and unlikely to be replenished from the air. Thus deprived of both air superiority and artillery support for the marines occupying Hill 1175, Barrow feared that his forces were spread too thinly. On February 5, he ordered Company G to vacate its position and head north. During their retreat, the marines from this company suffered an ambush that killed five members and wounded 18. With help from a relief company sent by the 2nd Battalion, Company G reached LZ Dallas just west of FSB Razor on February 8. Almost two weeks of stormy weather had deprived the marines of their momentum and enabled the NVA to prepare for their upcoming onslaught.

When the skies cleared on February 10, Colonel Barrow moved his headquarters from FSB Razor to Cunningham and quickly reinforced FSB Erskine, thus completing Phase II of the Dewey Canyon campaign. Within two days, the marines began Phase III, in which the three battalions advanced on Base Area 611. The 2nd Battalion retook Hill 1175 and moved forward along the Laotian border, while the 1st Battalion passed through FSBs Razor and Erskine in the center and the 3rd Battalion proceeded southward from FSB Cunningham on the eastern flank. By this time, all three units began to encounter enemy resistance. Most notably, the 1st Battalion battered an NVA unit sent from the base area to launch a raid on FSB Erskine. Aided by artillery support, the marines killed 25 Communists.

The marines entered Base Area 611 on February 18, where Communist resistance

Cunningham 3.7 miles (6 km) southeast of Razor.

Phase II involved securing the countryside between the Fire Support Bases and Area 611, followed by the establishment of another FSB within artillery range of the target. To the west, Company G from the 2nd Battalion headed southwest to secure Hill 1175 on the Laotian border as a Landing Zone (LZ). Climbing steep slopes, the company took the hill with little resistance from NVA skirmishers. To the east, the rest of the Marine expedition established FSB Erskine, 3.1 miles (5 km) south of Cunningham and Razor. With this accomplished, Barrow inserted the 1st Battalion into FSB Razor, a middle position between the other two battalions. The three

Vietnamization

Vietnamization was nothing new. Enabling the South Vietnamese to fight their own war had been mooted as a general idea as far back as in 1963 under Kennedy,, and the concept had taken shape even more under Johnson's presidency. Yet it was Nixon who, in 1969, gave the term its physical meaning.

Vietnamization was absolutely necessary: the U.S. public wanted its boys to get out of the war. But Nixon could not afford to simply pull out altogether and abandon South Vietnam to its fate. The answer to this problem, Nixon found, was the gradual, staged withdrawal of U.S. troops from South Vietnam, while simultaneously building up ARVN forces in terms of combat skills and military hardware. The theory was that by the time the U.S. had left the war entirely, South Vietnam would be more than capable of dictating its own destiny, a destiny that would be free from communism.

Nixon presented the policy of Vietnamization to President Thieu at a meeting on Midway island on June 8, 1969. Thieu, and much of South Vietnamese society, was nervous. Vietnamization sounded like abandonment, and Thieu argued that if it was to occur, then the South Vietnamese would need both time and substantial military aid. The terms agreed, that very month Nixon started pulling out U.S. troops – some 25,000 to start.

Yet on paper the prospects for the South Vietnamese looked good. The NVA had been decimated during the Tet offensive, whereas the South could still muster some one million troops (1970), and all were armed with the latest U.S. weaponry. And the weaponry poured in. Tanks, APCs, attack helicopters, ships, assault rifles – the tools of destruction were there in numbers. But paper strengths had no correlation with real abilities. The training of South Vietnamese forces in sophisticated U.S. weapons required a plentiful supply of translators. These were often not available, and ARVN troops frequently went into battle without fully understanding how to deploy their kit. Furthermore, the ARVN was not a cohesive body of troops. Its ranks were riven with corruption and factional in-fighting, and so many tactical lessons were lost to partisan attitudes. Secretary of Defense Clark Clifford felt after visiting Vietnam that many of the generals in charge did not even want the war to end as they received a seemingly inexhaustible supply of U.S. money while the war continued.

Vietnamization may not have been perfect in practice, but it was the only way forward for the U.S. Therefore, as a policy, it received general public approval. Many people in the U.S., however, saw the policy of Vietnamization overtly contradicted in U.S. actions which took place in Cambodia and bombing raids carried out over the North. Yet Nixon knew he could not pull out too quickly. To placate public dissatisfaction, he promised that U.S. forces would carry out heavy 'spoiling actions' against NVA troops prior to their final departure, with the effect that the South would have more time to take charge with confidence.

We now know that without U.S. protectorship, the South was doomed. It did make some promising demonstrations of military initiative, such as the Lam Son 719 incursion into Laos. Yet even this had some U.S. backing either from artillery or advisers, and eventually turned into a horrible rout for the ARVN troops. Vietnamization required a disciplined and ordered South Vietnamese army. This was never achieved. In hindsight, all Vietnamization did was open the way for the NVA's final victory.

ABOVE: The real face of Vietnamization? Although perceived as a largely American-fought war, the number of casualties – both civilian and military – was much higher for the South Vietnamese. Many South Vietnamese felt that the U.S. were simply abandoning them, despite constant American efforts to reassure them.

LEFT: Green Beret Captain Louis Kingsley training a group of ARVN soldiers. Although with Nixon's election the U.S. armed forces began a process of disengagement, the Special Forces responsibilities if anything increased, as efforts were redoubled to raise the standard of training, equipment and morale to enable the South to prosecute the war successfully on its own.

ABOVE: Sergeant Jane Szalobryt, one of the many American advisers who were stationed in South Vietnam. In this picture, she is shown serving as a drill instructor for members of the South Vietnam Womens Armed Forces Corps, and appears to be instructing the women in particular about the positions of their hands as they march. Confronted with the reality of disengagement, senior officers in the United States military implemented a program of aid and assistance to make the South Vietnamese armed forces a viable institution capable of defending the country after the American departure. Naturally, these programs would apply to the the female as well as the male elements of the force.

stiffened and led to four days of fierce combat. However, improved weather conditions enabled the Americans to employ air strikes and napalm drops onto NVA positions. On February 20, Company C of the 1st Battalion received such assistance when it attacked and captured a well-armed hilltop bunker containing two 122mm howitzers. Within two days, the marine battalions had driven the NVA out of the part of Base Area 611 that was in Vietnam. Ironically, they soon discovered that the bomb craters left by earlier American air strikes had made excellent storage bins for enemy munitions.

Despite the success of the raid within South Vietnamese territory, most of the base area was actually on the Laotian side of the border. Atop highland ridges, the marines peered into Laos, where they could see convoys of trucks hauling supplies through Route 922. Technically, they were forbidden to cross the border to deal with this activity unless first

attacked by the enemy. However, Colonel Barrows decided to violate this rule by ordering the 2nd Battalion to enter Laos and finish the objective of disrupting NVA logistical operations in the base area. He planned to justify his decision by arguing that the discovery of 122mm howitzers in enemy hands meant that NVA presence on the border constituted a clear and present danger requiring an immediate reaction. On February 22, the battalion's Company H led the way with an early morning ambush on a truck convoy on Route 922, destroying three vehicles. The next day, the rest of the battalion moved into Laos, beat back NVA resistance, and occupied Base Area 611 until March 3.

In the end, General Abrams accepted Colonel Barrow's rationale for violating the rules of engagement; and the marine officer went on to enjoy a distinguished career. Because the campaign had concluded at a time when Hanoi had decided to launch another Tet offensive, Barrow and Abrams had good reason to presume that the actions of the 9th Marine Regiment effectively constituted a preemptive strike preventing the NVA from invading Military Region 1. During the Dewey Canyon operation, the marines lost 130 killed and 920 wounded. In return, they killed 1,617 NVA personnel and captured an impressive collection of supplies: 16 artillery pieces, 73 antiaircraft guns, several hundred rifles and pistols, about a million rounds of ammunition, and 200,000 pounds of rice. However, three NVA regiments would reoccupy Base Area 611 and logistical activity would resume there within two months.

While the 9th Marine Regiment ripped into Base Area 611, the NVA launched the 1969 Tet offensive on February 22. Like the 1968 offensive, it was a coordinated series of assaults upon provincial capitals throughout South Vietnam. Once again, local Viet Cong guerillas served as the spearhead in the offensive, although the severe depletion of NLF forces from the 1968 onslaught required the NVA to participate to a greater extent. Apart from these similarities, the 1969 Tet Offensive differed from the earlier campaign in many important ways. This time, the Communists focused almost exclusively on American military targets in an effort to demoralize the Americans further with massive casualties and thus facilitate a hastened withdrawal from Vietnam. The Communists also switched to smaller-unit operations, making much greater use of suicide sapper units infiltrating American installations and performing acts of sabotage.

Another important difference in the 1969 Tet Offensive was the fact that the Americans were much better prepared for it than they had been the previous year. Since New Year's Day, the Military Assistance Command, Vietnam (MACV) had been aware of some 37,000 NVA troops and several trucks moving south on the Ho Chi Minh Trail. During the first month of 1969, AC-123 and AC-130 gunships destroyed about a thousand trucks on the trail, although many others still got through to their destinations. Aware that the NVA would be dependent

ABOVE: A member of the South Vietnam Womens Armed Forces Corps takes aim on a target. Her weapon is an old carbine. The South Vietnam Womens Armed Forces Corps was established as part of an effort by President Nguyen Van Thieu to mobilize the population of the country against the Viet Cong and the North Vietnamese forces who threatened their homeland.
RIGHT: A young recruit in the South Vietnam Womens Armed Forces Corps smiles in front of a camera. Along with the Regional and Popular Forces, this women's organization would serve as a reservist component to the South Vietnamese military in the fight against Communism.

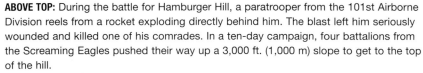

ABOVE TOP: During the battle for Hamburger Hill, a paratrooper from the 101st Airborne Division reels from a rocket exploding directly behind him. The blast left him seriously wounded and killed one of his comrades. In a ten-day campaign, four battalions from the Screaming Eagles pushed their way up a 3,000 ft. (1,000 m) slope to get to the top of the hill.

ABOVE: In the A Shau Valley, paratroopers from the 101st Airborne Division assail a North Vietnamese bunker at Hamburger Hill. In late May 1969, the division captured the summit of the hill after suffering about 300 casualties in 10 days.

RIGHT: Beneath an UH-1D Iroquois helicopter, soldiers from Company D, 2nd Battalion, 3rd Regiment, 199th Light Infantry Brigade advance on an area near Long Binh, north of Saigon. Some of the soldiers are riding on an M-113 Armored Personnel Carrier.

NEXT PAGE: Three paratroopers from the 101st Airborne Division cut loose with their M-16 assault rifles against communist positions on Hill 937. Although more accuarately named Ap Bia Mountain, Hill 937 rapidly acquired the sobriquet "Hamburger Hill."

ABOVE: A weary American serviceman attempts to find a moment of rest during a mission in the field, no doubt finding the blazing sunshine fairly uncomfortable. He is sporting a heavy bandolier of M-60 ammunition, draped over his shoulder. The majority of members of any unit would be responsible for carrying not just their own ammo but also belts for the unit's machine-gunner. The M-60, known as the "Pig" due to its weight, was a hungry weapon with a high rate of fire.

attacks or sapper infiltrations rather than pitched infantry battles. Near Saigon, Viet Cong sappers were especially destructive when they attacked the headquarters of the 25th Infantry Division, destroying or damaging 18 helicopters with satchel charges. The sappers did not carry rifles because their commander did not expect them to survive and thus saw no reason to sacrifice weapons along with his manpower. Ultimately, the 1969 offensive did not last as long as the previous one, petering out after three weeks of intense fighting. Nevertheless, the Communists succeeded in killing over 1,100 American servicemen while suffering only a third of the losses that they had sustained in the 1968 Tet Offensive.

Although the Communists succeeded in extracting their pound of flesh from their enemies, American commanders were able to find some signs of encouragement in the wake of the offensive. The lack of civilian targets in the campaign meant that there were few civilian casualties or refugees, thus indicating that the offensive had little if any adverse effect on the allied pacification campaign in the countryside. Moreover, most of the Communist invaders killed in action had actually met their deaths at the hand of ARVN forces. The good performance of South Vietnamese soldiers in the fighting provided General Abrams and other MACV officers with some hope for the future of the Saigon government.

Ambassador Bunker, General Abrams, Admiral John S. McCain, and other high-ranking officers were anxious to retaliate against the Communists. Alluding to an informal pact made between Hanoi and Washington during the last months of the Johnson administration, they noted that North Vietnam had agreed to refrain from launching attacks on the South in exchange for a pledge by the United States to stop bombing the North. Since the Communists had violated this agreement, these men urged a prompt reactivation of the air campaign on North Vietnam as a reprisal aimed at deterring Hanoi from future offensives. Within the White House, Kissinger agreed, claiming the United States could bring North Vietnam to its knees with a continuous

upon local NLF cells for security and reconnaissance, Abrams directed his field commanders to implement the new policy of deploying smaller patrol units to find and "beat the hell out of" Viet Cong cadres and guerilla forces. This vigorous patrolling technique forced the Communists to abstain from massing in formations larger than the company level if they wished to avoid detection before reaching their respective targets.

When the Communists struck, they hit more locations than they did in 1968. In fact, about 600 American bases and positions experienced a violent encounter. However, most of these incidents involved rocket and mortar

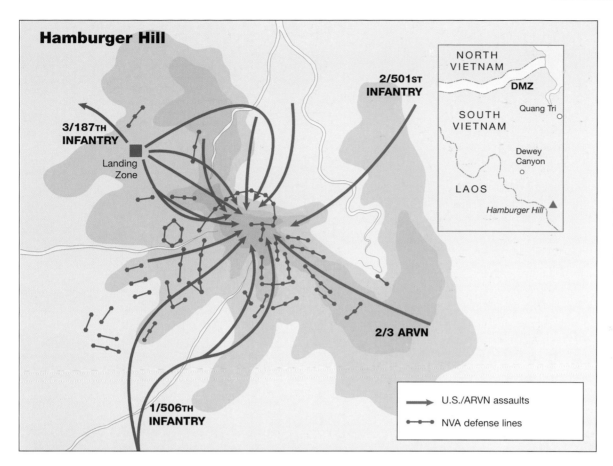

Hamburger Hill

3/187TH
INFANTRY

Landing
Zone

2/501ST
INFANTRY

2/3 ARVN

1/506TH
INFANTRY

NORTH
VIETNAM

DMZ

Quang Tri

SOUTH
VIETNAM

Dewey
Canyon

LAOS

Hamburger Hill

→ U.S./ARVN assaults

●—● NVA defense lines

BELOW: During the battle of Hamburger Hill, paratroopers from the 101st Airborne Division carry a wounded comrade – who is attached to a drip – to an evacuation helicopter. During the Vietnam War, the effective use of such aircraft brought wounded troops to medical facilities in relatively short periods of time and thus saved thousands of lives that would otherwise have been lost, although it exposed the helicopter crews to great risk.

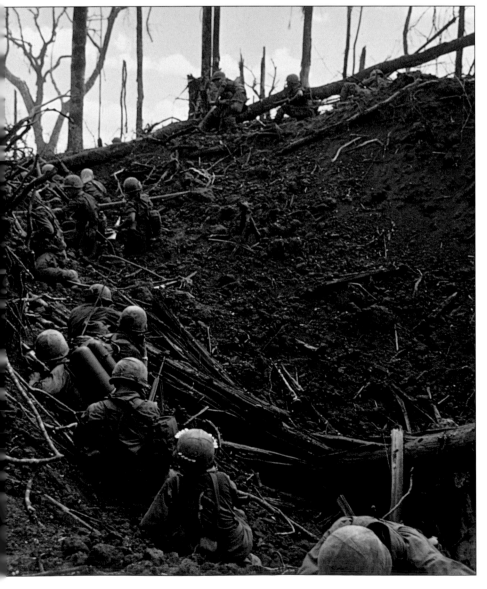

and aggressive bombing campaign. He even went as far as to claim that such an action would end the war with a favorable conclusion for the United States by 1970.

Nixon, however, declined to act on these suggestions, citing the likelihood of violent domestic protest to such a measure. Kissinger and other bombing advocates responded by arguing that Communist aggression had rendered swift retaliation an ethically justifiable action. Since Hanoi had drawn first blood, American antiwar activists had no moral right to protest any punitive measure initiated by the White House. Nixon rejected this advice, deciding to play it safe with the American public by refraining from reprisals, although in later years he agreed with Kissinger and cited this decision as the "greatest mistake" of his administration.

General Abrams did succeed in convincing Nixon to authorize a secret bombing campaign against Communist sanctuaries in Cambodia. Within that country, the NVA possessed a supply depot known to the Americans as Base Area 353. Located near the South Vietnamese border, the base area purportedly contained the fabled Center Office for South Vietnam (COSVN), which was the regional headquarters of the Vietnamese Communist Party. Some CIA analysts and other intelligence officers balked at this rumor, suspecting that COSVN was not a fixed installation, but merely a term collectively referring to the strategic planners of the Communist war effort in the South. However, the President believed differently. On March 18, Nixon launched Operation Breakfast, which consisted of 48 B-52 sorties on the base area.

Although the White House informed a few sympathetic Senators and Congressmen about the bombings, it took great pains to keep the American public from finding out about this clandestine action. In fact, the officers responsible for planning Operation Breakfast engaged in elaborate subterfuge to minimize the possibility of information leaks about it. On the ground, flight crews received orders to strike false targets in South Vietnam. Then, while they were en route to these locations,

FAR LEFT TOP: An unarmed Slick Huey transport helicopter and an escorting Cobra gunship fly over rice paddies. Introduced in September 1967, the AH-1G Cobra was designed specifically for attacking enemy targets. It could achieve a speed of 219 mph. (352 kmph) and its weaponry consisted of two 7.62mm miniguns, two 40mm grenade launchers, and several rockets.

FAR LEFT BOTTOM: American ground troops inch their way up a defoliated hill. One of them is armed with a flame-thrower, a weapon that was effective at burning enemy forces inside their bunkers. Not surprisingly, the men who were stuck with the duty of wielding this instrument were always priority targets for Communist marksmen during battles.

LEFT: On May 18, during the battle of Hamburger Hill, medics tend to a wounded paratrooper who had been injured in the face by a hand grenade. That day, the 101st Airborne Division had made considerable progress in its advance toward the summit, only to be thwarted by heavy rainfall that turned the barren slopes of the hill into rivers of mud.

NEXT PAGE: Weary and wounded paratroopers from the 101st Airborne Division move back down a slope of Hamburger Hill after conquering the area on May 20. In the foreground lies one "Screamin Eagle" who didn't make it. Angrily reacting to the carnage of this battle, the editors of an underground newspaper actually placed a fragging bounty of $10,000 on Lieutenant-Colonel Weldon Honeycutt, the commanding strategist of the battle. ("Fragging" was the practise of using a fragmentation grenade to kill your own officers, usually rolling the grenade into their tent while they slept.)

ABOVE: American medics treat wounded paratroopers waiting for evacuation helicopters during the battle of Hamburger Hill, which was part of a larger campaign aimed at clearing Communist forces out of the A Shau Valley, a hotbed of enemy activity near the Laotian border. .
RIGHT: A wounded paratrooper waits for evacuation in the A Shau Valley. In the spring of 1969, the Americans sought to deprive the North Vietnamese of this base of operations that kept Communist forces in the northern part of South Vietnam supplied.
FAR RIGHT: A member of the 101st Airborne Division surveys the A Shau Valley from the top of Hamburger Hill. During the 10-day battle, the Americans killed about 630 Communists, achieving a favorable kill ratio of 10 to one.

they received coded messages directing them continue until they reached their true bombing objective in Cambodia. Since the North Vietnamese denied possessing any sanctuaries on Cambodian soil, they would be in no position to protest the bombings without admitting that they actually had such facilities.

After the bombing crews finished their missions, MACV sent a 13-man team of Green Berets across the border to survey the damage inflicted upon the sanctuary. The upbeat commandos expected to find corpses, wreckage, and demoralized survivors strewn about the area. Instead, they parachuted into what their commanding officer described as a beehive that had been poked with a stick. Swarms of angry Communist soldiers quickly fell upon the Green Berets, killing all but two commandos who were lucky enough to reach a helicopter that returned them to South Vietnam. So far, the air war on the Communist presence in Cambodia did not seem to be very effective.

Nevertheless, Nixon continued with a fourteen month bombing campaign against

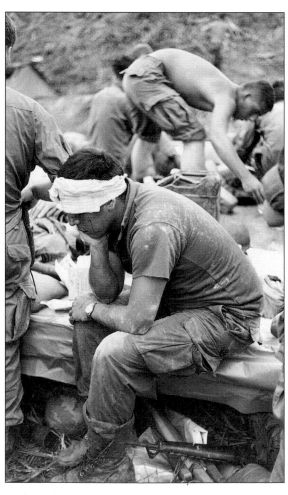

ABOVE: OV-10A "Broncos" flying over the Mekong Delta. They are equipped with jamming pods and flare dispensers to distract any surface-to-air missiles launched against them. The aircraft were used as reconnaissance and forward air control aircraft, controlling the air assets over a particular area of South Vietnam and deciding which assets to commit to any call for assistance from the ground troops. They often attracted ground fire from the Viet Cong, but could quickly call on air support if not immediately shot down.

NVA sanctuaries all over the Cambodian border. After Operation Breakfast came Operation Lunch, then Snack, then Dinner, then Dessert, and finally Supper. In May, someone within the White House or other relevant government agency leaked information about these "Menu" bombings to a *New York Times* reporter, who quickly published this piece of news. Not surprisingly, antiwar activists in the United States loudly denounced the expansion of the war into a neutral country.

The White House turned to international law to justify its actions. Specifically, Nixon cited a clause from the 1907 Hague Convention requiring neutral countries to prevent any warring power from occupying or making use of their land. If such countries failed to discharge this obligation, the other belligerent nation had a right to initiate an "appropriate counteraction" against this situation. Moreover, the White House claimed that the Cambodian ruler, Prince Norodom Sihanouk, had consented to sorties against NVA sanctuaries as long as they were carried out on unpopulated areas and in secret to

enable the prince to maintain his neutrality. Kissinger stressed that the United States Air Force did not bomb Cambodia itself, but only a group of North Vietnamese bases that were located in Cambodia against the wishes of that country's government. The fact that Prince Sihanouk had reopened full diplomatic relations with the United States during the bombing campaign underscored this point. At any rate, renewed NVA logistical activity in Cambodia indicated that the air campaign had at best a temporary effect that the White House had desired.

While B-52s attempted to shut down Communist operations in Cambodia, the Army's 101st Airborne Division found itself involved in a major battle about 3.1 miles (5 km) southeast of the Dewey Canyon campaign that had occurred earlier that year. Responding to a report of the 9th NVA Regiment moving toward Hue, the division's 3rd Brigade and the 4th Battalion from the 1st ARVN Regiment headed to the A Shau Valley to intercept this advancing column. Upon reaching its destination, the brigade broke up into company-size

RIGHT: An American serv-iceman aims his M-79 "Blooper" grenade-launch-er at an enemy target from behind the foilage within the jungle, while two of his comrades look on. This particular weapon fired a 40mm (1.57 in.) spherical projectile that would deto-nate on impact and hadf a kill radius of 5 yds. (4.5 m). In addition to these capa-bilities, the grenade-launcher could fire buck-shot, smoke, and tear-gas rounds. This is a fairly unusual photograph in that since 1963, most troops in Vietnam had not been equipped with this weapon, but rather with an M-16 assault rifle. Many of these weapons – as well as aircraft and rivercraft – would be inherited by the South Vietnamese after American forces had pulled out in 1973. As part of Vietnamization, the ARVN would be taught to use these weapons by American instructors, but as translators were in short supply, fighting with unusual pieces such as the blooper grenade-launcher would have limited effec-tiveness for the ARVN.

LEFT: American troops use sturdy palm trees as cover during a harsh firefight against an unseen, hidden enemy. Throughout the years of the Vietnam War, the elusiveness of Communist guerillas would serve to bedevil allied forces who, more accus-tomed to fighting with the tactics of open, conven-tional warfare, found these guerillas difficult to locate, and were themselves often sitting targets. The soldier in the foreground of this photograph keeps a pack of cigarettes secured under his helmet band, which was a common practice among combat troops in the field.

LEFT: A returnee from Vietnam receives a hero's welcome from his home town. By this stage of the conflict, as the anti-war movement gathered momentum, a soldier returning from the conflict was as likely to find cold indifference or downright hostility.
RIGHT: The message on his helmet cover shows exactly how much this soldier is going to miss South Vietnam. Although many American soldiers found Vietnam a very alien environment, some developed great affection for the country and its people during their tour of duty. Most American soldiers returned physically unharmed but the mental scars would affect all but a very few.
BELOW: In scenes reminiscent of the G.I.s leaving Europe after the end of World War II, American servicemen line the rail of a ship taking them back home to the United States.

Bringing them Home

Withdrawal became the dominant U.S. policy in Vietnam from 1969. Accepted by Johnson and then initiated forcefully by Nixon, withdrawal was based on the acceptance that the U.S. could no longer – politically or financially – afford to extend the war in Vietnam. The withdrawal of U.S. troops could not be achieved overnight without undermining the entire war effort, and fatally destabilizing the Saigon regime. Thus as Vietnamization took hold on the country, the U.S. began to hand over responsibility to the ARVN in a progressive, staged withdrawal, rather than a headlong rush for home.

However, the drop in U.S. manpower in Vietnam was prodigious, and the South must have started to feel an increasing sense of isolation, especially as the American assistance had lasted for years. In 1969, the peak of U.S. involvement, there were around 540,000 U.S. soldiers in Vietnam. With the official acceptance of Vietnamization, that number fell by 25,000 in a matter of just weeks. After that, the numbers were slashed every month. By 1970 the total had fallen to 415,000. By 1971 that figure had been almost halved: 239,000. The year 1972 continued the trend dramatically: only 47,000 remained, and in 1973 troop withdrawal continued at 14,300 troops a month until complete

withdrawal was achieved. From 1972 onwards, there were more U.S. logistical and advisory personnel than there were combat troops.

Nixon's pursuit of withdrawal satisfied the public that the years of bloodshed in Vietnam – for the U.S. at least – were being wound up. Yet the masses of troops coming home created an unforeseen problem. Combat soldiers returning from duty often received more suspicion and hostility than welcome. Vietnam had been an unpopular war, and massacres such as My Lai had painted U.S. troops in a harsh light. Ultimately, the irony was that although all wanted the U.S boys out of Vietnam, many did not want them home.

RIGHT: A U.S. soldier pauses in front of the camera during a patrol in the field searching for the enemy. He has used some of the local foliage to camoflage his helmet to aid him in keeping his presence hidden from them. He wears leather gloves to protect his hands, and a lightweight Flak jacket over his T-shirt. Patrolling in the jungle consisted of long periods of boredom. When excitement in the form of contact with the enemy came, it was usually over very quickly, with little indication of how many (if any) Viet Cong had been hit and a number of friendly casualties to be evacuated by a "Dust-Off" helicopter. After a while, the constant stress of waiting for an enemy attack would wear down the men in the field, and as a result they were frequently given opportunities for "R'n'R" (rest and recuperation) – but they were never far from the enemy, even in Saigon.

units and searched the countryside for the enemy. On May 10, Companies B and D from the 3rd Battalion, 187th Regiment reached a site on the Laotian border designated Hill 937, or Ap Bia Mountain. There they got into a firefight with members of the 39th NVA Regiment. This incident began an eleven-day campaign that the 101st paratroopers would call the Battle of Hamburger Hill.

The next day, Company B attempted to advance up the hill from the northwest, only to be hit with heavy losses by entrenched and well-armed enemy defenders who stopped the paratroopers in their tracks. During its ascent, Company B discovered a telephone network and documents indicating that Hill 937 was a major base of operations for the NVA regiment. Impressed with this information, the 3rd Battalion's commander, Lieutenant Colonel Weldon Honeycutt, committed the rest of his unit to an offensive on the enemy's positions. He sent Company C to assist the dwindling

ABOVE: Sporting a bandanna and necktie, a well-armed soldier negotiates his way through tall grass during a patrol near the Cambodian border. In addition to his M-16 rifle, he is armed with an M-26A1 fragmentation grenade, a device with a blast radius of over 10 yds. (9.1 m).

LEFT: A soldier from the 1st Infantry Division (The Big Red One) fills his canteen from a stream. In April 1970, this division returned to the United States. Like most troops in Vietnam, he is equipped with an M-16 assault rifle, the standard weapon of American infantry forces since 1963. Although light to carry in the jungle and effective at close range, it tended to jam when the chamber and gas tubes became dirty during battle.

LEFT TOP: A member of a local Peoples Self-Defense Force (PSDF) unit stands guard at a village while his neighbors harvest rice. During the process of Vietnamization, the Saigon government increasingly relied upon such auxiliary units to maintain security in the countryside.

RIGHT TOP: An American soldier with a bandolier of M-60 ammunition and a smoke grenade. Like the smaller M-16 rifle, the M-60 machine gun tended to jam when dirt or other particles accumulated over the chamber and gas tubes. The machine gun would sometimes keep firing when the shooter took his finger off the trigger.

OPPOSITE: Along a row of barbed wire, a patrolman and his German Shepherd dog keep watch at the perimeter of a base. Viet Cong and NVA sappers were good at infiltrating enemy facilities and wreaking havoc. The Communists also used bangalore torpedoes to breech defensive perimeters during ground assaults.

members of Company B, who were clearing LZs in their area to enable medevac helicopters to land and take their wounded comrades to safety. Meanwhile, Company D approached Hill 937 from the northeast and Company A stood back as a reserve unit. The advancing companies waited several hours while artillery and air strikes attempted to soften the NVA's positions.

The next day, Companies B and C attempted to coordinate an effective assault on enemy positions, only to be pummeled by gunfire that killed four paratroopers and wounded 33 by the end of the day. Throughout the night they hunkered down while AC-47 gunships strafed the slopes above them. On May 14, Companies B, C, and D moved forward again in an arc stretching across the northern and western slopes of the hill. Although Company B made good progress on the west, Company C bogged down in a particularly fierce gunfight to the north, prompting Honeycutt to order both companies to withdraw to more defensible positions. Then he sent in the rested members of Company A to relieve Company C and planned another assault for the following day. Meanwhile, the 3rd Brigade's commander, Colonel Joseph B. Conmy, Jr., sent the 1st

Battalion, 506th Regiment to hit Hill 937 from the southwest. Conmy reasoned that blocking off the entire western half of the hill would prevent NVA reinforcements and supplies from arriving via the Ho Chi Minh Trail in Laos.

On May 15, the 3rd Battalion paratroopers staggered past a network of claymore mines, reaching a point 450 ft. (150 m) from the crest of the hill. Honeycutt then ordered them to remain in place until the 1st Battalion arrived. The following day, the 3rd Battalion held its ground while the 1st Battalion struggled with stubborn NVA soldiers in its advance up the southwestern slope. On May 18, it joined with the 3rd Battalion in a coordinated assault to the top of the hill. The latter unit charged up slippery, muddy terrain into machinegun fire, rocket-propelled grenades (RPGs), and mines that inflicted heavy casualties. Despite such adversity, the 3rd Battalion came very close to the enemy's defensive perimeter at the top of the hill. Meanwhile, the 1st Battalion overcame similar obstacles to reach a good defensive position about a kilometer below the crest.

During the fighting, the 101st's division commander, Major General Melvin Zais observed the progress of the two battalions

LEFT: At the Special Forces Camp at Ben Het, a soldier watches out for enemy troops while applying a bandage to the head of a wounded comrade during a fight beyond the perimeter wire of the base. In May and June 1969, the Communists laid siege to the isolated camp, which was situated close to the Cambodian border. Immediate medical treatment in action like this saved men's lives, as it would help keep wounds stable until a helicopter could arrive and take the casualty to a medical center. A number of Special Forces men became casualties during the war, as they were always involved in the action.

RIGHT TOP: The scene only moments before, when the man now wounded in the left hand picture by a sniper's bullet is directing South Vietnamese colleagues in an operation to sweep the enemy away from the perimeter wire outside Ben Het.

from his helicopter. Determined to take Hill 937 even if the achievement required the deployment of his entire division, he ordered the 2nd Battalion, 501st Regiment, to attack the site from the northeast. He also sent two companies from the 2nd Battalion, 506th Regiment to reinforce the 3rd Battalion, 187th Regiment in the northwest. In addition, the 2nd ARVN Battalion, 3rd Infantry Regiment joined the fight, entering the field from the southeast. With these reinforcements thus helilifted into the offensive, the 101st Airborne's commanding officers planned a final push to take place on May 20. By this time, the stubborn enemy resistance on Hill 937 had convinced them that they had an important regimental command post in front of them. And with a gauntlet of American para-troopers and ARVN infantry "grunts" now forming a constricting gauntlet around this base, the NVA defenders had nowhere to go.

The night before May 20, 1st Battalion, 506th Regiment managed to reach a point about 600 ft. (200 m) below the top of the hill. The following morning, the Airborne/ARVN attack force began its coordinated assault upon

ABOVE: In preparation for a mission, Navy Sea, Air, or Land (SEAL) commando – on the right – briefs a helicopter pilot about the operation. One of the most elite units in the United States armed forces, the Navy SEALs performed clandestine operations from deep within enemy-held territory, and were engaged in various actions, ranging from surveillance to assassination. They were especially active during the conflict in the Mekong Delta.

LEFT: Aboard an Assault Support Patrol Boat, a sailor mans a machine gun turret. This particular machine gun is a double-barrel, 50-caliber model, and the look of concentration on the sailor's face shows how difficult this weapon was to wield in battle conditions. Belts of ammunition can be seen either side of the weapon. Also armed with two grenade launchers, one 18mm mortar, and one 20mm (0.78 in.) cannon, the craft which this machine gun armed, the Assault Support Patrol Boat, was capable of traveling at a speed of 16 knots. Its hull was about 16 yds. (14.6 m) long and was manufactured from steel.

RIGHT: A group of standard River Patrol Boats dock in the mud of a riverbank, catching the attention of several curious spectators, from children to older people, one of whom is peering onto the deck to get a better view, while another plays in a small canoe next to the boat. Although not as large or as heavily-armed as the Assault Patrol Boat or many other riverine craft, the River Patrol Boat was nevertheless relatively fast, and was capable of traveling at speeds of up to 25 knots. The Stars and Stripes flag hangs from both flagpoles identifying the craft to fellow travelers.

BELOW: Along the Mekong River, a lone sailor on the stern of a patrol boat points his heavy machine gun at a target somewhere on the shoreline, while strong waves roll in toward the shore. The many piles of spent shells lying around on the deck of the craft indicate that the sailor has recently been forced to make extensive use of his weapon. Near the center of the picture, a high wave can be seen at the shoreline, possibly created by a sailor who was firing from another vessel.

ABOVE: A local unit from the Peoples' Self-Defense Force patrols a pathway through an area near their community. Unlike other South Vietnamese reservist organizations, PSDF volunteers lacked state of the art weaponry, even having to share rifles with some of their comrades.

RIGHT: Riverine patrolmen watch out for enemy activity along the banks of the Mekong River. Atop a flagpole on their boat flies a Confederate battle flag. In many instances, river sailors displayed their state or regional banners, as well as displaying the flag of the United States.

FAR RIGHT: A field officer transmits some recently obtained information on a portable radio during an operation. Flying overhead, a reconnaissance helicopter gets ready to locate enemy forces.

what was left of the NVA base. By this time the Communists were severely depleted, and did not open fire until they could see the whites of their enemies' eyes. Aided by artillery and mortar fire, the paratroopers of the 3rd Battalion, 187th Regiment reached the top of Hill 937, only to find themselves struggling with tenacious adversaries who kept fighting until every bunker on the crest was destroyed. The other battalions reached the summit with only scattered instances of resistance. Miraculously, not a single American or South Vietnamese soldier died during this last offensive in the battle.

Like most other battles of the war, Hamburger Hill had produced a lopsided casualty count. Fifty-six Americans died during the engagement, while over 600 NVA soldiers met their death in the fighting. With some justification, Major General Zais claimed that the battle was a victory for the 101st Airborne Division's 3rd Brigade. After all, it had been sent to the A Shau Valley to find enemy forces in the area and destroy them; and it had accomplished exactly that feat. Back in the United States, antiwar politicians denounced the battle as a meaningless killing spree that did nothing to bring the war closer to a conclusion. In fact, Hamburger Hill seemed to be an indication that Nixon was continuing the old war of attrition strategy from the Johnson administration. Ultimately, both Nixon and

KIT CARSON SCOUTS

In the intelligence war against the VC and NVA, what was needed more than anything were people who knew how the Communists thought, who understood their motivation and tactics. These were the Kit Carson scouts. The scouts were VC and NVA defectors, individuals persuaded to cross sides with promises of amnesties, social support, and financial incentives. Their recruitment was part of the Chieu Hoi ("open arms") program. Initiated from 1967, Chieu Hoi drew out some 7,000 defectors or civilians from South Vietnam's border regions who were familiar with VC/NVA cross-border movements. From recruitment they were trained in counterinsurgency at the Kit Carson school in Quang Tri.

Once trained, the mission was betrayal. Many scouts were highly motivated once turned against the Communist cause, especially after Tet when many VC were appalled with the NVA tactics which had practically destroyed them. The scouts were able to reveal key Communist people, bases, and operating methods, leading to significant actions by U.S. special forces and the CIA. The scouts also participated in many U.S. Army and Marine Corps operations, killing their former comrades with little compunction.

What became of the scouts once Vietnam fell in 1975? For most of them, the future was bleak. When the war ended, 4,000 were still in Vietnam; half are believed to have met execution. The other half either fled to refugee centers in Thailand or the U.S. Either way, it was a poor repayment for a courageous service.

LEFT: A mixed team of American and South Vietnamese propagandists prepare for take off in a helicopter which is equipped with a collection of loudspeakers attached by the door. Two of the men are engaged in discussion, both carrying weapons, while on the floor of the aircraft, stacks of papers can be seen bundled together ready to be scattered from the helicopter onto the terrain below. During this kind of psychological warfare operation, the helicopter crew usually consisted of four Americans and three Vietnamese, and these personnel would be responsible for broadcasting messages through the outside speakers to enemy forces. This would have the effect of both demoralizing the enemy forces and bolstering the morale of any allies or pro-Saigon villagers who happened to be in the area. The Communists would spread their own propaganda on foot by night, either in printed form or face-to-face with civilians in villages without an American or ARVN presence.

MACV accepted this assessment; and the battle would be the last one in which the Americans defined their victory in terms of the enemy body count attained. For the rest of the war, American officers would eschew such search-and-destroy tactics in favor of the small-unit maneuvers championed by Marine Major General Raymond Davis.

By the time the battle of Hamburger Hill was winding down, the Nixon administration had developed its policy of Vietnamization into a two-phase plan. Phase I required the United States to maintain a military presence in South Vietnam sufficient enough to protect its client state for the time being. Phase II was to ensure that the South Vietnamese armed forces were strong enough to hold their own against both the NLF and the NVA. On June 8, Nixon met with Nguyen Van Thieu at Midway to articulate the details of this policy. The meeting resulted in a plan in which the United States would pull 25,000 troops out of

ABOVE: During a training session aboard a river patrol boat, an American sailor and his South Vietnamese pupil converse with local villagers. The patrolmen are operating along the Bassac River, east of the Mekong Delta and near the southern tip of South Vietnam.

LEFT: Ho Chi Minh (1890–1969), perhaps the most well-known political revolutionary in Southeast Asia, served as the first President of the Democratic of Vietnam. His death in 1969 did not discourage the North Vietnamese from continuing the war to unify the nation under Communist rule. During his reign, Ho governed with skilled politicians and military commanders, and these figures carried on the war effort after he was gone.

ABOVE LEFT: North Vietnamese volunteer workers rebuild a bridge damaged by an American air strike. Bridges were favorite targets for pilots to disrupt transportation within North Vietnam.

LEFT: NVA artillerists man an antiaircraft weapon supplied by the Soviet Union or China. The NVA deployed such emplacements within the Democratic Republic of Vietnam and at points along the Ho Chi Minh Trail in Laos and Cambodia.

South Vietnam immediately, followed by future withdrawals to be carried out in periodic increments. Meanwhile, the American armed forces still in South Vietnam would help the country increase the size of its military to about a million regulars, to be armed with state-of-the-art equipment and trained by American advisers.

Although the American advisers performed their roles well, they could only do so much to improve the quality of ARVN as an effective institution. In fact, they were well aware that Vietnamization could only succeed if the South Vietnamese government and armed forces were determined to make it succeed. However, South Vietnam's military culture possessed dysfunctional features that the Americans could not eradicate. Most ARVN soldiers were conscripts required to serve from the ages of 18 to 40. This long period of servitude along with the poor pay and lack of resting time from work caused about 125,000 desertions in 1969, with even higher numbers in subsequent years. Demographic differences between the officers and other ranks further contributed to morale problems. Most officers were affluent urban Catholics holding sway over privates tending tp be Buddhist peasants.

ABOVE: B-52 bombers or "BUFF"s as they were known, flew missions from the American military base on Guam in the Pacific Ocean. Originally intended as another base from which to strike at the Soviet Union in case of a nuclear attack, Guam saw a massive expansion program during the Vietnam war, as it was the only airfield with the facilities to service these huge aircraft. It had the added attraction of being invulnerable to North Vietnamese attack.

LEFT: In Washington, Congressional Representative Alexander Pirnie, a Republican from New York, picks the first capsule for the national draft lottery and prepares to announce from the stand the birthdate selected. All eligible American men who were born on the date chosen, September 14, were then liable to be drafted into the armed forces and these men would be sent on to Vietnam. To the left of Alexander Pirnie is Lieutenant-General Lewis Hershey, the outgoing Selective Service director who was in charge of administering the national draft at the time.

BOTTOM LEFT: At American University in Washington, a student named Scott Jenkins contemplates his future, sitting behind a railing on the campus grounds. He has just received his draft notice and faces the prospect of going to VIetnam and possible death. Despite Nixon's commitment to disengagement from the Vietnam War, the President continued implementing the draft until 1973, and with the introduction of the national draft lottery, fewer U.S. citizens could manage to dodge it.

OPPOSITE PAGE: A disgruntled Marine expresses his disillusionment with the war with graffiti which has been written on his uniform. By 1969, antiwar sentiment was not just becoming widespread among the people back home, but also among combat troops. Having seen many comrades die in action, and daily facing the prospect of death themselves, these combat troops were now beginning to question the necessity of killing and dying for a cause that their country was abandoning.

An artillerist uses the grisly remnants of an earlier Viet Cong attack to create an effective warning sign to discourage the enemy from returning for another attempt. Artillery firebases were protected with barbed wire and Claymore mines as well as perimeter fences, sentries, and often watchtowers. Vegetation and trees would be cut back to give an exposed "killing ground" which any attacker would have to cross before reaching the base itself. However such defenses could not prevent mortar attacks.

Within the officer corps, well-connected political officers often enjoyed more frequent promotions than did talented and experienced combat officers.

The Communists sought to expose the ineffectiveness to the South Vietnamese armed forces with a two-month siege of the Ben Het base near Cambodia and Laos. In May, the NVA descended upon the facility, which was occupied by a unit of South Vietnamese marines commanded by Colonel Nguyen Ba Lien. The marines performed well for about a month, aided by 500 American artillerists stationed at nearby Dak To. Then the marines grew tired of fighting and pulled back into the perimeter of their base, thus allowing the NVA intruders to control the surrounding countryside and threaten the American artillerists, who now had to guard their own perimeter.

A month into the siege, a group of American engineers accompanied by South Vietnamese guards occupied the road between Ben Het and Dak To in order to repair damages brought upon it. When the enemy attacked them, the guards fled, leaving the engineers to absorb a withering assault that killed 19 men and wounded another 120. After another month, while Colonel Lien maintained a safe distance from the action and marked time, the NVA withdrew, satisfied that it had made its point. In Hanoi, the Communists proclaimed that the incident revealed that the United States would never be able to use Vietnamese "puppets" to prosecute a successful war against their own countrymen.

While the NVA demoralized the South Vietnamese near Cambodia, its Viet Cong confederates harassed the Americans at Cam Ranh Bay. After losing so many guerillas in the Tet Offensives, the NLF had resolved to limit itself to small-scale terrorist strikes against its enemies. On August 7, a team of Viet Cong sappers infiltrated the north side of the American base at about midnight, probably with the aid of sympathetic insiders employed within the perimeter. While inside, the sappers tossed explosives into the base

hospital, opened fire with machineguns, and destroyed several other buildings before they left the way they came. Without losing a single guerilla, they killed two Americans, wounded another 98, and damaged 19 buildings. Like other sapper attacks, the raid on Cam Ranh Bay enabled the NLF to serve notice to the Americans in Vietnam and back in the "real world" that it was still a potent force capable of inflicting physical and psychological damage upon them.

This greater reliance on small-unit strikes was a logical response to the tactical changes enacted by the Americans. By operating as small cells, the Communists could avoid detection easier and maintain smaller and better-hidden caches of weapons and supplies. Moreover, the lack of noticeable concentrations

ABOVE: A close-up view of the business end of a M16 assault rifle, the standard issue weapon of both American and South Vietnamese servicemen at this time. It was much more sensitive to dirt and mud than its Soviet-designed (and Chinese-built) counterpart, the AK-47, examples of which were buried and left for days, before being dug up and fired without any problems – a level of reliability about which M16 operators could only dream.

My Lai

On March 16, 1968, a flight of helicopters landed the men of C Company, 1st Battalion, 20th Infantry Brigade near the hamlet of My Lai, in Quang Ngai province, Vietnam. What they went on to do there would shock the world, and would irrevocably alter international and domestic perceptions about who were the good guys in the Vietnam War, and who were the bad guys.

In the days leading up to March 16, the men of C Company had been literally pushed to their limit. Many friends of the company's troops had been mercilessly shot down in front of them by cunning VC snipers. Booby traps had stripped some men of their limbs and some of their lives. Fatigue and the desire for vengeance had conspired to cloud many soldiers' thinking. My Lai was supposed to be the place in which the U.S. troops could have their revenge. The hamlet was thought to be Viet Cong occupied and the soldiers were well prepared for a firefight. What they found instead in My Lai were nothing but civilians, these being mainly old men, women, and children. For reasons which are still debated by many to this day, the GIs nevertheless turned their guns on the Vietnamese hamlet's defenseless occupants.

The slaughter was horrific. The GIs filled trenches with terrified, pleading people and proceeded to machine gun them down without mercy, right down to babes clutched in their mothers' arms. Children and old men were bayoneted, and women were raped and shot within their homes. The indiscriminate blood lust went on for hours and hours, and by the time it had finished, up to 347 civilians had been slaughtered. The men of C Company then simply recovered their weapons and left.

The horror of My Lai might have lain undiscovered, had not a veteran, Ronald L. Ridenhour, written letters to Nixon and other government officials giving some outline of what occurred at the village. These letters were not written until over one year after the event and, following a report in the *New York Times,* the Army was compelled to investigate. A panel convened under the leadership of Lieutenant General William Peers and proceeded to bring charges against 15 officers involved in the assault. Particular focus would rest on Lieutenant William Calley, a young officer who was responsible for overseeing the horrific massacre of some 200 of My Lai's inhabitants, and he would later be the target of much outrage within the American media.

ABOVE: Lieutenant William Calley, seen by many as the scapegoat for the My Lai atrocity, attends his trial. As a result of his actions on March 16, he was sentenced to life imprisonment, a charge that was later reduced to twenty years. It is impossible to know whether My Lai was just a horrific aberration, or an example of something far more commonplace than the U.S. Army was willing to admit.

The press coverage of the trial was intense. America was stunned, unable to believe that its soldiers could have committed such atrocities. Yet more sinister was the implication that My Lai was not an exception during the Vietnam conflict. Search and destroy was a tactic that needed an end result, and such a result was achieved through body counts. With senior officers usually being isolated from actual field conditions, civilians provided one method of achieving these quotas. My Lai was reported at the time as an action in which 128 Viet Cong had been killed, but only three weapons had been captured. A sinister pattern of similar figures emerged from other engagements.

My Lai blew away naivete about what was going on in the jungles of Vietnam. Calley was sentenced to life imprisonment (later reduced to 20 years), but many felt that he was the tip of the iceberg and something of a scapegoat for the whole military system. Perhaps in recent times we have come to a broader understanding of the massacres in Vietnam as what happens when young men are traumatized by war and placed far from the rule of law.

RIGHT: One of the survivors of the My Lai massacre. The graphic accounts or apparently pre-meditated and organized butchery carried out by the men of the Americal Division in March 1968. In the years following John F. Kenedy's presidency, many Americans still saw the United States as the natural champion of democracy and the defender of the free world against commu-nism. The brutal treatment of civilians was something Americans associated with their communist enemies, or the excesses of Nazi Germany. The fact that American boys were capable of this treatment of peo-ple they had supposedly been sent to defend was a bitter pill to swallow.

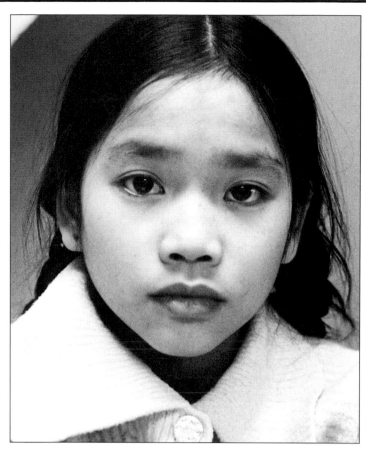

ABOVE: Soldiers preoccupied with the struggle to conquer an elusive enemy and often unable to tell civilian from guerrilla, often tarred all with the same brush. The uncertainty and terror etched on the faces of this South Vietnamese family speaks volumes about the treatment they expect.

LEFT: The armored might of the U.S. military represented here by M113 armored personnel carriers and M551 Sheridan tanks. Although of limited use in the rugged terrain of the Central Highlands or the deep jungle, armored formations played a vital role in the war. They were most often used keeping open South Vietnam's road network, a constant target for the communists as they attempted to disrupt communications within the south. Without the ability to maneuver the Allied forces were effectively "sitting ducks". However U.S. armored formations possessed a firepower which even the best equipped NVA units could not hope to match. The Sheridan main gun's "flechette" anti-personnel round in particular could decimate entire units. As such regular patrols by armored columns such as that shown here were an effective way of keeping the highways open.

RIGHT: Naval crewmen arm a rocket emplacement on a helicopter, the ubiquitous Huey. These weapons fired 2.75-in. (69.8 mm) projectiles at ground targets. Rocket types included standard explosives, white phosphorus, and anti-personnel rounds known as 'Nails'. The door gun, an M2 Browning 0.5 in. (12.7 mm) caliber weapon, is clearly visible on the right hand side of the photograph. Door guns were used to suppress enemy fire from the ground during an insertion or pickup. The gun, still in service today, was also used extensively in World War II.

of ground forces made it difficult for the Americans to employ B-52 carpet bombings against NLF guerillas operating in the countryside. The use of sapper attacks also fit in well with the overall Communist strategy of winning through attrition. Under this situation, all the Viet Cong fighters had to do was to endure and hasten the American departure by poking and stabbing their enemies with harassing actions.

However, not all Viet Cong operatives were willing to engage in high-risk infiltration actions for the benefit of the NVA. In fact, many of them became disillusioned at the lack of tangible progress being made in the direction of final victory, despite the enormous sacrifices made during the two Tet Offensives. This sense of frustration led some Southern Communists to suspect that the Hanoi government saw them as expendable resources. Thus, about 28,000 NLF guerillas "rallied" (defected) to the Saigon government during 1969, twice as many as in the previous year.

Despite this morale problem within the Communist ranks, circumstances back in the United States indicated that the war of attrition was going against the Americans. During the latter months of 1969, American casualty rates dropped steadily; and intelligence reports indicated that the Communists were not planning any major offensives for the rest of the year. Peace advocates in the United States interpreted these revelations as an indication that Hanoi was willing to de-escalate and negotiate an end to the war. Nixon himself responded by ordering MACV to refrain from dynamic military campaigns in favor of continuing the effort to strengthen ARVN. He would also pull over 60,000 American troops out Vietnam by the end of the year. Despite these concessions, antiwar activists planned a series of demonstrations in Washington and other cities to clamor for a quicker end to the conflict.

Meanwhile, Kissinger proceeded to Paris to begin secret peace talks with the North Vietnamese in August. He and Nixon retained a secret scheme to re-escalate hostilities if these talks should stall. Specifically, the White House threatened to mine Haiphong harbor,

ABOVE: In the Mekong Delta, pilots aboard a UH-1B helicopter prepare to take off from a tank landing ship and start another mission. These men are members of Light Helicopter Attack Squadron Three (HAL-3).

NEXT PAGE: In many ways the ultimate price of the conflict in Vietnam was paid by the civilian population rather than the military. Caught in the middle and at the mercy of both sides their suffering was incalculable. This scene of devastation would be repeated countless times before peace came.

RIGHT: A "Stars and Stripes" bearing a peace symbol flies in front of the Washington monument. Although highly visible and vocal, it is debatable whether the anti-war movement ever represented the views of the majority of Americans. Nixon's landslide victory in the 1972 presidential election, despite the expansion of the war into Cambodia and and Laos, and the heavy bombing of the former suggests that the "silent majority" may have had a somewhat different view.
RIGHT: Thousands of U.S. antiwar protestors march in front of the Capitol dome in Washington, DC. In this rally, many of the activists can be seen waving the flag of the National Liberation Front (NLF), which was then the political arm of the Viet Cong. Many of the more radical elements of the antiwar movement continued to openly sympathize with the National Liberation Front throughout the war, seeing this organization as the true political representative of the Vietnamese people. Several celebrities – such as Jane Fonda – would be prominent in these antiwar movements, and would attract much controversy by announcing their hopes that the enemies of the U.S. forces would defeat them. After the learning of the horrors of the 1968 Tet Offensive and the casualties which the American soldiers had endured there, domestic opposition to the Vietnam War became more organized, active, and widespread throughout the country. This public action served to create a siege mentality within the White House as Nixon expanded the war into other parts of Southeast Asia, and many U.S. citizens were placed under close surveillance.

impose a naval blockade, and unleash a relentless bombing campaign against any "military" targets throughout the North in the event of a stalemate in Paris. Kissinger went as far as to advocate bombing dykes on the Red River in order to flood the farmlands of North Vietnam. During this first round of talks, negotiations did indeed reach an impasse when the North Vietnamese representative demanded the immediate dissolution of the Saigon regime.

A month later, Ho Chi Minh died at the age of 79. Nixon and Kissinger hoped that Ho's death would create a leadership crisis in Hanoi. However, the North Vietnamese government remained in the able hands of Prime Minister Pham Van Dong and General Vo Nguyen Giap. In fact, Ho's deteriorating health had already enabled these men to assume much more power in earlier years. Although the death of Ho plunged North Vietnam into a state of mourning, it did not lead to an internal political struggle analogous to the infighting that had afflicted the Soviet Union after the death of Vladimir Lenin.

In November, the American homefront became more demoralized when several newspapers published an article written by Seymour Hersch detailing the massacres carried out by units from the Americal Division at My Lai and My Khe the previous year. At about the same time, the Army appointed a blue-ribbon commission headed by Lieutenant General William Peers to investigate the massacres. After 16 months of research, the Peers inquiry would determine that the killings were more than just scattered acts of excessive brutality, instead recognizing a premeditated atrocity ordered by Lieutenant William Calley at the site of the killings and tolerated by higher-ranking officers determined to maintain a cover-up. The public revelations of the massacres coincided with the "March Against Death," a three-day antiwar demonstration in Washington with 300,000 participants.

Disillusionment also sank in among the American troops still in Vietnam. Many of them were involuntary conscripts who had internalized the sentiments of antiwar activists back home and sported long hair, peace signs, and hippie beads. Increasingly, combat soldiers actively avoided fights with the enemy and became insubordinate when ordered into battle. In a few extreme instances, rebellious troops assassinated officers who attempted to preserve the chain-of-command. Others acquired an active dislike for the Vietnamese "gooks" and "dinks" who did not seem to appreciate the blood that Americans had been shedding in the war against Communism. This antipathy led many soldiers and marines to look upon all Vietnamese people as enemies and even as subhumans whose lives were unworthy of respect. Widespread opposition to the prosecution of Lieutenant Calley underscored this feeling. Not surprisingly, Vietnamese citizens responded with similar feelings of hostility. By the end of the decade, Vietnam had acquired a dysfunctional character that rendered Vietnamization a difficult task to accomplish. However, the curtailment of Communist activity in the South gave MACV much reason to believe that pacification was working in the countryside.

Bleeding Cambodia

At the end of the 1960s, American and South Vietnamese military commanders looked forward to the upcoming decade with feelings of guarded optimism. After the Tet Offensives and other costly battles, the National Liberation Front (NLF) had become so depleted that the main burden of carrying on the war had fallen into the hands of the North

Vietnamese Army (NVA). By 1970, at least two-thirds of the 125,000 Communist soldiers operating in the South were Northern regulars who were skilled fighters but lacked either the familiarity with the southern terrain or the friendly relationships with local villagers that NLF (Viet Cong) guerrillas had enjoyed. With the Viet Cong's political and espionage network disrupted by high casualty rates and vigorous counterinsurgency measures, the remaining Communists in the South had difficulty supplying themselves or moving in the countryside. Moreover, the hardships suffered by the NLF created morale problems among its surviving operatives. Told by their Northern comrades that they still had many struggles ahead of them before final victory, some Viet Cong insurgents surrendered or simply disbanded and returned to their villages under a guarantee of amnesty which had now been offered to them by Saigon.

Although the Phoenix Program had fostered a climate of oppression and abuse in the South Vietnamese villages, by 1970 it had proven itself a formidable counterinsurgency measure against the Viet Cong's system of infiltration and supply. In three years, it had ensnared over 19,000 suspected agents, 6,000 of whom were killed in action or executed. Communist officials conceded that the measure was an effective adversary that had exposed thousands of their operatives, liquidated several bases, and undermined the effectiveness of their operations. Frustrations engendered by the Phoenix Program and the Accelerated Pacification Campaign contributed to the NVA's decision to abandon large-scale campaigns like the Tet Offensives in favor of harassing skirmishes until the last of the American forces departed.

The Allies also employed more traditional methods to pacify the countryside. Early in 1970, the American Army's 9th Division tamed the Mekong Delta with a campaign of artillery bombardment, crop-defoliation, and population relocation. In the central region, American marines and Korean troops employed similar methods. Meanwhile, American soldiers organized into mobile strike-force units uncovered a large collection of enemy munitions in a cache northeast of Saigon in February. Collectively,

ABOVE: South Vietnamese troops masquerade as VC during a training exercise. As America disengaged, efforts were made to improve the training and equipment of the ARVN.
RIGHT: A Cambodian boy loads an American-made M-16 rifle for his father. By 1969, the war in Vietnam was spreading across the border as American bombers began bombing North Vietnamese sanctuaries within Cambodia.

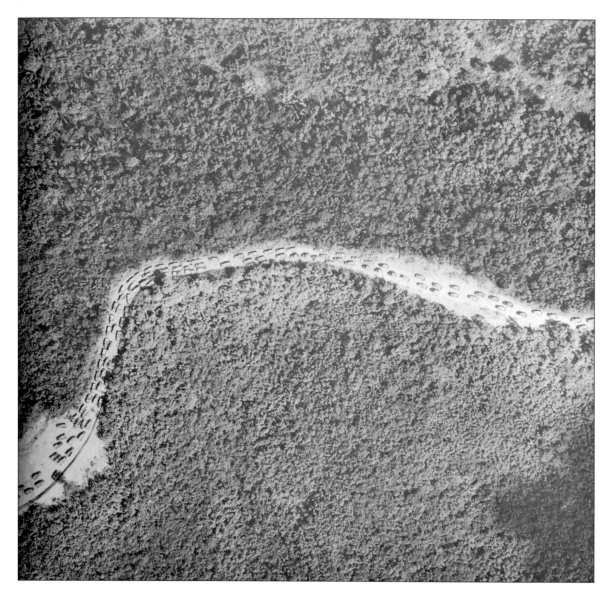

LEFT: An aerial view of the Ho Chi Minh Trail shows several trucks transporting supplies to Communist troops in Laos, Cambodia, and South Vietnam. During their war against France, the Vietminh had used this route when it was still a primitive footpath. In May 1959, the Hanoi government created an engineering unit called Group 559, which developed the trail into an impressive supply and communications highway.

BOTTOM LEFT: Attempts were made to clear sections of the Ho Chi Minh Trail of its protective covering of jungle, which concealed the VC supply convoys. The defoliation program was controversial, and the widespread use of chemical agents proved an ecological time bomb.

the raiders seized 150 tons of supplies. One booby-trapped arsenal called the "Rang-Rang Cache" contained rocket launchers, grenade rifles, ammunition, telephones, shovels, and tires.

Despite these achievements, lingering problems plagued the allied war effort. Although badly mauled and demoralized, the NLF underground was not completely broken and maintained some sympathy among villagers still resentful toward the Americans and their clients. The residents of Saigon and other population centers occasionally found themselves reminded of the Viet Cong's durability when Communist forces fired rockets and mortar shells into their neighborhoods from nearby areas. On July 11, Communist artillerists practically destroyed the pro-Saigon hamlet of Thanh My near Da Nang, killing 74 residents with brutal mortar fire.

To the north, crack troops from the 6th NVA Regiment drew blood at the A Shau Valley near Laos in July. At Firebase Ripcord they bombarded a unit of paratroopers from the American 101st Airborne Division for three weeks until the Americans evacuated the position. During the attack, the Communists killed 61 paratroopers and wounded 345. The NVA regiment then proceeded north to Firebase O'Reilly, which was occupied by the 1st Regiment of the Army of the Republic of Vietnam (ARVN). After sustaining a two-month assault, the ARVN unit retreated with heavy casualties in September. Although the Communists had difficulty operating in the interior of South Vietnam, they remained a formidable presence on the borders.

This presence on the edges of South Vietnam enabled the NVA to maintain its logistical system from Hanoi to the front.

Early in 1970 the Military Assistance Command, Vietnam (MACV) ascertained from its intelligence-gathering services that the American bombing campaign had not done enough to halt the flow of weapons through the Ho Chi Minh Trail. Although bombers had destroyed 50 percent more trucks in 1969 than the year before, the enemy still succeeded in sending about 4,000 tons of war materiel to Communist sanctuaries that year. During the same period, the NVA also received almost 2 tons of supplies at the port of Sihanoukville on the Cambodian coast.

The NVA was determined to protect its supply network from American bombers. It equipped many of its *binh trams* (fortified distribution units) on the Ho Chi Minh Trail with antiaircraft artillery pieces and surface-to-air missiles (SAMS). Thus equipped, the *binh trams* had become well-organized command

ABOVE: Sent from the Soviet Union, a cargo ship docks at a harbor in North Vietnam. Throughout the war, Haiphong and Vinh would serve as excellent ports at which the government in Hanoi was able to receive weapons and supplies from the Soviet Union and other Communist allies. Vessels sent from the Soviet Union and China carrying supplies for the NVA would often dock at the Cambodian port of Sihanoukville.

RIGHT: From an altitude of 3,500 feet (1,067 m), the crewmen from an American naval aircraft provide an aerial view photograph of part of the Ho Chi Minh Trail which ran through Laos. Although warplanes and helicopter gunships from the United States often managed to destroy hundreds of trucks on the trail every year, tons of supplies nonetheless were able to pass through, and these would go on to equip Communist troops which were operating in the South.

OPPOSITE TOP RIGHT: In the early days of the war, the Ho Chi Minh Trail was little more than a jungle path, and pilots faced little opposition. As the war progressed, increasing numbers of anti-aircraft guns and surface-to-air missiles were deployed by Hanoi, making the target a far tougher nut to crack.

OPPOSITE BOTTOM RIGHT: Thousands of missions were flown against the Ho Chi Minh Trail during the course of the Vietnam War, and many tons of equipment were destroyed. In comparison with the flood of materiel moving south, the quantities lost were inconsequential to the VC war effort. Short of a long-term deployment of large numbers of ground troops to physically block the Trail – politically unacceptable – the air campaign was the only option available to the United States in their struggle to sever this vital artyery of supplies.

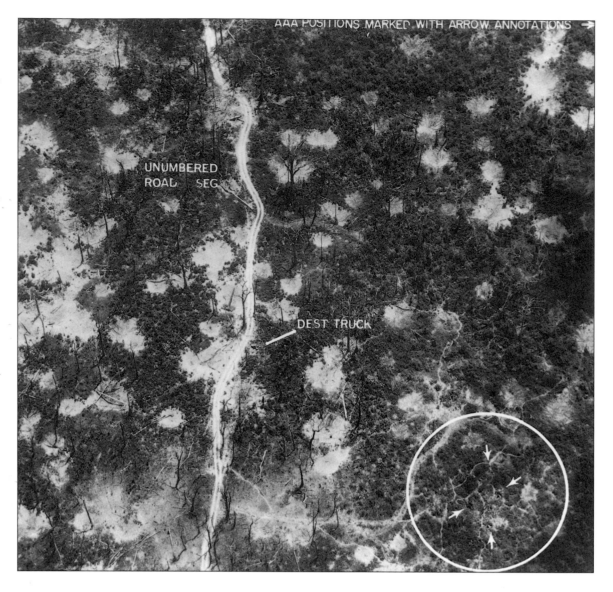

and supply centers, each one manned by a regimental-sized unit responsible for managing the necessary transportation, medical services, engineering, and antiaircraft facilities in its area. Collectively, about 40,000 NVA troops serviced the Ho Chi Minh Trail in Laos alone.

Confronted with these problems, General Creighton Abrams and other MACV commanders tried to keep as many troops in Vietnam as was possible, but politicians and antiwar activists in America agitating for disengagement proved to be more influential. During his first year in office, Nixon had placated most of these "doves" in the United States with his promise of troop withdrawals. After about 10,000 Americans and many more Vietnamese had been killed that year, many more "doves" came into open opposition to the White House. Under this domestic pressure to keep his promise to end the war, Nixon intended to

bring at least 140,000 troops home from Vietnam during 1970. He also sent Kissinger to engage in peace talks with the North Vietnamese diplomat Le Duc Tho in Paris on February 20.

Facing an inevitable end to American military aid, President Nguyen Van Thieu realized that the durability of South Vietnam required both military and political reforms aimed at generating popular support. Although he never succeeded in rooting out corruption either in the government or in the ARVN, he did initiate a sweeping land redistribution policy. In March 1970 he announced his "Land to the Tiller" program, in which his government would allocate about a million acres of arable land to 500,000 sharecropping families that had been renting it. With this action, about one-third of the country's cultivated soil passed into the hands of an emerging class of yeoman farmers. In two years, about 400,000 farmers collectively would own as much as 1.5 million acres of land.

Despite this achievement, American commanders realized that internal reforms would do little good unless the Saigon government had sufficient time to carry them out. Abrams and other Americans feared that their client state would not have enough of the required time while the NVA presence continued in Laos and Cambodia. As long as the enemy retained his supply and communication infrastructure in these two countries, South Vietnam remained vulnerable to a two-front invasion from the north and west. Fortunately for South Vietnam, events would furnish the Allies with the opportunity to become proactive in Cambodia.

In his attempt to maintain Cambodia's neutrality during the Vietnam War, Prince Norodom Sihanouk had succeeded in angering both belligerents. The United States resented his tolerance of Communist sanctuaries on Cambodian soil. When he acquiesced to American bombing sorties against these sanctuaries, he provoked the NVA into arming and training Khmer Rouge insurgents rebelling against the Cambodian monarchy. Although Sihanouk never cared for the NVA presence in his kingdom, his military was clearly too weak to evict it, and American commanders appreciated this reality. Thus, they relished the prospect of sending allied troops across the border to knock out the NVA presence in Cambodia personally.

Sihanouk also had significant domestic troubles. Although many of the rural peasants still venerated him, the urban middle classes had become alienated over misguided government expenditures which had an adverse effect on the Cambodian economy. The urbanites also favored moving Cambodia into the American camp in order to receive the transfusions of American cash that Saigon and Bangkok were enjoying. Likewise, Cambodian army commanders wanted an alliance with Washington in order to acquire the same military aid that South Vietnam was receiving. Some officers had already sent sol-

GENERAL LON NOL

For the first five years of the Vietnam War, Cambodia was a neutral bystander to the conflict, yet many believed it was neutral in name only. It was a major supply route for the VC and NVA operating in South Vietnam, with supplies coming down through the Cambodian section of the Ho Chi Minh trail or through southern Cambodian ports. Many in the U.S. felt something had to be done about Cambodia, and they had an ally within the country itself.

General Lon Nol was a stridently anti-communist politician and soldier. He had served under the French in Cambodia, fighting against communist guerrillas in the 1950s, before he became the Cambodian army's chief of staff (1955) and commander in chief (1960) under Prince Norodom Sihanouk, Cambodia's head of state. Sihanouk did his best to remain neutral, but Lon Nol was a powerful pro-U.S. figure waiting in the wings. During the 1960s Nol was successively deputy premier (1963), minister of defense (1968–69), and twice premier (1966–67 and from 1969), and with implicit U.S. backing he decided to act against Sihanouk. Having overthrown Sihanouk in March 1970, he straightaway ordered the NVA from his country, closed the Cambodian section of the Ho Chi Minh trail, and permitted U.S. and ARVN troops to operate against enemy forces within Cambodian territory.

Nol held the premiership of Cambodia until 1972, becoming President on March 10 of that year. Yet his presidency lasted only three years before Cambodia fell to the communist Khmer Rouge. Nol escaped with only a few days to spare, and naturally settled in the country he had so favored, the U.S.

diers to South Vietnam for training under American advisers.

With Communist forces swarming through the northeastern regions, and disaffected army officers and businessmen scheming in Phnom Penh, Sihanouk left the country in January 1970 in order to receive anti-obesity treatment at a clinic in France. In his absence, the pro-American Prime Minister, General Lon Nol, took the reins of government and quickly instigated hostility both to North Vietnam and the 400,000 Vietnamese residents living in the country. He issued a decree ordering the NVA to vacate its bases in the hinterland, and at the same time, rampaging mobs sacked the NVA and NLF legations in Phnom Penh and murdered Vietnamese civilians indiscriminately. Overseas, Sihanouk attempted to defuse the crisis in his kingdom by traveling to Moscow in a fruitless effort to persuade the Kremlin to help him force the North Vietnamese to leave Cambodia. While in Russia he learned that the Cambodian National Assembly had deposed his rule and installed Lon Nol as the new head of state. This revelation led Sihanouk into joining a tenuous alliance with the Khmer Rouge in a campaign to overthrow Lon Nol.

In late March, Cambodia degenerated into chaos. Rival gangs in Phnom Penh hacked and slashed each other in gruesome street battles in which cannibalistic combatants devoured the hearts and livers of their mutilated victims. Lon Nol's own brother suffered such a fate. Meanwhile, police-organized lynch mobs continued to terrorize the Vietnamese men, women, and children living in the country. Frustrated by their inability to dislodge the NVA and Viet Cong forces from Cambodia, Lon Nol's troops took their anger out on Vietnamese civilians by participating in the massacres. By mid-April, hundreds of Vietnamese corpses drifted down the Mekong River into Vietnam. In a rare show of solidarity, Hanoi, the NLF, and Saigon all condemned the new Cambodian government for its behavior.

Amid this turmoil, Viet Cong guerrillas operating in Cambodia moved their families out of the inhospitable country. Then the Vietnamese Communists and their Khmer

RIGHT: Cambodia attempted to walk the tightrope of neutrality, but lacking the strength to defend her position, she was inexorably sucked into the maelstrom of the war.
BELOW: At the beginning of 1970, this camouflage-clad young woman's country stood on the edge of an abyss. Caught between the combatants, Cambodia would ultimately pay the highest price of all.
NEXT PAGE: A U.S. armored column on the move. In Cambodia President Nixon finally gave his commanders the chance to take their gloves off. Congress revoked the Gulf of Tonkin resolution as a result, and from now on the administration's policy in Vietnam would be under far closer scrutiny.

Rouge confederates pushed deeper into Cambodian territory, attacking towns and isolated Cambodian forces. East of Phnom Penh, an NVA unit of 3,000 men laid siege to a Cambodian army post. Meanwhile, South Vietnamese forces and their American advisers secretly penetrated border areas. On March 27 and 28, an ARVN Ranger Battalion went 1.5 miles (3 km) into an area near the Parrot's Beak salient and destroyed a Communist base. Four days later, another South Vietnamese unit moved 10 miles (16 km) into Cambodia. On April 20, a raiding party of 2,000 soldiers invaded Parrot's Beak again, killing 144 Communists.

By mid-April, CIA agents had persuaded Lon Nol into requesting that American-ARVN ground forces help him deal with the Communists. To encourage him to join the American orbit in Southeast Asia, MACV also sent the Cambodian soldiers that it had armed and trained in South Vietnam back into Cambodia to support the new regime. Nixon

The Phoenix Controversy

Tacticians in the U.S. intelligence service were always looking for ways in which to break the organization of the Viet Cong and NVA before the South was left to stand on its own. Thus the Phoenix Program was born. Phoenix intended to go right to the heart of the communist organization. It was launched in 1968, and utilized earlier intelligence methods in which CIA operatives had united with South Vietnamese police and civilians to unearth VC members. At that time, the cooperation had proved successful in many districts, so between 1968 and 1972 the program was intensified.

Phoenix worked by penetrating deeply into Vietnamese society. U.S. troops, CIA officials, Vietnamese civilians, local detectives, and police were all brought into an efficient intelligence network which exposed VC at the deepest level. Once a VC suspect had been identified, the South Vietnamese police would move in to make an arrest. Yet Phoenix was an aggressive program. In four years of its operation, Phoenix personnel captured 34,000 VC suspects, but they also killed 26,000. Many of these deaths were highly questionable, and smacked of either kill-quota fulfillment or legalized assassination. In addition, corruption led many suspects to bribe their way out of the prison cells. Despite the high numbers of VC taken out of action by the Phoenix Program, the communist infrastructure remained functioning and in place. As Vietnamization continued to take hold, the Phoenix Program was wound up in a storm of controversy.

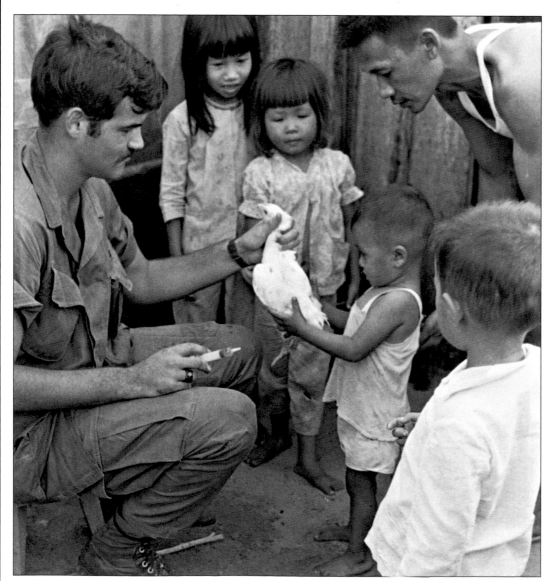

LEFT: Both the Americans and the South Vietnamese government knew that ultimately the outcome of the war depended less on battlefield victories, and more on their ability to separate the southern population from the influence of the communist cadres. Unless the civilian population could be persuaded that their best interests lay with the Saigon regime, the long term survival of South Vietnam as an independent political entity was unlikely. The Phoenix Program, as part of the wider pacification program, was a much more sophisticated approach to the problem than earlier "Hearts and Minds" policies.

contributed to this hasty cultivation of military ties by formulating a plan of aid in which American agents would furnish Cambodian troops with weaponry captured from the Vietnamese Communists at such places as the "Rang-Rang Cache." By the end of the month, Kissinger, General Abrams, and CIA Director William Colby finally got the president's formal approval for an invasion. Within the cabinet, Secretary of State William Rogers and Secretary of Defense Melvin Laird attempted to dissuade Nixon from extending American ground operations into a second country, but their words fell on deaf ears.

The Joint Chiefs of Staff (JCS) thus ordered MACV to launch a "limited incursion" into the country, in which American ground troops were permitted to travel no more than 18 miles (30 km) into Cambodia and could remain only until July 30. Beyond these restrictions, General Abrams insisted on total autonomy in executing the invasion. The JCS preferred to see the action carried out exclusively by ARVN units in order to minimize

ABOVE TOP: Australian troops fraternize with South Vietnamese villagers. From July 1962 to December 1972, almost 47,000 Australians served in the Vietnam War. During this period, their casualties included 496 killed and 2,398 wounded.

ABOVE: Allied troops consult maps and take notes during an offensive action. Under the supervision of General Creighton Abrams, American ground forces sought to increase South Vietnamese involvement in efforts to pacify the countryside in order to enable ARVN to become an effective organization which would be capable of resisting the Communists without American aid.

LEFT: M-48 Patton Tanks and armored personnel carriers from the 11th Armored Cavalry Regiment prepare to invade the Fishhook salient of Cambodia. In spring 1970, with massive air and artillery support, American and South Vietnamese troops chased Communist forces out of their sanctuaries and seized several munitions caches near the border.
OPPOSITE: The strain of the war shows on this airborne soldier's face as he is taken back to base after a patrol.
BOTTOM LEFT: An ammunition-festooned infantryman takes five minutes to himself to read the "funnies." Once across the Cambodian border, there would be no time for him to rest.
NEXT PAGE: South Vietnamese troops wait for helicopters. During the war, the UH-1 Huey was the primary mode of transportation for allied forces, inserting ground forces into battle zones and evacuating the wounded to medical centers.

American casualties and to show the fighting prowess of South Vietnamese soldiers. However, Abrams rejected this proposal in favor of a joint allied operation, presuming that the NVA fighters were so well entrenched in their bases that they might be tough adversaries, even for salty American veterans.

Among the 14 Communist sanctuaries located in Cambodia, three important sites were in the Parrot's Beak salient and two more were in another salient, the Fishhook. On April 29, 8,700 crack troops from the ARVN's III Corps spearheaded the allied invasion at Parrot's Beak. Under the command of Lieutenant General Do Cao Tri, this strike force consisted of two armored cavalry squadrons, two units from the corps' 5th and 25th Infantry Divisions, and four battalions from the 2nd Ranger Group. After two days of intense hand-to-hand combat and American

ABOVE: ARVN formations did perform remarkably well during the Cambodian invasion – indeed better than expected – and showed signs that "Vietnamization" could prove more than a pipe-dream. However, they were still hugely dependent on the kind of firepower and military muscle the U.S. alone could deploy. This vulnerability was revealed with painful clarity when the ARVN tried to "go it alone" the following year.

air strikes, the Communists evacuated the salient, losing 375 men. The victorious ARVN units lost 30 men killed and 70 wounded in the fighting. At the town of Ba Thu, the South Vietnamese looted Base Area 367, a sanctuary containing houses, bunkers, restaurants, and warehouses filled with supplies. They also occupied the town of Prascaut, where Cambodian soldiers had murdered about 90 Vietnamese civilians.

On the following day, an allied force consisting of 10,000 Americans from the 1st Air Cavalry Division and the 11th Armored Cavalry Regiment joined with 5,000 soldiers from the 1st ARVN Cavalry Regiment and the 3rd ARVN Airborne Brigade in an assault on Fishhook. After chasing the 7th NVA Division

and some Viet Cong guerrillas out of the salient, they secured Base Area 353, which American officers had identified as the site of the Central Office for South Vietnam (COSVN). Fifty Communists died in sporadic fighting. On May 1 the 11th Armored Cavalry headed north to the town of Snuol, a strategic hub where Routes 7 and 13 converged. Although the Americans wanted to take the town intact, stiffened NVA resistance forced them to pound it to pieces with artillery, napalm, and tactical air strikes before the Communist garrison sneaked out at nighttime.

During this operation, Nixon resumed bombing sorties on parts of North Vietnam. He also appeared on television, justifying the invasion as a measure aimed at protecting Lon

RIGHT: American troops engage in the construction of fortifications at a Fire Support Base (FSB). During offensive actions against Communist strongholds, the Allies relied heavily upon FSBs, such as this one pictured here, because they would provide the infantry forces with the effective artillery support they needed.

BOTTOM RIGHT: On national television, President Nixon explains the purpose of the Cambodian invasion in a broadcast which went out to the nation on April 30. Expressing confidence in the success of the action, during this broadcast the President went on to predict that the allied forces would overrun the Central Office for South Vietnam (COSVN), which was the Communist military and political headquarters for southern South Vietnam. It was claimed that the complete destruction of the Central Office for South Vietnam would help bring about a satisfactory conclusion to the war.

Nol's regime and ensuring the success of Vietnamization by obliterating enemy bases that threatened American personnel still in Vietnam. The president also proclaimed that the allied troops entering Cambodia were striking at COSVN itself, "the headquarters of the entire Communist military operation in South Vietnam." This bold claim contradicted the more modest objective enunciated by the MACV commanders overseeing the invasion, who knew that they could never permanently obliterate the Communist presence in Cambodia, but who aimed to disrupt it for long enough to provide Saigon with enough time to strengthen its military forces.

Meeting negligible resistance, American and ARVN units cleared most Communist

RIGHT: An American crew negotiates an M551 Sheridan Reconnaissance Tank through a smoke-filled battle zone. As a relatively fast armored vehicle, the Sheridan was a useful weapon in the Cambodian incursion.
BELOW: A Cambodian soldier assists a wounded comrade during a battle at Tang Kauk, 52 miles (84 km) away from Phnom Penh. Afflicted with poor leadership, government troops engaged in a desperate struggle against a well-organized Communist insurgency that steadily gained momentum after the overthrow of Prince Sihanouk.

forces out of the sanctuaries within a week. Before long, the Allies learned that the enemy had received orders to retreat before any invasion force could bog them down in a pitched battle. At the peak of the invasion, about 48,000 ARVN and 30,000 American fighters participated in ten operations that kept the NVA at arm's length while they descended upon its sanctuaries. When they secured the area, they initiated thorough searches on the ground and aboard helicopters for Communist supply depots.

The NVA's resolve not to fight enabled the invaders to carry out their mission with great effect, finding abandoned huts and fortifications stuffed with useful plunder. Just above Fishhook, a battalion from the 1st Air Cavalry uncovered a sanctuary called "the City," which contained 1,300 small arms, 200 artillery pieces, and 1.5 million rounds of AK-47 ammunition. The base also possessed a truck garage, a pig farm, and even a swimming pool. Another battalion found a place they called "Rock Island East" 25 miles (40 km) to the northeast – and took on May 6 after a firefight that killed seven Americans and left another 20 wounded – containing 329 tons of munitions, including 6.5 million rounds of antiaircraft ammunition, 500,000 rifle bullets, thousands of rockets, trucks, and telephones.

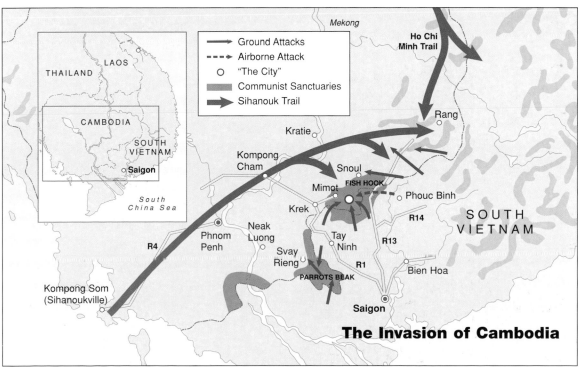

The Invasion of Cambodia

Map legend:
→ Ground Attacks
⇢ Airborne Attack
○ "The City"
▬ Communist Sanctuaries
➤ Sihanouk Trail

ABOVE: Close to the Demilitarized Zone (DMZ), a soldier from the 61st Infantry Division decorates himself with a peace symbol, a Pancho Villa, and a bandoleer. Like other young American citizens during the 1960s, some servicemen in Vietnam were caught up in the spirit of the times. After 1968, many combat troops were to become increasingly disillusioned with the war and sometimes expressed their ambivalent attitude,

PRINCE NORODOM SIHANOUK

As a leader in one of the most troubled, divided regions of the world, Prince Norodom Sihanouk was destined for political turbulence. Yet in many respects he was victim of his own attempts to keep Cambodia neutral in a sea of fighting and upheaval. From 1941 to 1955, he ruled as king of Cambodia. He tried to declare Cambodia independent from French rule during World War II, yet the French returned, and Sihanouk chose to sit and wait while they bled themselves white in the Indochinese conflict just across the border. The French left in 1954, and Sihanouk became head of state, president and prime minister until his overthrow in 1970.

It was the Vietnam War that brought down Sihanouk, like so many politicians across the world. Attempting to keep to the middle ground during the conflict, he refused U.S. aid and assistance, but he did allow covert NVA operations from within Cambodia's borders in return for their non-support of the Khmer Rouge faction fighting for a communist Cambodia. His nimble handling of international politics made Cambodia a relatively peaceful and prosperous state during the upheavals of the 1960s, yet the politics of the region caught up with even him, and he was ousted by the pro-U.S. Lon Nol in 1970.

Sihanouk continued to take an active interest in Cambodia's future, managing difficult alliances as president-in-exile and returning as king of Cambodia in 1993. His return to the royal palace constitutes a landmark in one of the most durable political careers in Southeast Asia.

During their two-month visit in Cambodia, the invaders collectively seized 9,300 tons of weaponry, ammunition, and other equipment, along with 7,000 tons of rice. The enormous amount of loot seized led to a race against the June 30 deadline to get these supplies back to South Vietnam in time. While bulldozers cleared about 2,000 acres of jungle into landing zones, helicopters and ground vehicles crossed the border continuously, transporting captured goods out of Cambodia. During this procedure, the NVA launched only one significant assault. In mid-May, the Communists attacked Firebase Brown near Snuol, only to be repulsed, with 52 of their fighters killed at close range. Meanwhile, two brigades from the American 4th Infantry Division invaded Cambodia at a point about 125 miles (200 km) north of Fishhook, slaying 184 Communists in eight days. Altogether, American and ARVN forces claimed 11,000 enemy soldiers killed and 2,000 captured, while suffering relatively modest casualties themselves.

The invasion also emboldened Lon Nol to close the port of Sihanoukville to the NVA for the rest of the war. This loss, along with the invasion, forced the Communists to shift their

LEFT: While General Lon Nol's coup brought the Cambodian government firmly into the U.S. camp and led to increased military aid, it also unleashed the full fury of the communists against the fragile regular army.
RIGHT: The firepower available to the U.S. and ARVN forces was awesome, but it was difficult to hit a target that chose not to stand and fight.
BELOW RIGHT: Armed with Communist-made weapons, Cambodian soldiers investigate the ruins of a government outpost near the Vietnamese border after it had been overrun by Viet Cong guerillas. NVA and Viet Cong guerilla action was common after Lon Nol sought to expel the Communists from their various sanctuaries from Cambodia.

base of operations into Laotian territory. For a while, they were much more dependent on this region to maintain their logistical operations south of the Demilitarized Zone. Meanwhile, the heavily-populated area around Saigon was temporarily relieved from Communist attacks, enabling the Thieu regime to develop and mobilize units to replace the departing American forces and to attempt political and economic reforms urged by Lon Nol.

Moreover, the performance of some ARVN participants in Cambodia offered moments of inspiration. The fact that South Vietnamese soldiers had successfully spearheaded the engagement at Fishhook and Parrot's Beak alone impressed American field officers. Two ARVN generals were particularly distinctive. Nguyen Viet Tanh, the commander of IV Corps, was the architect of the assault on Parrot's Beak. Unfortunately for South Vietnam, he perished in a helicopter crash during the action. The other rising star was Do Cao Tri, commander of III Corps, who became known as the "Patton of Parrot's Beak." Abrams realized that ARVN's performance in the invasion would provide a valuable boost in morale for its soldiers.

ABOVE TOP: South Vietnamese troops locate the remains of an NVA soldier in a hastily excavated foxhole. After 1968, the Communist war effort had gradually shifted from the depleted Viet Cong organization to such North Vietnamese regulars.

ABOVE: Members of the South Vietnamese Task Force 225 escort a Viet Cong captive to a helicopter. During the Cambodian invasion, the task force attacked a base area north of the Parrot's Beak salient. Although they captured 2,328 Communist soldiers, most retreated into the Cambodian interior.

RIGHT: The corpse of a Khmer Rouge rebel is recovered by Cambodian government troops in Kompong Spau province, west of Phnom Penh, and the site of intense combat. Cambodia's civil war was much more brutal than Vietnam's; neither side was willing to take prisoners.

NEXT PAGE: The chance to clear out the sanctuaries and hit the enemy on his "home turf" had its own price, as the exhaustion and trauma clearly etched on the faces of these soldiers illlustrates.

LEFT: At a supply base known as The City, members of the U.S. 79th Engineer Group inspect a pile of crates left by fleeing Communist troops. Located north of the Cambodian Fishhook salient, The City contained about 1,300 small arms, 200 crew-served weapons, and 1.5 million rounds of AK-47 ammunition.

RIGHT: Cambodian government soldiers surround the remains of 78 Communist guerillas during a campaign in Kompong Saila, a province 78 miles (126 km) north of the Phnom Penh. Aided by artillery, helicopter gunships, and airborne units, Lon Nol's forces had beaten back a Khmer Rouge offensive on a strategically important village in the area.

BELOW: The quantity of materiel captured in Cambodia was undoubtedly impressive, but the reality was that it could be replaced almost effortlessly by Hanoi's Communist mentors. The long-term significance of the strike on Cambodia was questionable.

While in Cambodia, Lieutenant General Tri tackled other missions, noting that South Vietnam was not bound by Nixon's 19 mile (30 km) restriction or the June 30 withdrawal deadline. On May 23, he led a 10,000-man armored column to relieve a garrison of 1,000 Cambodian troops besieged by NVA forces at Kampong Cham, 45 miles (70 km) northeast of Phnom Penh. The following day, the ARVN tankers reached a rubber plantation that had served as a headquarters for a Viet Cong unit. After the NLF guerrillas fled the premises, the ARVN soldiers confiscated anything that might be useful to the Communists. Two days later, the armored column lifted the siege of Kampong Cham, killing 98 NVA soldiers.

ABOVE: Two members of the 199th Light Infantry Brigade try and cool off in the heat of the Cambodian jungle. The Cambodian operation gave the Americans a morale-boosting chance to take out the Communist sanctuaries, which had remained tantalizingly out of bounds for so long.

Meanwhile, President Thieu attempted to rescue any surviving Vietnamese residents suffering persecution in Cambodia. With the consent of Lon Nol, a South Vietnamese naval force evacuated 3,400 refugees from the country. Loaded aboard two ships, the refugees proceeded down the Mekong River and reached Vietnam without any trouble. Although some Communist soldiers were still present in the areas around the river, they allowed the South Vietnamese crew to complete its mission of mercy unmolested.

The persecution of Vietnamese civilians did not prevent the ARVN from offering further aid to the beleaguered Cambodian army.

In mid-June, another South Vietnamese tank force consisting of 4,000 men descended upon Kampong Speu, a town just west of Phnom Penh that served as a strategic hub through which petroleum and other vital imports passed from Sihanoukville to the capital. The ARVN tankers joined with 2,000 Cambodian soldiers in an attempt to encircle the Communist forces occupying the town. However, the Communists evacuated Kampong Speu before the town was surrounded, allowing their enemies to retake it without opposition.

At the end of June, the monsoon season forced the ARVN expedition to stop operations and return to Vietnam at about the same time

RIGHT: Members of the 409th Radio Research Detachment occupy an M113 armored personnel carrier during the Cambodian incursion. The use of such vehicles enabled American and South Vietnamese forces to move quickly into the country and strike Communist sanctuaries before enemy troops had time to remove their supplies with them into Cambodia's interior.

BELOW RIGHT: The reaction of the "Stars and Stripes" to the Cambodian invasion was understandably rather more positive than the rest of the world's media. The incursion into Cambodia unleashed a storm of protest and exposed President Nixon to accusations that, far from disengaging, he was widening the war in Southeast Asia.

as the Americans. Despite the success of the invasion, it had little long-term effect on the Communist war effort. Although the number of seized munitions was impressive, the NVA eventually replaced these losses with the massive supplies that continued to flow from Russia and China. Moreover, most Communist forces had succeeded in avoiding serious injury simply by moving further into the Cambodian interior. With this withdrawal accomplished, they were able to set up a new supply route along the Mekong River. This network would be almost completely secure thanks to the inability of the Cambodian army to challenge the NVA presence. Finally, the

Near the central coastal town of Chu Lai, Sgt. John Autenreith reads Christmas mail from home. Adorned with a peace symbol tattooed onto his arm, this member of the 1st Infantry Regiment, 52nd Division has almost finished with his tour of duty.

performance of some ARVN troops proved to be less than admirable: during the campaign, desertion rates rose from 8,000 to as many as 12,000 per month.

In the United States, the invasion of Cambodia provoked a predictable public outcry. To citizens eager to see an end to the American involvement in Vietnam, Nixon's action constituted not only a repudiation of his promise to end the war but also an obvious attempt to expand the scope of American involvement in Southeast Asia. In reaction, Congress revoked the Gulf of Tonkin Resolution in May 1970, effectively ending the president's exclusive veto over affairs in Vietnam. Months later, Congress passed an amendment drafted by Senators John S. Cooper and Frank Church, which forbade any future introduction of American ground troops into Cambodia. Outside Washington, newspapers denounced the Cambodian incursion, as did prominent educators, clergymen, and celebrities.

ABOVE: Cambodian government troops give covering fire for their colleagues during a fight with Khmer Rouge guerillas.
LEFT: After a March 1970 antiwar sit-in protest, an Air Force ROTC cadet and a student protester exchange restrained words at Washington University, Missouri. After the Cambodian invasion, antiwar protestors assailed ROTC facilities in college campuses across the country.
NEXT PAGE: May 9: antiwar activists stage a demonstration in front of the White House, protesting over the expansion of the Vietnam War into Laos and Cambodia. President Nixon and members of his administration began to employ questionable surveillance methods against critics of their policy in Southeast Asia.

Massacre at Kent State

By 1970, the U.S. was a nation divided over Vietnam. Many polls showed that on the whole people were still in favor of some form of U.S. protection for Southeast Asia, yet the polls could not shout above the bubbling protest coming from American universities, always vociferous centers of national protest over Vietnam since the beginning of the conflict. Passions were running high, and violence was not an uncommon result on the campuses as police and college authorities tried to handle disruptions. Yet nothing compared to what happened at Kent State University in Ohio on May 4, 1970.

The announcement that U.S. soldiers had entered Cambodia in April 1970 brought thousands of students out in anger, not least in Kent State, where protest became loud and aggressive. A weekend of trouble resulted, with students spilling out of the campus and down into Kent's downtown area. Windows were broken and businesses disrupted. Scuffles broke out on the streets, followed by arrests. The city became worried at the mounting chaos, and called for assistance from the National Guard.

The Guard arrived on Saturday night, a night of mounting tension in which student protestors set fire to the campus headquarters of the Army Reserve Officers' Training Corps (ROTC). Yet Sunday broke with some measure of calm. The state governor announced that the University would stay open, and the National Guard force remained on standby. It would be Monday when matters took a dramatic turn for the worse.

Monday saw up to 3000 student gather in a vocal protest on the campus' commons area. After the turbulence of the weekend, the authorities felt they had had enough. Guard troops formed themselves into an offensive line and ordered the students to disperse, backing this threat with canisters of tear gas. Yet the students were staying, even replying with stones and taunts. Order broke down. Guardsmen advanced upon the students with fixed bayonets, forcing them to move backward across the campus. Then, for reasons still not entirely understood, when the Guard approached the crest of Blanket Hill, a contingent of them turned toward the Taylor Hall parking lot and opened fire with their rifles. In a matter of seconds, nearly 70 shots were fired. Four students were killed outright, and eight others were wounded. One student was permanently paralyzed.

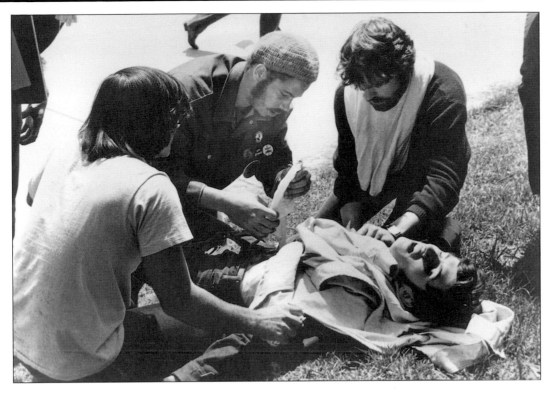

LEFT: Students struggle to save one of their wounded colleagues after the shooting. Even for a nation that had become inured to the violence of the war after five years of media coverage, the events of May 4 were a profound shock. Few had believed that this could happen in the heart of the United States itself.

The Kent State killings brought the trauma of Vietnam home to America in a very personal way. Violence towards civilians abroad seemed to be spreading into the U.S. The protest response was huge – some 100,000 people descended upon Washington on May 9 to decry the action. Shockingly, two more students were shot dead by the police only the following week at Jackson State University in Mississippi. The student killings were just one more element that fed the disillusionment sweeping the country over the Vietnam War.

If anything positive can be said for these university deaths, it is that the students achieved their aim of highlighting the conflict in Vietnam once more, although they paid dearly – with their lives.

LEFT: The violence at Kent State was symptomatic of the rising tensions which were building in the U.S. Opinion on the war was becoming increasingly polarized, and frustration was mounting on both sides. Was the struggle for democracy in Southeast Asia worth the sacrifice of American democracy?

FAR LEFT: National Guardsmen fire tear gas in an attempt to disperse the student protesters. The gas would be followed by live bullets, and Kent State became a watershed in the course of the campaign against the war.

Most visibly, university campuses throughout the country erupted in unrest when news of the Cambodian invasion reached America. In Ohio, this unrest reached a bloody crescendo at Kent State University after a gang of protesters torched a Reserve Officers Training Corps (ROTC) building on campus and then proceeded to hassled fire-fighters who were attempting to extinguish the flames. The state governor reacted by dis-patching the Ohio National Guard to the uni-versity, vowing to "eradicate" this activity. On May 4, a group of guardsmen opened fire on a crowd of demonstrators, killing four of them. This incident and other episodes of campus violence sent shock-waves throughout the United States and intensified student hostility both toward the war and toward the federal government.

Later that year, about 100,000 demonstra-tors marched on Washington, descending on the White House and other centers of govern-ment power. Although these activities would subside in the wake of the pullout from Cambodia and the return of more servicemen from Vietnam, Nixon responded to them by developimg a siege mentality. In reaction to growing fears of subversion against his authority, he established a cadre of domestic spies who were now charged with stalking political opponents. Members of the adminis-tration repeatedly warned Nixon about the legal and political trouble that he might create for himself by employing these kinds of extreme measures, but the President paid no heed to their advice.

Back in Vietnam, American and ARVN officers planned their next move in the wake of the Cambodian incursion, realizing that by the end of 1970 there would be fewer than 300,000 American troops in the country. In June, the United States government initiated a three-year plan to enlarge the ARVN to a size containing ten infantry divisions, one airborne division, and one marine division. In addition to this, the South Vietnamese armed forces would include 50 air force squadrons, 1,200 warships, and various specialized units, as well as artillery batteries armed with long-range howitzers and antiaircraft pieces. The goal of this enlargement was to make the South Vietnamese military powerful enough to fight independently and without the aid of American ground forces, and this was all to be achieved within three years.

At the end of the year, MACV strategists planned an invasion of Laos in which ARVN troops would fight on the ground, while the United States furnished air and artillery support. Specifically, General Abrams and his staff formulated a coordinated air-ground

action against NVA communication and supply lines around the town of Tchepone. As the planners were keen to stress the importance of speed to the success of the invasion, they noted that the weather conditions, as well as the deployment of antiaircraft weapons in that area, would conspire to prevent American air support from being used to its maximum effect.

The CIA went on to confirm this fear with a report warning about the strong presence of NVA infantry, armor, and artillery in the vicinity of Tchepone. Most ominously, the combination of well-placed air defenses on the Ho Chi Minh Trail and near the town and the rugged jungle terrain in the area would endanger any helicopter pilot who was making an attempt to fly over the area or to find an adequate landing zone.

Despite these warnings, MACV planners made their intentions clear. They would be launching Operation Lam Son 719 just after the Tet holiday in February 1971.

BELOW: At Valley Forge, Pennsylvania, actress Jane Fonda is photographed listening attentively among many at an antiwar rally. This rally was sponsored by an organization of Vietnam War veterans who, having come back to the U.S., had turned against the war. Although Fonda was one of many noted celebrities to advocate peace, she became particularly controversial in later years, especially as a result of a visit she paid to Hanoi when she actually sat in an antiaircraft facility which had been used to shoot down American aircraft during the conflict.

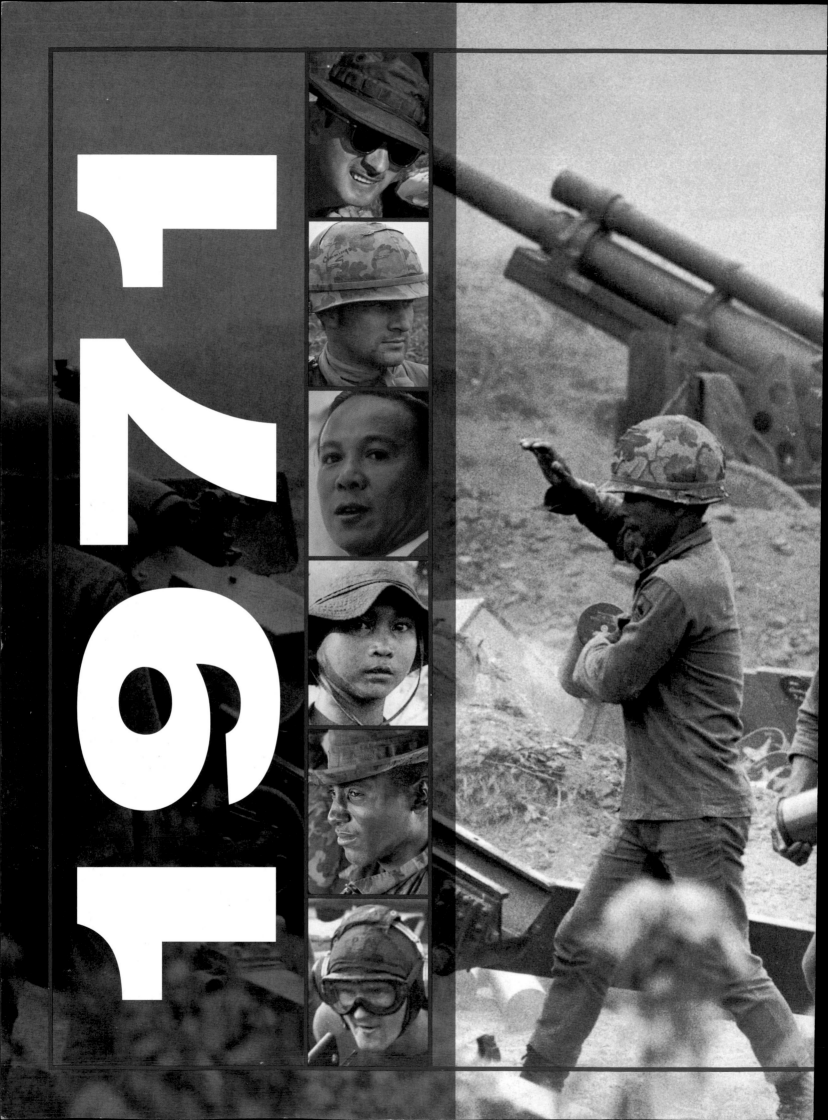

A Gamble in Laos

By late 1970, American and South Vietnamese military leaders became satisfied that the Communists were planning an offensive in the northern regions of South Vietnam. Nixon and Kissinger agreed with this prediction, suspecting that Hanoi might launch a campaign in order to gain leverage at the Paris peace talks and influence the outcome of the 1972 presidential election in the United States. Indeed, the buildup of North Vietnamese ground forces, artillery batteries, and antiaircraft emplacements indicated that Hanoi was beginning to favor the idea of striking while the American presence in Southeast Asia declined and the South Vietnamese armed forces were still in need of strengthening and improvement. To nip this suspected invasion in the bud, and to inflict serious injury upon the North Vietnamese logistical system that reinforced such plans, the allies planned their own pre-emptive strike into Laos: Lam Son 719.

Named after an ancient battle in which the Vietnamese had beaten back a Chinese invasion, Lam Son 719 was scheduled to begin in February 1971, just after Tet. In this campaign, the officers and soldiers in the ARVN would operate for the first time without any American troops fighting on the ground or even traveling along as advisers. If the ARVN

managed to succede in the execution of this campaign, it would emerge as a formidable military presence capable of holding its own against the Communists. The objective of Lam Son 719 seemed rather simple. An ARVN force consisting of infantry, airborne, armor, marine, and ranger units was to advance west along or near a road designated Route 9 until it reached the town of Tchepone, which was about 25 miles (40 km) into Laotian territory. Presumably, the town and the nearby environs served as the main warehouse and distribution center of war materiel for the North Vietnamese Army (NVA). Once the ARVN fighters reached Tchepone, they were to destroy all the munitions and other supplies they could find and hold the town until the start of the wet season in May. In effect, the goal of this mission was to sever a major artery in the Ho Chi Minh Trail long enough to disrupt all North Vietnamese military activity south of the DMZ for several months.

As in Cambodia, American field commanders expressed apprehension about an all-ARVN ground invasion on this scale. In fact, some of them even estimated that the successful execution of Lam Son 719 would require at least four divisions of 60,000 American combat veterans to dislodge and contain

---

ABOVE: Near the coastal military base at Da Nang, a soldier on patrol from the 23rd (Americal) Division balances his M-16 rifle on his shoulder. The Americal Division had a poor reputation as a haven for drug addicts and officers rejected from other units.
RIGHT: The South Vietnamese invasion of Laos was carried out without the direct support of U.S. ground forces, but the massive power of America's air assets were available and played a crucial role in the operation by pummelling NVA formations during both the invasion and the withdrawal.

RIGHT TOP: The plan for Operation Lam Son 719 was for the airmobile forces to "leapfrog" down Route 9 to the town of Tchepone while the ground units punched down the road itself. The airmobile forces would provide a screen protecting the infantry and armored units from attack from north and south of the road. If the supply lines to the south could be cut for long enough it would have a serious effect on communist operations in South Vietnam.

RIGHT BELOW: The Laotian invasion was the first major operation independent of U.S. support carried out by the South Vietnamese. The ARVN had performed well during the Cambodian operations of the previous year, their armored units in particular had shown aggression and determination. The hope was that the ARVN forces would display the same qualities when operating without the support of U.S. ground forces. It would be a major test of how deeply the changes that Vietnamization had made were taking root.

the expected enemy resistance. The entrenchment and reinforcement of NVA forces in the areas around the Laotian panhandle alone was an indication that the ARVN invaders faced an onerous task. Moreover, the heavily wooded and mountainous terrain in the region served as an ideal bailiwick for the Communist defenders.

North Vietnamese communications intercepted in January 1971 showed that Hanoi knew of an upcoming ARVN/American invasion. Although the Communists also suspected the possibility of an amphibious assault on North Vietnamese soil and diverted forces to the central region of their country in preparation, they still had plenty of manpower and hardware to contest any thrust into the Ho Chi Minh Trail. Altogether, the NVA possessed about 60,000 well-equipped troops in the Laotian panhandle, including five divisions

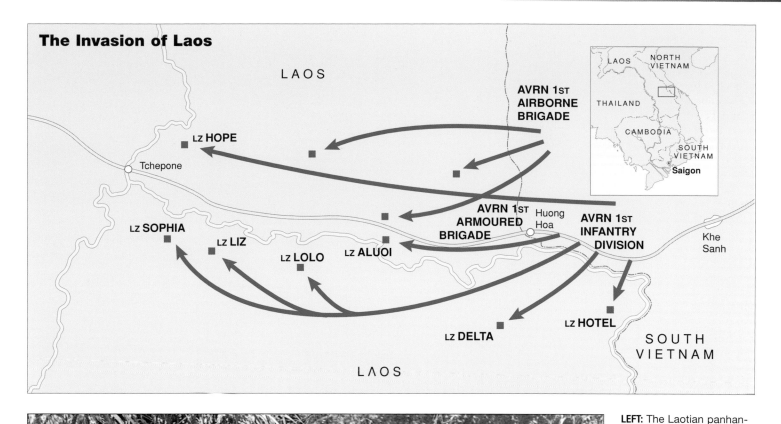

The Invasion of Laos

LAOS

AVRN 1ST
AIRBORNE
BRIGADE

LZ HOPE

Tchepone

LZ SOPHIA

LZ LIZ

LZ LOLO

LZ ALUOI

AVRN 1ST
ARMOURED
BRIGADE

Huong
Hoa

AVRN 1ST
INFANTRY
DIVISION

Khe
Sanh

LZ DELTA

LZ HOTEL

SOUTH
VIETNAM

LAOS

LAOS   NORTH VIETNAM

THAILAND

CAMBODIA

SOUTH VIETNAM

Saigon

LEFT: The Laotian panhandle constituted a key section of the Ho Chi Minh Trail which poured supplies south to communist bases in Cambodia and to units operating within South Vietnam itself. It was also a major staging area in its own right for operations in the northern provinces of South Vietnam around Quang Tri, Da Nang and Hue. Running supplies through nominally neutral Laos bypassed the heavily defended Demilitarized Zone and until 1971 prevented U.S. or ARVN ground forces from interfering.

NEXT PAGE: Although a poor country even by the standards of Southeast Asia, North Vietnam developed one of the most sophisticated and formidable air defense systems in the world. Vast amounts of weaponry and equipment were supplied by the Soviet Union and communist China, from relatively simple anti-aircraft guns such as that shown here, to complex radar-controlled surface-to-air missiles (SAMs).

ABOVE: When initially faced with the problem cutting the communist supply lines to the south, the United States aim had been to smash the Ho Chi Minh Trail with air power such as these F-105 Thunderchiefs. Massive efforts were made and vast amounts of ordnance dropped in an effort to sever this crucial communist artery of supplies.

RIGHT: The aftermath of a raid on the Trail – several destroyed trucks are visible. For every truck destroyed however, hundreds more were getting through; thousands of tons of supplies to feed the communist war effort in the south. One of the reasons for launching Lam Son 719 was the demonstrable failure to cut the Ho Chi Minh Trail with air power alone.

and two regiments of infantry, eight artillery regiments, three engineering regiments, three tank battalions, six antiaircraft regiments, eight sapper battalions, and numerous service and transportation units. In its first major ground operation, the ARVN was facing the greatest concentration of Communist forces in the war.

Despite excessive security precautions, Communist spies managed to obtain copies of the ARVN invasion plans and passed the information to Hanoi and the American news media by the end of January. Not surprisingly, newspapers and magazines back in the United States published the plans and urged American field commanders to abort the invasion. Ironically, many ARVN soldiers scheduled to participate in Lam Son 719 had not even heard about the planning details until this leak was publicized. The attempt by high-ranking American and South Vietnamese strategists to maintain secrecy thus prevented the participating units from carrying out vital preparations; nor were they able to communicate with each other to plan effective coordination during the invasion.

To aid the ARVN in its expedition, the 7th USAF launched a bombing campaign in the Laotian panhandle. Ordered by Abrams to devastate this area, the USAF commander General Lucius Clay warned that de-escalation and budget cuts might prevent him from exploiting his air power to maximum effect. In 1969, he recalled, he could call in about 30,000 B-52 sorties per month. In 1971, he could muster no more than 14,000 sorties per month. The air force dealt with this by focusing its bombers and tactical aircraft on four rectangular areas measuring 0.6 by 1.2 miles (1 by 2 km) on the Ho Chi Minh Trail. Intelligence analysts had identified these areas as bottleneck intersections through which enemy transporters passed en route to destinations in Laos and Cambodia.

The 7th Air Force group focused 27 B-52 sorties on the four boxes per day, while tactical aircraft struck these sites 125 times daily. During the next two months, air force crews would average about one hit on these areas every 20 minutes, 24 hours per day. By mid-January, pilots were knocking out record numbers of trucks in the four areas; but supplies to the south continued to flow. Meanwhile, the United States Navy created a diversion by dispatching a task force filled with marines to the Gulf of Tonkin in a feigned amphibious assault on North Vietnamese soil.

The chief strategist of Lam Son 719, Lieutenant General Hoang Xuan Lam of I Corps, ordered his forces to begin their march down Route 9 on February 8. Meanwhile, the American commander of Military Region 1, Lieutenant General James W. Sutherland,

BELOW: A U.S. Army M551 Sheridan tank on the South Vietnamese border with Laos. Although prevented by the Cooper-Church amendment from taking part in the operation, U.S. ground forces rolled right up to the border and South Vietnamese units were accompanied by U.S. advisors. The ARVN could also call on the powerful U.S. Fire Support Bases just across the border for artillery support, and in addition to the large number of air strikes flown by U.S. planes, American helicopter pilots took heavy risks resupplying ARVN units and airlifting the wounded to safety.

Marvin of the ARVN

Of all the armies in the Southeast Asia region in the 1960s and 1970s, none were more powerful on paper than that of South Vietnam. Yet by 1975, that army had been broken. Both Viet Cong insurgency and NVA invasions had killed thousands of its men and had also disrupted its tactical initiatives. So why the disparity between the evident military might of the Army of the Republic of Vietnam (ARVN), and its lack of competence on the ground?

Physically, ARVN had everything it needed to fight a modern war on land, sea, and in the air. Following the Geneva Accords in 1954, when Vietnam was split into north and south, the U.S. began to pour military equipment into the ARVN infrastructure. Every ARVN soldier came to possess the latest U.S. rifles, and light support weapons such as machine guns and 81mm mortars were actually supplied in greater numbers than to comparable bodies of U.S. troops. Yet there was a fatal flaw in the way that the U.S. equipped this burgeoning army. Most of the weapons and tactical assistance provided by the U.S. Military Assistance Advisory Group (MAAG) was for a different type of war than the one being fought. The Vietnam war was turning into a classic guerrilla conflict, not a conventional war of pitched battles and mass movement of troops. The U.S. at this time had no real experience of guerrilla war, and so it equipped ARVN more for the battles of World War II. Consequently, the Viet Cong took chunks out of ARVN on a weekly basis through slippery, piecemeal assaults, while ARVN retaliation proved weak and uncoordinated.

But there were other problems. In many ways, armies inherit the tendencies of their political leadership. This principle held true in ARVN. The South Vietnamese government was corrupt, preferential, and given to in-fighting, and as a result, the ARVN was the same. Throughout the 1950s and 1960s, ARVN was deeply involved with black-market trading and drug smuggling, and this culture permeated the ranks, right up to the senior officer class. Indeed the quality and nature of the officers was one of ARVN's major headaches. In the 1950s, there had been too few officers, as many of the best had fought on the side of the French. Thus the officer ranks were filled with cronies of the government, men who had friends in high places, but little, or even no, military talent. During Diem's reign, officers of this type were so conscious of pleasing the president that they were often

incapable of making their own decisions on the battlefield. The result was either inactivity or horrendous casualties. Furthermore, whereas 80 percent of South Vietnam was Buddhist, only five percent of ARVN officers were. This religious disparity led to partisan attitudes and these attitudes alienated many civilians from the army and left many soldiers demotivated. All of this was exacerbated to a great extent by the rates of pay. While high-ranking officers enjoyed good renumeration, the foot soldier was rewarded for his efforts by astonishingly low wages.

These problems dogged the ARVN until the fall of the country in 1975. Apart from one or two elite units, such as ARVN Marine or Airborne Regiments, U.S. soldiers had little respect for their South Vietnamese equivalents. The joke went that "Marvin" missions were "search and avoid" rather than "search and destroy." Even at the peak of its strength during Vietnamization, ARVN forces could not put together a convincing victory. After abortive invasions of Laos in 1973, the best ARVN could muster was an ill-considered defensive strategy. 400,000 ARVN troops, however, died in the Vietnam war, far in excess of the U.S. casualty figures. Individual ARVN troops did fight hard in the war, but their efforts were undone by a system which crippled the organization which was so badly needed to survive against the North.

LEFT: "Marvin the ARVN" had much in common with ordinary soldiers the world over; when led by good officers who did not squander the lives of their men, properly equipped, paid and fed, the South Vietnamese fighting man could demonstrate an aggression and stamina that shocked their communist opponents and astounded their American allies. During the Tet Offensive of 1968, in Cambodia in 1970 and again during the Easter Invasion of 1972, ARVN units showed courage and determination often in the face of formidable odds. Unfortunately, this was the exception much more often than it was the rule. More usually, the largely Buddhist common soldiers were officered by indifferent Catholic officers – corrupt political appointees with little or no military talent who embezzled the funds for their wages and supplies. The only real surprise under these circumstances is that so many of the rank and file continued to fight for as long as they did.

BELOW LEFT: When political pressure on the home front, particularly from an increasingly hostile Senate and Congress, made military withdrawal inevitable, the U.S. military began the process of "Vietnamization." South Vietnamese units were extensively re-equipped with the most modern weaponry, and efforts were made to bring their training and competence up to the same standard. Many of the basic social and political issues which undermined the effectiveness of the ARVN remained unresolved however. Nevertheless, following the Easter Offensive of 1972 and through 1973 the South Vietnamese probably had the best of the fighting and their were apparent grounds for optimism. Even as late as the first months of 1974 the ARVN retained the military initiative. Under the pressure of increasing NVA attacks and with the resolve of their political masters questionable, the ARVN began to disintegrate. They could match and even surpass the NVA's equipment with their U.S. backing, but they could not match its motivation.

TOP LEFT: Weary soldiers from the 3rd ARVN Division rest after a fight in a nearby village. An organization hastily assembled in 1971, the division suffered from poor leadership, inadequate training for the troops, and insufficient equipment. Two of its regiments, the 2nd Infantry and 11th Armored Cavalry, were crack outfits sent from the 1st Division; the other two were filled with criminals, recaptured deserters, and green reservists.

LEFT: One of the hilltop bases built in Laos as the ARVN swept towards the key town of Tchepone.

remained near the border to direct artillery support and maintain an advisory role via radio communication. The ARVN expedition advanced in a three-pronged movement. On Route 9, a 4,000-man column consisting of the 1st Armored Brigade Task Force and the 1st and 8th Airborne Battalions proceeded down the battered highway. The 21st and 39th Ranger Battalions rode American helicopters to observation positions near Route 92 to the north, where they were to perform holding actions against any attack from that direction. Between the ranger bases and Route 9, the 2nd and 3rd Airborne Battalions landed on Fire Support Bases (FSB) 30 and 31 to protect the right flank of the main column. Finally, crack soldiers from the 1st Infantry Division covered

the left flank of the main column by occupying a line of FSBs and Landing Zones (LZ) to the south of Route 9.

At the start of the invasion, the Laotian Prime Minister Souvanna Phouma issued a mild statement of protest in which he conceded that North Vietnamese had already violated Laotian neutrality with their longtime occupation of the Ho Chi Minh Trail. The tone of this protest suggested to American and South Vietnamese leaders that the Laotian government was simply making a gesture to avoid tensions with Hanoi. Meanwhile, the main column of the advance down Route 9 traveled 6 miles (9 km) during the first day of the campaign. The highway was torn and perforated from previous air strikes, so only the tanks and

ABOVE During the early days of the Laotian invasion all the signs were good. NVA resistance was negligible, signs of the damage inflicted by the air strikes was everywhere and the main hinderance to the ARVN advance was the weather and the poor state of the roads.

NEXT PAGE: The initial airmobile assault into Laos was succesful, the ground forces linking up with 9th Airborne Battalion on Day 3 of the invasion. All supplies had to be choppered in and losses began to mount as NVA anti-aircraft guns targeted resupply and casevac flights.

RIGHT: A South Vietnamese soldier pulls a crate of supplies from a bunker along the Ho Chi Minh Trail in Laos. At this facility, ARVN forces uncovered many caches of gasoline and uniforms, as well as weapons. Despite these gains, Communist troops and supply convoys reappeared in the area within a week after the Lam Son 719 campaign.

BELOW: As in Cambodia the NVA base areas which the ARVN overran proved to be a treasure trove of weapons and equipment. This time, however, the communists were not so willing to abandon their bases without a fight. As the momentum of the South Vietnamese operation faltered, the NVA began to strike back with increasing effectiveness. The original plan had called for the ARVN to remain in Laos until the beginning of May. In fact they would be back in South Vietnam by the end of March.

other tracked vehicles could negotiate the surface. Trucks could not penetrate further down Route 9, so fuel and spare parts for malfunctioning vehicles had to be airlifted to the armored units. This logistical situation became more serious when NVA anti-aircraft batteries attacked American helicopters.

On the second day of the advance, heavy rains swamped Route 9, allowing very little movement for the ARVN column on the ground, as well limiting the air support responsible for providing supplies and cover fire. The weather cleared up the following day, enabling the column to reach a rendezvous point halfway to Tchepone. There they linked with the 9th Airborne Battalion, which had been airlifted to FSB A Luoi by American helicopters. For the time being, the ARVN troops in the area set up camp and patrolled the surrounding area. To the south, patrols from the 1st Infantry Division uncovered large stashes of small arms, ammunition, recoilless rifles, gasoline, and rations. They also found corpses littered all over the countryside, the victims of American bombing and strafing.

For the first three days, Communist resistance to these incursions was almost negligible. However, the execution of Lam Son 719 quickly slipped into a state of confusion when both the chief planner and the chief logistician of ARVN I Corps were killed in a helicopter crash. The main column waited for orders to continue advancing on Tchepone, but received none for several days. Until early March the members of the ARVN expedition hunkered down while NVA resistance intensified. Most significant, day-and-night salvoes of mortar and rocket attacks were launched against FSB A Luoi. Confused and exasperated, Abrams and other advisers tried to discover why Lieutenant General Lam and his subordinates allowed the advance to stall; he had to persuade the ARVN commanders to stick with the original invasion plan before the NVA could move into the panhandle, consolidate, and counterattack the ARVN forces.

According to rumors that abounded during and after the Lam Son 719 campaign, President Thieu himself had ordered a halt to the advance if the expeditionary forces suffered more than 3,000 casualties. Thieu denied the rumor. But even if he had nothing personally to do with the pause in the ARVN advance, he presided over a military hierarchy that was hamstrung both by coordination problems and infighting among the generals who commanded the diverse units involved in the invasion. Some were strongly opposed to Lam Son 719, while others resented taking orders from Lieutenant General Lam. As a result, the problems that had been so endemic to the South Vietnamese armed forces at last made their presence known in the wooded highlands of Laos.

Fortunately for the ARVN soldiers in Laos, the NVA was slow to mount a counterattack, partly because Hanoi was concerned with another possible offensive closer to home. In the Gulf of Tonkin, American warships filled with marines moved suspiciously close to the North Vietnamese port of Vinh, while

NGUYEN VAN THIEU

It is ironic that a man who would become president of South Vietnam in 1967 had once been a member of the Communist Vietminh – the precursor to the Viet Cong who expelled the French from Indochina in the 1940s and 1950s. Yet Nguyen Van Thieu's flirtation with communism did not last long. He switched sides early in the war to fight for the French colonial masters, and from then on remained a committed and implacable enemy of the Communists to the very end.

As this early part of his life suggests, Thieu was an opportunist. Corruption and ambition coursed through his veins in equal measures and he married into a high-society Catholic family to give himself more social leverage. He was also unpredictable and would regularly rely on astrology rather than reason to make his decisions. Yet the U.S. authorities liked him, gave him military training, and pushed his advance. In June 1965 he became head of state, with Nguyen Cao Ky as prime minister, in what was possibly one of the most unreliable political pairings in history.

In 1963 Thieu was there at the front of the coup against Diem, and he snapped up the position of chief of state under Premier Ky. Despite his title, Thieu was relatively powerless compared to Ky. Acrimony broke out between the two men. This was resolved in 1967 when Thieu managed to secure the presidential position, and Ky fell into the vice-president's role. Thieu would stay in this office for the lion's share of the war, from 1967 to 1975. His rule was mercurial, and towards the end characterized by some bad decisions. In March 1975, with the U.S. protection gone, Thieu decided to withdraw most ARVN troops from the Central Highlands and deploy them around Saigon. What was meant to be a "tactical withdrawal" became the disintegration of the ARVN. Thieu resigned on April 21, 1975, passing the mantle of office to his vice president, Tran Van Huong. Shortly after, the South fell.

ABOVE: South Vietnamese troops drag a communist soldier from his hiding place. Those fragmented enemy units first encountered by the South Vietnamese in Laos had been pounded relentlessly by air strikes for days in advance and were in no condition to offer serious resistance.

OPPOSITE: South Vietnamese troops inspect the bodies of some of their less fortunate NVA adversaries. The aim was for a fast moving drive down Route 9 to seize the town of Tchepone and cut the supply lines running south. The speed of advance would keep the communists off balance. The death of two of the operation's key planners in a helicopter crash caused the advance to stall, however, allowing the NVA to recover.

American fighter planes crossed the skies overhead. Impressed with this elaborate bluff, the NVA diverted forces from the DMZ to Vinh. But later in February, as this threat waned, Hanoi refocused its attention to the Laotian panhandle. It dispatched the 70th NVA Division into the area and sent the 2nd NVA Division from southern Laos to Tchepone. By the end of the month, the NVA had about 36,000 soldiers in the Laotian panhandle, a two-to-one advantage over their enemies in the area.

In their campaign to crush the ARVN presence in Laos, the Communists developed a plan to exploit their numerical advantage. First, they would use their antiaircraft weapons to neutralize American air support for the ARVN expedition. Then the NVA would demoralize its adversaries by pounding their bases continuously with artillery, mortar, and rocket barrages. Finally, with these targets thus battered and softened, the Communists could then finish off the ARVN expedition by

engulfing its bases with waves of infantry assaults.

The South Vietnamese soldiers in Laos hoped that their artillery batteries in the FSBs and American air superiority would keep the NVA at bay. However, the ARVN howitzers had a shorter range than the 130mm and 122mm guns possessed by the Communists, and lacked fixed and visible targets to hit with any precision. Moreover, American tactical aircraft could only provide sporadic assistance in the face of foul weather and antiaircraft fire. The B-52 bombers were not deterred by these obstacles. But from their high altitude they could not strike NVA positions without risking nearby ARVN bases. As the NVA divisions moved closer to these bases, this danger became more manifest and effectively removed the heavy bombers as participants in the battles for Route 9.

Well-armed, the NVA struck hard on February 18 against the lightly-defended ranger and airborne bases north of Route 9.

RIGHT: Colonel Ho Trang Hau, deputy commander of the ARVN airborne, during operation Lam Son 719. As in Cambodia, some of the ARVN's more junior officers performed with distinction in Laos. The operation as a whole was severely undermined by the indecision and timidity of the man who was supposed to be driving it forwards – Lieutenant General Lam. President Thieu's attempts to replace him ended disastrously however, when General Do Cao Tri, one of the ARVN's best senior officers, died in a helicopter crash on his way to take command.
OPPOSITE TOP: Things begin to go wrong. South Vietnamese wounded await evacuation on a cold wet Laotian hilltop. The NVA began to pick off the ARVN Ranger bases which screened Route 9 one by one. If the screening bases were overrun the ground units would have to run the gauntlet of NVA attacks all the way back to the Vietnamese border.
OPPOSITE BELOW: At Fire Support Base 31 in Laos, North Vietnamese troops stand over the remains of a destroyed command bunker that had been occupied by the ARVN 3rd Airborne Brigade. After enduring a long pummeling by NVA artillery, the brigade commander and other occupants in the bunker surrendered in late February. As part of their surrender deal they were later broadcasted denouncing the Lam Son 719 operation on North Vietnamese radio.

Outnumbered by at least six-to-one, the 39th Ranger Battalion held its ground at Base North for three days before its commander ordered a retreat to Base South. When the NVA attackers moved into the fallen base, American gunships swept into the scene, killing over 600 soldiers and destroying or damaging almost 100 tanks. Meanwhile, the rangers battled their way to Base South in a savage fight, forced to use weapons and ammunition captured from the enemy because they had run out of bullets for their own rifles. By the time the 39th Battalion reached its objective, it had suffered a casualty rate of 75 percent and was down to about 100 combatants.

These remnants joined the 21st Battalion at Ranger Base South just in time to face another onslaught from the NVA. Fortunately for the Rangers, American airpower and ARVN artillery from the nearby airborne FSBs suppressed the Communist offensive long enough to enable American medevac helicopters to land on Ranger Base South and remove 122 wounded soldiers from danger. Two days later, Lieutenant General Lam determined that the ranger base was not worth maintaining and ordered the surviving defenders to retreat 3 miles (5 km) southeast to FSB 30, where they were airlifted back to Khe Sanh. Although beaten and almost annihilated as independent units, the ranger battalions succeeded in their holding actions long enough to give the rest of the ARVN expedition about a week to prepare for attacks from the north.

The chief strategist of Lam Son 719, Lieutenant General Lam, was wracked by indecisiveness and timidity, and in an attempt

ABOVE: A relaxed American serviceman with his M-16 casually slung across his shoulder. Apparently on patrol, he is presumably in an area considered secure, but is nevertheless taking a chance. There were precious few areas in South Vietnam where a soldier could feel completely safe from the communist guerrillas. After President Nixon took office U.S. units were increasingly instructed to avoid high-risk operations that might result in heavy casualtties.

OPPOSITE: At the Utility Tactical Transport Helicopter Company which was situated in Saigon, Captain Robert L. Webster examines an MXL Emerson Squad 4-machine gun emplacement on his UH-1B helicopter. This weapon had the technical advantage of being operated either by the co-pilot, or operated by remote control.

to salvage any success from the operation, President Thieu attempted to replace him with a more dynamic commander. Lieutenant General Do Cao Tri, the head of III Corps, had distinguished himself in the 1970 Cambodian invasion. He was ordered to proceed to Laos and take over direction of the Laotian adventure. However, Tri perished in a helicopter crash before he reached his destination. Thanks to yet another helicopter accident, Lam kept his job.

With the ranger bases liquidated, the NVA unleashed its wrath on Fire Support Bases 30 and 31, the last line of opposition between it and the ARVN armor column on Route 9. On February 25 a massive Communist ground force consisting of long-range artillery, tank formations, and 2,000 infantrymen attacked the 3rd Airborne Battalion at FSB 31, where its commander, Colonel Nguyen Van Tho, maintained his headquarters. Although the NVA lost many of its tanks to tactical aircraft strikes, it kept up its attack. Before the end of the day, the Communists overran the firebase and captured most of its defenders, including

Colonel Tho, and appropriated a battery of 105mm howitzers. During this assault, the NVA lost 250 soldiers and 11 tanks. To the east, the 2nd Airborne Battalion at Fire Support Base 30 lasted for another week. Fortunately for the ARVN defenders, the high slopes of their position protected them from enemy tanks, although NVA howitzers and mortars pounded the FSB relentlessly. By March 3, the Communists succeeded in disabling all of the 12 artillery pieces in the ARVN encampment, forcing the Airborne soldiers to evacuate.

Meanwhile, the main ARVN column on Route 9 moved from its positions around Fire Support Base A Luoi in a fruitless effort to assist the beleaguered Airborne positions on the North flank. South of FSB 31, an ARVN relief force of five M41 tanks, several APCs and some Airborne units fought three indecisive battles with NVA tanks and infantrymen from February 25 to March 1. During the course of the fighting, the ARVN forces and American air strikes destroyed 23 tanks and killed over 1,100 enemy soldiers, while the

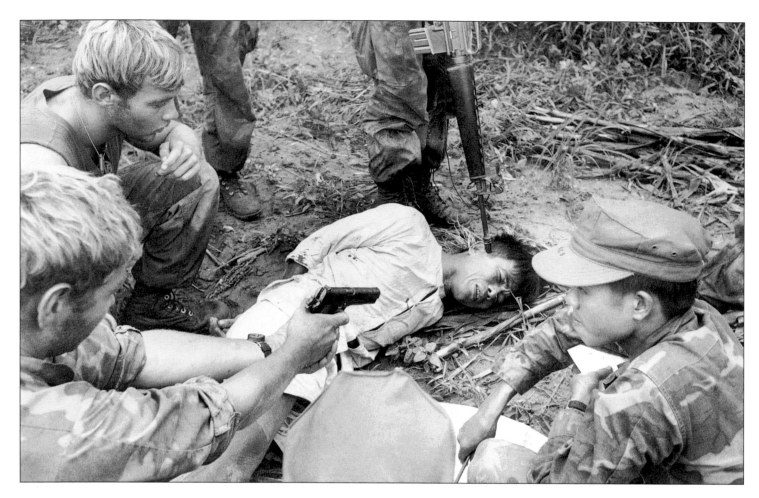

ABOVE: Near Da Nang, American Marines take a forceful approach interrogate this suspected Viet Cong prisoner during a patrol. The Marines are assisted in their interrogation by an interpreter who appears at the right of the photograph. In 1971 the war seemed to be swinging markedly against the Communists. While the controversial Phoenix Program – together with other counterinsurgency measures – had managed to capture and/or kill as many as 18,000 Viet Cong activists – most of whom were low-ranking cadres who had been operating in villages – during the same year, the South Vietnamese government claimed to have "rallied" some 20,000 former communists to the government side as part of their "Chieu Hoi" or Open Arms Program.

NVA succeeded in killing about 200 ARVN soldiers and destroying three tanks and 25 APCs. On March 3, the rest of the ARVN tank column clashed with an NVA infantry battalion and decimated it with the help of B-52 bombers. Along Route 9, the ARVN armored units and their American benefactors inflicted heavy losses on the NVA but failed to prevent the northern FSBs from collapsing and moved no closer to Tchepone.

By this time, the organizers of the campaign abandoned the original plan calling for the armored column to take Tchepone via Route 9 in favor of one that involved airlifting battalions from the 1st Infantry Division into the town as a victory gesture. On March 3, American helicopters transported a battalion to Fire Support Base Lolo, which was south of Route 9 and slightly closer to Tchepone than FSB A Luoi. From FSB Lola the 1st Division inched westward, inserting more battalions into LZs and FSBs closer to the town. Faced with stiff NVA resistance, the Americans lost several helicopters in these maneuvers. On March 6, a massive fleet of Huey transport

helicopters, protected by Cobra gunships and fighter planes, deposited the 2nd and 3rd Battalions of the division's 2nd Regiment onto LZ Hope, which was 2 miles (4 km) northeast of Tchepone. Within three days, the ARVN infantrymen entered the ruined town and its surroundings and destroyed caches of supplies stashed in the nearby mountain ridges.

Satisfied with this symbolic victory and fearful of a likely counterattack by the NVA, Thieu and Lam rejected the original plan to maintain an ARVN presence until May in favor of an immediate withdrawal. Abrams pleaded with his South Vietnamese confederates to keep the 1st ARVN Division in Tchepone and send the 2nd ARVN Infantry Division into the area to reinforce this occupation. Thieu offered to comply with this advice if Abrams sent a division of American soldiers into the Laotian panhandle, knowing that the Cooper-Church Amendment prohibited such an action. With Abrams thus stymied, ARVN strategists implemented a plan of withdrawal.

When the NVA learned that the ARVN invaders were retreating from their bases, it

LEFT: Bouam Long, a CIA-run mercenary camp in Laos. It was from bases such as these that the Secret War was waged. Throughout the 1960s the CIA carried out an array of "black" operations which if discovered could be denied by the U.S. government. As the scale of the involvement increased however, it became increasingly difficult to conceal and U.S. involvement was finally admitted in 1969. This did not bring the operations to an end and they continued up until the end of the war, and – many suspect – for some time after.

BELOW: This 15-year old boy-soldier served in the CIA-sponsored "secret army" which waged America's war in Laos. He had actually been fighting since the age of 13, denying him any kind of normal childhood.

Secret War in Laos

Laos was a real problem for the U.S. The Geneva Accords of 1954 had made Laos neutral, and also no superpower was allowed to enter the country under the terms of the agreement. Yet Laos was tactically and politically vital to the whole Southeast Asian region. Furthermore, from the mid-1950s it was constantly on the brink of falling to the Communists, and the U.S. could do little more than pour in financial help and military advisers.

By 1960, however, more substantial U.S. interventions were taking place, headed by the CIA. Elections in April 1960 were rigged by vast amounts of CIA-distributed bribes. There began a dangerous tug-of-war over Laos between the U.S. and the Soviet Union, each backing different regimes, personalities, and forces in the hope of establishing a sympathetic government. By the time Kennedy stepped into the White House, many thought that Laos, and not Vietnam, would be the site of a forthcoming war.

While an overt U.S. military invasion of Laos was out of the question, covert operations were not. Enter the CIA again. The CIA had actually been in Laos since 1951, training forces through a cover organization called the Overseas Southeast Asia Supply Company. Yet in the 1960s, at Udorn in neighboring Thailand, the CIA established a fictitious commercial airline called Air America which actually performed reconnaissance and supply missions into Laos for the benefit of pro-U.S. troops. CIA operatives joined and trained special counterinsurgency units, and worked dangerous behind-the-lines actions. To compound their vulnerability, they were told that if they were discovered, then the U.S. government would disavow their presence in Laos. In 1969 the truth of U.S. involvement in Laos was publicly revealed, but that did not stop CIA agents heading into the hinterlands of Laos on missions we can only guess at.

RIGHT: A long-range recon-naissance patrol (Lurp) team descends upon a landing zone. Often oper-ating deep inside enemy territory, these units seized prisoners, collected infor-mation, and ambushed Viet Cong trails in the jun-gle. Early in the war, Special Forces outfits per-formed such missions, then went on to teach their techniques to the regular American and South Vietnamese army units.
BELOW: A "Tiger-Stripe" clad member of a Special Operations Group checks his PRC-25 radio set is working. SOG units were often inserted deep behind enemy lines, and if they got into trouble their radio was the only contact with the outside world.

RIGHT: A Huey prepares to recover a damaged Hughes OH-6 Cayuse light observation helicopter. Although the helicopter is probably the most resonant icon of the war, Vietnam was a far from helicopter-friendly environment. More than 3,000 helicopters of various types were lost during the conflict and replacing them made millions of dollars for corporations like Bell and Hughes. The vulnerability of helicopters in a modern combat environment as demonstrated graphically in Vietnam, led to the development of specialized, armored attack helicopters such as the AH-1 Cobra. This process would ultimately lead to the appearnce of the modern battlefield attack helicopter as epitomized by the AH-64 Apache which performed with such distinction in the Gulf War over 15 years later.

SECRET BOMBS
Secret bombing in Cambodia

It's hard to believe that it would be possible to keep around 3,630 B-52 bombing raids secret from the outside world. Yet that is exactly what the U.S. military and government managed to achieve in March 1969. The destination was Cambodia, a country set aside as neutral by the Geneva Accords in 1954. The ruler of Cambodia, Prince Norodom Sihanouk, had attempted with some difficulty to walk the independent line between South Vietnam, the U.S. and their Communist opponents. Yet Sihanouk ignored the Viet Cong's use of Cambodia's northern frontier for the Ho Chi Minh Trail. Later, following his conviction that there was a CIA plot to overthrow him, Sihanouk started to allow NVA shipping to use the southern port of Sihanoukville; from there supplies could be taken across the Cambodian border into South Vietnam.

The U.S. decided to act. The "Menu Series" of raids were massive airstrikes directed at key NVA troop buildups and supply routes in Cambodia. However they had to be kept secret from the outside world. This was made more feasible by a sudden change of heart from Sihanouk, who began to want the heavy Communist presence removed from his country. The bomber pilots themselves would take off, expecting a raid within South Vietnam, only to be re-routed during the flight to Cambodia. When they landed, Pentagon officials would falsify the records of their missions.

The Menu Series had a profound impact on NVA movements in Cambodia, but when the raids came to light in the 1970s, there was an outcry. Cambodia would receive many more bombs before the end of the war – some 540,000 tons in total – but from 1973 onwards there was no more secrecy.

wasted no time counterattacking. At FSB Lolo, the Communists surrounded and decimated a battalion from the 1st Infantry Division. At FSBs Delta and Hotel to the southeast, they tore into brigades of South Vietnamese marines until American air strikes repulsed the attackers. Along Route 9, the surviving remnants of the armored column fought their way past ambushes before limping back into South Vietnam on March 23. Two days later, most of the ARVN expedition was back home. However, the NVA kept up its counteroffensive on the other side of the border. Communist sappers penetrated the American-ARVN base of operations at Khe Sanh, killing three Americans and destroying several helicopters. When artillery salvoes rained down upon the base, its commanders decided to abandon it on April 7, after the last of the ARVN expedition was back from Laos.

Not surprisingly, both sides claimed victory in the campaign. The allies cited the massive

LEFT: A corporal serving in a reconnaissance battalion reflects for a moment as he prepares for a mission. He has taped over the barrel of his M-79 "Blooper" grenade launcher to prevent dirt getting in. He also carries a smoke grenade, and has a combat knife taped to his webbing at the right shoulder. The "Boonie hat" he wears was more comfortable than the issue helmet and preferred by many soldiers, particularly in recon or long-range patrol units. The United States Congress was forced to clamp down upon cross-border operations due to political pressure (as well as public outrage) and the activities of long-range scouting units had been greatly curtailed by 1971.

RIGHT: A convoy of patrol boats of the Mobile Riverine Force on the Mekong River. In December 1965, the United States Navy assumed responsibility for clearing Viet Cong forces from the river. The river had become an important route for moving men and supplies and ARVN attempts to take control of the South's waterways had been largely unsuccesful. Two years later, in 1967, the 2nd Brigade, 9th Infantry Division joined the "brown water" navy to pro vide a little added "muscle." As the U.S. withdrawal gathered pace, the Americans handed over responsibility for the river patrols to the South Vietnamese.

ABOVE: The huge drum this U.S. serviceman is wrestling with contains the controversial but extremely effective napalm. Although used in both World War II and Korea, it was only during the Vietnam conflict that this substance achieved notoriety. Although its effects were horrific, they were no more so than countless other weapons in the U.S. and South Vietnamese arsenal – which in the end is all napalm was, a weapon.

quantities of enemy supplies destroyed and the 13,000 NVA soldiers killed during the fighting. However, the NVA ultimately succeeded in driving its adversaries out of Laos well before May, killing 9,000 ARVN fighters and 253 American pilots in the process. And despite the damage inflicted on the Communist supply lines, North Vietnamese logistical activities on the Ho Chi Minh Trail resumed and thrived within three months.

The results of Lam Son 719 also did not sit well with the citizens of South Vietnam, who were already chafing under appalling economic conditions. The campaign led many of them to believe that Vietnamization was merely a process by which South Vietnamese soldiers would kill and die in a holding action while their American confederates abandoned the region. This realization led to widespread expressions of hostility, both to the United States and President Thieu. Students, Buddhist monks, disfigured veterans, war widows, and even Catholic priests took to the streets in protest in the months leading up to the

October 1971 presidential elections. Meanwhile, the National Liberation Front (NLF) became a stronger political and military presence in the countryside.

Two other candidates beside Thieu ran for president – General Duong Van (Big) Minh and the vice-president, General Nguyen Cao

ABOVE: An American lies low in thick vegetation in preparation for an ambush. Under the changes introduced by General Creighton W. Abrams, United States ground troops operated in small units and employed tactics that emphasized stealth and speed over size and sheer brute force.

LEFT: At Da Nang, American troops uncover a booby trap which had been left by Viet Cong guerillas. in this case it is an unexploded artillery shell which has been rigged to detonate when a victim picks up a helmet left on the ground. About 66 percent of American casualties in the Vietnam War were due to such trickery, requiring the United States Marine Corps and other service branches to initiate training on how to deal with land mines, booby traps and other explosives.

Ky. While Thieu maintained his hardline anti-communist ideology, Ky and Minh openly advocated a negotiated settlement with the NLF and its recognition as a political party. Not surprisingly, the United States embassy actively supported Thieu's re-election. At the same time, the Americans also wanted to see a well-contested election that would show how well western-style democracy worked in South Vietnam. However, Thieu was more interested in keeping his job, and set about removing his adversaries from the running. He persuaded the legislature to invoke a legal technicality that disqualified Ky's candidacy, then mobilized his political machinery into a campaign of electoral fraud in which pro-Thieu voters would perform multiple votes. When Big Minh confronted Ambassador Ellsworth Bunker with evidence of this maneuver, Bunker attempted to bribe Minh into remaining in the election as a token opponent. Offended by the gesture, Minh withdrew his candidacy. Faced with an unopposed referendum on the Thieu administration, Ky, the NLF, and other critics called for a boycott. In response, the Saigon government implemented measures forcing citizens

ABOVE: The anti-war protests probably reached their peak in 1970–71 as the protestors reacted to invasions of Cambodia and Laos and the apparent widening of the war.

RIGHT: Members of Vietnam Veterans Against The War stand with supporters in front of a post office. On December 28, 1971, the organization occupied the Statue of Liberty, hoisted an upside-down American flag on top of the monument, and sent a letter to President Nixon demanding an evacuation from Southeast Asia.

OPPOSITE: Police officers arrest two antiwar protestors during a May 3, 1971 demonstration in Washington, DC. The activists were attempting to block traffic on a bridge. During this confrontation, thousands of their comrades went to jail.

RIGHT: The Armed Forces Day parade in full swing in downtown Saigon on June 19, 1971. This important public event – which was watched by many of Saigon's civilian population – had been staged by President Nguyen Van Thieu. The impressive spectacle was the first such demonstration since November 1967 when Communist forces had launched an attack during his Presidential inauguration day parade.

BELOW: During the latter years of the U.S. involvement discipline became an increasing problem. Nobody wanted to be the last soldier to die in Vietnam, particularly when America was getting out. Morale suffered, and it would not be until the Reagan administration that the U.S. armed forces would truly recover.

to vote in the referendum. As a result, the vast majority of eligible voters participated, re-electing Thieu by an overwhelming margin. Not surprisingly, the Hanoi government and the NLF both repudiated the results of this election and walked away from the Paris peace talks for several months.

Back in the United States, troubles continued to afflict the Nixon administration. In the wake of Lam Son 719, about 200,000 demonstrators marched on Washington. In June, the *New York Times* began to publish excerpts from the Pentagon Papers, a collection of documents from the Johnson administration detailing the internal squabbling and indecision that had plagued the politicians and generals involved with the planning of the war. With some justification, Nixon and Kissinger both feared that the publication of these documents would undermine American bargaining power in any future negotiations with Hanoi. And although the Nixon administration had scored a major foreign policy achievement by

opening diplomatic relations with China in July, it could not dissuade Beijing from continuing to provide military aid to North Vietnam.

The American armed forces also had their problems. On March 29, Army Lieutenant William Calley was convicted in a court martial for his role in the 1968 My Lai massacre. His trial had revealed a conspiracy within his company to cover up the atrocity. Among the 140,000 servicemen remaining in Vietnam by the end of 1971, heroin addiction had become a widespread problem. The dependency on this and other drugs was symptomatic of the feelings of malaise, resentment, and frustration held by many of the American personnel in the country. Other symptoms included increased racial tensions within the ranks, insubordination, and "fragging" incidents in which rebellious soldiers ridded themselves of an unwanted officer by tossing a grenade into his tent. At last, the antiwar fever that had overtaken Americans back home had reached the troops in Southeast Asia.

BELOW: At Lang Vei, near the Laotian border, a peace flag flies from a U.S. self-propelled gun. During the 1968 Tet Offensive, armored units from the NVA had overrun the Special Forces base then at Lang Vei, killing about 200 Americans, as well as Montagnard tribesmen who were defending it. By 1971 the Americans were as far as possible avoiding exposed and vulnerable positions of this sort which were all too easily targeted by the communists. As the ARVN shouldered the lion's share of the burden of the war, the U.S. forces increasingly took a back seat. President Nixon was under mounting pressure as a result of the Cambodian and Laotian operations and wanted to demsontrate his strategy was succeeding with lower casualty figures.

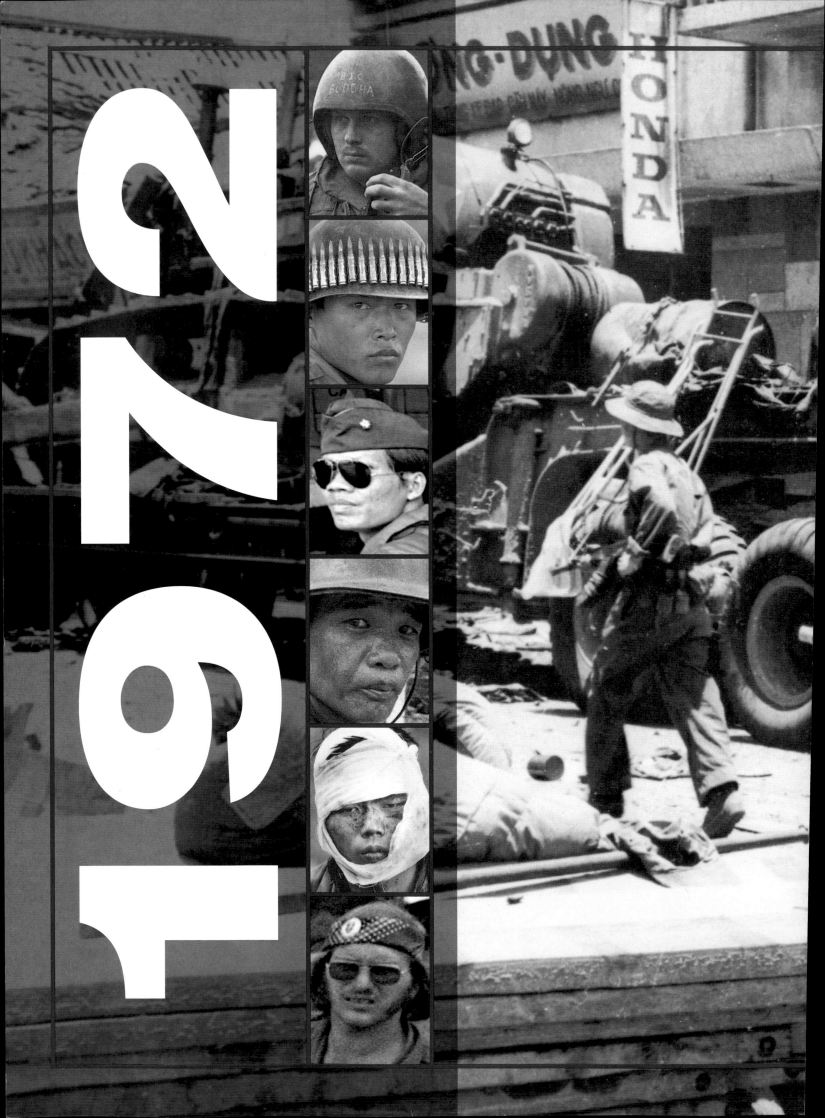

The Easter Offensive

Late in 1971, the NVA moved about 1,000 tanks to the DMZ and other areas bordering South Vietnam. The following January, American intelligence sources interpreted further Communist troop buildups to be an indication of yet another Tet Offensive. Presumably, invasions would occur both along the DMZ and in the central highlands, where mediocre ARVN forces were widely dispersed. Fortunately for the Allies, the Tet holiday came and went without incident, thus providing the ARVN with more time to prepare for a possible attack.

The task of defending Military Region 1 (MR 1) near the DMZ had fallen into the hands of the 3rd ARVN Division of I Corps. Commanded by Brigadier General Vu Van Giai, the division was a hastily assembled force that included crack infantrymen from the 1st Division and an armored cavalry unit combined with two regiments made up of criminals, recaptured deserters, and green reservists. Although Giai was a capable field commander, he was afflicted by the presence of junior officers who had been rejected from other units. By 1972, this and other ARVN divisions also suffered from the problem of having too few American advisers to provide crucial help with the coordination of artillery, logistics, and air support.

Faced with two enemy divisions on the other side of the DMZ, Giai worked feverishly to transform his division into an effective fighting force. He implemented accelerated training regimens for the inexperienced units, introduced mobile, small-unit tactics, and rotated the regiments through various bases in their area to make all of his men familiar with MR 1.

Unfortunately, the division lacked the necessary trucks to move many units at a time. On March 30, the crack 2nd Regiment and the green 56th Regiment were intermingled into a disorganized mob awaiting transportation during a rotation at Cam Lo, when an artillery round struck Ai Tu base, the divisional headquarters, just north of Quang Tri city. Armed with long-range 130mm howitzers, the NVA followed through with a six-day barrage against ARVN bases all over MR 1. The Easter Offensive was underway.

The superior range of the NVA guns prevented ARVN artillerists from responding in kind; and poor weather hindered air strikes against Communist positions in the DMZ. These advantages enabled about 30,000 NVA troops and 200 tanks to move quickly on the ARVN bases. To the south, another 20,000 Communist soldiers prepared to invade from their bases in Laos and Cambodia. Altogether, 14 Communist divisions would participate in the Easter

ABOVE: Major-General Phan Van Phu, the commander of the crack 1st ARVN Division, presents a Vietnamese Cross of Gallantry medal to a member of Company A, 1st Battalion, 327th Regiment, 101st Airborne Division during stand down ceremonies.
RIGHT: At Chon Than, an ARVN paratrooper adorns his helmet with a band of bullets while he prepares to travel down Highway 13. Situated 40 miles (65 km) north of Saigon, Chon Than was the location of the headquarters for the 6th Paratrooper Battalion, which had recently been involved in a battle with Communist units near the capital.

Offensive on three fronts at the peak of the fighting. The NVA objective was to divert as many ARVN units as possible to MR 1, while Communist divisions to the south swept through the central regions of South Vietnam and took Saigon itself.

At first, the 3rd ARVN Division handled the offensive rather well. While American warships off the coast bombarded the advancing NVA column, the division set up defensive lines at Camp Carroll to the west and Dong Ha to the east. Aided by a battalion of South Vietnamese marines and the 20th Tank Regiment, the ARVN defenders at Dong Ha beat back an approaching NVA armored column, while two American advisers blew up the bridge across the Cam Lo River that led to the town. This forced the Communist tankers to spend several hours taking a 7 mile (12 km) detour to the town of Cam Lo to the west. The detour provided allied air and artillery forces with enough time to prepare strikes against the NVA invasion.

The ARVN position at Camp Carroll was even better than at Dong Ha. Occupied by the 56th Regiment, the base had a large artillery

battery, including four 175mm howitzers that had a longer range than the NVA's 130mm guns. However, after three days of shelling, on April 2 the commanding officers unexpectedly surrendered their command to the Communists and later appeared on Radio Hanoi, urging all South Vietnamese servicemen to surrender to the NVA. In the face of this treachery, 33 ARVN soldiers escaped with their American advisers aboard a helicopter. The bloodless takeover of Camp Carroll gave the NVA uncontested control over the town of Cam Lo and its bridge, and forced all ARVN forces in the area to pull back several miles to the southeast. Within two days, the South Vietnamese reestablished cohesive defensive lines from the coast to the Thach Han River 6 miles (10 km) south of Camp Carroll. For three weeks, ARVN resistance stiffened while antitank crews wreaked havoc upon advancing NVA armored units.

By this time, Nixon and Kissinger finally appreciated the seriousness of the situation in MR 1 and worried that all of South Vietnam might collapse. On April 4, they unleashed Operation Linebacker, a two-month bombing

RIGHT: A member of a U.S. special rescue and reconnaissance unit divests himself of a variety of weapons and ammunition on his return to his base at Lai Khe. The unit had just returned from Loc Ninh, where they had assisted in the evacuation of a number of U.S. advisers wounded in the fighting there. Airlifted out shortly before the city was overrun, they were the last Americans to leave.

LEFT: At a village which is situated 6 miles (9.7 km) west of Phu Bai, an American soldier, still wearing his bullets, uses his helmet to drink the water which he has scooped up from a nearby stream. Located in the proximity of Hue, the village was also not far from a large base for the 2nd Brigade, 101st Airborne Division. Like many American troops during the Vietnam War, the 101st Airborne Division displayed its outstanding qualities of endurance, such as in July 1970 when at Firebase Ripcord a unit of its paratoopers withstood an NVA bombardment for three weeks before evacuating its position.

LEFT: Now fighting on their own, the Easter Offensive was the ARVN's first test against a major NVA attack. Their determination and resilience came as a surprise, not least to the North Vietnamese.

BELOW: From the South China Sea, the battleship USS *New Jersey* – seen here participating in a night action – served as a floating firebase. From where it was stationed, it was able to pound at the Communist forces, utilizing 16 in. (41 cm) shells that could travel distances of about 25 miles (40 km). A warship that had been in service with the United States Navy since World War II, the USS *New Jersey* was sent out to Vietnam in 1968.

campaign on North Vietnam that would include 100 B-52s, hundreds of tactical war-planes, and four aircraft carriers. During the first two weeks, bombers struck supply depots, fuel sites, and other relevant targets in Hanoi, Haiphong, Vinh, and other localities. Later in the month, when the skies cleared over South Vietnam, American aircraft terrorized NVA ground forces, forcing the Communists to avoid massing for attacks during the daylight. Nixon and Kissinger also planned to mine Haiphong harbor in May, after Kissinger had time to convince Moscow and Beijing that the action was merely a defensive measure aimed at blunting an unprovoked invasion.

Nixon's aggressive response to the DMZ crossing did nothing to deter the Communists from opening up two more fronts in its inva-sion. On April 5, the 5th NVA/Viet Cong Division crossed the Cambodian border from Snuol to attack the Loc Ninh base, which was occupied by about 2,000 ARVN rangers and infantrymen. Although the defenders repelled five assaults, NVA tanks eventually overran

ABOVE: An American tank crewman expresses his negative feelings about the war through the graffiti scrawled on his gun mount. Photographed here, he is part of an armored unit which is making its way back to its combat base. On September 30, 1971 – the day on which this photograph was taken – the United States Senate had voted for a total withdrawal of American forces from Vietnam, a withdrawal scheduled for completion by the spring of the following year.

the base and killed or captured most of its occupants. The liquidation of Loc Ninh enabled the NVA to advance 15 miles (25 km) due south down Highway 13 to An Loc, the capital of Binh Long province.

In Saigon, the Joint General Staff (JGS) dispatched two divisions to the area. The 5th ARVN Division moved into An Loc, while the 21st Division occupied a point south of the city to serve as a second line of defense between the Communists and Saigon. Meanwhile, the 7th and 9th NVA Divisions, along with a tank regiment, swept in from the Fishhook salient, surrounded An Loc, and shelled the city just as the ARVN forces arrived. The three Communist divisions then

settled into a siege and predicted that they would take An Loc by April 20.

The NVA divisions attempted to make good on this prediction on April 13. Their advancing units suffered a rain of American artillery shells, rockets, and air strikes as they advanced on the city. Although the Communists seized An Loc's airfield, their advance stalled when ARVN antitank crews demolished several NVA vehicles. By this time, the South Vietnamese possessed an area occupying only 0.38 square mile (one square kilometer); but they held their position well past April 20, thanks in part to American air and artillery support and an aerial supply route. Meanwhile, the 21st ARVN Division

NVA – Men from the North

While it was the Viet Cong that caught the public imagination during the Vietnam War, it was the North Vietnamese Army (NVA) that finally secured victory. The NVA grew out of the Chu Luc, the force developed to combat the French during the first Indochinese war. The Chu Luc was organized like any regular army – a structure of battalions, regiments, and divisions – and had a tight political command. The French, whatever their attitudes to rule, were overwhelmingly impressed by the Chu Luc. Their vigor in the fight bordered upon suicidal, and their endurance at times seemed supernatural.

These qualities they took forward into the NVA, formed when Vietnam was split in two after the Geneva Accords. In particular, they proved their endurance during many desperate journeys down the Ho Chi Minh trail. A typical example comes from the 66th NVA Regiment in the fall of 1965. The entire regiment marched for two months down the trail from North Vietnam to Ia Drang, each man carrying over 22 lb. (10 kg) of food. Malaria, poisonous animal bites, and dysentery killed significant numbers every day, and U.S. airstrikes were a hideous daily occurrence. To complete the journey ,once they arrived at their destination they fought for over a month against U.S. troops in the battle of Ia Drang, losing 3,561 of their number.

The journey to Ia Drang illustrates the tenacity built into the NVA psyche. But they did not fight by courage alone. The NVA was in every sense a modern army. Its main suppliers – China and the Soviet Union – saw to it that they had the firepower to take on even the might of the U.S. NVA artillery could rival the U.S. equivalent easily on range and accuracy. Each NVA soldier, at least by the end of the 1960s, had Chinese or Soviet assault rifles which gave lethal close-quarters firepower. The antiaircraft system in North Vietnam was one of the most sophisticated that the

world had, or has, seen. Add to this package the T54 battle-tanks and the SAM-7 shoulder-launched antiaircraft missiles and the traditional image of the underdressed, primitively armed North Vietnamese soldier doesn't match up.

In the final analysis, the NVA was a tightly disciplined force whose fighting spirit bordered on the fanatical. Yet they suffered appallingly. North Vietnam suffered one million war dead, many of them NVA kililed far from home in the South or wiped out by airstrikes above the DMZ. What is disturbing is that casualties did not seem to swerve the political will of Ho and his government, except inasmuch that numbers of men had to be found to fight. Ho's revolutionary war was a long and costly game, but he knew that the death of a single U.S. soldier would have more political consequence than the deaths of 100 NVA troops.

FAR LEFT: The Americans were simply the next in a long line of adversaries against whom the Vietnamese had struggled, almost constantly, for 2,000 years. They had seen the Chinese, French, Japanese and French again all come and go, and they had paid a price in blood every time. From experience they knew that there would be no quick end to the war. General Westmoreland had vowed to bleed the North Vietnamese white, but ironically it was the United States that found the long war unsustainable. North Vietnam proved capable of taking far higher casualties than the United States with little apparent effect on their determination to prosecute the war. The North Vietnamese government and people were psychologically prepared for a long war in the way that the Americans simply could not be.

ABOVE: For many NVA soldiers, there were months of suffering to endure even before they had the chance to come to grips with their foe. A significant proportion succumbed to the depredations of the Ho Chi Minh Trail on the route south, without ever seeing the land they had vowed to liberate. Those that survived the journey south, however, proved to be hardened and tenacious fighters.

RIGHT: Along Highway 13, a South Vietnamese soldier hurls a hand grenade at a Communist sniper position situated just 27 miles (43 km) north of Saigon. Combat in this area raged in late 1972, while both sides were anticipating a cease-fire agreement between Washington and Hanoi, and thus competed for as much territory as they could get. North Vietnam's leaders had hoped that the ARVN would collapse under the pressure of the 1972 offensive. The Americans were withdrawing, and the improvements in training, organization and equipment of the South's armed forces were not yet complete. The ARVN did not prove as brittle as the North hoped, and the impact of U.S. air power has been underestimated.

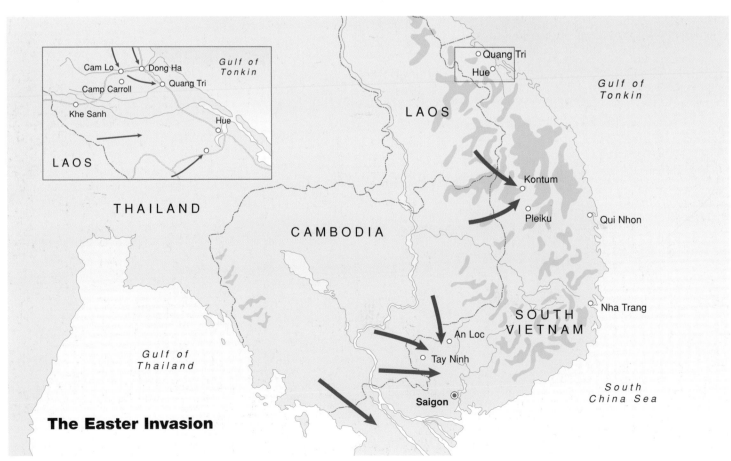

The Easter Invasion

advanced up Highway 13 to relieve the beleaguered city, only to be stopped by the 7th NVA Division's defensive line along the road. However, 120 soldiers from the 13th Regiment, 9th ARVN Division did manage to slip around the left flank of the NVA division, sustain an artillery barrage from the north and the south, and reach An Loc to help with the defense of the city.

On April 12, the Communists opened the third front of their offensive at a remote area in the central highlands. Near the border town of Dak To, the 320th NVA Division shoved a group of South Vietnamese rangers and paratroopers from a ridge just south of three ARVN bases after four days of combat. By this time, three regiments from the 22nd ARVN Division had moved into the bases and were supposed to be prepared for an assault. A week later, the

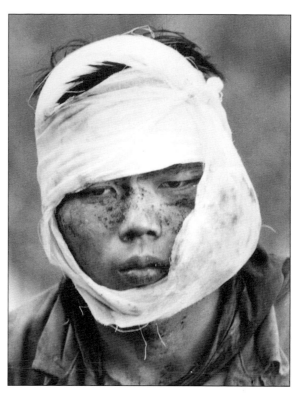

LEFT: A wounded ARVN Ranger waits for an ambulance unit to evacuate him from a rice paddy. During the Easter Offensive, South Vietnamese Rangers played an active role in the defense of An Loc. During the war, the Saigon government usually deployed these forces in border regions.

BELOW: During the battle for An Loc, wounded South Vietnamese soldiers try to get out of the area on the skids of a Huey helicopter while its pilot attempts to take off after delivering fresh troops to the town. During this operation, the Communists shot down one helicopter with several soldiers aboard.

ABOVE: An ARVN soldier helps a refugee from Quang Tri City down from the truck which has just evacuated her and other members of her family. The NVA attacks in the Demilitarized Zone, and the problems encountered by the ARVN in stemming these attacks, caused many to flee from their homes.

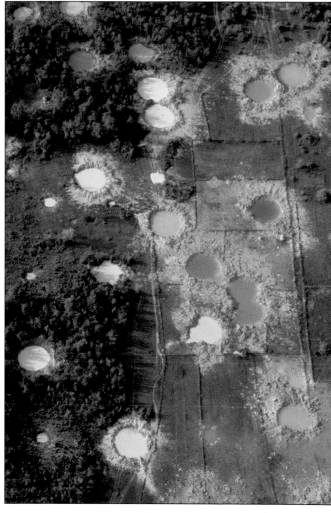

2nd NVA Division swept in from the north, encircled the bases, and pounded their occupants with artillery strikes. At the Tan Canh base, the commander of the ARVN regiments panicked and fled the scene in an American helicopter, while the soldiers in his command broke up into small units and retreated 15 miles (25 km) south to the town of Kontum. The NVA was in a perfect position to sweep into Kontum while its enemies were in disarray, but failed to exploit this opportunity.

At the end of April, the NVA also made further progress in the DMZ theater of operations. Within the ARVN defensive line below the Cam Lo River, a rumor circulated about an enemy breakthrough on the western end. Although the rumor did not faze Brigadier General Giai, it did bother his superior officer, Lieutenant General Hoang Xuan Lam, the commander of I Corps and architect of the Lam Son 719 campaign. Without consulting Giai, Lam dispatched the 20th Tank Regiment from its position along the front line to the

southwest in order to intercept this fictitious NVA breakthrough. Infantry units adjacent to the tank regiment interpreted this move as a retreat and immediately headed south, leaving a huge gap in the ARVN defensive line.

South Vietnamese marines succeeded in restoring order when they intercepted these retreating soldiers on the north bank of the Thach Han River and redeployed them on a new line at the divisional headquarters at Ai Tu. They ordered this makeshift force to cross to the more defensible south bank, only to be overruled by the JGS back in Saigon. These conflicting orders further confused and demoralized the division's regiments and sent them on another general retreat down Route 1, where soldiers and civilian refugees mingled in a disorganized mob. Thus confronted with a tempting target, NVA artillerists pummeled the highway mercilessly, turning it into a corridor of mangled corpses and smashed vehicles.

By this time, Giai had abandoned hope of maintaining control of his division and gave

ABOVE RIGHT: B-52 Stratofortress bombers destroy the Vietnamese countryside to save it from the Communists. As well as the devastation brought by American military hardware, the landscape of South Vietnam sustained heavy damage from Agent Orange and other chemical defoliants.

ABOVE LEFT: Four miles (6.4 km) south of Quang Tri City, a distraught refugee pulls his dead son from a truck that had been driven over a land mine. The blast had killed about 40 people and injured another 60, while they had been trying to flee the battle in the city.

NEXT PAGE: An A-7E Corsair II ready for launch on the flight deck of USS Constellation, April 25 1972. U.S. air power played a major role in blunting the NVA offensive.

LEFT: South Vietnamese troops stand guard over a machine-gun nest belonging to Viet Cong forces that had been recently demolished by advancing American soldiers. After holding off enemy troops for several hours, the Communist guerilla who was repsonsible for maintaining the position was mortally wounded and then died en route to an American medical facility.

BELOW: South Vietnamese Marines find time to relax and take a break in the vicinity of Hue Castle after having been withdrawn from combat in Quang Tri. While ARVN commanders established a new line of defense, American warplanes and offshore vessels hammered the advancing Communist forces in May 1972.

his soldiers permission to make their own way back to yet another defensive line along the My Chanh River, 8 miles (13 km) south of Quang Tri city. Giai himself commanded a rearguard force consisting of marine units and the 20th Tank Regiment, which held on to the city long enough to cover the ARVN retreat. On May 2, Giai's force then began an evasive maneuver, heading east to the coast, then south to the My Chamh River. For over a day, his units successfully eluded the enemy until they approached the river and came under an NVA artillery bombardment. From the Gulf of Tonkin, the Americans replied with naval gunfire and air strikes which kept the Communists at bay long enough for Giai's party to cross the river to the safety of the new ARVN lines.

With MR 1 stabilized once again, South Vietnamese military justice quickly asserted itself. On May 2, President Thieu "punished" Lieutenant General Lam by reassigning the

ABOVE: ARVN paratroopers from the elite Presidential Guard head toward a landing zone near Chon Thanh. Their mission was to help raise the Communist siege of the provincial capital of An Loc, located in Binh Long province near the Fishhook salient of Cambodia. Stalled by heavy artillery and mortar fire en route to the town, the paratroopers were helilifted into an area east of it.

LEFT: An ARVN soldier searches the body of an NVA regular. The losses suffered by the North Vietnamese in 1972 meant it would be some time before they could renew their attack on the South.

Operation Linebacker I & II

In March 1972, the North Vietnamese threw themselves into another major invasion of the South. They hoped that the withdrawal of U.S. ground troops would open the way for an easy victory. What they hadn't banked on were the Linebacker raids.

Linebacker I ran between May 8 and October 23, 1972, and was the most destructive and intensive bombing campaigns seen since the days of "Rolling Thunder." In a magisterial 41,000 sorties, B-52s slammed 155,000 tons of bombs into North Vietnam, while F-4 Phantoms took out bridges and oil depots with the new 'smart bomb' technology, and A-6 Intruders and A-7 Corsairs laced Haiphong harbor with 2,000 lb. (907 kg) sea mines. Supply routes from mainland China were also left looking like the face of the moon.

The devastation was awesome. Before Linebacker I, 25,000 tons of supplies each month came into North Vietnam's harbors. After Linebacker, that figure was reduced to almost zero. Supplies originating from China decreased by an incredible 140,000 tons a month. North Vietnam was brought to the negotiating table but three weeks of talks ended in failure. As a result, Linebacker II was initiated on December 18 in order to give the U.S. proposals greater force.

Linebacker II was almost more extreme than its predecessor. 49,000 tons of munitions were dropped, B-52s working the night and lighter bombers working the day. This round-the-clock bombing shattered Hanoi. There was no electricity or water, and no transport system. Thousands died in the bomb blasts. In response, the northern air defenses fired over 1000 SAM missiles and shot down 26 U.S. aircraft. Linebacker II ended on December 30, and North Vietnam was back at the negotiating table with its infrastructure shattered. Only by 1975 had it recovered enough to muster an invasion of South Vietnam, and the soldiers fighting during that period must have rejoiced not to hear the distant thunder of B-52 engines.

LEFT: The destructive power of the Linebacker raids was incredible, and the effect on North Vietnam was catastrophic. Whether Hanoi was bombed back to the negotiating table is disputed by some, but there is strong evidence to show that President Nixon's bombing offensive was effective in a way that President Johnson's "Rolling Thunder" campaign never was. The ruthlessness with which Richard Nixon employed the huge strength of the United States Air Force against North Vietnam shocked world opinion, but left little doubt as to his ongoing determination to support the South as well as to seek a permanent settlement.

LEFT: An SA-2 "Guideline" surface-to-air missile (SAM) site on the outskirts of Hanoi. With weaponry and equipment supplied by the Soviet Union and China, North Vietnam developed the most sophisticated and formidable air defense system in the world at that time. The Vietnamese fired nearly 1,000 surface-to-air missiles during the Linebacker raids, and succeeded in bringing down 26 U.S. aircraft, of which 15 were B-52 Stratofortresses.

RIGHT: Individual air raid shelters on the streets of Hanoi. The effect of the bombing on the North Vietnamese attitude to the war is almost impossible to gauge, but for the first time the population of North Vietnam's major cities felt the full force of the wrath of the United States. The American bombing systematically destroyed North Vietnam's infrastructure around Hanoi. Massive B-52 strikes and attacks by other U.S. aircraft using laser-guided "smart bombs" reduced the supplies flowing into South Vietnam by an immense 155,000 tons (157,500,000 kg) per month.

RIGHT: Seven miles (11 km) due east of Hue, three soldiers from the South Vietnamese forces carelessly drag a dead Viet Cong guerilla through the dust on a chain like an animal carcass. The casual brutality with which the Vietnamese combatants treated each other was the product of long years of war. Civilians look on, kept in check by other South Vietnamese troops. This photograph was taken at Huong Tra where, during a battle, the South Vietnamese had killed another 13 Communists.

LEFT: A South Vietnamese veteran advances cautiously in the aftermath of the battle for Bong Son, his weapon ready. The tension clearly etched on his face, he is shown here picking his way through the debris of a wrecked section of town after the Viet Cong had been driven out of it. Located halfway between Quang Ngai and Qui Nhon, Bong Son was a town on the coast that had temporarily fallen into Communist hands during the Easter Offensive.

BELOW RIGHT: A South Vietnamese soldier helps patch up a wounded buddy. Although ARVN performance in the war was mixed, by and large the individual soldiers fought well. The determining factor was more often the quality – or lack of it – of their leadership.

well-connected corps commander to a bureaucratic post in the Ministry of Defense. Command of I Corps then fell into the hands of Lieutenant General Ngo Quang Truong. Brigadier General Giai did not fair so well, receiving a conviction for desertion and a five-year jail sentence from the JGS. Thus, he spent the rest of the war in prison, only to be relocated to a "re-education camp" by the Communists after the fall of Saigon in 1975. Meanwhile, other ARVN forces moved in to relieve the 3rd Division from the responsibility of repelling the Communist offensive.

In Moscow, Kissinger met secretly with Secretary-General Leonid Brezhnev and persuaded the Soviet leader to pressure Hanoi into ending its Easter campaign. In addition, Brezhnev agreed to approach his Communist ally with a proposition from the United States offering to end the bombing of North Vietnam

in exchange for an NVA withdrawal from southern territory. Kissinger also suggested a meeting with Le Duc Tho in Paris, scheduled on May 2. When the two diplomats met, the NVA's favorable military situation caused Tho to flout Kissinger's overtures and to gloat over the beating that ARVN forces were taking from Communist soldiers who were merely retaliating against unspecified provocations. With their diplomatic efforts thus stifled,

Kissinger and Nixon turned to a greater use of force.

On May 8, the White House ordered the mining of North Vietnamese harbors, despite reservations about the adverse effect that the action might have on the friendly relations that the Nixon administration had cultivated with China and Russia. In the Gulf of Tonkin, a squadron of warplanes from an aircraft carrier dropped 36 mines into Haiphong harbor without losing a single jet to antiaircraft fire. The presence of these explosives kept 27 ships bottled up in the area. Within three days, Navy and Marine Corps pilots also mined the harbors of Thanh Hoa, Phuc Loi, Quang Khe, Dong Hoi, and several inland waterways. Much to the relief of the White House, Moscow and Beijing issued only mild protests to these actions. In fact, Nixon and Brezhnev held a successful summit meeting in Moscow later that month.

Meanwhile, the military situation began to improve for the Allies. At An Loc, documents captured from a slain NVA political officer had revealed serious problems for the Communist offensive. High casualties, the lack of supplies, and disease had taken their toll on the morale of the NVA participants. Moreover, the NVA high command had reprimanded and replaced the chief strategist of the 9th Division

LEFT: Two F-4 Phantoms sit atop the deck of their carrier, USS *Constellation*. The F-4 Phantom was produced to a design by the US company McDonnell-Douglas which made its first appearance in 1958. As a long-range high-altitude interceptor, this model of aircraft initially saw action in Vietnam in 1964 as part of the retaliatory actions which were taken in response to the Gulf of Tonkin incident. Throughout the Vietnam War, American forces came to rely increasingly heavily upon F-4 Phantoms to carry out tactical strikes against the enemy positions on the ground. The USS *Constellation* was one of six American carriers which were operating in the area to help blunt the Communist invasion, in addition to a number of U.S. Navy destroyers and cruisers shelling the coast.

BOTTOM LEFT: Lieutenant "Randy" Cunningham explains to members of his squadron how he downed three MiG-17 fighters during a mission over North Vietnam. Both he and his RIO (Radar Intercept Officer) were forced to parachute from their F-4 Phantom into the Gulf of Tonkin after their triple kill. They were picked up by a U.S. destroyer and returned to the carrier, where they were congratulated by their colleagues on becoming the first aces of the war.

RIGHT: In the sky over North Vietnam, a F-105D Thunderchief belonging to the United States Air Force shoots down an enemy Soviet-built MIG-17, which is seen here diving to earth in a blaze of gunfire. The photographs of this dogfight were taken using a gun camera which had been mounted specifically for this purpose on the American F-105 Thunderchief.

Escaping Reality

By 1969, morale in the U.S. forces in Vietnam had hit an all-time low. The experience of the fighting man wavered between hour upon hour of numbing boredom and sudden moments of horror and violence. Some fighting units would experience combat in some form almost every single day, an extremely wearying experience. The lack of public support back home in America had filtered through to the forces, and a sense of isolation set in.

With morale falling, the intake of illegal drugs rose at an alarming rate. Generally speaking, the 1960s was a decade of drugs for most western societies, and in America especially, taking drugs was a cultural choice linked with psychedelic music and ideas of mind liberation. But in Vietnam, the impact of drugs on military units was a serious matter. Marijuana use was the most prevalent form of abuse: in 1969, a survey of soldiers finishing their tour of duty revealed that 60 percent had regularly used this drug during their period in Vietnam. The consequences of this in terms of reduced combat awareness, accidents, and discipline problems is not fully documented, but in 1970, some 11,000 U.S. servicemen were arrested on drug-related charges, and it is known that 1,146 of these were users of hard drugs. Here was a much more serious problem. Again in 1970, medical reports showed that there were as many as two deaths per day from heroin overdose within the U.S. forces. Around 35,000 confirmed heroin addicts were reported in 1971, and the number of legal cases for hard drug use climbed to 7,026.

Reports of drug abuse naturally reached home via the media and the already damaged reputation of the GI took a further downturn. Yet the combination of a relentless, traumatic and frequently bizarre war, and the easy availability of drugs, was destined to produce men wanting to flee the reality of the world around them.

RIGHT: Drugs were not exclusively a Vietnam-related problem; they were as much a part of American culture of the late 60s and early 70s. The deterioration in morale within the U.S. armed forces as a result of the war did lead to widespread abuse, and members of the services returning home from Vietnam would bring back their habit with them. In Vietnam itself, most drugs could be obtained easily, and at relatively low cost, encouraging abuse. However discipline remained high when patroling in the field – the danger of a combat situation deterred all but the most addicted of users from indulging while on active combat duty.

RIGHT: A flight of F-105 Thunderchiefs over Vietnam. While the mighty B-52 Stratofortresses shouldered the burden of night attacks during the Linebacker raids, lighter attack aircraft like the Thunderchief struck at North Vietnam during the day. Some two-seat Thunderchiefs were adapted to the "Wild Weasel" role; these aircraft were designed to knock out the North Vietnamese air defenses to protect the main strike force.

for failing to take the city. Encouraged by this evidence, the Americans implemented continuous B-52 sorties over Communist positions around An Loc for 25 hours on May 11. On the ground, American and ARVN observers could see NVA tankers climbing out of their vehicles and fleeing from the rain of bombs. Tattered and demoralized, the 5th NVA Division launched one more attack on May 14. When this effort failed, the Communist expedition retired back to Cambodia.

On May 16, the 320th NVA Division and several other regiments attached to it advanced on Kontum from the north, only to be mauled by B-52 bombings. When the American pilots finished their mission, soldiers from the 23rd ARVN Division jumped out of their trenches to attack their softened adversaries, only to find mangled corpses scattered around and terrified survivors fleeing the scene. For two weeks, this pattern continued, shredding the NVA attack force into tatters. At the end of the month, the Communists had penetrated the ARVN perimeter at Kontum when American helicopters armed with tube-launched, optically tracked, wire-guided (TOW) missiles appeared and destroyed 24 tanks in three days. Meanwhile, many other NVA vehicles ran out of gasoline after B-52 bombers had destroyed

Communist logistical lines. By now in full retreat, the Communists absorbed brutal counterattacks both on the ground and from the air on their way back to Cambodia.

Back in MR 1, Lieutenant General Truong began a protracted counterattack in mid-May, when he sent two marine brigades behind enemy lines to disrupt logistics, terrorize rear echelon soldiers, and harass NVA front-line fighters from behind. While tactical aircraft wreaked havoc upon NVA batteries, trucks,

ABOVE: Bomb craters perforate the area around a supply base. During the Easter Offensive, American air power played a decisive role in blunting Communist attacks on Binh Long City, Kontum, and other areas. Later in the year, President Nixon used B-52 Stratofortresses to great effect on North Vietnam during peace negotiations in Paris.

and massed formations, the South Vietnamese marines tore their way back to the ARVN lines. A month later, Truong unleashed Lam Son 72, a two-division campaign to retake Quang Tri province. West of Hue, the 1st Division struck the NVA lines in an attempt to draw the Communists out of their positions in the province. During this diversion, the

Airborne Division surprised NVA troops in their bunkers on the north bank of the My Chanh River in a nighttime assault that cracked the Communist line. Truong then helilifted four marine battalions behind the invasion force to cut off reinforcements. These maneuvers forced NVA forces to rush back to a new defensive line at Quang Tri City.

Truong wanted to leave the NVA soldiers in the provincial capital while his forces secured the surrounding countryside and starved out the Communists in a siege. However, President Thieu wanted Quang Tri retaken immediately and ordered him to seize the city in a massed assault, despite the network of bunkers, machinegun nests, and a central citadel within its limits. On July 11, American helicopters dropped South Vietnamese marines into the northern outskirts, where they beat back NVA tanks in a three-day battle, cut off the last road north, and surrounded the city on three sides. Eleven days later, the Airborne Division launched an attack on the citadel that went well until South Vietnamese pilots mistakenly bombed the

TOP LEFT: Seven jubilant South Vietnamese para-troopers raise their guns and handgrenades aloft in Quang Tri City. They are celebrating the fact that they have just succeeded in destroying a building known to have housed soldiers who were fighting on the side of the Communists. Although the ARVN would eventually go on to recapture Quang Tri City, the NVA forces would nonetheless manage to retain control of all the ter-ritory which was situated on the west side of the Thach Han River.

RIGHT: After having driven Khmer Rouge guerillas out of an area situated along Route 5, Cambodian gov-ernment troops make a grim discovery – the remains of murdered sol-diers and villagers – in a location 67 miles (108 km) northwest of Phnom Penh. Pictured here, they are about to begin the recov-ery of the remains. During the Vietnam War, grue-some spectacles such as these would not only shock the troops, but would also serve as an indication of the horror that was to come, and that would engulf the entire country of Cambodia within the fol-lowing three years.

BELOW LEFT: Thirty-five miles (56 km) south of the Demilitarized Zone, situat-ed near Cam Lo, several destroyed and burnt out T-54 Main Battle Tanks, property of the North Vietnamese, are pictured cluttering Route 9. The wrecked vehicles shown here were the victims of a severe pummeling by South Vietnamese war-planes and ground forces. The North Vietnamese were known to have first employed these T-54s – which were built and sup-plied by the Soviets – in massed formations during the Easter Offensive.

ABOVE: While the Democrats nominate George McGovern as their Presidential candidate for the forthcoming elections of 1972 at their Miami Beach convention, disillusioned Vietnam War veterans demonstrate outside of the convention hall. Even before the Vietnam War had taken its course, some of its veterans had acquired a distinct feeling that their own government had betrayed them by sending them into what they saw as an unnecessary and unjust conflict. The slogans adorning their banners – which call for an end to the conflict and advocate victory to the NLF – communicate their antiwar message loud and clear, while on the far left, one veteran can been seen with injuries sustained during combat.

paratroopers and forced them to withdraw. They had incurred heavy losses.

On September 9, the South Vietnamese began a final assault on the citadel. Five marine battalions attacked from three directions and took it after a week of combat. The rest of the city fell the following day. Thieu then ordered Truong to stop advancing past Quang Tri City and to allow the NVA to keep its gains north of that point. This decree to end the ARVN counterattack enabled the Communists to keep about 10 percent of the South Vietnamese countryside, but at an enormous cost. During the course of the Easter Offensive, the NVA had lost about half of the 200,000 troops which had been committed to the campaign; and its overall size was now smaller than the South Vietnamese armed forces. Faced with this reality, Hanoi determined that it would not be able to mount another significant offensive action for at least three years. They had incurred heavy losses.

During the ARVN counterattack, Kissinger met with Le Duc Tho on several occasions in Paris. Not surprisingly, Kissinger found the North Vietnamese progressively friendlier as their offensive deteriorated. On October 8, Tho offered Kissinger almost everything that the United States had demanded: a ceasefire, the release of war prisoners, and a willingness to refrain from interfering with internal political conflicts in South Vietnam. Kissinger quickly accepted this overture and the two men planned to sign a formal peace treaty at the end of the month, after their negotiators worked out minor details in the agreement.

However, President Thieu derailed this process by rejecting the terms of the treaty out of hand, primarily because of provisions allowing the Communists to keep the land that they had seized in South Vietnam. He also denounced the peace treaty publicly and accused the United States of deserting him. Kissinger then notified Hanoi that the United

States could not impose this treaty upon an unwilling ally. After Nixon won a spectacular victory in the presidential election, Kissinger and the North Vietnamese resumed negotiations in November and December. This time, the Communists became intransigent, and demanded more and more concessions that Kissinger refused to accept.

To effect a change of heart, Nixon unleashed Linebacker II, a vigorous bombing campaign against military targets in northern North Vietnam that began on December 18 and lasted 11 days. During the course of the operation, about 1,600 civilians were killed; and the destruction brought by these "Christmas bombings" provoked international and domestic outcry. When the campaign ended, Kissinger and Le Duc Tho agreed to meet again in January 1973. To what extent Nixon succeeded in bombing the North Vietnamese back to the negotiating table remains unclear.

ABOVE: American Specialist-4 Merle Schonortz and Specialist 4 Lloyd Ryan, an Australian, Ron Lovelock, and Tu Du Streetbar girls listen to the 1972 Presidential election results. Nixon's victory was one of the greatest electorial landslides in American history.
ABOVE TOP: At a hangar in Bien Hoa, a South Vietnamese pilot stands in front of an American-built Northrop F-5, one of many pieces of hardware supplied by the United States under the Enhance and Enhance Plus programs, aimed at restoring the South Vietnamese armed forces to their pre-Easter Offensive levels.

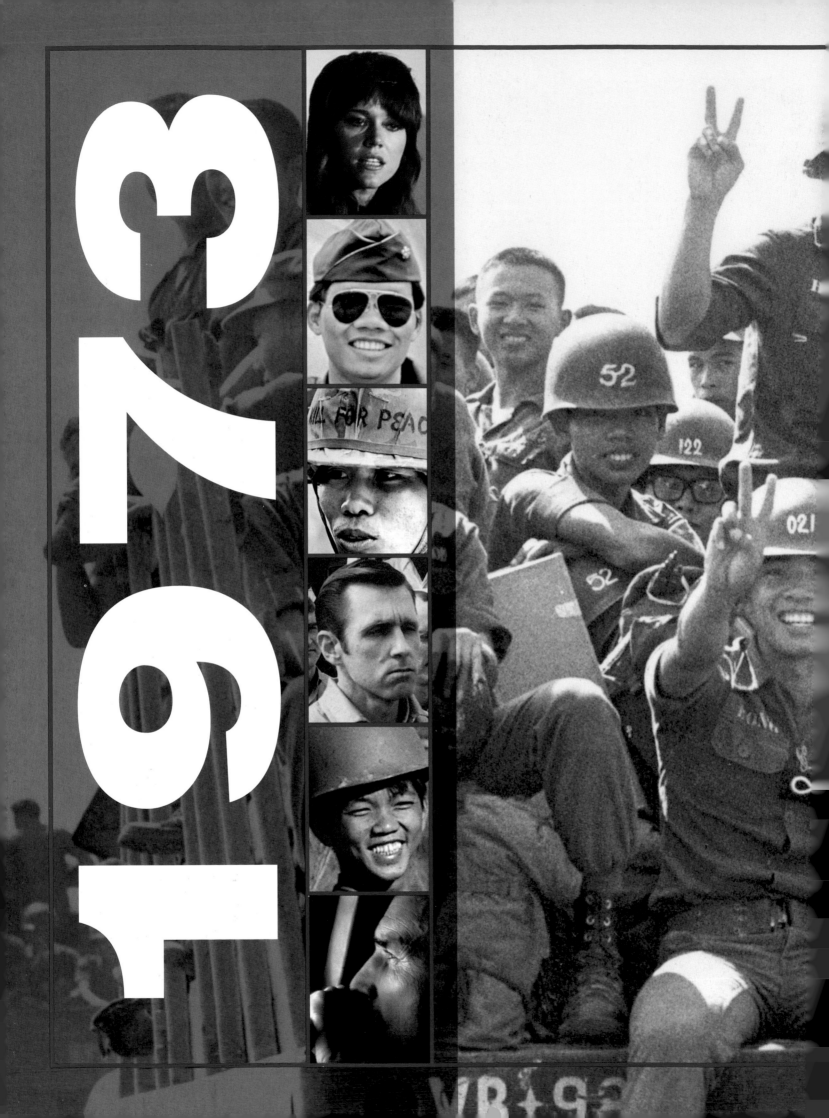

1961

Peace at Last?

At the beginning of the year, Henry Kissinger and Le Duc Tho met in Paris again to work out the final details of a treaty ending the American involvement in Vietnam. Overall, the results of these final talks tended to favor the Communist cause. The North Vietnamese Army (NVA) won the right to retain the land it occupied south of the DMZ. In return for this concession, Hanoi promised to pull 30,000 troops out of southern territory and agreed to extend the ceasefire to Laos. However, the North Vietnamese claimed that they had no influence over their Khmer Rouge confederates and thus refused to offer any guarantees about ending hostilities in Cambodia.

The final draft of the Paris treaty also called for the establishment of an International Commission of Control and Supervision (ICCS), an assembly of Polish, Hungarian, Canadian, and Indonesian military officers charged with ensuring that both belligerents adhere to the terms of the peace agreement. However, the North Vietnamese ensured that the ICCS would merely be a token force containing no more than 1,160 participants, a much smaller number than Kissinger had wanted. Also included was a clause mandating the creation of a National Council of National Reconciliation and Concord (NCNRC), a panel of pro-Saigon and Communist activists assembled to organize future local and general elections in

South Vietnam. Presumably, the National Liberation Front (NLF) would be allowed to compete as a legal party. Finally, the treaty included provisions for the return of American prisoners of war at a rate which was commensurate with the withdrawal of American servicemen from Vietnam, as well as for the removal of mines from North Vietnamese harbors.

In Saigon, President Thieu threatened to veto the "Agreement on Ending the War and Restoring the Peace" by refusing to sign it. Nixon responded by declaring that the United States planned to ratify the Paris treaty with or without Thieu's approval. When he realized that Nixon was not bluffing, Thieu consented to the agreement six days before Kissinger and Tho staged a formal signing ceremony on January 27, 1973. Officially, the American war in Vietnam came to an end on this date. However, the struggle was far from over for the Vietnamese people.

The two Vietnamese armies lobbed artillery, rocket, and mortar fire at each other right up to the moment when the Paris peace treaty took effect on January 28 at 8 a.m. At An Loc, an NVA rocket killed an adviser, Lieutenant Colonel William B. Nolde, the last official American casualty in the war. When the hour of the ceasefire arrived, the two armies on the opposite banks of the Thach Han River at Quang Tri fell abruptly quiet. Among conventional forces near

---

ABOVE: President Thieu (left) meets to discuss the implications of the peace agreement with President Nixon (middle) and Henry Kissinger (right). By this stage the U.S. was firmly committed to leaving Vietnam with as much honor and dignity as possible.
RIGHT: Near Quang Ngai on the central coastal region of South Vietnam, the young son of a soldier sits among a large stack of live artillery rounds. The boy and his father are living within the perimeter of a military outpost.

the DMZ, the war seemed to be over. Below this area, the fluid character of the battle lines and the guerrilla presence in the countryside meant that hostilities were to persist in scattered areas. Specifically, a land-grabbing campaign emerged, in which units from the ARVN competed with Communist forces for control of villages.

Early in the year, Saigon's prospects looked good. In a contest for 400 hamlets across South Vietnam, ARVN forces exploited their numerical superiority against thinly spread Communist units to seize all but 23 of the villages two weeks after the ceasefire had taken effect. The South Vietnamese established forward outposts throughout the countryside to create a semblance of authority and to bait Viet Cong guerrillas into attacking, thus violating the peace treaty. This proactive activity enabled ARVN to control 90 percent of the

RIGHT: At Da Nang men from the 3rd Regiment, 3rd Marine Division queue on the dock, preparing to board the USS *Iwo Jima* which will take them home. On March 29, 1973, Nixon finally pulled the last of the American ground forces out of Vietnam. Since taking office as President in 1969, Nixon had been under almost constant pressure to pull troops out of what many in the U.S. saw as a foreign war with little relevance to their country. In March of 1973 that moment had finally arrived.

LEFT: In the central city of Pleiku, a convoy of jeep-mounted TOW anti-tank misslies supplied by the U.S. stops and waits for soldiers to change a flat tire. This high tech equipment was typical of the increasingly sophisticated hardware being shipped to South Vietnam and added to ARVN's arsenal as the U.S. ground forces progressively disengaged. Although the equipment flooding in from the America was turning the ARVN into a well-equipped military force, it still faced a formidable task. By 1973, almost all of the territory west of Pleiku city was under Communist control.

BOTTOM LEFT: Delegates to the Paris Peace Talks around the negotiating table. This picture, taken at a meeting on January 13, 1973, shows delegates ironing out the final details of a treaty designed to end the war in Vietnam. Le Duc Tho, the chief negotiator of the North Vietnamese government, is positioned in the center of the left-hand side of the table, directly facing his American counterpart at the talks, Henry Kissinger.

Paris Peace Conference

ABOVE: The signing ceremony held in front of the media at the Paris Peace Conference. The ratifying of the treaty saw the U.S. committed to withdrawal from Vietnam, which was a major success for the North Vietnamese.

The Paris Peace conference ended the U.S. involvement in Vietnam. It catapulted the names of Henry Kissinger and Le Duc Tho into the limelight and saw them receive the Nobel Peace Prize for their efforts. Yet, in retrospect, the Peace Accords were just a breathing space for North Vietnam. Once the U.S. were gone, then the South was there for the taking.

By 1972 Kissinger, the U.S. Assistant for National Security Affairs, and Le Duc Tho, the North Vietnamese negotiator were already in secret discussions about ways out of the Vietnam impasse. On October 8 , Le Duc Tho placed a series of proposals on the table. He advocated immediate ceasefire, the complete withdrawal of U.S. forces from Vietnam within 60 days, and an exchange of POWs. The areas controlled by the North following the Easter Invasion were to be retained, and an interim coalition government was to be formed from the Saigon regime, the communist People's Revolutionary Government (which

was formerly the National Liberation Front), and an independent party was to oversee subsequent reunification elections.

Kissinger did not accept the package outright, but an interim agreement was signed. This was much to the fury of Thieu's government who had not been consulted, and so Thieu refused to sign. After the re-election of Nixon, the negotiations resumed, but broke down again. The U.S. then resorted to force in the Linebacker II bombing raids, driving the North back to the negotiating table. Hanoi returned to the negotiations and the Paris agreement was signed by all parties, including Thieu, on 27 January 1973.

Thus ended the U.S. involvement in the war. But in retrospect, the agreement signed in Paris achieved a number of Hanoi's war aims. The U.S. had been ousted, the Communists now held substantial territories in South Vietnam, and they were free to complete their conquest of the south.

population and 80 percent of the territory of South Vietnam. For several months, the NVA was in no position to challenge this hegemony because of the losses it had sustained in the Easter Offensive and the Christmas Bombings.

Despite these ominous indications of renewed warfare, the United States remained committed to disengagement, which was tied to the return of 653 American POWs from North Vietnam. In February, Hanoi released 163 captives to American officials as a good-will gesture to facilitate the withdrawal of the 24,000 American military personnel still in Vietnam. The following month, on March 29, Hanoi released the remaining captives the same day when the last 5200 American ground troops departed the country. After this date, the American presence consisted of 209 officers and enlisted personnel, serving primarily as embassy guards, ceasefire monitors, and other noncombatant functions.

With the prospect of future encounters with American ground troops now gone, North Vietnam began rebuilding its military forces and economic infrastructure in anticipation of a future showdown with South Vietnam. During the course of the year, the Communists revived and expanded their logistical network along the Cambodian–South Vietnam border, created seven reserve divisions, and replenished units devastated in the Easter Offensive. In effect, they turned the western frontier of the Saigon regime into a "Third Vietnam," a separate political entity with its own government bureaucracy. Hanoi sustained this new regime by sending at least 70,000 troops down the Ho Chi Minh Trail in violation of the Paris accords, as well as civilians to populate and develop the area. The noncombatants included political cadres, schoolteachers, health officials, and peasants charged with growing rice for the NVA.

North Vietnam eventually connected the "Third Vietnam" to itself by constructing a paved highway and a fuel pipeline that ran parallel to the Ho Chi Minh Trail. The presence of 22 antiaircraft regiments along this road effectively deterred air strikes against trucks and tanks traveling on it. Although South Vietnam

ABOVE: "They make a wasteland and call it peace." A South Vietnamese soldier waves his nation's flag at the news of the end of the fighting. The hopes of a genuine negotiated end to the war would soon be shattered.

RIGHT: Despite the optimism of this ARVN soldier victory was to prove even more elusive for the South than peace. The "peace" ushered in by the treaty was little more than an uneasy truce. Although in some places the fighting did halt, at least temporarily, elsewhere ceasefire violations were the norm.

RIGHT: The South
Vietnamese flag flies above
this village as members of
a South Vietnamese unit
hope for more peaceful
days ahead. Despite
President Thieu's clear
reservations about the
treaty signed in Paris,
there was some real opti-
mism in the South that it
might form the basis of a
lasting peace with North
Vietnam. Events were to
prove that it represented,
at best, a breathing space
for the two combatants to
gather their strength for
the final struggle. In his
memoirs, General
Westmoreland accused
Nixon and Kissinger of giving too much away in
Paris. The North
Vietnamese read this as a
lack of real commitment to
defend the South, encour-
aging them to push for
complete victory and
undermining the long term
viability of the settlement.

LEFT: Although the Paris treaty was supposed to end the war, small-scale fighting quickly broke out between ARVN and Communist forces as both sides sought to secure as much territory in the South as possible. This attempt to seize and control as many villages as possible became known as the war of the flags.
BELOW: South of Saigon, these Viet Cong guerillas pose with their armament having occupied territory near Cai Lai on Highway 4. Shortly before the signing of the Paris peace treaty, the Communists had secured this location along with many other areas between Saigon and the Cambodian border.

possessed a large air force, its warplanes lacked the electronic equipment that American aircraft had possessed to help pilots evade surface-to-air missiles. Near the DMZ, the Communists developed Dong Ha into a thriving port that served as a military depot to help support future incursions into the South.

While the two belligerent nations set out to consolidate the control they had over their respective areas within South Vietnam, fighting broke out in several disputed areas. In March, the NVA besieged the Tong Le Chan Ranger Base in Military Region 3 (MR 3) and shelled the area throughout the summer. The Communists also attacked the town of Hong Ngu near the Cambodian border in an effort to secure hegemony over the border regions for the "Third Vietnam." However, South Vietnam's military superiority during the first half of the year enabled ARVN to exercise much more initiative in contested areas for at least a few months.

LEFT: Some of the first American prisoners-of-war to be released as a result of the Paris Treaty at Gia Lam Airport. Most of the captives shown here are pilots and crewmen who were shot down during air missions over North Vietnam during the conflict. From left to right, they are: Captain John W. Clark, USAF; Captain Joseph Crecca, Jr., USAF; Major Hubert K. Flesher, USAF; Lieutenant-Commander Fred R. Purrington, USN; and Captain John J. Nasmyth, Jr., USAF; TSGT Eddie P. Boaz. It is notable that the faces of these men show no emotion; it was only when they had boarded the aircraft taking them home that the men allowed their feelings to come through.
FAR RIGHT: A returning POW emerges from the aircraft that has flown him home into the full glare of the media spotlight. These men were instant celebrities and after years of captivity and isolation many of them found the overwhelming attention difficult to cope with. Many had spent long years in North Vietnamese camps and during that time their country had changed out of all recognition, to a large degree as a result of the very war they had been fighting. Coping with the culture shock of their homecoming would prove an ongoing struggle.
BELOW RIGHT: As part of the terms of the peace treaty the United States committed to assist the North Vietnamese in clearing the huge numbers of mines that had been sown around the North Vietnamese coast and particularly the major ports such as Haiphong. The U.S. had at its disposal sophisticated mine-detection equipment which North Vietnam did not possess.

Saigon was especially concerned with maintaining control of such heavily populated regions as the Mekong Delta and the coastal lowlands. South Vietnam planned to settle at least half of the 600,000 refugees in Hue and Da Nang who had fled from the Easter Offensive, into areas that it hoped to seize from the Communists. In Quang Tin province just south of Da Nang, the 2nd ARVN Division cleared the coastal areas of scattered Viet Cong guerrillas, then joined with a Ranger battalion to pursue the fugitives into the western hills. Below the Mekong Delta, the poorly led 21st Division was supposed to dislodge Communist cells from the rice-producing Chong Thien province. However, the divisional commanders gave this responsibility to reservist Territorial Forces that were unable to accomplish the task.

Upriver and close to the Cambodian border, the 7th ARVN Ranger Group and the 4th Armor Group had more success in the Seven Mountains Region in Chao Doc province. In early July, the two units attacked a network of bunkers occupied by the 1st NVA Division. After over a month of inconclusive fighting, when they lost about 900 men to combat and disease, the Communists retired to Cambodia.

These losses caused Hanoi to deactivate the division. The ARVN's success in Seven Mountains gave South Vietnam another important rice-producing area that had served as the southern terminus for the Ho Chi Minh Trail. Throughout the spring and summer of 1973, ARVN scored numerous other victories in smaller engagements that "pacified" more hamlets, bringing several hundred thousand civilians into South Vietnamese jurisdiction.

Later in the year, the North Vietnamese realized that keeping their forces in fixed defensive positions made their units static and vulnerable to enemy assaults. However, Hanoi also feared that resuming aggressive military actions in South Vietnam might provoke the United States into more B-52 sorties against NVA positions. Although the Watergate scandal and an antiwar majority in Congress were eroding the warmongering powers of the White House, the North Vietnamese still perceived Nixon as a ruthless and unpredictable maniac who might initiate another Linebacker campaign if the NVA went on the offensive. However, the possibility of losing the "Third Vietnam" to ARVN forces due to inaction proved to be a bigger risk that provoked Hanoi into authorizing dynamic actions in the South.

In June, the NVA attacked Trung Nghia near Kontum. After three months of bloody combat, the 23rd ARVN Division drove the invaders from the area. Southwest of Saigon, Communists moved into old fortifications in the Tri Phap Swamp and launched raids against nearby South Vietnamese bases. Toward the end of the summer, the ARVN IV Corps retaliated and inflicted heavy casualties on its enemies, although it failed to challenge Communist control of the swamp. Meanwhile, NVA and Viet Cong units employed sapper attacks, assassinations, and terrorist actions to undermine the South Vietnamese pacification campaign, especially against refugee centers and resettlement hamlets in the coastal regions of MR 1. On September 6, Communist forces fired mortars, rockets, and incendiary grenades into An Tinh village, burning over 300 houses in the process.

Later in the month, NVA infantry, artillery, and armored units overpowered the Le Minh Ranger camp 45 miles (72 km) west of Pleiku. Days later, Communist forces produced similar results against an ARVN outpost at Bach Ma near Da Nang. Northwest of Saigon, NVA activity persisted throughout Tay Ninh province. In addition to maintaining their long-time siege of Tong Le Chan, the Communists

Return of POWs

'**G**od bless the President and God bless you, Mr and Mrs America, you did not forget us.' So ran the words of Lieutenant Commander Everett Alvarez, one of the first U.S. soldiers to be captured in Vietnam and one of the first to be released under Operation Homecoming.

Homecoming was the fruit of the Paris Peace Accords, signed on January 23 ,1973 and withdrawing the U.S. from its long and bloody experience in Vietnam. Written into the agreement was the requirement for exchange of prisoners on both sides. U.S. military authorities knew of around 600 confirmed POWs either in North Vietnam itself, or who were

believed to have been held prisoner by the Viet Cong in remote areas of the South. Now they could come home.

The actual release of U.S. prisoners was described by many witnesses as one of the most emotional events of their lives. Some prisoners – particularly airmen shot down during the early stages of "Rolling Thunder" back in the 1960s – had been in prison for nearly eight years. For many, torture had been a common occurrence. Isolation, disease and squalor had become part of their lives. Yet early February saw the move towards their release. Those in the infamous Hanoi Hilton were allowed to clean and dress in civilian clothes. After this they were taken to Hanoi's Gia Lam airfield in camouflaged buses. Photographs from this event show the soldiers marching with crisp military discipline, showing that they had not been beaten and keeping their faces impassive. It was only once they had boarded the C-141 aircraft set to take them home that the tears and smiles came.

Most of the prisoners were flown to the USAF Hospital, Clark Air Base, Republic of the Philippines, where they received a medical evaluation and treatment where necessary. They were also able to experience the joy of a fresh, clean bed, something some had not felt and enjoyed for years. But it was the welcome they received that lodged in many of their memories. Thousands of servicemen greeted them off the aircraft with cheers. At the bottom of the aircraft steps they were met by dignitaries such as Admiral Gayler, the commander of all U.S. forces in the Pacific. Thus their war came to an end, and they were once more brought back into the fold of their country and their units.

Homecoming did not satisfy all, however. For some, the figures just didn't seem to add up. During Operation Homecoming the communists released some 512 POWs, 53 soldiers previously identified as missing in action, and one man whom the U.S. believed had been killed in action. Yet by 1976 the Department of Defense still listed 36 men as POWs not returned. Even more worrying, 795 men remained as MIAs.

To this day, many groups in the U.S. still claim that significant numbers of U.S. soldiers remain captive, imprisoned in remote areas of Vietnam, hidden from the sight of the world. By now, it is unlikely that they are right, and Homecoming is most probably the final chapter in the POW story.

ABOVE: Cheering American POWs depart Vietnam. President Nixon took office in 1969 with a commitment to bring the war to an end. Faced with a Congress increasingly hostile to the war, the pressure to withdraw from Vietnam was tremendous.

LEFT: A POW contemplates his return to "the World." The prospect of release had been what had kept many of the men going during their captivity, but the actual reality of the event could be traumatic.

FAR LEFT: Major Charles R. Tyler arrives at March Air Force Base, California. Like several of his comrades Major Tyler had spent almost six years as a prisoner of North Vietnam. The joy of his wife at the return of her husband is clear, but some men returned to loved ones who had become strangers during their long years away. Others had been so changed by their experiences that picking up their lives was difficult.

bombarded ARVN positions at Soui Day and Nui Ba Den Mountain with artillery and mortar fire. The NVA rendered this area and Phuoc Long province to the northeast increasingly isolated from Saigon through a campaign of continuous harassment against ARVN positions and units using the roads that connected these provinces to the capital.

On November 4, the NVA began a campaign in Quang Duc province, 93 miles (150 km) northeast of Saigon, when its 205th Regiment overran ARVN positions at Bu Prang and Bu Bong near the Cambodian border. Two days later, while Communist units fired rockets into the Bien Hoa airbase near Saigon, the 271st NVA Regiment seized another ARVN post at Dak Son, 9 miles (15 km) northeast of Bu Bong. The 205th Regiment then headed south and besieged the town of Kien Duc, which was 12 miles (20 km) west of

AND KILL MIGS

LEFT: Air Force personnel relax and take a break from operations at a base in Thailand. From left to right, they are Captain Jeff S. Feinstein, Operations Specialist Chief Gene P. Barnes, and Captain John A. Madden. Both Feinstein and Madden are members of the 432nd Tactical Fighter Reconnaissance Wing MIG Killers, a group which was charged with shooting down the Soviet-made warplanes which were flown by the North Vietnamese in bombing operations during the conflict.

OPPOSITE TOP: Actress Jane Fonda with her future husband Tom Hayden, both vocal opponents of U.S. involvement in Southeast Asia. The final withdrawal of U.S. forces did not bring an end to the anti-war movement, but the intensity of the protest did diminish. The agony of Vietnam was about to be eclipsed in the U.S. by the scandals of Watergate which would ultimately bring down the President himself.

OPPOSITE BOTTOM: South Vietnamese military police prepare to release Communist captives to their adversaries on the other side of the Thach Han River. In March 1973, both sides implemented a prisoner exchange as part of the peace agreement. In preparation for their return, the Communists have removed their prison garments. Altogether, the Saigon government released 25,000 enemy soldiers.

NEXT PAGE: South Vietnamese Airmen pose for the cameras, standing in front of the warplanes recently given to them by the United States Air Force after its withdrawal. When the Americans departed the country, they turned over 150 Northrop F-5 fighters to their ally, in addition to other equipment.

Gia Nghia, the provincial capital and head-quarters of the 23rd ARVN Division. While a South Vietnamese regiment was digging in at Kien Duc, ARVN II Corps sent reinforcements to the troubled areas. On November 28, the 44th ARVN Infantry Regiment retook Dak Son. A week later, the 205th NVA Regiment temporarily seized Kien Duc, only to lose it to a punishing counterattack mounted by the 45th ARVN Regiment.

At the end of the campaign, the NVA retained only Bu Bong and Bu Prang. However, Hanoi did enjoy another important result from this offensive. Unlike earlier years, American bombers and warplanes did not show up to tear apart Communist ground forces or North Vietnamese urban centers. In fact, the Quong Duc campaign had unfolded at a time when the United States Congress had passed the War Powers Act over Nixon's veto. Enacted on November 7, the new law required the president to notify Congress within 48 hours after sending troops into any theater of action, and required him to halt such actions if

LEFT: At Prek Cak Par, 7 miles (11 km) southeast of Phnom Penh, Cambodian government troops in an armored personnel carrier attack a group of Communist rebels through a screen of smoke. The Cambodian government soldiers were retaliating against an ambush which had been staged by Khmer Rouge guerillas. These guerillas had attacked the Zeo Brigade as they were traveling along Highway 30.
BELOW LEFT: A young Cambodian soldier hauls a mortar into battle on his shoulder, a look of anxiety in his eyes as he glances over to action taking place in another part of the field. By 1973, troops loyal to Lon Nol struggled for survival as the Khmer Rouge insurgency gained momentum and the American air support for the Cambodian government ended that summer.

he failed to gain legislative approval within 90 days. Months earlier, lawmakers had also forced Nixon into accepting August 15 as a deadline for any bombing action in Southeast Asia. By the end of the year, the North Vietnamese government realized that American disengagement from Southeast Asia was permanent and that the NVA could strike the South with impunity.

While South Vietnam struggled for survival without American intervention, the Lon Nol regime in Cambodia teetered on the brink of destruction. Unlike the North Vietnamese and the Pathet Lao, the Khmer Rouge was not interested in signing a ceasefire agreement. In February, the Communist insurgents had beaten demoralized government troops in almost every engagement and reached the outskirts of Phnom Penh when B-52s appeared and devastated the attackers. A month later, Nixon expanded the bombing campaign from Khmer Rouge positions to the South Vietnamese border, hoping to knock out NVA logistical networks that were not supposed to exist, according to

the Paris treaty. By this time, the Khmer Rouge and the North Vietnamese had little to do with each other.

As the year progressed, the ranks of the Khmer Rouge grew to include 50,000 disciplined fighters, while the government army degenerated into a state of disorder and corruption. In April, the Communists again approached Phnom Penh and showered the city with rockets and mortars. Nixon then ordered more bombings on Khmer Rouge positions, knowing that he had to end these air strikes on the August 15 deadline. Although the rebels were aware of this deadline, they chose not to wait until it passed. Instead, they massed for an attack on Phnom Penh, only to be torn to ribbons by B-52 bombs. This inexplicable miscalculation forced the Khmer Rouge to retire and lick its wounds, although it retained a strong presence beyond the capital and wreaked havoc on government bases throughout the country. By 1974, Communist forces on both sides of the border enjoyed distinct military advantages over their enemies.

ABOVE At Kompong Cham, Cambodia, a government soldier expresses his attitude toward the Khmer Rouge with inscription on his helmet loaded with irony and which shows the lengths he is pepared to go in order to eradicate the rebels who have shattered the peace of his country. As the practice of decorating their helmets was common in the U.S. forces – though officially forbidden – so their Southeast Asian allies copied the habit. Like their former comrades they used the slogans to demonstrate their feelings about the conflict. In August 1973, the Khmer Rouge rebels and the Cambodian government forces met head on in a fierce battle for the city of Kompong Cham, which came to an end only when the Communists were forced to retire due to lack of ammunition.

1974

The Third Indochina War

By the end of 1973, both Hanoi and Saigon had concluded that a political settlement to their conflict was impossible and turned to military force to resolve their competition for territory in the South. The following January President Thieu proclaimed the beginning of a new Indochina war in which the ARVN would act openly against areas of Communist occupation before the NVA could use them as a launching pad for future invasions. Meanwhile, the North Vietnamese developed a plan

to regain the land they had lost since the 1973 cease-fire and implemented a campaign that would undermine the Saigon regime by striking and demoralizing both the ARVN and the civilian population. First, the Communists planned to attack depots, airfields, roads, and outposts to disrupt the South Vietnamese transportation and communication system and inflict heavy losses on ARVN forces. Then the NVA would move the war from isolated bases into areas which were densely populated.

Early in the year, the initiative seemed to be with the South Vietnamese. In January they learned that the 5th NVA Division was moving from Tay Ninh to Dinh Tuong province in the Mekong Delta in an attempt to block Route 4, which was Saigon's only link to the region. If the division reached the otherwise

lightly defended Communist bases in the Tri Phap swamp, it would be difficult to dislodge. In mid-February, certain members of the 7th and 9th ARVN Divisions descended upon these bases before the NVA division arrived, surprised the defenders, and sent the Communists reeling with heavy losses of men and equipment.

Fighting then erupted throughout this area as well as upriver in Kien Tuong province, most of which went well for the South Vietnamese. In an effort to divert the ARVN campaign in Tri Phap, the Central Office for South Vietnam (COSVN) launched terrorist raids upon isolated ARVN outposts and civilian targets such as schools and churches. Despite the mayhem inflicted upon soldiers, schoolchildren, and parishioners, ARVN forces continued their six-week campaign in the swamp, killing about 1,000 Communists and seizing 5,000 tons of food, and over eight tons of weapons and ammunition. ARVN engineers then constructed fortifications for reservist Regional Forces (RFs) to occupy. NVA units briefly captured these bases in late April, only to lose them in an ARVN counterattack the following month. By June, South Vietnam maintained a firm hold on the swamp and deprived the 5th NVA Division of an important base area for operations in the delta.

ABOVE: In the early months of 1974 a resurgent ARVN won a string of victories over their communist opponents. Perhaps the South's armed forces had finally come of age – they had certainly had the best of the fighting since the 1973 ceasefire.
RIGHT: A South Vietnamese soldier mans a sandbagged guard post outside the Presidential Palace in Saigon. Apparently abandoned by his erstwhile US allies and beset by communist enemies and internal opponents, it is hardly surprising that President Thieu developed something of a siege mentality. But at the beginning of 1974 it seemed his regime might still have the resilience to weather the storm.

Thus stymied in Military Region 4 (MR 4), the 5th NVA Division fell back to the Parrot's Beak salient in Cambodia and staged cross-border strikes upon enemy positions. On March 27, it besieged a base at Duc Hue, provoking the ARVN II Corps commander, Lieutenant General Pham Quoc Thuan, into assembling a 20-battalion expeditionary force against Communist units in the salient. Late in April, the 49th ARVN Infantry Regiment and the 7th Ranger Group entered the eastern side of the salient, thus beginning the Svay Rieng operation, while South Vietnamese warplanes struck suspected NVA sanctuaries in the area. To the southwest, two RF battalions crossed into Cambodia from Moc Hoa, advancing on the 5th NVA Division's headquarters.

On April 28, the 275th NVA Regiment and the 25th Sapper Battalion attacked the border town of Long Khot, just west of Parrot's Beak, in an effort to divert the ARVN expedition. Unimpressed with this maneuver, the South

ABOVE: Wearing their distinctively tightly tailored uniforms, soldiers from the South Vietnamese army move nervously out from under the cover of a building. By 1974 many had become increasingly reluctant to close with the enemy and were totally dependent on U.S. firepower – including armor, artillery, and air power – to fight their war.

RIGHT: In the placed water of a river, a wrecked Bailey bridge sags, destroyed during the fighting between North and South Vietnamese troops. In the foreground, a soldier of the ARVN VI Corps looks at the muddy and battered foxhole in which a North Vietnamese soldier fought and died. The North had become aware that the United States, tired of the war, would no longer commit ground troops to assist the South, and therefore knew that a conventional attack against the South was a viable option.

FOLLOWING PAGE: As the year progressed communist pressure built in a series of offensives, and the ARVN's military position began to unravel with alarming speed.

Vietnamese sent three armored units from Go Dau Ha into the salient. Moving quickly to the west, the tank column headed straight for the 5th NVA Division's headquarters, forcing the Communists to pull away from Long Khot to defend their beleaguered base area. ARVN infantry and armored cavalry units then crossed the border from Moc Hoa and interdicted the NVA regiment before it could return to its headquarters. With the entire Communist division thus divided and pinned down, the ARVN battalions swept through the salient, disrupting NVA logistical lines, killing 1,200 of the enemy, taking 65 prisoners of war, and capturing hundreds of weapons while losing fewer than 100 soldiers before returning to South Vietnamese territory in early May.

Although the success of the Svay Rieng operation provided the South Vietnamese with encouragement for the future, it turned out to be the last hurrah of the Saigon regime. As the year progressed, the tide of the war turned in

GENERAL DUANG "Big" Minh

By nature, General Duong Van Minh was a man who would much rather take life easy, playing tennis and growing flowers, than shape policy. Yet "Big" Minh – his nickname due to his size of personality and physique – would be at the heart of some of Vietnam's major political events.

Duong Van Minh made his reputation as an army officer during the early reign of Diem, defeating the Binh Xuyen gangster-militia which formed a Saigon-based threat to Diem's rule, and publicly guillotining its leader. Despite this act, the President did not trust him, and Minh became Diem's military adviser between 1962 and 1963. This was, in effect, a powerless post. Yet Duong Van Minh was a man who wanted status and influence. As U.S. discontent with Diem's reign grew, he was approached with regard to leading a coup. So in November 1963, Minh and a body of other ambitious generals overthrew and executed Diem. Minh established himself as Chief of State and head of a new 12-man Military Revolutionary Council, lasting only two months before himself being ousted by Major General Nguyen Khanh. This did not end his political career, however. He spent the next nine years floating in and out of positions of power, and providing a determined opposition to President Thieu.

Minh did achieve his return to the position of President. The year was 1975, and the North Vietnamese were knocking on the gates of Saigon. On April 21, President Thieu resigned and passed power over to his vice president, Tran Van Huong. By this stage presidential power had lost much appeal, and Huong resigned. Minh stepped in and took up the reigns of ebbing power. He called for a ceasefire and negotiations, but was ignored by the eager NVA. Minh surrendered Saigon to the Communists on April 30, and afterward went into detention. The position he had always craved had proved his final undoing.

RIGHT: At a funeral held at Mount Olivet Cemetery on April 20, 1974 for U.S. Air Force Captain Bob Weskamp, his son Timothy (7) and daughter Cecily (8) hold the folded Stars and Stripes flag on his coffin. Captain Weskamp was killed during an attack on targets near Hanoi in 1967. Seven years after burial in Vietnam, his body was disinterred and returned to the United States for burial with full military honors. At the funeral – attended by his widow Mrs. Patricia Bowers, mother Mrs. James Roberts, children, and brother Major Dick Weskamp USAF – there was a fly past of U.S. combat aircraft in the "missing man" formation.

ABOVE: Cambodian government troops carry a wounded comrade past an M113 Armored Personnel Carrier. In the 1970s the Cambodians were finally dragged into the Vietnam War. The Khmer Rouge fought using many tactics of the Viet Cong.

BELOW: A South Vietnamese Marine wounded during the period of the "truce" signed in January 1973. Between then and January 1974, 13,788 South Vietnamese soldiers, 2,159 civilians, and 45,057 Communists died in the fighting.

favor of the NVA. In April and May, the Communists began a series of offensives that engulfed all four of South Vietnam's Military Regions. Near Saigon, NVA swarmed throughout MR 3, attacking ARVN bases north, west, and east of the capital. Early in April, the 7th Division seized Firebase Chi Linh, severing Route 13, an artery that connected Saigon to Phuoc Long province. Near the Fishhook salient, the Tong Le Chan Ranger base fell to the Communists after a 15-month siege.

East of Saigon, two NVA regiments drove RF units out of their positions along the Long Kanh-Phuoc Tuy provincial border near

Highway 1, although ARVN regulars eventually dispersed the regiments and retook the areas. The Communists then seized Bao Binh village on May 24 and the Rung La refugee settlement on June 11. The occupation of these two positions 31 miles (50 km) east of the capital enabled the NVA to block Highway 1. On June 17, ARVN forces retook Rung La and pushed the Communists away from the road. However, the NVA and Viet Cong still held Bao Binh and were able to launch raids from there into Rung La and against ARVN vehicles riding down Highway 1.

In May, the 9th NVA Division overran three ARVN positions on the northern tip of the Iron Triangle region 20 miles (32 km) northwest of Saigon. The 7th NVA Division then moved in from Chi Linh and reinforced this newly acquired area while ARVN forces arrived from the south to protect the rest of the Iron Triangle. In a bloody campaign that lasted until November, the 18th ARVN Division eventually cleared the Communists out of the area. If the NVA had retained the area, it would have been able to fire artillery barrages into Tan Son Nhut air base and ARVN positions at Cu Chi, Phu Cuong, and Lai Khe.

In the Central Highlands the NVA began a campaign to batter and demoralize the two ARVN units in MR 2, sweep them out of their

Nixon's Fall

On June 17, 1972 five men broke into the offices of the Democratic National Committee at the Watergate complex in Washington D.C. They were caught, and so began a spiraling scandal which eventually forced the resignation of President Richard Nixon on August 9, 1974.

The five, it transpired, had been hired by the Republican Committee to Re-Elect the President (CRP or "Creep") headed by former U.S. Attorney General John Mitchell. He resigned, and effectively shouldered the blame for the incident. His sacrifice seemed to work: Nixon was convincingly re-elected president against the Democratic candidate George McGovern. The scandal could have stopped there. A grand jury investigation of Watergate identified several key figures implicated in the break-in, and on April 30, 1973 Nixon accepted the resignations of or dismissed several key figures of his administration. These included White House Chief of Staff H.R. Haldeman, White House Assistance on Domestic Affairs John Ehrlichman, and, crucially, the U.S. Attorney General Richard Kleindienst.

The new Attorney General ordered a sweeping investigation of the Watergate incident, under special prosecutor Archibald Fox. As proceedings got underway, shocking revelations started to emerge. White House Counsel John Dean, dismissed by Nixon over Watergate, implicated the White House at the highest levels, even stating that Nixon had bribed the burglars to keep their silence.

Nixon, of course, fought back vehemently. But the scandal was snowballing. White House aide Alexander Butterfield revealed that all presidential conversations were recorded on a tape system installed by Nixon himself. Nixon was subpoenaed by Cox to hand over eight particular tapes. Nixon refused on grounds of national security, and there began a battle through the courts to acquire these recordings. The courts consistently found against Nixon, but he did not release the tapes, and sacked Cox. His new appointment to special prosecutor was Leon Jaworski, and Nixon finally handed over a batch of heavily doctored tapes. Over 18 minutes had been deliberately erased from one. It looked like a coverup, and in March 1974, a grand jury indicted seven White House staff – including Mitchell, Hadleman, and Ehrlichman – and explicitly implicated Nixon. More tapes or transcripts were unearthed, and 64 more were dragged from Nixon by a Supreme Court ruling.

The evidence devastated Nixon and exposed crimes even outside of Watergate. It revealed a White House which had authorized a burglary, deliberately covered up evidence, received illegal campaign contributions, falsified documents. Worse, it had even tried to damage reputations of opposing politicians through spreading slanderous rumors. The portrait was of a corrupt and devious administration. The Supreme Court brought three counts of impeachment, yet before he could go to trial, Nixon resigned on that infamous day in August 1974, giving himself legal immunity. He escaped prosecution, but he could never be free from the ignominy.

LEFT: In a rather contrived photograph, some visitors to the White House are shown holding copies of the *Washington Star-News*. The edition in their hands is announcing that President Richard Nixon would be resigning that evening in a groundbreaking television broadcast which would be seen by the entire nation.
BELOW LEFT: With his wife, his daughter, and his son-in-law standing behind him, an utterly exhausted President, undone by the Watergate scandal and facing impeachment, announces his intention to leave office on August 9. Significantly it was President Nixon who understood that, at a fundamental level, war is a contest of wills. During negotiations to extricate the United States from the ground war, he was prepared to put his words into action by backing President Thieu. He promised that the United States would "Vietnamize" the war by building up the South Vietnamese capabilities and that it would use diplomacy to drive a wedge between the North and its Chinese and Soviet allies. However, Nixon was also prepared to use airpower as a stick to back up the carrot of negotiations. When the North Vietnamese attempted to take advantage of the U.S. withdrawals in its Easter Offensive in March 1972, he not only ordered a massive and devastating U.S. air campaign against the attacking ground troops, but also resumed the bombing of North Vietnam that his predecessor, President Johnson, had halted three and a half years before. In a memorable statement, he was known to have said that "the bastards have never been bombed like they're going to be bombed this time." This was a policy that the Chinese know as "fight-fight-talk-talk," and Nixon's tough approach to the North impressed the leadership of the South. Consequently when, following the Paris Peace Agreement, Nixon told Thieu "You have my absolute assurance that If Hanoi fails to abide by the terms of this agreement, it is my intention to take swift and severe retaliatory action," the South felt that they were in safe hands.

RIGHT: A boy soldier, wearing simple peasants clothes, holds his weapon at the ready. This boy is a member of the Forces Armèes Nationale Khmer (FANK), the Army of the government of General Lon Nol who had deposed the wily Cambodian leader Prince Norodon Sihanouk on March 18, 1970. The North Vietnamese had used Cambodia as a base and also as a route for infiltrating supplies and thousands of men down the Ho Chi Minh Trail that ran through its eastern border and the port of Sihanoukville. When – with U.S. backing – Lon Nol began to take a more aggressive approach to these North Vietnamese operations, the North Vietnamese responded by assisting the Communist Khmer Rouge in their attacks on the FANK and the government in Phnom Penh. Unfortunately for FANK, they lacked the training and equipment – as well as sufficient skilled leadership – to resist the aggressive Khmer Rouge. The North Vietnamese were also angry that Prince Sihanouk had tacitly agreed to the "secret" bombing by the USAF of the base areas along the border, in operations which were codenamed Operation Menu and had started in March 1969. It was this extension of the Vietnam war – undertaken by Nixon without the agreement of Congress – that spurred the demand for the impeachment of the President.

positions, and isolate Kontum and Pleiku. Near Pleiku two regiments from the 320th NVA Division attacked Outpost 711 in April but the South Vietnamese defenders held out long enough for the 22nd ARVN Division and a ranger group to drive the Communists out of the area after a month. The NVA had more success in isolated outposts. On May 12, Division 324B besieged Dak Pek and overran it in four days. Ten days later, two Communist battalions seized Tieu Atar, south of Pleiku.

Communist aggression also occurred in South Vietnam's northern provinces. In Quang Tin, NVA units captured the town of Ky Tra on May 5. From this point the attackers fired rockets into the 2nd ARVN Division's headquarters at Chu Lai and Tam Ky airfield, both of which were on the coast. Heavy fighting also broke out in other coastal provinces within MR 1. At Tien Phuoc NVA units mauled three ARVN battalions mercilessly before retiring in mid-June. Further north, the Communists sent 11 battalions on a sabotage mission through Quang Nam, destroying bridges along Highway 1 and dilligently harassing nearby towns and bases.

The following month NVA III Corps launched a campaign to take the Khe Le Valley, south of Da Nang, in order to gain more access to the populated areas on the coast. On July 18 the Communist artillery, rocket, and mortar units pounded ARVN bunkers and firebases in the area out of existence. The NVA corps then occupied the hills surrounding the valley and fired more rounds into the Da Nang airfield and a base at Duc Duc. On July 29, the 29th NVA Regiment attacked Thuong Duc, a district capital and the westernmost ARVN post in Quang Nam. The 79th ARVN Ranger Battalion held on to the town in the face of fierce infantry and artillery assaults, but had to evacuate the area when the rangers ran out of ammunition.

As the year progressed, South Vietnam began to disintegrate in the face of the Communist offensives. Rampant corruption, economic problems, growing public opposition to the Thieu regime, chronic shortages of vital

RIGHT: Dwarfed by his M16 rifle, a boy soldier from FANK waits by a track in Cambodia. The M16 – which was designed by Eugene Stoner for Colt Fire Arms Inc – was made from alloys and plastic, and therefore was an ideal weapon for the lighter build of the Asian soldiers in Indochina. It was only 35 in. (990 mm) long, weighed only 7 lb. (3.18 kg), and with a muzzle velocity of 1,070 yds. (990 m) per second, it had a low recoil force. The 5.56 mm ammunition was light, compact, and easy to carry. On full automatic, the rifle could be fired at between 150 and 200 rounds per minute (rpm), or semi automatic at 45–65 rpm. The basic design was also modified as the Colt Commando, a carbine version which had a telescopic butt that could take the weapon down to 27 in. (711 mm). One drawback of the Commando was that it had a distinctive muzzle flash when it was fired. This could attract hostile fire and earned the Colt Commando the reputation of being an "unlucky" weapon, since many men armed with it were easily spotted, and killed or wounded.

LEFT: One soldier lies seriously injured while another sits shocked and wounded in the chaos of a South Vietnamese Army Aid Post. Even when the U.S. was fully committed to the war, the medical resources for the South Vietnamese were not always of a comparable standard to those available to U.S. servicemen. Tragically, corruption was mainly responsible for the misdirection of drugs and resources, particularly galling when charities in the United States gave aid. It was common sight in the cities to see ex-soldiers as amputees still wearing their uniforms trying to survive and often support a young family by begging.

ABOVE: A South Vietnamese Army Biet Dong Quan Ranger officer confers on the radio during street fighting. Units like the ARVN Rangers, Airborne, and Marines were well trained and motivated and enjoyed high morale. Unit pride was reflected in insignia like the Rangers' Black Panther patch on the left shoulder. The Rangers also favored red or maroon berets, as well as brightly colored company bandanas and camouflaged uniforms in different patterns. ARVN Marines wore green berets with an anchor insignia.

supplies, and dwindling American aid all took their toll both on ARVN and the civilian population. In the United States the dominance of the antiwar Congress over the federal government reached its zenith when the Watergate scandal forced Nixon to resign in August 1974. Most senators and congressmen were now opposed to further aid to South Vietnam, or too preoccupied with other issues to bother with Southeast Asian affairs. Both Hanoi and Saigon perceived Nixon's departure as a significant turning point. He had been the only powerful American politician determined not to allow South Vietnam to be conquered.

Satisfied that the new American president, Gerald Ford, lacked the will to save the Saigon regime, the North Vietnamese capitalized on their gains. By September the NVA boasted ten divisions within the South, with seven more in reserve in the Demilitarized Zone (DMZ), totaling 200,000 soldiers. The Communists also possessed over 700 tanks, 450 howitzers with ranges superior to those of ARVN, and 20 anti-aircraft regiments well-equipped to neutralize the South Vietnamese Air Force. These forces also enjoyed access to a logistical system that improved continuously.

Thus the NVA tightened the noose around South Vietnam. Toward the end of the year the Communists attacked several ARVN positions in MR 3, but their successes were less spectacular here because the South Vietnamese were more determined to protect the areas around Saigon. In MR 2 the NVA was more successful, using its superior firepower to overwhelm most ARVN bases, including Chong Nghia, the last major outpost in Kontum province, which fell on October 3. Further north the Communists made further inroads in MR 1 until ARVN forces stabilized their lines around Hue and Da Nang late in the year.

By the end of 1974 the Communists had won most of the delta, isolated Tay Ninh and Phuoc Long provinces from Saigon, and pushed the ARVN to the coastline of MR 1, leaving many populated areas throughout the country vulnerable to artillery strikes. The

LEFT: In the heat of the midday sun, a sobbing South Vietnamese child refugee staggers alone through a holding area. This small boy appears to have been fortunate enough to have a label with his name and address; however, combat and the disruption of war split up families and orphaned children. At the close of the war, there was a concerted drive to evacuate orphans from Vietnam. Twenty or more years later, these young men and women who had grown up in the United States and Europe would return to visit Vietnam in an attempt to give their lives and their origins some structure.

initiative had now fallen into the hands of the NVA, while the South Vietnamese hunkered into defensive positions and waited for their doom. While Communist units continued to envelop isolated ARVN bases, the North Vietnamese high command developed the "Resolution for 1975," a plan for a final assault on the Saigon regime that would begin in December against enemy positions in the Central Highlands and the delta. On December 13, the 7th NVA Division attacked Don Luan in Phuoc Long province. Although he was not there to see it, Ho Chi Minh's long struggle for Vietnamese unification was in its final stage.

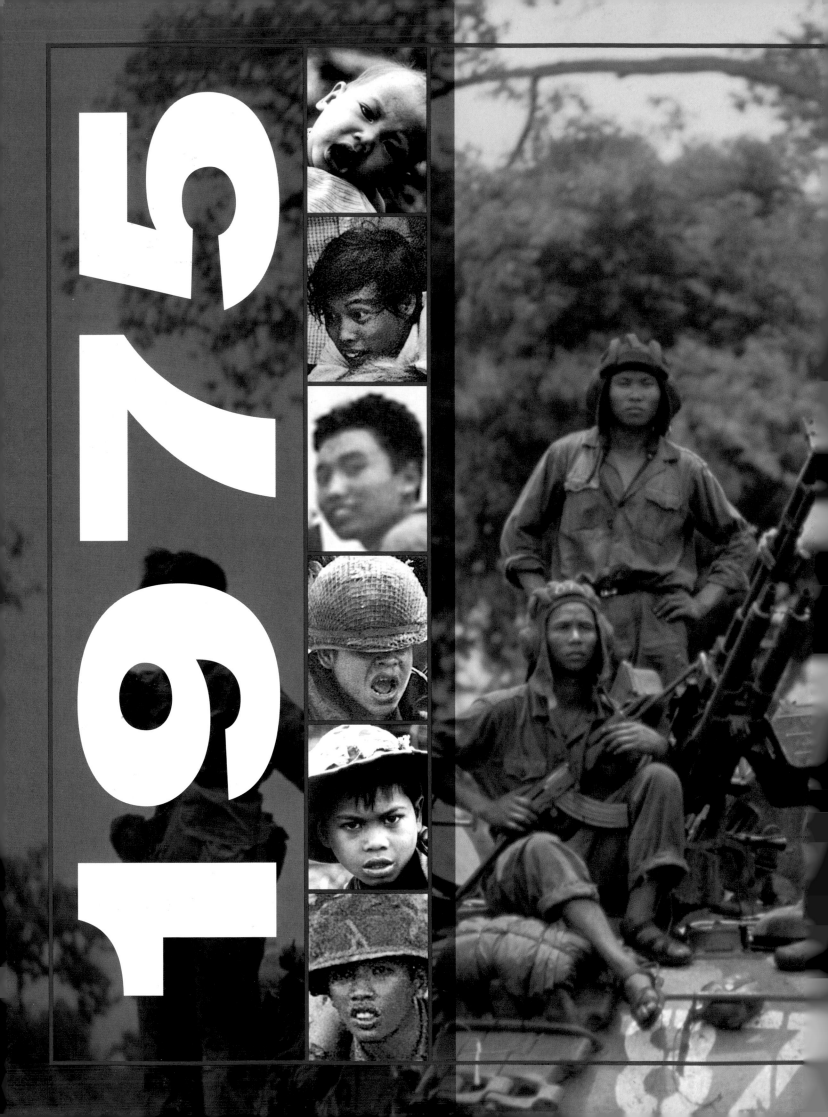

1975

The End of the Road

By January 6, less than a month after the offensive opened, the NVA controlled Phuoc Long Province north of Saigon. The NVA employed what it called its "blooming lotus" or "paratroop" tactics whereby, according to General Van Tien Dung, Chief of Staff of the NVA – who had employed the same tactics against the French in 1952 – the NVA would "send our troops in, avoiding enemy positions in the outer perimeter ... and unexpectedly struck right in town, wiping out the nerve center of the enemy command, taking the town in one day and only then sending the troops out to destroy the perimeter outposts." This process was used throughout the NVA's final campaign in the winter of 1974 and spring of 1975.

The South Vietnamese government responded by sending the elite 8th Ranger Group to An Loc on January 5. Unfortunately, they did not have any armor and, while they fought bravely, were no match for the NVA's Soviet-supplied PT-76 and T-54 tanks. Clearly America's willingness to support the South Vietnamese had waned. Hanoi set out a two-year timetable to absorb the South. As events turned out, they required only a few months.

As the 200,000-strong North Vietnamese prepared their well-equipped forces for the attack, they faced a South Vietnamese Army which numbered approximately 192,000 soldiers and marines. The NVA devised a strategy of attacks directed toward My Tho in the Mekong Delta, Ban Me Thout and Tuy Hoa in the center of the country, and Hue and Da Nang in the north. The objective was to seize major cities and destroy the ARVN's offensive capabilities.

The main attack would be directed against what Hanoi considered to be the weakest link in the South Vietnamese Army's defensive chain, Military Region 2, the most thinly defended area in South Vietnam. This decision was not made lightly, as the ARVN had the majority of its forces poised in the north of the region in the vicinity of Pleiku and Kontum. Therefore General Dung decided to strike first at Ban Me Thuot, a city in Darlac Province in the south of MR 2. He codenamed the operation "Campaign 275."

The final offensive against South Vietnam began on March 1, 1975. This was the date when the NVA's 968th Division struck ARVN outposts west of Pleiku in MR 2. General Dung's Campaign 275 had managed to exploit the ARVN's decision to concentrate its forces in the Pleiku-Kontum area, while at the same time leaving Ban Me Thuot thinly defended and open to invasion.

ABOVE: A South Vietnamese soldier supports a wounded comrade during the fighting in An Loc in early April. In 1972 the city had been the scene of a South Vietnamese triumph, halting attacks by the North Vietnamese. For two weeks in 1975 it again held out against huge NVA forces.
RIGHT: Vietnamese Air Force CH-47 Chinooks that have dropped off ammunition at An Loc pick up refugees and soldiers on Highway 1 on April 13. The city had come under sustained heavy artillery fire during the day.

While the battle for Ban Me Thuot was in progress, President Nguyen Van Thieu ordered General Phu to evacuate the Highlands and concentrate his defenses around the populated centers along the coastal lowlands. This proved to be ill-advised as it simply ceded a good portion of South Vietnam to the enemy.

In later years Thieu argued that, given the state of preparations of the NVA, and the unwillingness of the United States to honor its commitments to South Vietnam, it was the only thing he could do in order to allow the ARVN access to more defensible terrain. Thieu based his decision on the hope that the ARVN could "hold the line." While some ARVN units fought a brief delaying action, most began an organized withdrawal, and civilian refugees began to clog the roads, preventing the ARVN from moving troops to mount a sustained counterattack.

On March 21, elements of the NVA's 320th Division virtually annihilated the 23rd ARVN Ranger Group at Cheo Reo along Route 7B, as well as battering the ARVN II Corps. During the fighting and subsequent retreat, II Corps lost over 75 percent of its 20,000 troops, only

5,000 soldiers making it to the coast at Nha Trang. The Rangers likewise suffered heavy casualties. Of the original 7,000, only 900 made it to the coast in what can only be described as one "of the worst and certainly most poorly executed withdrawals in the history of warfare." Not only did individual soldiers abandon the battlefield, but so too did their senior officers. By the time the NVA had annihilated the II Corps, individual battalion and group commanders were all that remained to lead whatever nearby troops would still obey orders and fight.

Sensing victory, the North Vietnamese continued to press toward the coast, and in the process captured tons of supplies and thousands of troops. They quickly took advantage of the confusion, though some ARVN units continued to resist. With the destruction of the ARVN II Corps, the NVA turned its attention toward MR 1 where "they hoped to continue their success."

In Quang Ngai Province the NVA and reconstituted Viet Cong units continued to launch small-scale operations against ARVN forces, though "spoiling attacks" by the 2nd ARVN Division and Ranger forces delayed the NVA's elite 52nd Brigade which had briefly moved southward toward Binh Dinh Province.

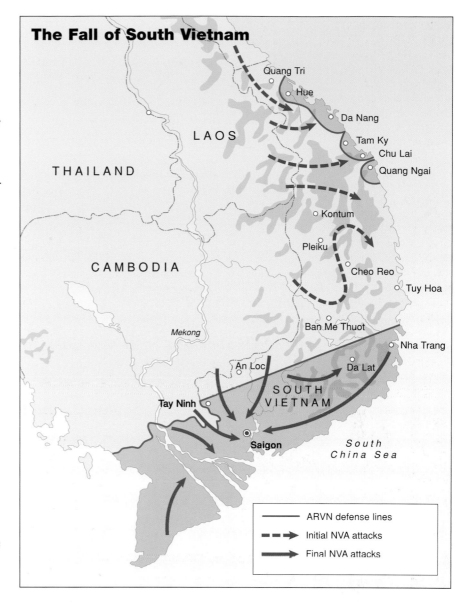

The Fall of South Vietnam

- ——— ARVN defense lines
- - - -▶ Initial NVA attacks
- ———▶ Final NVA attacks

RIGHT: South Vietnamese troops pass equipment over the U.S. Embassy fence in Saigon while civilians beg to be let through to the waiting helicopters evacuating the selected few to the carriers waiting off the Vietnamese coast. **FOLLOWING PAGE:** A Vietnamese boy carries his little brother as he joins the crowds of refugees and flees from Pleiku City in the Central Highlands. On President Thieu's orders, the ARVN withdrew from the city in March.

Creating the Killing Fields

In 1967 a guerrilla force was created that would go on to commit one of the greatest genocides in the history of the 20th century. Entitled "Khmer Rouge," they were formed as the military wing of the Communist Party of Kampuchea. Their aims were simple: overthrow the neutralist government of Norodom Sihanouk and establish a communist state. Yet in the late 1960s, their power was limited. Sihanouk was popular amongst the peasant classes – the very people the Communists hoped to enlist – and militarily they were isolated. Yet after Sihanouk was ousted from power in 1970, the Khmer Rouge ascendancy began. A five-year civil war ensued. Inch by inch, the Khmer Rouge extended their ruthless control. By 1975 they were at the very door of the Cambodian capital, Phnom Penh. In April they finally swept away the last vestiges of opposition and took Cambodia, renamed Democratic Kampuchea in 1976.

Kampuchea was anything but democratic. Its new ruler was Pol Pot, the son of a farmer and leader of the Khmer Rouge throughout its years of underground struggle. With the capture of Phnom Penh, he became Kampuchea's prime minister and personally launched a period of the most hideous murder and displacement in Cambodia's history. The whole country was forced to relinquish private property, money, and their clothes (everyone had to wear the same peasant dress). No one could travel without permission, and all schools and places of learning were shut.

Fear swept the nation. The new regime set about resettling all the urban populations into rural concentration camps.

These concentration camps were the "killing fields," as history has named them. This name was highly appropriate. On the most ludicrous suspicions, people were executed on the spot, or tortured to death in the most horrific manner. The Khmer Rouge, with Pol Pot's sanction, intended to eradicate every trace of the former "bourgeois" ideology by slaughtering those who were implicated in it. Even the wearing of glasses could bring death, as the Khmer Rouge construed it as a sign of capitalist intellectualism. Some 1.5 million of Cambodia's people are estimated to have been killed in the years of genocide. The Khmer Rouge even started to prefer to conduct executions by suffocating people in plastic bags; there were so many people to kill that ammunition supplies could not keep up.

The period of Khmer Rouge horror finally ended in 1979 when Vietnam invaded Cambodia. After the Vietnamese took over the country, the forces of the Khmer Rouge were once more expelled into the political and literal wilderness. From this wilderness, they continued with guerrilla actions until the mid-1990s. Ironically, in 1997 the Khmer Rouge actually expelled Pol Pot from their ranks and put him under house arrest. He died of natural causes in 1998, thus escaping the justice which was needed to satisfy over one million deaths.

LEFT: Khmer Rouge dressed in olive green Chinese uniforms and the distinctive red and white krama, the traditional Cambodian scarves associated with the movement. They are armed with the AK47, a weapon that came to dominate the war in Indochina. Designed by the Russian engineer Mikhail Kalashnikov shortly after World War II, the AK47 weighed 10.3 lb. (4.69 kg) loaded with 30 rounds. The folding stock version in the photograph had a minimum length of 2.53 in. (64.5 cm) On automatic, the AK47 had a range of 327 ft. (300 m) and 436 ft. (400 m) on semi automatic. It had a practical rate of fire of 100 rounds per minute (rpm) on automatic and on semi of 40 rpm.

FAR LEFT: The smiling face of the leader of the Cambodian Communists or Khmer Rouge, Saloth Sar, who styled himself on Pol Pot. He had studied in Paris where his political views had made him anti-intellectual and in favor of a world of agrarian simplicity. When the Khmer Rouge took over in Cambodia, they renamed it Kampuchea and forced the urban population out into the country where, in a world in which money was banned, they embarked on a brutal social experiment in agrarian revolution. Opposition, even perceived opposition, was brutally suppressed, and over 1.5 million died during the rule of the Khmer Rouge.

Despite this rare display of military prowess, the destruction of II Corps in the Highlands proved to be the fulcrum upon which South Vietnam's fate rested. On March 8, fierce fighting broke out in MR 1. Certain elements of the 2nd NVA Division and 52nd Brigade had attacked and then proceeded to overrun the district capitals of Hau Duc and Tien Phuoc. Simultaneously, Quang Tien's provincial capital of Tam Ky was threatened by these Communist forces.

At the same time, President Thieu became concerned about the security in and around Saigon, and ordered a reluctant General Truong to release the 1st Airborne Brigade. Thieu also ordered ARVN's III Corps (Lieutenant General Nguyen Van Toan) to withdraw his forces from An Loc and employ them in MR 3 or "wherever they were needed." These moves ripped the heart out of General Truong's defenses in MR 1, and reversed the ARVN's greatest victory in the last months of the Vietnam War. To replace the Airborne Brigade and III Corps, Thieu ordered the Vietnamese Marine Corps Division (VNMC) to Da Nang to shore up Truong's defenses.

Even this proved too little, too late, as on March 19, the NVA struck hard against the former U.S. Air Base at Da Nang. It fell on March 29, and with it tons of recently arrived U.S. equipment. On March 24, Lieutenant General Truong, bowing to pressure from President Thieu, ordered the evacuation of Hue as resistance in MR I came to an end. ARVN resistance in the city of Quang Tri proved hopeless as the retreat from the region turned into a rout. The ARVN suffered what can only

RIGHT: A T-54 tank of the NVA 203rd Armored Regiment flying the flag of the National Liberation Front crashes through the gates of the Presidential Palace in Saigon. By 1974 the NVA had four armored regiments equipped with 900 T-34, T-54, and Type 59 medium tanks, as well as amphibious PT-76 light tanks. At the end of the war, according to Pentagon estimates, the NVA captured over $5 billion of U.S. supplied equipment, including 550 tanks, 73 F-5 jet fighters, 1,300 artillery pieces, and 1,600,000 rifles, as well as soft skin vehicles. Some captured M113 APCs were supplied to an East German Army covert force that, dressed and equipped like West German soldiers, would penetrate NATO lines in the event of a war in Europe.

be described as a military catastrophe as MR 1 fell to the North Vietnamese. As many as 16,000 ARVN troops were extricated, but they were unable to take their heavy equipment with them due to the rapidity of the Communists' advance.

By April 3, 1975, the North Vietnamese Army held most of MR 2. Qui Nhon, Nha Trang, and Dalat had been abandoned. Combat began in MR 3 in Tay Ninh Province where the NVA launched a heavy combined arms attack against ARVN positions along Route 1 and Route 22 in the east of the region. Fighting soon shifted on April 9 to Xuan Loc, the capital of Long Khanh Province, where four NVA divisions attacked the 18th ARVN Division to gain control of Highway 1, the main access route into the Bien Hoa/Saigon area. Organized from the survivors of the various ARVN military units, the South Vietnamese soldiers who fought at Xuan Loc proved surprisingly effective. The ARVN 18th Division, commanded by Brigadier General Le Minh Dao, counterattacked on April 10 and retook a considerable part of the city. This ARVN victory renewed hopes in South Vietnamese and U.S. government circles that the NVA's spring offensive could be halted and Saigon saved.

By April 20, however, the NVA was able to retake Xuan Loc and resume its attack westward toward Bien Hoa. Other NVA forces moved to the south from Xuan Loc to block the main Bien Hoa-Vung Tau Highway (Route 15) north of Long Thanh. The loss of Xuan Loc and the effective interdiction of Routes 1 and 15 signaled the end of major organized ARVN resistance in eastern MR 3, opening the way for attacks against Bien Hoa and Saigon.

On April 21, 1975, President Nguyen Van Thieu resigned and fled the country. He was succeeded by Vice President Tran Van Huong who initially assumed a militant policy of continued resistance, but only a few days later surrendered the presidency to former General Duong Van "Big" Minh, who began to negotiate a ceasefire with the North Vietnamese. When several of their preconditions for a ceasefire were rejected, the NVA launched its final assault of the Vietnam War on April 26,

1975. Their three-day offensive destroyed remaining ARVN resistance and Saigon was now left defenseless.

As the NVA fought the remnants of the ARVN, on April 29, CH-53 and CH-46 helicopters evacuated U.S. citizens, their dependents, and South Vietnamese civilians from the U.S. Embassy compound and Defense Attaché's office. Dubbed Operation Frequent Wind, 682 sorties were flown by marine helicopters until the final evacuation of the marine embassy guards from its rooftop just as NVA tanks rumbled through the gates. When Frequent Wind ended on April 30, 1975, over 6,968 people had been lifted from Saigon.

The U.S. Embassy in Phnom Penh was evacuated on April 11–12, 1975 as the Lon Nol government finally fell to the Khmer Rouge offensive. Yet the agony was not over for the United States. On May 12, 1975 the container ship SS *Mayaguez* was captured in international waters off Cambodia by Khmer Rouge soldiers. On May 15, President Ford ordered the Marines to retake the vessel. At the cost of 18 American lives, it was recovered.

While the outcome of the war can only be considered a failure, the performance and service of U.S. troops was outstanding. South Vietnam was lost to the Comunists, but the U.S. military was never defeated on the field of battle by the NVA and VC. Instead, it fought bravely to the end and remained committed to South Vietnam's defense, despite the sheer hopelessness of the struggle.

ABOVE: To the victors the spoils. North Vietnamese Army soldiers take a break in the office of the President of South Vietnam. Behind the main desk is a large South Vietnamese flag made from lacquer. Initially, when the NVA arrived in Saigon, the population feared that there would be mass arrests and executions. The traders closed shop and the exotic night life disappeared. When it became clear that this would not happen, the city came back to life and the sophisticated and cosmopolitan Saigonese found the gauche Boi Doi – the ordinary foot soldiers from the North, who were now confronted by temptations of the flesh – figures of quiet ridicule. It was a shortlived illusion; the patrons of the North, China and the USSR, withdrew their military and financial support now that the U.S. had been humiliated and their Cold War aim had been achieved. Vietnam suffered economic stagnation; as the Hanoi leadership asserted control over the whole country, even the Liberal leaders once opposed to the Thieu government were arrested and the Viet Cong were marginalized by the Northern party organization.

AFTERMATH

Aftermath

In terms of size, scope, and human cost, the Vietnam War is not by any means the most significant conflict in American history. Unlike the War of 1812, the United States did not have to fight a single battle on its own territory or anywhere close to its borders. In 1862 almost as many Americans perished in a single day at the battle of Antietam as during the entire period of American involvement in Southeast Asia. And although North Vietnam was a repressive, one-party state, it possessed neither the power nor the inclination to constitute a global threat on the scale of Japan and Nazi Germany during World War II. However, the significance of the Vietnam War in American history is twofold. First, the conflict was the first unambiguous military defeat suffered by the United States. Second, the war generated unprecedented disillusionment among Americans who had been raised to believe that their country was invincible and that it served a special mission to bring democracy to the entire world.

Amid the malaise of defeat, observers and participants in the war sought explanations for the loss of Vietnam. Opinion polls at the end of the war indicated that most Americans regarded it as a mistake, but believed that the United States government should have committed all of its resources to win once the commitment had been made. Many veterans echoed these feelings, arguing that they could have won the war if the government had allowed them more freedom of action against the enemy, especially against the Communist sanctuaries in Laos and Cambodia. General Westmoreland articulated this view in his memoirs. He also blamed Nixon and Kissinger for offering too many concessions at the Paris peace talks, and accused members of the news media of skewing their coverage of the war in favor of the Communists in order to turn American public opinion against it.

Many military officers shared Westmoreland's bitterness toward the news media. They also faulted President Johnson for failing to rally the American public behind the war and the rotation system that returned experienced fighters from the front after serving only a year in Vietnam. Others cited strategic failures in the American war effort. Some air force commanders believed that a more rigorous and continuous bombing campaign would have hammered Hanoi into submission. Admiral Thomas Moorer asserted that the United States could have won simply by taking the war directly to North Vietnam, where American combatants would have fought conventional battles akin to those in Europe during World War II. Meanwhile, civilian critics attributed the American failure in Southeast Asia to the Cold War mindset that

ABOVE: A Cambodian father holds his badly wounded child as his wife screams for help after a Khmer Rouge rocket landed in Phnom Penh during fighting in May 1975.
RIGHT: South Vietnamese who have fled from Vietnam on an overcrowded fishing boat struggle up a scrambling net lowered over the side of a U.S. Navy warship.

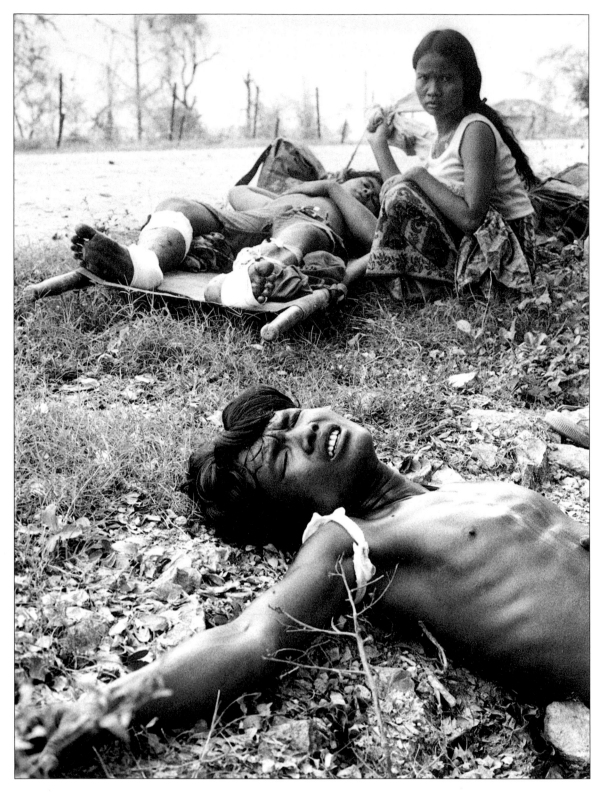

RIGHT: Close to Phnom Penh, the wife of a Cambodian soldier fans her wounded husband to protect him against the heat as he waits for medical attention. This soldier is one of the FANK. In the foreground, an unattended comrade who has been wounded by the same Rocket Propelled Grenade (RPG) attack screams in acute pain. The medical support and the evacuation of casualties was a rudimentary service in Cambodia, and the climate and conditions in that country led to wounds becoming quickly infected. The government, led by Lon Nol, came under increasing attack from the Khmer Rouge and in response to this, the U.S. decided to withdraw its remaining personnel. Accordingly, on April 12, 1975 in Operation Eagle Pull, all U.S. diplomatic and military personnel as well as their dependants remaining in Cambodia were withdrawn to safety. Helicopters from the U.S. 7th Fleet were responsible for the evacuation of 276 people, including 159 Cambodians, 82 Americans, and 35 other foreign nationals. At that point, the U.S. permanent military presence in Cambodia had been a scant one. It was limited to a small joint armed forces contingent called the Military Equipment Delivery Team, Cambodia. This was a force which had been organized in Saigon on January 30, 1971, and was set up in Phnom Penh on October 9.

prevented any constructive dialogue with Ho Chi Minh, and the hubris that caused many Americans to underestimate the determination of his followers to obtain national unity at any cost.

These autopsies on the American defeat in Vietnam reflected pervasive postwar feelings of doubt among citizens about the credibility of their country as a world power. Henry Kissinger believed that this sense of doubt also took root in American diplomacy, rendering the United States government timid in its dealings with other countries and in future conflicts. Called the "Vietnam Syndrome," this skittishness prevented the United States from becoming more proactive in crises that occurred in later years. Most notably, President Jimmy Carter failed to rescue the Shah of Iran from overthrow in 1979 and let a hostile Islamic regime to seize power of that strategically

LEFT: On Chinese supplied trucks, men of the NVA drive through Saigon in a victory parade. Following its capture, Saigon was renamed Ho Chi Minh City after the North Vietnamese leader who had died on September 2, 1969. However, just as Leningrad has reverted to St Petersburg, so too Saigon has retained its distinct identity. About 56 miles (90 km) upriver from the South China Sea, it is in effect two cities: Saigon to the north of the river and the Chinese suburb of Cholon to the south. The airbase and airport Tan Son Nhut is outside to the north, and the Bien Hoa Airbase about 50 miles (80 km) north along Highway 1.

important country. During the administration of Ronald Reagan, this new-found isolationist impulse continued through the 1980s in Congress and in American public opinion when the president unsuccessfully attempted to escalate American involvement in the civil war in El Salvador.

The Vietnam War also created problems for the American armed forces that lingered many years after the disengagement from the conflict. The unpopularity of the war had cost the military a great deal of its prestige, which frustrated recruiting efforts and created manpower shortages within the ranks. This shortage worsened when Nixon ended the draft in 1973, forcing the service branches to compete with the civilian sector in luring employees. The money spent on waging the Vietnam War, along with the funds required to offer attractive salaries for potential recruits in later years, left little spare for important technological innovations that the military needed to modernize itself. Military leadership also suffered during and after the conflict when universities throughout the country developed an aversion to Reserve Officer Training Corps (ROTC) programs on their campuses. The prestige and quality of the armed forces finally recovered during the Reagan administration in the 1980s.

Like other wars, the Vietnam conflict left numerous veterans with physical and psychological scars from their experiences. Advances in medical science had the ironic effect of ensuring that combatants were more likely to survive severe wounds, only to spend the rest of their lives crippled or mutilated. In addition, some veterans suffered from the serious effects of Agent Orange, a chemical defoliant that aircraft had dropped over wooded areas to deprive Communist forces of natural camouflage. On some occasions, this toxin had landed on American ground troops, promoting cancer, skin disease, and other afflictions.

ABOVE: An informal Khmer Rouge victory parade enters the Cambodian capital Phnom Penh. Under Pol Pot there was a concerted drive to erase the past and reconstruct society, and the interrogation, torture, and murder of anyone who was not a committed believer in the Khmer Rouge's destruction of books, temples, and any evidence of Cambodia's history. The Khmer Rouge operated through committees, but it was Pol Pot who provided them with methods and motivation.

ABOVE: In the days before the Khmer Rouge turned Cambodia into a concentration camp, children wait to receive food at a refugee center run by the Catholic Relief Services.
BELOW: The telegram that informed the parents of 21 year old Corporal Charles McMahon Jr, USMC, of Woburn, Massachusetts that their son's body would be arriving in the United States almost a year after his death. Killed on April 29, 1975, Cpls McMahon and Darwin Judge (19) were the last U.S. servicemen to die in Vietnam.

Psychological problems also plagued many veterans. Ten to fifteen years after returning home to resume a seemingly normal life, many of them suffered from post-traumatic stress disorder, a delayed effect on the mind that included anxiety, panic attacks, and rage, and which often led individuals to divorce, drug abuse, or suicide. Although American soldiers had faced deadly and terrifying situations in many earlier wars, the Vietnam conflict possessed unique characteristics that exacerbated the mental strain imposed on its combatants. Unlike the two world wars, the Vietnam War did not possess a neat set of battle lines that showed precisely where the enemy was located; troops permanently existed in a state of danger, and were constantly threatened by anything from booby traps in the jungle to schoolchildren tossing grenades into taverns frequented by American personnel. Not surprisingly, this state of continuous anxiety wreaked havoc upon the human mind and led some veterans to lash out at the Vietnamese population.

LEFT: A jumble of bones and emaciated bodies litter a trench in Cambodia. The murder of political enemies by the Khmer Rouge was prompted by the denunciations of politicized children as well as Communist party officers. The killings were by clubbing, shooting, and suffocation using plastic bags. Prior to these killings the "enemies" were interrogated in improvised centers – like schools – photographed, and their details listed. Long after the bodies of these victims have been lost, the photographs remain, showing terrified or haunted faces staring at the camera. The attribution of "Guilt" was often quite arbitrary with, for example, the victim being selected because they wore spectacles that marked them as an anti-Communist "intellectual." Those that were not killed were often worked to death in agricultural projects outside the cities. It was very difficult to escape from these projects and the automatic punishment was a ghastly death. The capital Phnom Penh became a ghost town as it was emptied of its population and, as part of the social experiment, the use of money was forbidden. Paper money swirled in the empty streets. Cambodia's reconstruction after the war was hampered by the murder of a middle class who might have reforged links in the world of commerce, administration, health, and education.

Vietnam veterans also tended to be younger than those who had fought in earlier wars; and the trauma of combat often inflicted more permanent psychological damage upon youthful soldiers. Added to these problems was the cool reception that Vietnam veterans received from the American public upon their return to the United States, usually ranging from indifference to open hostility expressed by antiwar activists who denounced them as "baby killers." Unlike earlier heroes who had returned from triumphant wars against Nazis, imperialists, or secessionists, Vietnam veterans had to struggle to gain the gratitude from their country that they deserved. On November 11, 1982, they achieved this goal with the consecration of a national monument erected in Washington, DC. A simple, granite wall inscribed with the names of the 57,939 Americans killed or missing in action, the

RIGHT: A former South Vietnamese soldier or civil servant accompanied by a warder carries a trash can across the churned ground adjoining bomb damaged buildings in Vietnam. As their world collapsed, some men could not face the prospect of capture and imprisonment. Journalists in Saigon saw a Lt Col of the South Vietnamese police walk to a war memorial in the park near the National Assembly building. The man's eyes filled with tears, and he cried out "Fini! Fini!" before saluting the memorial and then putting his pistol to his head and shooting himself.

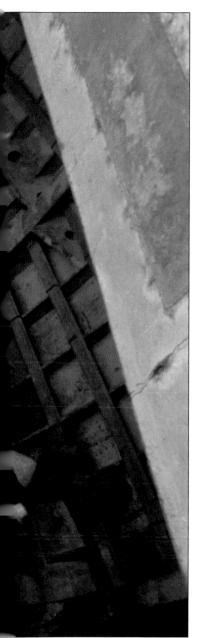

LEFT: "Boat People," who have escaped from Vietnam in a freighter, are lifted from the hold in a cargo net. For many radicals who had opposed the U.S. involvement in Vietnam and had seen the Viet Cong and North Vietnamese as the underdogs in the war, the mass of refugees who attempted to escape posed a moral dilemma. Some refused to criticize the policies of the Hanoi leadership that had prompted this exodus. However, others could see that all was not well in the united Vietnam. Would-be escapers were prey to unscrupulous middlemen who found often unseaworthy craft. Once they were at sea, they were prey to pirates who would kill, rob, or rape the refugees. Even those who made it to the then British Hong Kong found themselves in grim, fenced camps.

RIGHT: In traditional Viet Cong "uniform" of black twopiece clothing, lacquered straw "cooly" hat, and armed with a captured American-supplied M1 Carbine, a member of the National Liberation Front guards a public building in Saigon after its capture.

memorial served as an emotional catharsis for the veterans who attended its unveiling.

Although the United States confronted significant problems as a result of the war, they were not nearly as severe as the hardships inflicted on the people of Vietnam. Altogether, the war had killed or wounded about four million soldiers and civilians on both sides, including 600,000 Communist soldiers. Those escaping death or disfigurement confronted a ravaged countryside, disrupted economy, wrecked social order, and a corrupt, repressive government plagued by ineptitude. Bombings, artillery strikes, and Agent Orange had reduced much of the country's cultivated areas, hamlets, and picturesque scenery to wasteland that was often reclaimed by the jungle.

South Vietnam also experienced traumatic cultural dislocation as a result of the war. Traditionally the region had been an agrarian society centered on the family unit and the village. During the course of U.S. involvement in the war, these foundations practically disintegrated under the strain of war and policies of forced relocation. As a result, millions of farming villagers found themselves eking out meagre existences in any form of menial employment they could find in the cities. Much of this employment was tied to the American presence in Vietnam, so the work they found was tenuous at best. Not surprisingly, the rapid influx of rural folk into the cities quickly led to overcrowding and very unhealthy living conditions in Saigon and other population centers. The urbanization of South Vietnam also broke down many of the provincial identities that had existed in the country before the American entry into the war, turning the people into a more homogenized mass, which had no distinctive regional characteristics.

In the immediate aftermath of the conquest of South, it appeared that the victorious Communists would reconstruct their nation with malice toward none and charity for all. This chimera quickly vaporized when the North Vietnamese government set up a network of agents and informers that created a climate of oppression and fear across Saigon (now renamed Ho Chi Minh City) similar to that of Bucharest, Pyongyang, and other Eastern-bloc cities. In July 1975 Hanoi also required veterans and bureaucrats from the Saigon government to attend "re-education camps" that would to turn them into good Communist citizens. Theoretically, common soldiers from the Army of the Republic of Vietnam (ARVN) could graduate from the camps within three days, while ARVN officers

and bureaucrats required a month of indoctrination. However, the Communists soon extended the periods of "training" so that inmates from all social stations served time for several years.

Eventually, Hanoi obliged many other citizens who had no connection to the Saigon government – including Buddhist and Catholic monks, teachers, students, disaffected peasants, and even Viet Cong veterans who had become resentful toward their northern comrades – to undergo detention. The Communists also incarcerated doctors, scientists, engineers, economists, accountants, and other educated citizens who could have provided invaluable assistance in the recovery of Vietnam's infrastructure. Altogether, anywhere from 500,000 to a million Vietnamese citizens wound up in re-education camps until the government closed the worst of its facilities and released several political prisoners in 1986. Ironically, some served their time in prisons that had been built by the Saigon government.

Living conditions in the camps varied. The worst facilities were in the remote northern

LEFT: The former South Vietnamese National Police Chief Nguyen Ngoc Loan with his wife in the burger, pizza, and Vietnamese restaurant he managed in Burke, Washington after escaping Vietnam. Honest Vietnamese officials and soldiers settling in the U.S. were often forced to take quite menial jobs as unlike others, they were innocent of corruption and therefore had no money waiting in overseas accounts.

ABOVE: Khmer Rouge soldiers in the typical "uniform" of the organization keep guard in the ancient temples of Angkor Wat, built in the 12th Century in Cambodia. The temple complex suffered badly during the conflict in Cambodia, and carvings are still being looted even today. The men in the photograph are armed with a B40 Rocket Launcher, a copy of the Soviet RPG7. The launcher weighs 13.8 lb. (6.3 kg) and fires a 3.8 lb. (1.75 kg) 85 mm caliber antitank rocket. An experienced crew of two can fire between four and six rounds a minute and hit a stationary target at 1640 ft. (500 m).

NEXT PAGE: Smiling Vietnamese pass a U.S. supplied ARVN M48A3 tank. The NVA's deployment of Soviet supplied wireguided 9M14M Malyutka "Sagger" antitank missiles, along with a lack of ammunition and spares, helped

CHILDREN OF VIETNAM
The American-Asians of Vietnam

They are perhaps the greatest forgotten legacy of the Vietnam War. It is estimated that around 35,000 American-Asian children were born during the Vietnam War, the product of short romances, a permissive lifestyle in a wartorn country and, in some cases, what were genuine relationships that continued well after the war.

The status of many of these children is indicated by the term "dust of life" applied to them by the Vietnamese. These children were visually distinctive, with lighter or darker skin than most Vietnamese (depending on the father) and eyes of a more oval shape. Thus distinguished, they and their mothers were often ostracized by their own communities and families, and faced unpredictable persecution from the government with the Communist takeover in 1975. Many ended up on the streets as beggars or orphans, and the females were prey to prostitution.

The reasons behind this explosion of American-Asians during the Vietnam War are easy to see. Over one million U.S. servicemen passed through Vietnam in ten years. Far from home, many of them struck up ill-advised relationships with local girls, relationships which had little future when the tour of duty ended. Furthermore, prostitution was rife. By the time the U.S. troops left in 1973, there were up to 500,000 prostitutes working in South Vietnam. They, like many Vietnamese women, found some escape from Vietnam's poverty through American dollars and support, and some must have hoped for U.S. citizenship as a way out of a country dissolving in war. Few such dreams were realized, and the children they bore to U.S. fathers faced a difficult future. With their origins written clearly on their faces, they would have to be strong enough to face prejudice and rejection for many years.

ABOVE: A Chinese Peoples' Liberation Army (PLA) 122mm M-1955 Field Howitzer opens fire against Vietnamese troops during the invasion of northern Vietnam on February 17, 1979. This devastating attack was to be the low point of deteriorating relations between the two countries, which was caused in part by Vietnam's invasion of Cambodia following the Khmer Rouge abuse of the ethnic Vietnamese in that country, as well as several cross-border attacks. Despite Pol Pot's appalling record, he still enjoyed Chinese patronage, and China's attack was carried out in part to support the Khmer Rouge. Between 200,000 and 300,000 Chinese troops – backed by aircraft and artillery – crossed the border into territory that had not seen any ground combat since the struggles of the early 1950s, when Vietnam was a French colony.

locations and often lacked adequate food or medicine. Not surprisingly, malnutrition led to epidemics of malaria, dysentery, and other diseases among the inmates. The camps were also overcrowded, unsanitary, and manned by brutal guards. Punishments for even trivial or fabricated offenses included solitary confinement for several years, hard labor, slow starvation, and executions. Guards regularly used torture; prisoners were beaten and often left manacled under the tropical sun without water. Like South Vietnamese jailers in earlier years, the Communists utilized "tiger cages," which were small confinement cubicles lacking enough space for occupants to stand.

Conditions in postwar Vietnam were even worse for those who were not purely Vietnamese. As relations between Hanoi and Beijing deteriorated during the late 1970s, the country became an increasingly inhospitable place for the numerous Chinese residents living in Ho Chi Minh City and other urban areas. Many of them left, either across the Chinese border in the north, or aboard vessels with Vietnamese refugees. Altogether, about a million Vietnamese and Chinese "boat people"

fled the Hanoi government by sea. Although most of them reached countries willing to grant asylum, as many as 50,000 died from drowning, exposure, or pirate raids. The 50,000 Amerasians in Vietnam were another ethnic group to suffer under Communist rule. Many of the offspring of American servicemen and Vietnamese women possessed blonde hair, blue eyes, black skin, or other distinguishing physical features that led to them being ostracized and marginalized economically. During the 1980s the Vietnamese government allowed some of these people to migrate to the United States.

In economic policy the Hanoi regime tried to follow standard Marxist doctrines, with unfortunate results. After the war it implemented a five-year plan in order to develop an industrial base in the country. However, the plan failed because the government failed to secure enough aid from its wartime allies and because of bureaucratic red tape imposed upon European companies attempting to initiate business ventures in the country. Customs officers at Haiphong and other ports also hindered international trade by extracting large bribes

LEFT: The rain- and mist-shrouded hills of northern Vietnam, where fighting between Vietnam and China took place. The Chinese penetrated 50 miles (80 km) into Vietnam and seized the provincial capital of Langson ostensibly as "punishment" for 700 alleged "provocations" along the border in six months. The Chinese may have had the advantage of numbers; however, they were not as battlehardened as the Vietnamese, making their claim that they inflicted 50,000 casualties and suffered only 20,000 a questionable one. **BELOW:** A PLA Type 59 tank lies abandoned on a roadside in Vietnam. With a crew of four and armed with a 100 mm (3.9 in.) gun and three machine guns, the Type 59 is a Chinese copy of the Soviet T-54 that was supplied to China.

RIGHT: The corroded identity tags of U.S. servicemen killed in Vietnam. Normally one tag on a chain around the serviceman or woman's neck remained with the body and one on a smaller chain was detached and forwarded to records; a body buried in the field could be located, identified, and reburied. In Vietnam, bodies were normally recovered and though many were shipped back to the mainland U.S., many were buried in Hawaii. In Vietnam, soldiers often had a third ID tag threaded through the laces of a boot, reasoning that if they were decapitated by a blast, they might lose their ID tags, but it was unlikely that their feet would be destroyed as well.

BELOW: Two USAF senior NCOs compare flight details and aircraft type with photographs of a remote crash site. Aircraft wreckage and markings can indicate the squadron and type, and thus the pilot or crew.

from foreign ships seeking to unload their cargo. In addition, Vietnam failed to revive its coal industry because it lacked the necessary machines and vehicles to do so.

Agricultural policies created even more problems. During the war, many southern peasants had joined the National Liberation Front (NLF) in order to achieve a land reform policy that would have left them with their own plots to till. Instead, they confronted a collectivization program that required them to live in rural cooperatives that were closely controlled by party functionaries. This effort to bring Communism to the countryside led to noticeable decreases in crop production, which caused food shortages throughout the country. Many farmers also slaughtered their draft animals before government agents could confiscate them. Even seafood became a scarce commodity after many fishermen fled Communist rule in their boats, and fuel shortages prevented the remaining fishermen from working effectively. Before long, southerners came to resent living under northern domination, while northerners questioned the dedication of their southern

comrades to the cause of the national Vietnamese revolution.

Amid these problems, high-ranking Communist officials ruled and lived much like feudal mandarins from an earlier age, despite the egalitarian rhetoric they espoused. Vietnam remained one of the poorest countries in the world during the 1980s, while many other nations in the region enjoyed great prosperity. In addition to food, such basic consumer goods as soap and aspirin became scarce and expensive commodities. This relentless poverty led many people to turn to the resources afforded them by black market capitalism, especially in the South. Refugees in western countries often sent cigarettes, whiskey, and other goods to their relatives back in Vietnam via Air France flights. After bribing corrupt officials, the recipients then sold their merchandise to the many vendors who hawked these wares on street corners in Saigon and other cities.

During the 1970s, Vietnam practically became an economic dependency of the Soviet Union. In fact, most cargo ships docking in Haiphong harbor were Russian vessels carrying oil, grain, and other vital supplies. The two nations also developed a military relationship similar to that which had existed between South Vietnam and the United States. The Russians saw Vietnam as a place where they could bolster their strategic presence in Southeast Asia and thus moved in to occupy the old American base at Cam Ranh Bay and other areas. Unfortunately for the Vietnamese, the Soviet personnel at these facilities lacked the cash of the American servicemen. During the following decade Vietnamese diplomacy suffered a serious setback when Moscow became friendlier toward the Chinese and sharply curtailed aid to Hanoi.

In 1979 the Vietnamese Communist Party conceded the failure of Marxist economic dogma, and began to encourage a degree of free enterprise in the country. The government allowed farmers, artisans, and merchants to pursue profits and thus stimulate the economy with an increased output of goods and also services. Dramatic improvement took a great deal of time simply because of the scarcity of resources required to stimulate economic growth. Throughout the 1980s, the liberalized economy suffered from inflation, lingering shortages, and hostility from idealists who were committed to the Communist revolution. After about a decade, conditions improved with the appearance of western corporations offering employment and inexpensive commodities for Vietnamese citizens.

While Vietnam struggled with postwar economic problems, Cambodia, under the Khmer Rouge, degenerated into a hellish

BELOW: U.S. Navy and Marine Corps staff work through the details of men Missing In Action (MIA) The issue of the MIAs has continued to dog relations between Vietnam and the U.S. As a result of cataclysmic explosions, the bodies of some men were completely destroyed while others were lost in deep jungle. In World War II they would have been classified as "Missing, Presumed Dead."

MIAs

Operation Homecoming – the mutual return of prisoners following the Paris Peace Accords – did not satisfy everyone. There still remained the issue of those classified as Missing in Action (MIA). Though the U.S. war had come to an end, military records still listed 2,387 U.S. servicemen as unaccounted for, and numbers of veterans and politicians claimed that these men were still being secretly held by the North.

It was to be a complex, emotive, and long-running issue, one which is still kept alive today by several veterans' pressure groups. They point to the fact that the 600 servicemen returned home in Operation Homecoming make no account of the MIAs who – more than likely – were taken prisoner. Also they add that the joint U.S./Vietnamese team set up to monitor prisoner release had quickly broken down in its cooperation, thus both sides had shown restraint in the numbers they released.

In 1976 the fact that U.S. PoWs were still held captive seemed to be confirmed in a House Select Committee on Missing Persons in Washington D.C. Reports had filtered through that both PoWs and some of the 21 journalist MIAs had physically been seen in remote camps in North Vietnam. However, the matter was underinvestigated as many in the U.S.administration wanted to put the ghosts of

Vietnam far behind them. Later, President Ronald Reagan was moved to pledge his support to continuing investigations into the matter. This renewed interrogation of the problem came to a head in the early 1990s during hearings held by Senator John Kerry. By this time U.S./Vietnamese

ABOVE: An MIA memorial medal, one of the many ways in which Americans remember servicemen whose remains have not been recovered, or who were reported alive as prisoners of war but have not returned. Some men were lost in long range patrols or aircraft flying over Laos or Cambodia, and until recently, the search for their remains has been more difficult than the retrieval of bodies from Vietnam.

LEFT: In a parade to remind the public about the MIA issue, an automobile which bears the name of a USAF pilot who had been shot down and missing in action in July 1972 drives past a group of Veterans of Foreign Wars.

RIGHT: On the lawn of the Pentagon, color parties are shown from the U.S. Navy, U.S. Marine Corps, U.S. Army, and U.S. Air Force. These color parties include the distinctive flag of the POW/MIA organization.

relations had warmed enough for the two countries to begin cooperation over the MIA issue. Accordingly, teams of investigators headed back into Vietnam's now silent and haunted battlefields.

Their work in Vietnam has borne fruit. Diligently tracking the last known movements of MIA soldiers, they have uncovered either the remains of many men (which can be identified through either dog-tags or DNA testing), or the truth of their demise. For Vietnam was an easy war in which to go missing. Soldiers would be injured and die in the dense jungle undergrowth, hidden from view for decades. Covert operatives would disappear into remote corners of Vietnam, Laos, and Cambodia, their presence so secret that even their government would disavow their presence if they were killed or captured. And like any other war, high-explosive weapons could sometimes cause individuals to vanish as if into thin air.

We are now at the stage in history where we can confidently say that the possibility of MIAs remaining captured in Southeast Asia is remote. All but one of the MIAs have now been accounted for, though many feel that the government still hides the truth about of their real whereabouts.

One day the issue will be finally laid to rest, but the fact that many still remember the MIAs of the Vietnam War at least continues the memory of what could be the forgotten soldiers.

LEFT: U.S. Navy pilots at the Navy Flight Weapons School at Miramar Naval Air station in California walk through a classroom that is decorated with the silhouettes and dates of Navy and Marine Corps "kills" over North Vietnam. The intense tactical flying raining program run by the U.S. Navy using U.S. air-craft with a similar per-formance to the Soviet designed types operated by the North Vietnamese became known by the popular name of the "Top Gun Program." Its success prompted the U.S. Air Force to follow a similar course. After the Vietnam War, the U.S. Army set up the National Training Center (NTC) at Fort Irwin for realistic tactical training against an Opposing Force (OPFOR). The NTC was a factor in the U.S. forces' 1991 success in the Gulf.

ABOVE: An honor guard salutes the casket of a U.S. serviceman on its way to Hawaii, either for burial in the military cemetery, or onward movement to the United States. Unlike U.S. soldiers in Europe, those killed in Vietnam were brought back to the U.S.

Cambodia. Although his party would rule the country for less than four years, it committed perhaps the most heinous and bizarre atrocities in modern history.

When the Khmer Rouge marched into Phnom Penh on April 17 1975, it immediately ordered the city's residents to evacuate the area. Citing the possibility of American bomb-ing raids against the city, the Communists asserted that the evacuation was merely a tem-porary safety measure. The residents left with little trouble, many of them with personal belongings. At first the Khmer Rouge troops managed to behave with a measure of restraint, confining their brutality to captured soldiers and bureaucrats from Lon Nol's regime when the evacuees reached temporary detention camps.

From these camps, the Khmer Rouge resettled these urbanites into rural communes throughout the countryside, then instigated tensions between them and the local peasants who had been living under Communist rule for several years. In effect, Pol Pot created a two-tier caste system in which the "patriotic" peas-ants enjoyed economic and social privileges

nightmare. Its new dictator, Pol Pot, launched perhaps the most ambitious campaign to achieve true Communism that any Marxist ruler had ever attempted. During his period of rule he abolished money, private property, and traditional social distinctions. Pol Pot also depopulated entire cities, which he had identi-fied as the source of class antagonisms in

Signs at the scene read:

NOTICE! We The People Who Vote Will Put up No Longer With People We put In Office! Who Are For Themselves and Rich only: 1. The President...

CHANGE The Name OF Nuclear Submarine CoRPuS CHRiSTy (Body of CHRIST) IT's A SACRaLiDge In FacT SCRAP ALL Weapons The Billions of Dollars Can Be used...

WAKE up! AMeRiCA. Recognize ALL CoMBaT VeTS Who FougHT and Died For $ou. MANY W.W.1-2 KoReA, VieTNaM HaVe Been Ripped OFF of Service- ConnecTed Disabili Ties Because of NeGLecT of MiLiTary MedicaL DepT and V.A.

For All DesTroyed! and InCoMpLeTe MiliTary Records Many Many VeTeraN's WHo've FougHT The Wars ReaL WeLL, Came Home WiTH Wounds and illness. BuT our GoverNmenT gave Them HeLL. For WHen They TRieD To geT Their DUe There Were No BeneFiT's on Them, Through The MiLiTary and VA Neglect WaS WHaT The GovernmenT Gave 'em, SuFFerinG ALL These Years Gone By WiTH Pain and Sorrows, Never RecievinG WHaT is Theit's, These Days! and The ToMorrow's By Joseph C.Petti

over the urban "new people." To prevent the new people from organizing into a hostile force, he relocated them continuously into far-flung regions throughout Cambodia. He also forced them into closely supervised "work brigades," chain gangs that performed hard labor in distant jungles and mountains. His goal was to keep the new people in a state of constant oppression, isolation, and poverty so that they could never rise up as a cohesive force to threaten his revolutionary program. In addition, Pol Pot wanted to kill off all those too weak to endure harsh conditions.

Like Josef Stalin, Mao Zedong, and other Communist nabobs, Pol Pot became paranoid about plots against his rule. In September 1976 he launched a series of purges against party members who showed too much leadership potential, thus threatening his hegemony. In this witch-hunt atmosphere, cadres tortured victims into admitting that they were agents of the CIA, then executed the "traitors." In one district, at least 40,000 Cambodians suffered this fate. By mid-1978, Pol Pot's paranoia became a self-fulfilling prophecy when disaffected party chiefs in the eastern region

ABOVE: Vietnam veteran Joseph Petti on a cross in Lafayette Park close to the White House in March 1982. He is one of many who claims that Agent Orange destroyed his health, but also protests about the lack of recognition for Vietnam veterans.
NEXT PAGE: Draped in the Stars and Stripes, caskets containing the remains of U.S. servicemen are lowered from a modified school bus during their journey back to the U.S.

AFTERMATH
AFTERMATH

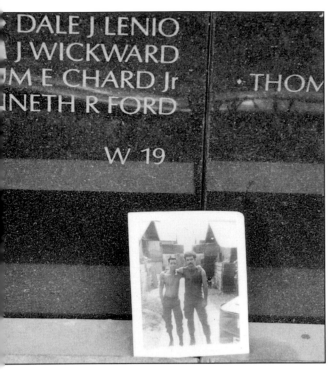

DALE J LENIO
J WICKWARD
M E CHARD Jr
NETH R FORD   · THOM

W 19

LEFT: A comrade recalls the friendship destroyed by war with a photograph placed close to the name of his friend on the Vietnam Veterans War Memorial. The memorial has become a shrine for veterans and their families and, in the center of Washington, is a hushed corner of a busy city. The tributes placed at the memorial are collected at the close of each day and housed at the Smithsonian. **BELOW:** John L. Steer, a U.S. Army veteran from Special Forces who lost his right arm in Vietnam in 1967, places a rose in the panels of the Vietnam Memorial on Veterans Day on November 11, 1986.

launched a rebellion. Although Pol Pot quickly smashed the uprising, some rebels slipped into Vietnam and established the Front for National Liberation.

Not surprisingly, Pol Pot carried out harsh reprisals throughout the eastern region. While relations with Hanoi were deteriorating, he accused the inhabitants of the area of being collaborators with Vietnam, and massacred at least 100,000 of them late in 1978. During this activity Khmer Rouge forces exterminated entire villages and relocated survivors to distant areas, where they were killed off through excruciating labor and harsh living conditions. Altogether, about 1.7 million easterners perished from this abuse. By this time, Pol Pot's regime had descended into a homicidal frenzy, and was drafting peasants into killing squads

that performed indiscriminate massacres throughout the country. Altogether the Khmer Rouge might have killed as many as 3.8 million people throughout the 1970s, about 26 percent of the population. By 1979, 42 percent of all Cambodian children had lost at least one parent, and the social dislocation wreaked by Pol Pot and his minions plagues Cambodia to this day.

On Christmas Day 1978 Vietnam invaded Cambodia after their armies had exchanged gunfire across the border for several months. In less than two weeks, 100,000 Vietnamese troops and 20,000 Cambodian allies defeated Khmer Rouge forces and took Phnom Penh. Although many Cambodians welcomed the Vietnamese as liberators, Hanoi had invaded the country for more selfish reasons. After

three years of acrimonious relations with Pol Pot, the Vietnamese had concluded that he was a pawn of the Chinese and an expansionist who sought to annex the Mekong Delta. Motivation aside, the invasion finally ended his atrocious rule. Vietnam occupied Cambodia until 1991, then turned it over to a coalition government that included Khmer Rouge participants.

In February 1979, yet another war broke out when China attacked Vietnam. Relations between the two countries had worsened since Beijing had become friendly with the United States in 1972. Conditions had deteriorated further since the fall of Saigon when Vietnam moved closer to the Soviet Union, despite attempts by the Chinese to pull Hanoi into their orbit. Vietnamese abuse against Chinese

BELOW: The year by year involvement in Southeast Asia shows clearly in the V-shaped Vietnam War Memorial. Where the wall is highest, the polished black granite reflects back the years in the late 1960s and early 1970s, when huge numbers of sailors, Marines, soldiers, and airmen were involved in the fighting. After the war, Congress ended the Draft and the U.S. Armed Forces became an all-volunteer force of career servicemen and women. The Vietnam war, the first war that the United States had lost, temporarily crippled national confidence, making bold foreign policy moves a thing of the past.

Life after Nam

During the height of the siege at Khe Sanh in 1968, there was a poignant note pinned to the U.S. Command Post noticeboard there. It read "For those who fight for it, life has a flavor the sheltered never know." To be a Vietnam veteran is to be set aside. Most of the men who fought in Vietnam averaged around 19 years of age during their tour of duty. They entered an alien world, a world where the jungle canopy set them in a green twilight full of beauty and danger, a culture with no resemblance to that of home, a war during which death could be encountered almost every single day.

Many veterans confess to having enjoyed Vietnam, despite the harrowing times. It was a period of strong emotion, rushes of adrenaline, and spectacular sights. It was a lawless time, in which every day brought something new and strange. Many veterans describe the experience of combat as if being in a world of hyperreality, where senses and thoughts work with a clarity and speed unobtainable in civilian life. This level of experience caused tremendous problems for many of the veterans returning home. Civilian

experience seemed to many trivial and lackluster, without the bursts of energy that Vietnam had given. Yet for others, the problems stemmed from what they had witnessed – recent estimates place 85,000 veterans as suffering from Post Traumatic Stress Disorder (PTSD). Years later, a sudden noise or a flash of light shining through vegetation could replay terrifying memories and shocking incidents.

This is understandable. One minute these veterans were in a ferocious firefight; twenty-four hours later they could be at home with their family in the U.S., their tour having come to an end. Families noticed the change, and often felt they had little in common with the son or husband who had returned. More painfully, many veterans received abuse by the public, and taunts of "baby killer" followed them down the streets. Almost no veteran received the heroes' welcome given to soldiers of former conflicts.

Yet time has healed some of the wounds. The idea that the majority of Vietnam veterans became dysfunctional on their return home is just not true. Many became very successful businessmen and leaders. Furthermore, interest in

FAR LEFT: Veterans carrying signs which serve to identify their states parade through Chicago in a "Welcome Home" parade in 1985. For many who had finished their 365-day tour in Vietnam, their subsequent return home was a shock and a disappointment, and reactions to these servicemen and women varied, from indifference to active hostility. The antiwar movement castigated them almost as war criminals, and it was not uncommon for those who had been crippled to be told that their injuries were deserved.

LEFT: A veteran's hands hold the Silver Star, Bronze Star, and Purple Heart awards for gallantry and injury in action that he received in the Vietnam War. During the final years of the war in Vietnam, the shock of the sight of the Vietnam Veterans Against the War – many of whom were disabled – hurling their decorations at the steps of Congress was one of the factors that turned a complete withdrawal from Southeast Asia from a political debate into a political necessity.

Vietnam blossomed in the 1980s and 1990s. Films such as "Platoon" hinted at what veterans had experienced, and more people came to understand horrors like what happened at My Lai in the context of a war that served to perpetuate brutality.

The Vietnam War memorial in Washington D.C. has become one of the most visited attractions in the United States, and more schoolchildren now learn about the conflict as part of their standard curriculum. Though it has come late, perhaps now those who fought in Vietnam feel that they live in a country that respects them, if not for what they achieved, at least for what they endured.

RIGHT: Vietnam veteran Bob Sutton on crutches outside the Federal Courthouse in Brooklyn during a protest against the proposed $4,120 million Agent Orange medical settlement. This was the first of five nationwide hearings that began in August 1984 to establish whether a better settlement could be agreed. A chemical in Agent Orange, called dioxin, caused cancers in veterans and birth defects in their children, but during the war, men had been assured that it was harmless. One of the "rites of passage" for men of the Ranch Hand operation that sprayed the herbicide was to drink a glass of Agent Orange.

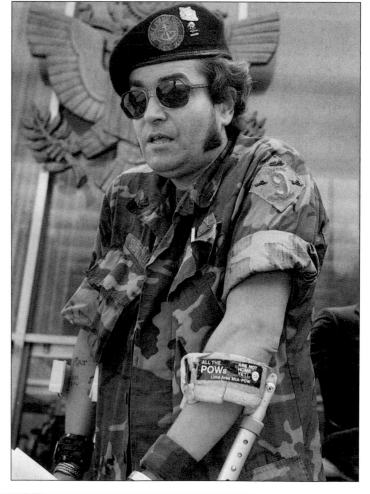

RIGHT: The remains of an unknown serviceman who died during the Vietnam War are carried across the Memorial Bridge to Arlington National Cemetery on May 28, 1984. In front are honor guards from each of the four services, and behind are the limousines of the heads of the government and armed services. On that day, the route was lined by many thousands of people who had come to pay their respects. For some, it was an act of catharsis, an opportunity to express their grief and their respect in public. For those who had avoided the war or had opposed it, it was a chance to reexamine the attitudes which they had held more than ten years earlier. The effort that had gone into finding and identifying the bodies of men missing in action meant that it was hard to find a body in Vietnam that could be identified as that of a U.S. serviceman, but which could not then be traced and named. However, from World War I, the Unknown Soldier has been an important symbol for all parents and widows who do not know where their next of kin are buried.

FAR RIGHT: Two days before he was laid to rest at Arlington, the coffin of the Unknown Serviceman lay in state in the Rotunda of the U.S. Capitol with a guard from each of the four services. For the men who had fought in Vietnam and returned, the memorials and monuments were aptly summed up by the inscription on the New York Vietnam Veterans Memorial. It was taken from a letter which had been sent home by a U.S. soldier, who wrote: "One thing worries me – will people believe me? Will they want to hear about it, or will they want to forget the whole thing ever happened?"

residents also angered Beijing when they began streaming across the border to escape persecution. When China withdrew its technical assistance and aid to Vietnam in the summer of 1978, this persecution started to increase. Finally, the Vietnamese invasion of Cambodia proved to be the last straw for the Chinese government.

With Vietnam in the Soviet bloc, Beijing had seen Pol Pot's regime as its sole ally in Southeast Asia. From 1976 the Chinese had poured money, arms, and advisers into Cambodia to bolster a friendly regime. After Vietnam had toppled the Khmer Rouge dictatorship, China sought to teach its neighbor a lesson. On February 17, 1979, Deng Xiaoping

sent at least 75,000 Chinese troops across the border in a punitive expedition aimed at sacking Vietnamese bases and provincial capitals and subduing local enemy forces before returning quickly to claim victory and avoid heavy losses or long-term commitment. The Chinese army inflicted significant damage to many of its targets, including the border town of Lang Son, which the Vietnamese preserved in its ruined state as a monument. However, the invaders suffered higher casualties than expected and failed to intimidate Hanoi into withdrawing from Cambodia. The invasion also provoked Laos into expelling Chinese advisers from its soil, thus ending almost all of Beijing's influence within Southeast Asia.

The resumption of the ancient animosity between Vietnam and China created a strange variation of the "domino theory" that had been advanced in earnest by the American "Cold Warriors" in earlier decades. Instead of monolithic Communism spreading from Southeast Asia into neighboring areas, the region saw competing nationalistic forces which were imbued with Marxist doctrines and engaging in old-fashioned power politics. However, the conflict between these competing nationalistic forces meant that while the brotherhood of proletarian dictatorships broke apart, American relations with former adversaries gradually improved. Throughout the 1980s the United States found itself siding with an anti-Vietnamese Cambodian coalition based in Thailand that included both the Khmer Rouge and Prince Norodom Sihanouk.

LEFT: Protestors standing behind a crowd fence wave MIA/POW flags, jeer, and shout their disapproval of the U.S. President Bill Clinton's appearance at the Vietnam Memorial on May 31, 1993. Former Marine Corps Sergeant Charles Coster holds up a sign that sums up the pro-testors' anger at Clinton's efforts to avoid being drafted while he was a Rhodes scholar at Oxford. When he became President, he instructed that the correspondence relating to his efforts to avoid conscription should be traced and destroyed. However, copies of the correspondence had by that time already entered the public domain. In 1994 Clinton had the added humiliation of meeting an earlier generation of veter-ans, the men who had landed at D-Day and fought in Europe.

BELOW LEFT: The conflict – or at best tension – in Southeast Asia seems to be almost endless. In this photograph, officer cadets of the Khmer People's Liberation Front attend a parade in a refugee camp close to the Thai Cambodian border.

RIGHT: U.S. Marines stand guard outside the U.S. Consulate building in Kuwait following its libera-tion in Operation Desert Sabre, the land phase of the attack on the Iraqi forces which had occupied Kuwait in 1990. Many men who held senior positions in the U.S. Armed Forces in the operation between 1990 and 1991 had, like General Norman Schwarzkopf, the com-mander of the Coalition ground forces, served as company commanders in Vietnam. It was a new, more confident force with clear, achievable goals that these commanders were now directing; their men knew that they had the full sup-port of people back home.

During the following decade, after the gradual collapse of the Soviet Union and the end of the Cold War, diplomacy between Washington and Hanoi even took a turn for the better, despite the ongoing controversy that continued to surround the estimations that as many as 1,498 American servicemen were still missing in action.

Almost a generation after the fall of Saigon, the two countries finally established normal diplomatic relations. President Bill Clinton affirmed this new era of cordiality when he visited Vietnam in November 2000, proclaiming an end to the years of hostility between the two countries in optimistic speeches in front of cheering crowds.

ABOVE: The bronze sculpture of three servicemen who represent the European, African, and Hispanic elements of American society that stands facing the Vietnam Memorial in Washington. The men appear to be searching for the names of friends written on the black granite.

RIGHT: A moment of intense personal grief as, after searching for a year and then scanning the names, a veteran finds the name of a comrade killed in action. Every day, over 10,000 people file past the granite walls that bear the names of the 58,022 Americans killed or missing in Vietnam.

1945

9–11 MARCH—The Japanese occupiers of Indochina declare an independent Vietnam with Emperor Bao Dai as its leader.

15 AUGUST—Japan surrenders

2 SEPTEMBER—Ho Chi Minh's communist Viet Minh soldiers seize power and declare a Democratic Republic of Vietnam.

22 SEPTEMBER—French troops return to Indochina and fighting begins between them and the Viet Minh.

1946

MARCH—France makes a token recognition of Vietnam as an independent state in the Indochinese Union.

23 NOVEMBER—French warships shell Haiphong harbor.

19 DECEMBER—The Viet Minh attack French troops in the north of the country and the eight-year Indochina war begins.

1949

8 MARCH—Bao Dai is established as the nominal ruler of Vietnam.

19 JULY—France accepts Laos as an independent state associated with France.

8 NOVEMBER—France accepts Cambodia as an independent state associated with France.

1 OCTOBER—People's Republic of China is founded.

1950

JANUARY—Ho Chi Minh's Democratic Republic of Vietnam is recognized by both China and the Soviet Union.

8 MAY—U.S. government announces pro-French military aid to Vietnam, Laos and Cambodia.

26 JULY—$15 million of war aid is advanced from the U.S. to the French forces in Indochina.

1953

OCTOBER–NOVEMBER—Both Laos and Cambodia declare their independence from France.

1954

7 MAY—French troops are defeated by Ho Chi Minh's communist Viet Minh at the battle of Dien Bien Phu, thus bringing to an end French rule over Indochina.

16 JUNE—Ngo Dinh Diem is appointed as Premier of South Vietnam and organizes his government.

20–21 JULY—The Geneva Accords are signed, formally ending the First Indochina War. Vietnam is split at the 17th parallel into a communist-controlled north under the leadership of Ho Chi Minh and a U.S.-backed south under Diem. Both sides agree on reunificatory elections at a further date.

8 SEPTEMBER—South-East Asia Treaty Organization (SEATO) established as a protective community for South Vietnam against the North.

24 OCTOBER—President Eisenhower pledges U.S. aid to support South Vietnamese anti-communist military and political activity.

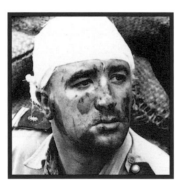

1955

MAY—U.S. aid begins to arrive in South Vietnam, including financial assistance, military equipment, and U.S. military personnel acting as advisors to South Vietnamese forces.

16 JULY—Fearing Ho's popularity, Diem rejects the Geneva Ac-cords and withdraws from the reunificatory elections. Communist insurgency subsequently increases.

23 OCTOBER—Emperor Bao Dai's office is annulled. Diem becomes the South Vietnamese head of state and subsequently declares the Republic of Vietnam.

1956

31 MARCH—Prince Souvanna Phouma becomes the Prime Minister of Laos.

28 APRIL—The U.S. Military Assistance Advisory Group (MAAG) takes formal responsibility for training South Vietnamese forces in the fight against the communists.

1957

29 MAY—Communist Pathet Lao guerrillas attempt to seize power in Laos.

SEPTEMBER—Diem's position is consolidated after winning a general election.

1958

JANUARY—Communist attacks increase around Saigon.

1959

MAY—The movement of communist troops and supplies down the Ho Chi Minh trail from North Vietnam begins.

JUNE–JULY—The Pathet Lao insurgents in Laos begin to receive military aid from North Vietnam.

8 JULY—Two U.S. advisors are killed at Bien Hoa during a communist attack.

1960

APRIL—Universal conscription introduced in North Vietnam.

5 MAY—MAAG strength is increased to 685 personnel from 327.

8 NOVEMBER—John F. Kennedy secures the U.S. Presidency.

11 NOVEMBER—Diem survives a coup attempt by South Vietnamese army groups.

DECEMBER—The communist National Liberation Front for South Vietnam is formed. This is called the Viet Cong (short for 'Vietnamese communist') by forces in the south.

1961

JANUARY—A pro-U.S. government is formed by Prince Boun Oum in Laos.

11–13 MAY—Vice-President Johnson visits South Vietnam.

He decides that an increase in U.S. aid to South Vietnam is necessary.

1–4 SEPTEMBER—Viet Cong launch attacks in Kontum province

18 SEPTEMBER—A Viet Cong battalion achieve the temporary capture of the provincial capital of Phuoc Vinh, 55 miles from Saigon.

8 OCTOBER—Opposing factions in Laos agree to the formation of a coalition government under Souvanna Phouma.

11 OCTOBER—Kennedy's chief military advisor, General Maxwell D. Taylor, goes on a fact-finding visit to South Vietnam.

NOVEMBER—Kennedy increases aid to South Vietnam on the basis of Taylor's report.

1962

3 FEBRUARY—The 'Strategic Hamlets' programme begins.

7 FEBRUARY—U.S. military personnel in South Vietnam number 4000.

8 FEBRUARY—MAAG is renamed as the U.S. Military Assistance Command, Vietnam (MACV) led by General Paul Harkins.

27 FEBRUARY—President Diem's palace is attacked by two South Vietnamese aircraft. He escapes unhurt.

JUNE—U.S. military personnel now in South Vietnam number 12,000.

AUGUST—Soldiers from the Australian Military Aid Forces (MAF) arrive in Vietnam.

1963

2 JANUARY—Viet Cong soldiers impose a defeat on South Vietnamese troops at the battle of Ap Bac.

MAY–AUGUST—Riots and demonstrations against Diem's government by South Vietnam's Buddhist community begin in Hue and then spread across the country into Saigon. Seven Buddhist monks burn themselves to death in protest at anti-Buddhist policies.

1–2 NOVEMBER—Diem and his brother Ngo Dinh Nhu are murdered in a military coup. The presidency is taken by General Duong Van Minh.

22 NOVEMBER—John F. Kennedy is assassinated and Lyndon B. Johnson becomes president.

1964

30 JANUARY—Duong Van Minh is deposed by a junta led by General Nguyen Khanh.

20 JUNE—General William C. Westmoreland replaces Harkins as commander of U.S. MACV.

1–4 AUGUST—Several engagements in the Gulf of Tonkin are reported between North Vietnamese patrol boats and the USS Maddox and USS C. Turner Joy.

5 AUGUST—North Vietnamese military targets are bombed by U.S. aircraft in retaliation for the incidents in the Gulf of Tonkin.

7 AUGUST—The U.S. Congress accepts the Gulf of Tonkin resolution. This enables President Johnson to take any necessary measures to defend U.S. forces and, crucially, to prevent further communist actions.

24 DECEMBER—A Viet Cong bombing in Saigon kills two Americans and wounds 52 others.

31 DECEMBER—The number of U.S. personnel in Vietnam number 23,000.

1965

8 JANUARY—2000 South Korean troops are deployed to Vietnam.

7 FEBRUARY—The U.S. base at Pleiku is attacked by the Viet Cong.

8 FEBRUARY—U.S. and South Vietnamese aircraft launch retaliatory attacks against North Vietnam.

10 FEBRUARY—23 U.S. soldiers die in a Viet Cong bombing at Qui Nhon.

13 FEBRUARY—The extended strategic bombing of North Vietnam—known as Operation Rolling Thunder—is authorized.

2 MARCH—Rolling Thunder begins.

8 MARCH—Two U.S. Marine battalions land at Da Nang as the first dedicated U.S. combat troops to be deployed in Vietnam.

JUNE—Nguyen Cao Ky becomes the South Vietnamese Prime Minister. U.S. troops in Vietnam number over 50,000 by the end of the month.

18 JUNE—B52 bombers used for the first time against Viet Cong targets.

27 JUNE—Large-scale U.S. operations are conducted by 173rd Airborne Brigade against Viet Cong units northeast of Saigon.

OCTOBER–NOVEMBER—U.S. units conduct the first major search-and-destroy operation into the Ia Drang valley.

25 DECEMBER—Rolling Thunder is paused with the hope of negotiations.

31 DECEMBER—U.S. troops strength in Vietnam exceeds 180,000.

1966

31 JANUARY—Rolling Thunder begins again after its hiatus.

APRIL—Operation Game Warden is launched in the Mekong Delta, attempting to sever riverborne Viet Cong supplies.

12 APRIL—B52s strike for the first time within North Vietnam.

23 JUNE—South Vietnamese troops attack and seize the Buddhist headquarters in Saigon to stop nationwide Buddhist rioting.

31 DECEMBER—U.S. troop strength in Vietnam reaches 385,000 personnel.

1967

8 JANUARY—Operation Cedar Falls is launched against communist forces in the Iron Triangle area near Saigon.

22 FEBRUARY—U.S. troops launch Operation Junction City, a huge S&D operation in Tay Ninh province.

28 FEBRUARY—The Mobile Riverine Force (MRF) is formed in the Mekong Delta.

1 MAY—U.S. troop strength reaches 436,000.

8 MAY—The NVA launch attacks against the Marine base at Con Thien, just south of the DMZ.

3 SEPTEMBER—General Nguyen Van Thieu becomes President of South Vietnam after a general election.

8 MAY—Con Thien, a U.S. Marine base just south of the DMZ, comes under NVA attack is subsequently held under siege.

4 OCTOBER—U.S. forces finally break the siege at Con Thien.

OCTOBER–DECEMBER—Khe Sanh air base near the DMZ comes under increasing NVA assaults.

1968

22 JANUARY—The siege at Khe Sanh begins and will last for 77 days.

31 JANUARY—The Tet offensive—the NVA's wholesale invasion of the South—begins.

16 MARCH—The My Lai massacre occurs.

31 MARCH—Tet severely damages President Johnson. He limits U.S. bombing of the North Vietnam and declares that he will not run for president again.

14 APRIL—The Khe Sanh siege is lifted.

3 MAY—The conditions for preliminary peace talks between U.S. and North Vietnam are accepted by both parties.

13 MAY—U.S. and North Vietnamese delegates meet in Paris to begin negotiations.

11 JUNE—General Creighton W. Abrams takes over as commander of the MACV, replacing General William Westmoreland

23 JUNE—The Khe Sanh base is abandoned.

5 NOVEMBER—Richard Nixon is elected U.S. President. He declares a shift in U.S. policy towards steady troop withdrawals from Vietnam.

31 DECEMBER—U.S. troop numbers in Vietnam hit their peak at over 536,000.

1969

25 JANUARY—Negotiations for a truce begin in Paris.

23–24 FEBRUARY—Communist forces launch major artillery and rocket attacks on 115 urban and military targets throughout South Vietnam.

18 MARCH—U.S. aircraft begin the secret bombing of communist targets in Cambodia.

8 JUNE—President Nixon announces a planned withdrawal of 25,000 U.S. personnel from South Vietnam over the next three months.

4 SEPTEMBER—In Hanoi, the death of Ho Chi Minh is publicly announced.

15 SEPTEMBER—President Nixon declares that 50,000 U.S. troops will be withdrawn from Vietnam by 15 April 1970.

OCTOBER–NOVEMBER—The U.S. is shaken by huge anti-war demonstrations, most of them concentrated in Washington D.C.

16 NOVEMBER—The My Lai massacre is revealed to a shocked U.S. public.

31 DECEMBER—U.S. troop strength in South Vietnam is down to 474,000.

1970

10 FEBRUARY—In Laos Souvanna Phouma states that he will not take action against supply movements down the Ho Chi Minh trail if the NVA withdraw its troops from the country.

20 FEBRUARY—Secret talks begin in Paris between Henry Kissinger and North Vietnamese negotiator Le Duc Tho.

18 MARCH—General Lon Nol overthrows Prince Norodom Sihanouk of Cambodia in a coup.

4 APRIL—50,000 people march through Washington D.C. in support of President Nixon's policy over Vietnam.

29 APRIL—MACV announces that U.S. forces joined South Vietnamese troops during offensive actions into Cambodia.

9–10 MAY—Up to 100,000 people flood Washington in protest against the war and against the shooting of four students at Kent State University by the National Guard.

29 JUNE—U.S. forces operating in Cambodia are withdrawn back into South Vietnam.

15 OCTOBER—President Nixon announces the further withdrawal of 40,000 U.S. troops for the end of December.

31 DECEMBER—The U.S. Congress repeals Gulf of Tonkin resolution. U.S. troop strength in Vietnam has now fallen to 335,000, down from 474,000 from the year previously.

1971

8 FEBRUARY—South Vietnamese forces mount Operation Lam Son 719, an invasion of Laos aimed at severing the Ho Chi Minh trail.

25 MARCH—Lam Son 719 ends in an ignominious and costly withdrawal for ARVN troops.

18 AUGUST—Australia and New Zealand state that they will withdraw all troops from participation in the Vietnam War.

9 SEPTEMBER—South Korea commits itself to complete troop withdrawal by June 1972.

OCTOBER—Nguyen Van Thieu is re-elected as president during South Vietnam's elections.

26–30 NOVEMBER—U.S. aircraft strike against NVA troop concentrations on South Vietnam's borders.

1972

5 FEBRUARY—A U.S. peace plan proposed on 25 January is rejected by North Vietnam.

30 MARCH—The Easter Invasion, North Vietnam's invasion of South Vietnam, is launched.

6 APRIL—U.S. airstrikes against North Vietnam begin in response to the Easter Invasion.

8 MAY—Nixon announces that North Vietnam's Haiphong harbor has been mined by U.S. aircraft.

26 APRIL—President Nixon declares that U.S. troop numbers will be reduced to 49,000 by 1 July.

12 JUNE—The siege at An Loc is finally broken by ARVN troops.

12 AUGUST—The last U.S. combat troops leave South Vietnam.

16 SEPTEMBER—Quang Tri city is recaptured by ARVN, though the province is far from pacified.

18 DECEMBER—Nixon launches Linebacker II, a heavy bombing campaign against North Vietnam north of the 20th Parallel. The raid follows several abortive peace negotiations.

30 DECEMBER—The Linebacker bombing is ceased following a successful truce between the U.S. and North Vietnam.

1973

15 JANUARY—U.S. military operations against North Vietnam are ceased based on progress in the negotiations between Kissinger and Le Duc Tho.

27 JANUARY—A peace agreement is formally signed by the U.S. and North Vietnamese representatives.

29 MARCH—The last U.S. troops finally leave South Vietnam.

15 AUGUST—Following a Congressional resolution in July, U.S. airstrikes against Cambodia are stopped.

14 SEPTEMBER—Communist Pathet Lao officials form a provisional administration with members of the Laotian government.

1974

4 JANUARY—President Thieu explains that the Vietnam War is not over. He points to over 57,000 deaths since the cease-fire.

15–28 JANUARY—Phnom Penh, the capital of Cambodia, suffers heavy casualties during shelling by communist rebels.

5 AUGUST—The U.S. Congress set a limit of $100,000,000 on military aid for South Vietnam in the 1975 fiscal year.

9 AUGUST—Following the gradual revelation of the Watergate scandal, President Nixon resigns.

1975

JANUARY—The NVA expands its troop numbers and strategic positions within South Vietnam, and maintains an increasing pressure on ARVN troops.

1 JANUARY—In Cambodia the Khmer Rouge launch a major attack against Phnom Penh.

4 MARCH—The NVA begin a series of offensives in the Central Highlands.

10–15 APRIL—NVA troops capture An Loc, a city only 38 miles from Saigon.

17 APRIL—Phnom Penh falls to the communist Khmer Rouge in Cambodia.

21 APRIL—Tran Van Huong takes over as South Vietnam's president after Thieu resigns.

28 APRIL—After only seven days, Tran Van Huong is replaced by Duong Van Minh as South Vietnamese president.

30 APRIL—The Vietnam War ends with the fall of Saigon to communist forces.

24 AUGUST—Laos falls to the Pathet Lao guerrillas. It becomes a communist state on 3 December.

DECEMBER—Cambodia is renamed Kampuchea after resistance to the communist Khmer Rouge finally crumbles.

1976

APRIL—Up to 50,000 refugees have up to this point spilled into Thailand from Cambodia in an attempt to escape Pol Pot's horrifying social engineering.

15 NOVEMBER—The U.S. uses its veto to prevent Vietnam becoming a member of the UN.

1977

17–18 MARCH—Vietnam hands over the bodies of 12 missing U.S. pilots as part of slowly warming relations between the two countries.

30 JUNE—The South-East Asia Treaty Organization (SEATO) is dissolved.

6 August—The Thai government announces that the Kampuchean military have committed over 400 cross-border actions to this date. Relations between the two countries deteriorate dramatically and fighting increases.

31 December—Vietnam launches major military attack into Kampuchea.**1978**

June—To this month it is estimated that some two million Cambodian civilians have been slaughtered under Pol Pot's genocidal regime.

August—Vietnamese/Kampuchean relations reach the brink of outright war.

25 December—Vietnam launches a full-scale invasion of Kampuchea, resulting in the overthrow of Pol Pot.

1979

January—An international trade embargo is placed upon Vietnam in response to its invasion of Kampuchea.

February—China makes an invasion of Vietnam. Fighting continues into March before China withdraws, though border actions continue for some time.

1982

11 November—The Vietnam War memorial is unveiled in Washington D.C. It lists all the names of more than 58,000 U.S. war dead.

1988

Vietnam begins the process of withdrawing troops from Kampuchea, a process that would be completed in 1989.

September—The U.S. and Vietnam conduct joint investigations into U.S. MIAs.

1992

April—Following a warming of relations between the U.S. and Vietnam, some conditions of the trade embargo are lifted.

December—U.S. companies are given government authorization to establish companies within Vietnam.

1993

Economic sanctions are further eased by the U.S., and the U.S. also withdraws its opposition to Vietnam's access to international capital through the IMF.

1994

3 February—U.S. economic sanctions against Vietnam are completely withdrawn following Vietnam's agreement to help over MIA issues

1995

31 May—Vietnam gives information about U.S. servicemen killed or missing during the war.

1998

15 April—Pol Pot dies of natural causes, though ironically as a prisoner of the Khmer Rouge he took to power.

VIETNAM STATISTICS

U.S. fatalities
Hostile deaths: 47,359
Accidental deaths: 10,797
Total deaths: 58,202

U.S. wounded
Wounded: 303,704 (153,329 required a period of hospitalization)
Severely disabled: 75,000, including 23,214 totally disabled; 5283 suffered single limb amputations; 1081 sustained multiple amputations

Missing in Action/POWs
January 1973, U.S. DoD figures: Total missing: 3309 (1380 actual MIA and 1929 unaccounted for)
POWs: 766 (114 died in captivity)
Operation Homecoming (the exchange of prisoners between North Vietnam and the U.S.) returned 512 POWs and 53 MIAs

Draftees
Draftees as percentage of total U.S. force: 25 per cent (648,500)
Draftees as percentage of U.S. combat deaths: 30.4 per cent (17,725)
Total draftees 1965–73: 1,728,344
Percentage of total draftees who served in Vietnam: 38 per cent
Marine Corps draft: 42,633

Racial composition of U.S. military personnel in Vietnam
Caucasian: 88.4 per cent
African American: 10.6 per cent
1 per cent listed as others.
Caucasians as percentage of war dead: 86.3 per cent
African Americans as percentage of war dead: 12.5 per cent
Number of Hispanics in Vietnam service: 170,000

Socioeconomic status of U.S. military personnel in Vietnam
Personnel from lower middle/working class backgrounds: 76 per cent
Personnel from mid-range income levels: 50 per cent
Personnel with fathers in professional employment: 23 per cent
Personnel with high school education: 79 per cent

TOTAL SOUTH VIETNAMESE FORCES AND VIETNAM-BASED U.S. FORCES, 1959–1971

	South Vietnam	United States
1959	279,200	650
1960	243,000	900
1961	240,000+	3200
1962	240,000+	11,300
1963	300,000+	16,300
1964	514,000	23,300
1965	500,000+	184,000 (December)
1966	500,000+	485,300
1967	643,000	485,600
1968	820,000	536,100
1969	897,000	474,400 (December)
1970	968,000	335,800
1971	1,048,000	250,900 (June)

COMPARATIVE STRENGTHS, 1975 (SPRING OFFENSIVE)

	North Vietnam	South Vietnam
Total military manpower	375,000	662,600
Tanks and APCs	600	1230
Aircraft	342	1673
Naval craft	39	1507

Figures in **bold** *refer to illustrations and their captions*

A

A Luoi 333
A Shau Valley 88, 331-334, **332**, 336, 415
Abrams, General Creighton W. **333**, 333, 417, 433
    advocates bombing campaign 372
    and ARVN withdrawal from Laos 474
    and the invasion of Cambodia 423, 424
    and the Laos border violation 364
    and Operation Lam Son 719 467
    plans invasion of Laos 449
    problems facing 414-416
    replaces Westmoreland 62, 337
    strategy 333, 337, 339
    tactics 355
    Tet Offensive, 1969 370
    and third Tet Offensive 341
Accelerated Pacification Campaign (APC), the 339, 341, 412
Acheson, Dean 323
African Americans **129**, **180**, **181**, **302**, 302, **303**
Agent Orange 197, 569, 573, **591**
Agnew, Spiro T. (1918-) 345, **348**
agriculture **113**, **308**
    post war 580
Ai Tu 488, 499
Air America 475
air strikes **55**, **56**, 145, 173, 177, 179, **230**
    at Dak To 98
    Hill 881 172-173
    at Hue 306
aircraft **45**
    Boeing B-52 Stratofortress **56**, **230**, 239, **394-395**
    Cessna 0-1 Bird Dog **295**
    Douglas A-1 Skyraider **94**, **215**
    Douglas AC-47 **264**
    Douglas C-47 Dakota **234**
    Fairchild AC-119G Shadow 229
    gunships **229**, 229, **264**
    at Khe Sanh **228**
    Lockheed AC-130 Spectre 229
    Lockheed C-130 Hercules **195**, **232-233**
    losses **233**
    McDonnell Douglas A4 Skyhawk **54**, **110**, **326**, **327**
    McDonnell Douglas F4 Phantom **55**, **126-127**, **204**, **301**, **508**
    Mikoyan-Gurevich MiG-17 **509**
    Mikoyan-Gurevich MiG-21 **328-329**
    North American RA-5 Vigilante **205**
    Northrop F-5 **532-533**
    Republic (Fairchild) F-105 Thunderchief **458**, **509**, **511**
    Rockwell International OV-10A Bronco **378**
    Vought A-7 Corsair **500-501**
    Vought A-7 Corsair II **326**
    Vought RF-8G Crusader **156**
Alvarez, Lieutenant Commander Everett 528
American-Asians **575**, 575, 578
An Khe 57
    and Tet 261
An Lao valley 89, 91
An Loc 493, **497**, 497, **503**, 508, 511, 518, **554**, 554, 562
Angkor Wat, temples of **574-575**
Annam 10
Annamite Mountains, the **62-63**
Ap Bac 35-36
Ap Bia Mountain *see* Hamburger hill, battle of
Apocalypse Now, film **343**
Archer, Neil 153
armored fighting vehicles **402-403**
    LVTP5A1 amphibious assault vehicle **188**, **192**
    M113 APC **157**, **248**, **330**, **441**
    ONTOS **105**
Army of the Republic of Vietnam (ARVN) 25, **44-45**, 89, **113**, **115**, **423**, 460, **460-461**, **496**

1st Airborne Battalion 463
1st Airborne Brigade 562
1st Armored Brigade 463
1st Cavalry Regiment 428
1st Infantry Division 132, 180, 184, 286, 291, 309, 463, 466-467, 474
1st Regiment 378, 415
2nd Airborne Battalion 463, 472
2nd Division 108, 132, 192, 194, 526, 557
3rd Airborne Battalion 463, 472
3rd Airborne Division 325
3rd Airborne Regiment 428
3rd Division **462**, 488, 490, 507
3rd Infantry Regiment 336, 387
4th Armor Group 526
5th Division 493
7th Battalion 137
7th Division 538
8th Airborne Battalion 463
9th Airborne Battalion 466
9th Division 538
18th Division 544, 563
20th Tank Regiment 499, 503
21st Division 493, 497, 526
22nd Division 497, 548
44th Infantry Regiment 534
45th Regiment 534
49th Infantry Regiment 540
51st Regiment 132
at An Loc 493, **497**, 497, **503**, **554**
at Ap Bac 35-36
at Base South 470
at Ben Hat 399
at Bong Son **506**
in Cambodia 419, 423-424, **428**, 428, 429-430, **434**, 434-435, 440, 443
at Camp Carroll 490
casualties **308**, 311, 460, 474, 481, **507**, **544**, **548**, 556-557
in the Central Highlands 56, 556
at Chu-Lai 137
and civilian population **360**
conditions of service **313**, 460
conduct **112**
conscripts 395
at Dak To 155
at Dong Ha 336
and the Easter Offensive 488, 490, **492**, 492-493, **497**, 497, 499, 503, 508, 511-512
enlargement of 449
enters Cambodia 419
evacuates the Highlands 556
failure of 40
final offensive 554, 556-557, 562, 563
at Fire Support Bases 30 and 31 472
at Firebase O'Reilly 415
Hac Bo (Black Panther) Recondo Company **270**, 283
at Hue 283, 286, 291, 295, 301, 305-306, 309
I Corps 507
II Corps 556-557, 562
III Corps 424, 428, 562
invades Laos **462-463**, 463, 466-468
and the invasion of Cambodia 423-424
in the Khe Le Valley 549
at Khe Sanh 232, 325, 327
at Kien Duc 534
at Kontum 511
lack of U.S. support **540**
land grabbing 520, 523, **525**
in Laos **454**, **462**, **462-463**, 463, 466-468, 468, 470, **471**, 472, 474
at Long Knot 540-541
Marines **44**, 132, **247**, **257**, **308**, **311**
medical resources **548**
military strength 132
and the National Radio Station 271
at Nui Loc Son Basin 189
officers **247**, **254-255**, 311, **361**, 395, 399, 460, 557, 574
and Operation Hastings 113
and Operation Hickory 184, 186, 189
and Operation Junction City 146
and Operation Lam Son 72 512

and Operation Lam Son 719 452, **454**, 458-459, 463, 466-468, 472, 474, 481
and Operation Prairie 134
paratroopers **53**, **489**
and the Paris peace treaty **523**, **524**
performance 433, 443, 460, **507**
post war **572**, 574
problems 460
in Quang Duc province 530, 534
at Quang Tri City **502**, **512**, 512
Rangers 132, 151, 169, 194, 232, **248**, **249**, **253**, 275, **314-315**, **331**, 419, 463, 470, **497**, 526, 540, **548**, 549, 554, 556, 557
re-education 574
relief of Khe Sanh 325, 327
reputation 314
resistance collapses 563
and Saigon 212, 275, **314**
in the Seven Mountain Region 526
success 160
and Tet **248**, 256, 258, 265, **268**, 271, 275, 278, 314
and Tet, 1969 370
and the Third Indochina War **538**, 538, 540, 544, 548, 549, 550
at Toumorong 96
training 20, 24, **412**
U.S. aid 20, **32**, 460
U.S. equipment **520**
at Van Tuong Peninsular 73
and Vietnamization 362
weapons **76**, 180, 460
withdraw from Laos 474
at Xuan Loc 563
ARVN *see* Army of the Republic of Vietnam
ARVN Joint General Staff Compound, Saigon 266-267
assassination 333, 422
Australian forces 50, 51, **53**, **140**, **141**, **178**, **212**, **269**, 269, 342, **423**
    casualties **140**, 269
Autenreith, Sergeant John **442**

B

Ba Thu 428
Ban Me Thout 554
    and Tet 253
Bao Binh 544
Barnes, Chief Gene P. **531**
Barrow, Colonel Robert H. 357, 360, 364
Base Area 353 372, 428
Base Area 367 428
Base Area 611 357, 360, 364-365
Base South 470
Ben Hai River 184
Ben Hat, siege of **386**, **387**, 399
Ben Suc 140, **143**, 145, 146
Ben Tre, and Tet 265
Bien Hoa **54**, **64**, 151, 530, 563
    and Tet 274
Binh Dinh Pacification campaign 89
Binh Dinh Province 89, 91, 91-92
Binh Xuyen gangster-militia 541
Blessing, Colonel Patrick 173, 179
boat people **567**, **572-573**, 578
Boaz, TSGT Eddie P. **526**
body bags **169**
Boi Loi woods 52
Bong Son **506**
    and Tet 261
Bong Son plain 89
booby traps **89**, 100, **308**, **481**
Bouam Long **475**
boy soldiers **547**, **548**
Bradford, Sergeant First Class Emmanuel **202-203**
Bradley, General Omar Nelson (1893-1981) 323
Brezhnev, Leonid, Soviet Secretary-General (1906-82) 507-508
bridges **394**
Brinks Hotel, Saigon, car bomb attack **36**
Browne, Malcolm 152
Browning, Glen **154-155**
Bu Bong 530, 534
Bu Prang 530, 534

Buddhist community
    insurrection **98**, **98-99**, 261
    protests **33**, 36
    re-education 574
Bunker, Ellsworth, U.S. ambassador **312**, 352, 370, 482
Burrows, Larry 152

C

Ca Lu 325
Ca Mau, and Tet 265
Calley, Lieutenant William 400, **400-401**, 408, 485
Cam Lo 490
Cam Lo River 499
Cam Ranh Bay 399, 581
    and Tet 261
Cam Son Secret Zone 154
Cambodia 46, 417-419, **419**, **443**, **544**, **566**, **568**, **570**
    bombing of 372, 376, 378, **478**, 478
    border operations 86, 88
    boy soldiers **547**, **548**
    and China 592
    invasion of **420-421**, 423-424, **428**, 428-430, **430**, **431**(map), 432-433, **433**, **438**, **440**, 440-441, **441**, 443
    Khmer Rouge and 417, 418-419, **513**, 518, **534**, **535**, 535, 563, **569**, 581, 584-585, 588-589
    the Killing Fields 560-561, **571**
    Nixon and 355
    Vietnam invades 589, 592
    Vietnamese residents evacuated 440
    Westmoreland requests permission to cross the border 102
Camp Carroll 237, 490
Camp Holloway 238
Campaign 275 554
Can Tho, and Tet 265
Carango, Private First Class Dominic J. **271**
Carfort, medecin-lieutenant Patrice de 22-23
Carter, Jimmy, President (1924-) 568-569
casualties 193, 276, **358-359**, **544**, 573
    African Americans 302
    Army of the Republic of Vietnam **308**, 311, 460, 474, 481, **507**, **544**, **548**, 556-557
    Australian forces **140**, 269
    Cambodia **568**, 585, 588-589
    civilian **41**, **97**, **106**, **111**, **253**, 280, 311, 400, **406-407**, 499, 513
    at Dien Bien Phu **30**
    evacuation **28**, **122**, **164**, **325**, **331**, **342**, **371**, **376**
    field hospitals **268**
    first aid **29**, **75**, **373**
    at Hue 309, 311
    Ia Drang Valley, campaign 66
    at Khe Sanh **228**
    the Killing Fields 560
    NVA 91, 113, 134, 137, **178**, 186, 189, 197, 198, 200, 311, 365, 391, 432, **469**, 472, 481, 495, **503**, 512, 526
    ratios 116, 242
    recovery of **278**, **290**
    special forces 324
    Tet **245**, 256
    U.S. Army 150, 159, **169**, **240**, **246**, 311, 391
    U.S. forces 116-117, **128**, 201, 370, 481, 518
    U.S. Marines 134, 136, 137, 189, 200, **228**, 311, 365
    U.S. Navy 470
    Viet Cong 91, 103, 116, 134, 136, 137, 139, 145, 150, 159, 198, 200, 201, 256, **258**, **507**
ceasefires 349, 518, 520, 563
    Tet 212, 214
Central Highlands, the 54, 56, 95, 154-155, 159
    ARVN evacuates 556
    NVA in 212, 336-337
    operations in 88, 96, 139
    and Tet 253, 256
    and the Third Indochina War 544, 548

U.S. forces in 57, 106
Central Office for South Vietnam (COSVN) 145, 151, 372, 428, 429, 538
Chapelle, Dicky 152
Chau Phu, and Tet 265
Cheatham, Lieutenant- Colonel Earnest C. 305, **306**
Cheo Reo 556
Chieu Hoi (Open Arms) program, the 333, 391
China, People's Republic of 166, 485, 494
    aid to Viet Cong 29
    and Cambodia 592
    invasion of Vietnam **578, 579**, 589, 592, 594
    and the USA 589
Cholon 262, 267, **316-317**, 336, 337
Chon Than **489**
Chong Nghia 550
Chong Thien province 526
Chu Lai 40, 132, 137, 138, 548
    and Tet 259
Chu Luc, the 494
Chu Pong Massif, the 65, 66, 102
CIA (Central Intelligence Agency)
    and Cambodia 419, 423
    and Laos 449, 475
cigarettes 305
Citadel, the, Hue 283, 284, 295, **295, 304**, 305
    fighting for **287**(map), **296**, 296, **297**, **298**
    U.S. Marines assault **282**, 309
"City, the", Cambodia 430, **438**
Civic Aid Program **48**
Civilian Irregular Defense Groups 35, 96, 103, **124**, 124
civilian population 58-59, 89, **91, 338**, 408, **498**
    Cambodia **432-433**, **570**
    casualties **41, 97, 106, 111**, 253, 280, **406-407, 499**
    children 178, **256, 263, 282, 339, 413**, **519, 549, 558-559, 570, 575**, 575, 578
    fear of **252, 330, 401**
    Hue 280, 286, 311
    massacre of 280, 311, 400
    and "mini Tet" 337
    and Operation Lam Son 719 481
    re-education 574
    relocations 145
    resettlement of 526
    resignation of **312**
    rural life **82**
    South Vietnamese evacuation of Cambodia 440
    stature **96**
    support for Vietminh 13
    and Tet 278, 280, 311
    women **265**
Clark, Captain John W. **526**
Clark Air Base 528
Clay, Cassius. see Muhammad Ali
Clay, General Lucius 459
Clifford, Clark 323
climate **193, 259**
Clinton, Bill, president
    at the Vietnam Veterans War Memorial **594**
    visits Vietnam 595
Cochin China 10
Coffin, Jerry D. **170-171**
Colby, William 339
collectivization 580
Collins, General J. Lawton **21**
combined action platoons 79
Con Bi Than Tan Valley 136
Con Thien 189, 192, **198**, 198, 200
Conmy, Colonel Joseph B. Jr. 384
Consolidation, USS **500-501**
Constellation, USS **508**
consumer goods, post war scarcity of 581
Cooper, Sergeant Johnny **64**
Coster, Charles **594**
COSVN see Central Office for South Vietnam
counterinsurgency 79

Country Joe and the Fish **182**
Crecca, Captain Joseph, Jr. **526**
Cronkite, Walter **250**, 250-251, 321
Crows Foot 91
Cu Chi 52, 86, 88, 544
    tunnels 100, **100-101**
Cu Loc 207
Cu Lu 194
cultural dislocation, post war 573-574
Cunningham, Lieutenant Randall H. **328**, **508**

D
Da Lat, and Tet 261, 265
Da Nang 40, **42**, 43, 132, 137, 139, 194, **238**, 526, 554
    fall of 562
    and Tet 253
    and the Third Indochina War 549, 550
Dabney, Captain William H. 231, 232
Dak Pek 154, 548
Dak Seang 154
Dak Song 530, 534
Dak To, battle of 96, 98, 154, 155, **159**, 159, **162-163**, **165**
Dalia, Private First Class Ronald **234**
Daly, Edward **556**
Dang Van Huong **243**
Dang Xuan Teo 270
Davidson, Brigadier-General Phillip B. 256
Davis, Major General Raymond A. 355, 357
de la Croix de Castries, Brigadier General Christian Marie Ferdinand **27**
De Lattre de Tassigny, Marshal Jean 17, **21**
Dean, John 546
defoliation **197**, 197, **414**, 569
Demilitarized Zone (DMZ) 92, 113, 171, 180, 184, 192, 499
Democratic Republic of Vietnam 20
    air defense system **456-457**
    fear of U.S. reprisals 526
    and Nixon's peace plan 355
    and Operation Linebacker 504
    peace requirements 354
    and peace talks 404
    perception of Nixon 526
    reconstruction of South Vietnam 574
    and the Third Indochina War 538, 550
    and the "Third Vietnam" 523, 526
    and U.S. disengagement 535
Deng Xiaoping 592
Dewey Canyon 357
Diem, President. see Ngo Dinh Diem, President
Dien Bien Phu, battle of, 13th March-7th May 1954 19-20, **27, 29, 108**, 248
DMZ see Demilitarized Zone
Do Cao Tri, General 428, 433, 472
Domino Theory, the 71, 594
Don Luan 551
Dong Ha 336, 490, 525
Dong Hoi **508**
draft dodgers **114, 170-171, 180**, 313, **347**
draft, the **114, 313**, 313, **396**, 569
Droung Due Dhuy, Lieutenant **102**
drugs 236, 485, **510**, 510
Duc Co 102
Duc Duc 549
Duc Hoa, and Tet 274
Duc Hue 540
Duong Van Minh, General 261, 481, 482, **541**, 541, 563

E
Eagles Claw 91
Easter Offensive, the, 1972 488, 490, **492**, 492-493, **496**(map), 497, 499, 503, 508, **511**, 511-512
Eaton, Sergeant **238**
economy 113
    post war 578, 580, 581
Ehrlichman, John 546
Eisenhower, Dwight D. (1890-1969), President 20
El Salvador 569
Ellsberg, Daniel 321

English, Major-General Lowell E. 112, 252, 253
Enterprise, USS **54**, 109

F
fatigue **105, 190-191, 197, 200**, 307, 370, **425, 436-437**
Feinstein, Captain Jeff **531**
field hospitals **268**
films 591
Fire Support Base 30 472
Fire Support Base 31 **471**, 472
Fire Support Base A Luoi 466, 467, 472
Fire Support Base Cunningham 357, 360
Fire Support Base Erskine 360
Fire Support Base Gold 147
Fire Support Base Lolo 474, 478
Fire Support Base Razor 357, 360
Firebase Brown 432
Firebase Chi Linh 544
Firebase O'Reilly 415
Firebase Ripcord 415
Fisher, Professor Robert 171
Fishhook, the 428
flak vests **65**
flame throwers **77, 372**
Flesher, Major Hubert K. **526**
Flower Power **260**
Flynn, Sean 152
Fonda, Jane 447, **530**
Ford, Gerald, President (1913-) 550, 563
Forrestal, USS **109**
Fort Polk **135**
Fox, Archibald 546
"fragging" 485
France 10, 218
    and Cambodia 432
    requests US intervention 20
    and the Vietminh 13
Freedom Bridge 184
French forces **11, 12, 13**, 13, 17, **20, 21, 24**, **25**
    at Dien Bien Phu 19-20, **27, 29, 30**, **30-31**, 248
    French Foreign Legion **14-15, 18, 19**, **22-23, 30**
    tactics 17
    Vietnamese troops **24, 29**
French Indochina 10
Fulbright, Senator William James. **321**, 323

G
Geneva Accords, the 20, 460, 475
Gia Dinh 274, 331
Giai, General see Vu Van Giai, General
Giap, General see Vo Nguyen Giap
Gilder-Sleeve, Lieutenant Elmer J. **156**
Go Vap ARVN Artillery and Armored Military Complex, Saigon 266
Grandes, Joseph Des **234**
Gravel, Lieutenant-Colonel Marcus 291
Great Britain, anti-war protests **184, 185**
Green Berets **35**, 35, **90**, 91, 124, 323, 324, **363**, 376
    in the Central Highlands 56
    creation of 35
Greene, Wallace M. Jr, General 138
Grice, Corporal R.G. **74**
Gulf of Tonkin Resolution 37, 70
    revoked 443

H
Hai Lang National Fortress 200
Hai Van Mountains 132
Haig, Lieutenant Colonel Alexander M. 140
Haiphong Harbor 128, 129, 404, 492, 581
    mine clearance **527**
    mined 504, 508
Halberstam, David 152
Haldeman, H.R. 546
Hamburger Hill, battle of 366, **368-369**, **371**(map), **373, 374-375, 376**, **377**, 383-384, 387, 391
Hanoi 15, 29, 128
    anti-aircraft defenses **504**
    bombing of 504, **505**
Hanoi Hilton, the **206**, 206-207, **207**, 528
Harriman, Averell 324

Hau Bon, and Tet 261
Hau Duc 562
Hau Nghia Province 151
Hayden, Tom **530**
"hearts and minds" **48**, 79, 110, **234**
helicopters 66, **477**
    Bell Huey AH-1G Cobra **372**
    Bell Huey UH-1B **72, 264, 322, 331**, **332-333**, 342, **343, 366-367, 404**, **426-427, 473**
    Boeing-Vertol CH46 Sea Knight **164**, **198**
    Boeing-Vertol CH47 Chinook **73, 89**, **176-177**, 342, **555**
    gunships 342
    Hughes OH-58A Kiowa 342
    Hughes OH-6 342
    invasion of Laos **464-465**
    jungle pickups **150**
    pilots **405**
    role **72, 342**, 342
    Sikorsky H-19 **28**
    Sikorsky H34D Seahorse **78**
    Sikorsky HH-3E 342
    tactics **64**, 89
helmets 106
heroin addiction 485, 510
Hersch, Seymour 408
Hill 881, Khe Sanh **186, 187, 216**, 222, 226, 229, 231, 231-232
Hill 937 see Hamburger Hill, battle of
Ho Bo 52
Ho Chi Minh (1890-1969) **16**, 16, 124, **393**, 495
    death of 408
    and the French 13, 15
    and Giap 218
    resistance to Japanese 10
    strategy 117
Ho Chi Minh City (Saigon) 574
    Chinese residents 578, 589, 592
Ho Chi Minh Trail, the 30, 54, 92, 119, 166-167, **167, 167**(map), 212, 229, **414**, 415-416, **416, 417**, 418, **455, 458**, 459, 466, 494, 523
Ho Trang Hau, Colonel **470**
Hoa-Binh 17
Hoa Lo Prison see Hanoi Hilton, the
Hoan Thanh Chieu **63**
Hoang Xuan Lam, General 459, 470, 472, 474, 499, 503, 507
Hocmuth, Major General Bruno 170
Hoffman, Abbie **318**
Hoi An 75
    and Tet 253
Honeycutt, Lieutenant Colonel Weldon 383, 384
Hong Ngu 525
Hope, Bob, Christmas show **83**
hostilities, end of 595
House Select Committee on Missing Persons 582
Hue 212, 526, 554
    air strikes 306
    allies encircle 301
    casualties 309, 311
    the Citadel **282**, 283, 284, **287**(map), **295**, 295, **296**, 296, **297, 298, 304**, 305-306, 309
    communist massacre **280**, 280, 286, 311
    evacuation of 562
    Gia Hoi 280
    Imperial Palace of Peace 283, 284, **294, 304**, 306, 309
    the New City 301, 305
    Nguyen Hoang bridge 291, **294**
    NVA attack 283-284
    Quon Hoc High School **277, 286**
    snipers **281, 287**, 291
    tactical zones 295, 301
    tanks **274-275, 292-293**
    and Tet 261
    and the Third Indochina War 550
    University of **282**
    U.S. Marines in **272-273, 275, 278**, **279, 284, 288-289, 290**, 307
    U.S. Marines assault the Citadel **282**, 306

U.S. relief column 291
Hughes Colonel Stanley 305
Humphrey, Hubert H., presidential campaign 345-346, 349

I

I Corps Tactical Zone (ICTZ) 73, 92, 132, 180
Ia Drang Valley, campaign 65-66, 73, 86, 116, 159, 494
identity cards **94**
identity tags **580**
Imperial Palace of Peace, Hue 283, 284, **294**, **304**, 306, 309
International Commission of Control and Supervision 518
international trade, post war 578, 580
Intrepid, USS **327**
Iran, hostage crisis 568-569
"Iron Triangle", the 139, 144-145, **145**, **146**, 146, **146-147**, **310**, 544
Iwo Jima, USS **521**

J

Jackson State University 182, 447
Japanese occupation **10**, 10, 16, 218
Jaudon, Sergeant Arnold **60**
Jaworski, Leon 546
Jenkins, Captain Harry 231, 232
Jenkins, Scott **396**
Johnson, General Harold K. 45, 46
Johnson, Lyndon B. (1908-73), President 70-71, **71**, **125**, 201
    authorizes bombing 45
    cabinet pressure on 323
    failure of 566
    increases US commitment 35, 43, 48, 321
    and Khe Sanh 248, 252
    orders air strikes 40
    peace overtures 323-324
    public opinion and 321
    retires from politics 324
    and Tet 282, **319**
    and Westmoreland **70-71**
Joint United States Public Affairs Operation (JUSPAO) 152
Jolley, Lance Corporal Perry M. **172**
Joint Chiefs of Staff 79
Judge, Corporal Darwin **570**
jungle clearances 144-145

K

Kampong Speu 440
Kampuchea 560-561
Karch, Brigadier General F.J. **40**
Kellison, Sergeant Phillip C. **12**
Kennedy, John F. (1917-63), President 36, **71**
    increases US commitment 30, 35
Kennedy, Senator Robert F. 321, 323, 345, **346**
Kent State University, massacre at 182, **446**, 446-447, **447**, 448
Kerry, Senator John 582
Khan Duc 337
Khe Le Valley 549
Khe Sanh 134, 165, 192, **213**, **222**, 478
    evacuated 329
    first battle of 169-170, 172-173, 177, 179, 179-180, **186**, **187**
    Hill 558 226
    Hill 861 222, 226, **227**, 231
    Hill 881 **216**, 222, 226, 229, 231, 231-232
    Hill 950 222
    Marine Air Traffic Control Unit **232**
    siege of, 1968 214, **215**, **216**(map), 216-217, **217**, 222, **224-225**, 226, **228**, 229, **231**, 231-232, 236-237, 239, 240-241, 244, 247-248, 252-253, **270**, 324-325, 327, 329, 590
Khmer People's Liberation Front **594**
Khmer Rouge **560-561**, **574-575**, 581, 594
    atrocities **513**, 560-561, **571**, 584-585, 588-589
    and Phnom Penh 535, **569**
    defeat of 589

and the Killing Fields 560-561, 584-585, 588-589
NVA aid 417, 518
and the SS *Mayaguez* 563
victory parade **569**
Khrushchev, Nikita, Soviet General Secretary 30
Kien Duc 530, 534
Killing Fields, the 560-561, **571**
Kim Son valley 89
King, Martin Luther (1929-68) **344**, 345
Kingsley, Captain Louis **363**
Kissinger, Henry 352, 355, 452, **518**
    advocates bombing campaign 370, 372
    and bombing campaign 378
    and the Easter Offensive 490, 492
    meeting with Brezhnev 507-508
    and Nixon 352, 354, 404
    and peace talks 404, 408, 416, 512, 512-513, 518, **520**, 522
    and the Pentagon Papers 485
    and the "Vietnam Syndrome" 568
Kit Carson Scouts, the **391**, 391
Kittyhawk, USS **109**
Kleindienst, Richard 546
Kompong Saila campaign **439**
Kon Tum, and Tet 253
Kontum 499, 511, 548
Korean forces 50, 89, **139**, 139, 192, 412
    2nd Korean Marine Brigade 137
    2nd Korean Marine Corps 132
    Marines **195**
    and Tet 261
Krulak, Lieutenant General Victor H. 46, 79
Kuwait **595**
Ky, Nguyen Cao *see* Nguyen Cao Ky
Ky Tra 548

L

La Than Tonc, Lieutenant 226
Lahue, Brigadier-General Foster 286, 291
Lai Khe 544
Laird, Melvin, Secretary of Defense 352, 423
Lam, General *see* Hoang Xuan Lam, General
Landing Zone Bird 92-93
Lang Son 592
Lang Vei special forces camp 323, 324, **485**
Laos 19, 167, 355, 432-433, 475
    ARVN withdrawal from 474
    Base South 470
    bombing of 166
    border violated 364
    expels Chinese advisers 592
    invasion of **454**, **455**(map), **462-463**, 463, **464-465**, 466-468
    invasion planned 449
    NVA presence 454, 458
Le Duc Tho 508, 512, 513, 518, **520**, 522
    peace negotiations 416
Le Minh Dao, Brigadier General 563
Le Nguyen Khang, General **99**
League for the Independence of Vietnam 10
Leary, Doctor Timothy **318**
Lehman, First Lieutenant Alfred E., Jr. **202-203**
LeMay, General Curtis 346
Lewis, Lieutenant Dave **341**
Liberation Army, the 13
Linebacker bombing campaigns 129, 490, 492, 504, **505**, 513, 522
Loan, Nguyen Ngoc, General. *see* Nguyen Ngoc Loan, General
Loc Ninh 159, 201, 492-493
Lodge, Henry Cabot 323
Lon Nol, General **418**, 418, 419, 432
Long Binh, and Tet 274
Long Knot 540-541
Long Range Reconnaissance Patrols **176**, **476**, **478**
Lovelock, Ron **515**
Low Altitude Parachute Extraction System **232-233**, 241, 244
Lownds, Colonel David E. 217, 226

M

M274 Mechanical Mule **135**
M728 Combat Engineer vehicle **138-139**

MACV Tigers, the 275
"Mad Minute", the **116**
Madden, Captain John A. **531**
Malone, Corporal James **50**
marijuana 236, 510
Mayaguez, SS 563
McCain, Admiral John S. **352**, 370
McCarthy, Senator Eugene 323
McCauley, Sergeant William **77**
McConnell, General John P. 124
McMahon, Corporal Charles Jr. **570**
McNamara Line, the 161, 165, 171
McNamara, Robert, Defense Secretary 40, 75, **79**, 79, 116, 124, 171, 323
    Honolulu conference 122
media, the 45, **152-153**, 152-153, **250-251**, 250-251, 485, 566, 591
    and the invasion of Cambodia **441**, 443
    and Khe Sanh 247
    and My Lai 400
    and Operation Lam Son 719 458
    and Tet 267, 270, 278, 282, 318
Mekong Delta, the 136, 235, 331, **354**, 412, 526, 589
    and Tet 265
    and the Third Indochina War 538, 550
Mekong River Development program 124
Mendoza, Private First Class Michael J. **148-149**
MIAs (missing in action) 528, **580**, **581**, **582**, 582-583, **583**, 595
    memorial medal **582**
Michelin Rubber Plantation, the 52
Military Assistance Group Vietnam (USMAAG) 20
Military Region 1 488, 557, 562, 562-563
Military Region 2 554, 563
Military Region 3 563
mines **138**, **327**
Minh, General *see* Duong Van Minh, General
Mitchell, John 546
Mobile Riverine Force, the **118-119**, 151, 154, **160**, **235**, 235, **354**, **388**, **389**, **390**, **393**, **479**
Moc Hoa, and Tet 265
Monmeyer, General William 237, 239
Montagnards, the 25, 35, 56, **64**, 106, 124, 323
Moorer, Admiral Thomas 566
Muhammad Ali **180**, 313
My Chanh River 503, 512
My Khe, massacre 408
My Lai, massacre 311, 400, **401**, 408, 485
My Tho 554
    and Tet 265

N

napalm **125**, **222**, **480**
Nasmyth, Captain John J. **526**
National Council of National Reconciliation and Concord (NCNRC) 518
National Liberation Front of South Vietnam (NLF) 25, 242, 275, 284, 286, 399, 412, 414, 481, 518, **573**, 580
National Radio Station, Saigon 267, 270-271
Navarre, General Henri 17, 19
New Jersey, USS **492**
New York Times 485
New Zealand forces 50
Ngo Dinh Diem, President of South Vietnam 20, **31**, 31, 36, 541
    failure of 24
Ngo Quang Truong, General 283, 286, 507, 511, 512, 562
Nguyen Ai Quoc *see* Ho Chi Minh
Nguyen Ba Lien, Colonel 399
Nguyen Cao Ky 99, **261**, 261, 267, 467, 481-482
Nguyen Chi Thanh, General 73
Nguyen Hoang bridge, Hue 291, **294**
Nguyen Ngoc Loan, General **266**, 280, 282
    in the USA **574**
Nguyen Van Thieu, President of South Vietnam 51, 212, 261, **312**, 339, **467**, 467

and Cambodia 440
evacuates the Highlands 556
and the fall of South Vietnam 562
introduces conscription 315
land redistribution policy 416-417
meets Nixon 395
and Nixon's peace plan 355, **518**
and Operation Lam Son 72 512
and Operation Lam Son 719 467, 472, 474
and the Paris peace treaty 518, 522
peace requirements 354
and the presidential election, 1971 481-482, 485
punishes General Lam 503, 507
rejects peace treaty 512
resignation of 541, 563
and Tet 256, 258
and the Third Indochina War 538
and Vietnamization 362
Nguyen Van Tho, General 472
Nguyen Viet Tanh, General 433
Nha Trang 253, 256, **556**
Nixon, Richard Milhous (1913-), President 70, 129, 182, **348**, 352, 352, **355**, 355, 404, 452
    approves invasion of Cambodia 423
    and bombing campaign 372, 376, 378
    and Cambodia 423, 428-429, **429**
    and the Easter Offensive 490, 492
    ends the draft 569
    and the Khmer Rouge 535
    and Kissinger 352, 354, 404
    launches Operation Breakfast 372
    launches Operation Linebacker 490, 492
    meeting with Brezhnev 508
    North Vietnamese perception of 526
    orders mining of North Vietnamese harbors 508
    and the Paris peace treaty 518
    and peace negotiations 513
    peace plan 354-355
    and the Pentagon Papers 485
    presidential campaign 345, 349
    pressure to end war 416
    re-elected 513, **515**
    resignation of 546, **546-547**, 550
    resumes bombing campaigns 428
    siege mentality of 448
    and Thieu **518**
    and Vietnamization 362, 395
    and the War Powers Act 534-535
    and Watergate 546
    withdrawal policy 380
NL *see* National Liberation Front of South Vietnam
Nolde, Lieutenant Colonel William B. 518
Norodom Sihanouk, Prince 417-418, **432**, 432, 478, 560, 594
North Vietnam *see* Democratic Republic of Vietnam
North Vietnamese air force 45
North Vietnamese Army (NVA) 48, **494**, 494-495, **495**
    1st Division 526
    2nd Division 468, 499, 562
    3rd Regiment 189
    5th Division 492, 511, 538, 540
    6th Regiment 415
    7th Division 428, 493, 497, 544, 551
    9th Division 493, 497, 544
    9th Regiment 378
    12th Sapper Battalion 283
    21st Regiment 137, 189
    25th Sapper Battalion 540
    29th Regiment 549
    39th Regiment 383
    52nd Brigade 557, 562
    66th Regiment 325, 494
    70th Division 468
    205th Regiment 530, 534
    230th Division 226
    271st Regiment 530
    275th Regiment 540
    304th Division 226
    320th Division 336, 497, 511, 548, 556

324th Division 112
325th Division 226
800th Battalion 283
802nd Battalion 283
804th Battalion 284
968th Division 554
in the A Shau Valley 332-333, 336
abandon large scale operations 412
at An Loc 493, 497, 511, 518
anti aircraft guns 166, **300, 394**
and ARVN withdrawal from Laos 474, 478
attack Fire Support Bases 30 and 31 472
attack Landing Zone Bird 92-93
attack Tong Le Chan 525
at Base Area 611 357, 360, 364
at Ben Hat 399
binh trams 415-416
in Bong Son 91
build up for the Easter Offensive 488
build up of forces 160, 452
in Cambodia 372, 376, 417, 418, 419, 428, 430, 432, 440, 441
captured equipment **562**
casualties 91, 113, 134, 137, **178**, 186, 189, 197, 198, 200, 311, 329, 365, 391, 432, **469**, 472, 481, 495, **503**, 512, 526
in the Central Highlands 88-89, 159, 212, 336-337
at Con Thien 198
at Cu Lu 194
at Dak To 96, 98, 154, 155
Division 324B 548
at Dong Ha 336
and the Easter Offensive 488, 490, 492-493, 497, 499, 508, 512
final assault 563
final offensive 554, 556, **557**(map), 557, 562, 563
at Hamburger Hill 383, 384, 391
at Hill 881 173, 226, 229
and the Ho Chi Minh Trail 166, 167
at Hue 283, 284, 291, 295, 296, 301, 306, 309
the Ia Drang Valley, campaign 65, 66, 73
K4B Battalion 284
at Kampong Speu 440
in the Khe Le Valley 549
at Khe Sanh 222, 226, 229, 232, 236-237, 241, **270**, 325, 327
at Kontum 511
land grabbing 520, 523
at Lang Vei 323, 324
in Laos 432-433, 454, 458, **466**, 467, **468**, 468, **469**, 470, 472, 474, 478
at Long Knot 540-541
"mini-Tet" 336, 337
at Nui Loc Son Basin 189
and Operation Attleboro 114
and Operation Hastings 112, 113
and Operation Hickory 184, 186, 189
and Operation Lam Son 72 512
and Operation Lam Son 719 454, 458, 467, 468, 481
and Operation Prairie 134
in Quang Duc province 530, 534
at Quang Tri City 512, 514
rebuilds forces 523
in Saigon 337
in the Seven Mountain Region 526
at Soui Day 530
in South Vietnam 412
strategy 88-89, 95, 160-161, 554
supplies 415-416
tactics 554
and Tet 253, 259, 261
Tet Offensive, 1969 365, 370
at Thach Tru 75
and the Third Indochina War 538, 540, **542-543**, 544, 548-549, 550, 550-551
at Thon Cam Son 194
victory **563**
victory parade **569**
at Xuan Loc 563

North Vietnamese militia groups **217**
nuclear weapons 214
Nui Ba Den Mountain 530
Nui Loc Son Basin 189

O

Ohanesian, Lieutenant Colonel Victor **102**
Oklahoma City, USS **300**
Ong Dong jungle 151
Operation Adair 189
Operation Allegheny **102**
Operation Attleboro 114
Operation Bastion Hill 200
Operation Beacon Star 170
Operation Beaver Cage 165, 169
Operation Benton 197
Operation Blue Marlin 75
Operation Breakfast 372, 376
Operation Castor 19, **21, 28**
Operation Cedar Falls 139, **143**, 144-145, 146
Operation Chinook 134, 136
Operation Cimarron 189
Operation Cochise 194
Operation Deckhouse **136**
Operation Delaware/Lam Son 332, 336
Operation Desoto 136
Operation Eagle Pull **568**
Operation Eagle's Claw **96**
Operation Fairfax 151
Operation Frequent Wind 563
Operation Gadsden 146
Operation Golden Fleece 79
Operation Hades 197
Operation Hastings 112-114
Operation Hickory 180, 184, 186, 189
Operation Hickory II 192
Operation Homecoming 528, 582
Operation Hood River 192, 194
Operation Independence 136
Operation Junction City 145-147, **150-151**, 150-151
Operation Kingfisher **200, 201**
Operation Lam Son 72 512
Operation Lam Son 719 167, 449, 452, **454**, 454, 458-459, 463, 466-468, 470, 472, 474, 478
claims of success 478, 481
Operation Lawrence 137
Operation Lien Ket 169
Operation Malheur 192
Operation Market Time 92
Operation Masher **93, 117**
Operation Medina 200
Operation Nathan Hale **97**
Operation Niagara 214, 237, 239
Operation Pegasus **322**, 324, 325, 327
Operation Piranha 73
Operation Prairie 132, 134, 137
Operation Quyet Thang (Resolve to Win) 331
Operation Ranch Hand 197
Operation Starlight 73
Operation Swift 197
Operation Thayer **137**
Operation Toan Thang (Complete Victory) 331
Operation Tran Hung Do 278
Operation Tucson 146
Operation Union 165
Operation Wallowa 198
Operation Wheeler 197-198
"Oregon Trail", the 91
Oriskany, USS **94, 156**

P

pacification program 79, 92, 108, 110, 113, 266, 312, 333, 339, 341, 408, 412
Page, Tim **155**
Panang, Buddhist insurrection in **98**
Paris peace talks, the 337, 404, 408, 416, 508, 512, 513, 518, **520, 522**, 522, 528, 566
Paris, First Lieutenant James **60**
Paris treaty, the 518
Parrot's Beak, the 419, 424, 428, 540-541
Patchin, Corporal Charles **145**
Pathet Lao 535

peace negotiations 337, 349, 404, 408, 416, 452, 507-508, 512, 513, 522
see also Paris peace talks
Peers, Lieutenant General William 400, 408
Pentagon Papers, the 485
People's Revolutionary Government 522
Peoples Self Defense Force (PSDF) 339, **340, 384, 390**
Petti, Joseph **585**
Pham Quoc Thuan, Lieutenant General 540
Pham Van Dong 408
Phan Huy Quat, Premier 261
Phan Thiet, and Tet 261
Phan Van Phu, Major-General **488**
Phnom Penh 418, 535, 563, **566, 569**, 584, 589
Phoenix Program, the 312, 333, 339, 341, **422**, 422, **474**
success of 412
photojournalism 152
Phu Bai 40, 132, 286
and Tet 259
Phu Cuong 544
and Tet 274
Phu Loc, and Tet 259
Phu Tho racetrack 283
Phu Vinh, and Tet 265
Phu Yen 106
Phuc Loi 508
Phuoc Le, and Tet 274
Phuoc Long 550, 554
Pirnie, Alexander **396**
Platoon, film 591
Plei Djering 103, 106
Plei Mei 63, 102
Plei Trap Valley 103, 106
Pleiku 96, **520**, 548
and Tet 253, 256
Pol Pot **560**, 560, 561, 584-585, 588, 589
paranoia of 585, 588
Post-Traumatic Stress Disorder 200, 590
Prascaut 428
Prek Cak 534
press, the 152
prisoners of war **103, 267, 268, 310, 311, 336**
blindfolds and **74, 93, 158, 334-335**
exchange of **530**
final offensive **562**
the French and **13**
the Hanoi Hilton **206**, 206-207, **207**
interrogation 51, **208, 249, 474**
return of U.S. 518, 523, **526, 527, 528**, 528, **529, 582**
treatment of **74, 80-81, 93, 112, 261**
propaganda **110**, 274-275, 302, **392**
see also psychological warfare
prostitution 575
protests **258**
anti-Diem **33**, 36
anti-war 70, **77, 114, 170-171, 180**, 182, 182, **183, 184, 185**, 247, **318**, 321, **346, 347, 348, 349, 408**, 408, **409, 443, 444-445**, 446-447, 448, **482, 483**, 485, **514, 530**
veterans **585, 591**
psychological injuries 200, 570-571, 590
psychological warfare **60**
see also propaganda
Vietminh **26**
Purrington, Lieutenant-Commander Fred R. **526**

Q

Quang Duc province 530, 534
Quang Khe 508
Quang Nam Province 132, 136, 548
Quang Ngai 108, 557
Quang Tin 108, 132, 548
Quang Tri City 170, **512**, 512, 514
evacuation of 562
and Tet 261
Quang Tri province 132, 526
Quon Hoc High School, Hue **277**

R

Rach Gia, and Tet 265
Radio Hanoi 212, 286, 490

Rao Lao River 336
re-education camps 574, 578
Reagan, Ronald, President (1911-) 569, 582
Recon by Fire **148-149**
reconstruction 574
Red River Delta 15, 19
refugees. *see* boat people
Regional and Popular Forces 151, 339
Regional Forces 538
religion, U.S. forces **88**
Republic of Vietnam 20, **57**(map), 523, 525
consolidates 525-526
democratic political process **208**
disintegration of 549-550
employment 573-574
fall of 554, **555**, 556-557, **557**(map), 562-563
fear of communists 313-314
land redistribution 416-417
military culture 395
pilots **532-533**
presidential election, 1971 481-482, 485
and the Third Indochina War 538, 549-550
transfer of military hardware **515**
urbanization of 573-574
"Resolution of 1975" 551
rest and recreation 104, **105**
Richardson, Elliot 352
Ridenhour, Ronald L. 400
Ridgeway, General Matthew B. 20
"Rock Island East" 430
Rockpile Firebase 237
Rogers, William, Secretary of State 352, 423
Rolling Thunder 45, 119, 122, 128-129, 528
Rosson, Lieutenant-General William B. 332
Rung La 544
Rung Sat swamps 52
Rusk, Dean, Secretary of State 116, **320**, 323
Ryan, Lloyd **515**

S

Sa Dec, and Tet 265
Saigon 17, 51, 212, 414, 433
African Americans in 302
Armed Forces Day parade **484**
ARVN Joint General Staff Compound 266-267
Brinks Hotel **36**
fall of **557, 562, 563**, 563
Go Vap ARVN Artillery and Armored Military Complex 266
"mini-Tet" 336, 337
National Radio Station 267, 270-271
NVA victory parade **569**
Presidential Palace **539, 562**
renamed Ho Chi Minh City 574
and Tet **220-221, 236**(map), **237, 244, 245, 248**, 259, 266-267, 270-271, 282-283
and the Third Indochina War 544, 550
third Tet Offensive 341
U.S. Consulate **237**
U.S. Embassy **41, 244, 245, 249**, 259, 267, **557**, 563
Viet Cong infiltrate 266
Sawada, Kyoichi, photographer 60, **164**
Schonortz, Merle **515**
Seaman, Lieutenant Colonel J. 145
search and destroy tactics 116-117
SEATO (Southeast Asia Treaty Organization) 269
Seltz, John **77**
Seven Mountains Region 526
Sharp, Admiral Ulysses S.G. 46, 79
Honolulu conference 124
Sihanouk, Prince Norodom. *see* Norodom Sihanouk, Prince
Sihanoukville, port **415**, 415, 432, 478
smoke, use of **147**
snipers **226**
at Hue **281, 287, 291**, 295
radio operators **120-121**
Snuol 428
Soc Trang, and Tet 265

Son Tay 207
Song Be 159
Song Con, battle of 63
Song Con Valley 57
Song Yen River **50**
Soui Day 530
South Vietnam *see* Republic of Vietnam
South Vietnam Womens Armed Force **364**, **365**
Southeast Asia Resolution, the 37
Southeast Asia Treaty Organisation (SEATO) 269
Souvanna Phouma, Prime Minister of Laos 463
Soviet Union 166, 418
　　aid to North Vietnam **415**, 494
　　aid to Viet Cong 29
　　collapse of 595
　　post war relationship with Vietnam 581, 589, 592
Special Operations Group **476**
Special Youth Shock Groups 166
Spock, Dr Benjamin **182**
Stars and Stripes **441**
Steer, John L. **588**
Stone, Dana 152
strategic hamlets **32**
Sutherland, Lieutenant General James W. 459, 463
Sutton, Bob **591**
Svay Rieng 540-541
Szalobryt, Sergeant Jane **364**

T
Ta Bai 333
tactics
　　Abrams 335
　　French 17
　　Giap 15, 17
　　at Hue 305
　　NVA 554
　　U.S. Army **60**, 62, **64**, 66, **67**, 98, 102, **116**
　　U.S. Forces 93, 95, 116-117, 355, 393, **481**
　　U.S. Marines **246**, 355, 357
　　Viet Cong 63, 75, 242, **337**, 399, 404
　　Viet Minh 17
　　Westmoreland 62
Tally Ho, aerial interdiction campaign 114
Talmanson, Robert A. **114**
Tam Ky 75, 194, 548, 562
　　and Tet 261
Tan Canh 499
Tan Son Nhut airport **246**, 336, **353**, 544, **556**
　　and Tet 266
Tang Kauk, battle of **430**
tanks **155**, **576-577**
　　French 14-15
　　M24 Chaffee **19**
　　M47 Patton **230**, **341**
　　M48 flame thrower **262**
　　M48A3 Patton **256-257**, **274**, **292-293**, **309**
　　M551 Sheridan Reconnaissance Tank **430**, **459**
　　PT76 light amphibious tank **323**
　　T-54 Main Battle Tanks **512**, **562**
　　Type 59 **579**
Task Force Delta 112-113
Task Force Oregon 138, 192, 194, 197-198
Task Force X-ray 132, **134**, 136, **272-273**, 286
Tay Loc airport 283
Tay Ninh 145, 550, 563
　　and Tet 274
Taylor, General Maxwell D. 36, 252
　　Honolulu conference 124
Thach Han River 499
Tchepone 466, 468, 474
television 152, **152-153**, 153, **250-251**
　　influence of 45, 250-251
　　and Khe Sanh 247
　　and Tet 267, 270, 278, 318
terrain **173**, **176**, **178**, **194**, **356**, **379**, **382**, 454

Tet Offensive, the 100, 117, 159, **247**(map), 253, 256, 258, 265, 296
　　of 1969 365, 370
　　casualties 311
　　causes of failure 271, 274, 312-315
　　Giap and **219**
　　in cities 261
　　media presentation 153, 250-251, 282
　　in the Mekong Delta 265
　　reprisals 280, 282
　　in Saigon **220-221**, **236**(map), **237**, **244**, **245**, **248**, 259, 266-267, 270-271, 274-275, 282-283
　　third offensive 341
　　U.S. Embassy **244**, **245**, **249**, 259
　　and U.S. public opinion 315, 318, 321
　　Viet Cong losses
　　Viet Cong planning 266
　　Westmoreland and 62, 212, 214
Thach Tru, battle of, 22nd-23rd November 1965 75
Thai Nguyen iron and steel complex 128
Thailand 475, **531**
Than Hoa Bridge 128
Thang Binh 189
Thanh Dien forest 144, **310**
Thanh Hoa 508
Thanh Hoa bridge **204**
Thanh My 414
theatre of operations 57(map)
Thieu, President *see* Nguyen Van Thieu
Third Indochina War, the 538, **540-541**, 540-541, 544, 548-551
"Third Vietnam" 523, 525, 526
Thon Cam Son 194
Thrasher, Corporal D. **235**
Thrasher, Sergeant Jimmy **235**
Thua Thien Province 132
Thuong Duc 549
Ticonderoga, USS **83**
Tien Phuoc 548, 562
Tieu Atar 548
Tiger Island 122
Tims, Private First Class James A. **157**
Tong Le Chan 525
　　fall of 544
Tonkin 10
Tonkin, Gulf of 459, 467-468, 503
　　crisis 37, 37
Toumorong 96
tour of duty, U.S. forces 48
training **135**
Tram Bang 152
Tran Van Huong 541, 563
Tri, General *see* Do Cao Tri, General
Tri Phap swamp 538
Truong, General *see* Ngo Quang Truong, General
Tully, Corporal Lester A. **306**
tunnel rats **61**, 100, **100-101**, **145**, 145
Turner Joy, USS 37
Tuy Hoa 554
　　and Tet 261
Tyler, Major Charles R. **528**

U
U Minh forest 331
United States of America 40, 404
　　and Cambodia 419
　　and China 485, 589
　　and Chinese intervention 102
　　commitment to disengagement 523
　　congressional opposition to war 323
　　costs 45
　　effect of Tet 267, 270, 315, 318, 321
　　end of the war 518
　　evacuation of Saigon 563
　　foreign policy 568-569
　　foreign relations 594-595
　　French request for intervention 20
　　and Hamburger Hill 391
　　intervention 40
　　and the invasion of Cambodia 443, 448
　　involvement in Laos **475**, 475
　　and Khe Sanh 247, 329
　　memorial 571, 573

military advisors 20, 24, 25, **32**, **34**, 35, 36, **44**, **364**, 395, 488, 518
military funerals **545**
military strategy 45-46
opens diplomatic relations with China 485
policy towards Vietnam 36-37, 40
presidential election, 1968 345-346, 349
presidential election, 1972 452
public opinion **266**, 341, **408**, 408, **409**, 447, 485, 566, 571
race relations 302, 341, **344**, 345
relations with Hanoi 595
relations with Vietnam 582-583
riots **344**, **345**
Senate Foreign Relations Committee 320
support for Vietminh 10, **12**
and the Third Indochina War 550
the Unknown Soldier **592**, **593**
and the veterans 571, 590
and the "Vietnam Syndrome" 568-569
and the Vietnam war 566
and Vietnamization 362
withdrawal **556**
U.S. Air Force **234**
　　7th Air Force 114, 237, 459
　　432nd Tactical Fighter Reconnaissance Wing **531**
　　bombing campaign **108**, 122, 124, 128-129, 349, 372, 376, 378, **394-395**, 459, 478, 490, **499**, 566
　　bombs An Loc 511
　　bombs Cu Chi 100
　　bombs Kontum 511
　　crash sites **580**
　　and the Easter Offensive **511**
　　and Khe Sanh 237, 239, 240-241, 244
　　Linebacker bombing campaigns 492, 504, **505**
　　at Loc Ninh 201
　　"menu series" raids 478
　　mining operations 508
　　and Operation Attleboro 119
　　and Operation Breakfast 372, 376
　　and Operation Junction City 150
　　and Operation Lam Son 719 **453**, 459, 468
　　pilots **126-127**
　　Rolling Thunder 43
　　strategy 119, 124
　　targets 128-129
U.S. Army 48, **62-63**, **72**
　　1st Cavalry (Air Mobile) Division 48, 54, 57, 63, 65-66, 73, **74**, **86**, 86, 89, 91, 92, **93**, 103, **117**, **142**, 155, 198, **240**, **259**, 301, 309, **322**, 325, 327, 332, 333, 342, **357**, 428, 430
　　1st Infantry Division 48, 52, **56**, **107**, **133**, 140, 146, 147, **150**, 150, 151, **157**, **174-175**, **196**, **197**, 201, **383**
　　2nd Infantry Brigade 140, 146
　　3rd Infantry Brigade 144
　　4th Infantry Division 103, 106, 139, 154, 339, 432
　　5th Cavalry 146
　　7th Cavalry 66
　　9th Infantry Division 147, 151, 154, **308**, 412
　　11th Armored Cavalry 140, 144, 146, 147, **424**, 428
　　13th Regiment 214
　　20th Infantry Brigade 400
　　23rd (American) Division 198, **452**
　　25th Infantry Division 86, **89**, 89, 98, 102, 106, 137, 140, 146, 147, **170**, 201
　　26th Infantry Regiment 140
　　35th Ranger Battalion 144
　　61st Infantry Division **431**
　　101st Airborne Division 48, 57, 63, 96, 98, 103, 106, **138**, 138, 139, **148-149**, 197, **332-333**, 333, **334-335**, **341**, **366**, **368-369**, **371**, **374-375**, 378, 415, **491**
　　173rd Airborne Brigade 43, 45, **46**, **47**, 51-52, **115**, 140, **142**, 144, **145**,

146, **150-151**, 154, 155, **159**, 159, **162-163**, **165**, 168, **169**, **330**
　　187th Regiment 383, 387, 391
　　196th Light Infantry Brigade 137, 140, 146
　　198th Light Infantry Brigade 200
　　199th Light Brigade 283, **366-367**, **440**
　　242nd Chemical Detachment 145
　　409th Radio Research Detachment **441**
　　501st Regiment 387
　　503rd Infantry Regiment 144, 146
　　506th Regiment 387
　　716th Military Police Battalion 275
　　in the A Shau Valley 332, **332**, 333
　　African Americans in 302
　　artillery **67**, **73**, **89**, 132, **159**, **176-177**, **189**, **324**, **398**
　　at Ben Hat **386**, **387**
　　in Binh Dinh Province 92
　　in Cambodia 428, **440**, **441**
　　Cambodian border patrol 383
　　U.S. Army 150, 159, **169**, **240**, **246**, 311, 391
　　casualties 54, 56, 57, 63, 88-89, 96, 106, 139, 154-155, 159
　　at Dak To 96, 98, **159**, 159, **162-163**, **165**
　　engineers **101**, **138**, **138-139**
　　at Firebase Ripcord 415
　　Green Berets **35**, 35, 56, **90**, 91, 124, 323, 324, **363**, 376
　　at Hamburger Hill **366**, **366-367**, **368-369**, **371**, **373**, **374-375**, **376**, **377**, 383-384, 387, 391
　　at Hue **287**, 301
　　I Field Force 102-103, 154
　　the Ia Drang Valley, campaign 65-66, 73
　　and Khe Sanh 216-217, **322**, 325, 327
　　at Landing Zone Bird 93
　　at Loc Ninh 201
　　massacres 400, 408
　　at My Lai 400, 408
　　and Operation Attleboro 114
　　and Operation Cedar Falls 140, 144, 144-145
　　and Operation Junction City 146-147, **150-151**, 150-151
　　protest within **258**
　　radio operators **95**, **115**, **154-155**, **260**
　　rear echelon troops **144**
　　reinforcements **52**
　　relief of Khe Sanh **322**, 325, 327
　　religion **88**
　　and Saigon 212, **237**
　　Special Forces 35, **35**, 35, 56, **90**, 124, **236**, 323, 324, **363**, **386**, **387**, 490
　　tactics **60**, 62, **64**, 66, **67**, 98, 102, **116**
　　and Tet **236**, **237**, 283
　　tour of duty 48
　　weapons **47**, **91**, **214**, **259**, **379**, **383**, **384**, **399**
U.S. Consulate, Saigon **237**
U.S. Embassy, Saigon **41**, **244**, **245**, **249**, 259, 267, **557**, 563
U.S. forces 35, 339, 449
　　age 590
　　armored fighting vehicles **402-403**
　　artillery **280-281**
　　build up 86, 138
　　in Cambodia 417, **420-421**, 423-424, 429-430
　　casualties 116-117, **128**, 201, 370, 481, 518
　　causes of failure 566-568
　　disillusionment of **397**, 408, **431**, **484**, 485, 510
　　equipment **134**
　　Fire Support Bases **429**
　　firepower **433**
　　and the Ho Chi Minh Trail 166-167
　　at Hue 284, 301
　　identity tags **580**
　　intelligence 132
　　invade Cambodia **420-421**, 423-424
　　KIAs returned to the USA **584**, **586-587**

Long Range Reconnaissance Patrols **176**
loss of prestige 569
luxuries **173**
military strength 45, 50, 70, 201
and Operation Lam Son 719 452, 454, 470, 474
performance 563
problems 63, 95-96, **106**
racial tensions **129**
resources 116
rest and recreation **104**, **105**
results 79
rotation system 48, 566
in Saigon 275, 278
special rescue and reconnaissance unit **491**
success 160
tactics 93, 95, 116-117, 355, 393, **481**
tasks facing 129
and Tet 261, 275, 278
Tet Offensive, 1969 365, 370
in the U.S. Embassy 267
weapons **356**
withdrawal of 355, **380**, 380, **381**, 393, 395, 416, **493**, 518, 523
U.S. Marine Corps **49**, **66**, 89, **90**, **123**, **129**, **179**, **220**, 412
1st Engineers **288-289**
1st Marine Air Wing 132, 172-173, 177, 179
1st Marine Division 43, 106, 108, 132, 136, 165, **172**
1st Marine Regiment 200, **279**, 286, 305, 311, 325
3rd Marine Division 112, 132, 169, 170, 172, 184, 192, **200**, **216**, 339, 357
3rd Marine Regiment 325
4th Marine Regiment 186, 189, **223**
5th Marine Regiment 137, 165, 169, 189, 194, 197, **277**, **282**, **286**, **298**, 305, 306
7th Marine Regiment **122**, **134**, 139
9th Division 136
9th Marine Expeditionary Brigade 40
9th Marine Regiment **135**, 136, 169, 184, **190-191**, 194, **227**, 232, 325, 357
26th Marine Regiment 134, 136, 192, 198, 214, 217, 226, **227**
African Americans in **303**
arrival in Vietnam 40, **42**
artillery **216**, **217**
at Base Area 611 357, 360, 364, 365
and Ben Hai 399
casualties 134, 136, 137, 189, 200, **228**, 311, **325**, 365
at Con Thien **198**, 198, **199**
at Cu Lu 194
at Da Nang **43**, **176**
at Dewey Canyon 357
disillusionment of **397**
deployment 1972 132
at Dong Ha 336
helicopters **78**
and Hill 110 169
and Hill 881 172-173, 179-180
at Hue **272-273**, **274-275**, **277**, **278**, **279**, **281**, **282**, **284**, **285**, 286, **287**, **291**, 291, **292-293**, 295, 295, **296**, 296, **297**, **298**, **304**, 305, 306, **307**, 309
III Marine Amphibious Force 43, 79, 92, 132
at Khe Sanh 169-170, 172-173, **186**, **187**, **215**, 216, **217**, 217, **222**, 222, **224-225**, 226, **227**, **228**, 229, **231**, 231-232, 236, 237, 241, 244, 324-325
in Kuwait **595**
land at Da Nang **42**
medics **276**
military strength 132
at Nui Loc Son Basin 189
and Operation Blue Marlin 75
and Operation Chinook 134, 136
and Operation Colorado **87**

and Operation Deckhouse **136**
and Operation Hastings 112-113
and Operation Hickory 180, 184, 186, 189
and Operation Independence 136
and Operation Prairie 134, 137
and Operation Starlight 73
and Operation Union 165
pacification program 108, 110
pilots **82**
and prisoners of war **158**
radio operators **122**
river patrols 118-119
snipers **120-121**, **281**, **291**
on the Song Yen River **50**
Special Landing Force 200
tactics **246**, 355, 357
Task Force X-ray 132, 136, **272-273**, 286
in the U.S. Embassy 267
at Van Tuong Peninsular 73
weapons **57**, **68-69**, **78**, **118**, **188**, **199**, **279**, **338**
withdrawal of **521**
U.S. Navy 35, **326**, 331, **479**, 503
African Americans in 302, **303**
aircraft carriers 109, **109**
casualties 109
munitions **55**
and Operation Lam Son 719 459
and Operation Market Time 92
pilots **82**, **327**, **328**, **584**
River Patrol Force 235
SEALs **387**
Task Force 71 92
Task Force 77 **110**
Task Force 115 92
USMAAG *see* Military Assistance Group Vietnam

V
Van Tien Dung, General 554
Van Tuong Peninsular, assault on 73
veterans **482**, **514**, **585**, **590**, 590-591, **591**
and Agent Orange 569
disabilities 569
memorial 571, 573, **588**, **589**, **596**, **597**
protests **591**
psychological injuries 570-571
Viet Cong 24, **34**, 242, **258**, **299**, **336**
1st Regiment 137
2nd Go Man Battalion 266
6th Binh Tan Battalion 267
9th Division 145, 151
70th Regiment 147
101st Regiment 266
267th Battalion 266
269th Battalion 266
272nd Regiment 147
attack Landing Zone Bird 92-93
attack U.S. Embassy 259, 267
in Binh Dinh Province 92
in Bong Son 91
C-10 Sapper Battalion **249**, 259, 267
at Cam Ranh Bay 399
in Cambodia 418-419
casualties 91, 103, 116, 134, 136, 137, 139, 145, 150, 159, 198, 200, 201, 256, **258**, **507**
causes of failure of Tet 271, 274
in the Central Highlands 54, 56-57, 63, 88-89, 154, 155, 159
command system 29
control of the countryside 36
at Dak To 159
depletion of 412
disillusionment of 404
final offensive 557
at Ia Drang 116
intensify struggle 36
at Khe Sanh 169-170
and Korean forces 139
land grabbing **525**
at Loc Ninh 201
in the Mekong Delta 241, 265, 331
"mini-Tet" 337
and the National Radio Station 270-271

numbers 242
objectives 57
and Operation Attleboro 114
and Operation Cedar Falls 144
and Operation Chinook 136
and Operation Junction City 147, 150, 151
and Operation Prairie 134
organization 24-25, 242
and the Paris peace treaty 520
political officers 25
problems 63
raids 75
reasons for success 460
reoccupy pacified areas 159
in Saigon 266-267, 270-271
strategy 95
strength 30, 46, 48
supplies 29, 54, 56, 92, 166-167, 412, 414
tactics 63, 75, 242, **337**, 399, 404
at Tam Ky 194
target Americans 40
and Tet 62, 242, **249**, 253, 256, 258-259, 261, 265, 266, 271, 274-275, 278, 280, 283, 312
Tet Offensive, 1969 365, 370
and the Third Indochina War 544
tunnel systems **61**
tunnels 100, **100-101**, **145**, 145, **341**
uniform **93**, **573**
at Van Tuong Peninsular 73
in War Zone D 52
weapons 137, **239**, **242-243**, 370
women **241**
Vietminh, the 10, 13-15, **14**, **17**, 24, **30-31**, 218-219
at Dien Bien Phu 19, 20
organization 10, 12-13
supplies **28**
tactics 17
weapons **25**
Vietnam Peoples Air Force **328-329**
Vietnam, post war 573
Vietnam Veterans War Memorial **588**, **589**, 591, **596**, **597**
Vietnamese Naval Training Center 253
Vietnamization 124, 182, **333**, 341, 352, 362, **362-363**, 380, 393, 395, 408, 422, **461**, 481
Vin Loi woods 151
Vinh Huy 189
Vinh Long, and Tet 265
Vinh, port 467, 468
Vinh Thanh Special Forces Camp 91
Vo Nguyen Giap 10, 13, 212, **218**, **219**, 239, 315, 408
background 218
and Dien Bien Phu 19, 20
failure at Tet 313
and the French 15, 17
and the Ia Drang Valley 73
strategy 13, 14, 219, 296
tactics 15, 17
and Tet **219**
Vu Van Giai, General 488, 499, 503, 507

W
Wallace, Governor George 346, 349
Walt, General Lewis W. 73, 75, 113, 132, 137
strategy 79
war correspondents **118**, 152-153, **164**
War Powers Act, 1973 534-535
War Zone C 145, 147
War Zone D 51-52
Watergate scandal 355, 526, 546, 550
weapons
AK47 **560-561**
ARVN **76**, 180, 460
bayonets **240**
B-40 rocket propelled grenade launcher **242-243**
Degtyarev light machine gun **239**
flame throwers **77**, **372**
Khmer Rouge **560-561**
M14 rifle **47**, **188**

M16 assault rifle **56**, 180, **188**, **279**, **383**, **399**
M20 Rocket Launcher **118**
M60 machine gun **56**, **68-69**, **76**, **78**, **338**, **356**, **384**
M79 grenade launcher **91**, **379**
mines **138**, **327**
mortars 137, **199**, **214**
Type 56 assault rifle **103**
U.S. Army **47**, **91**, **214**, **259**, **379**, **383**, **384**, **399**
U.S. Forces **356**
U.S. Marines **57**, **68-69**, **78**, **118**, **188**, **199**, **279**, **338**
Viet Cong 137, **239**, **242-243**, 370
Viet Minh **25**
Winchester Trench Gun **259**
Weathermen, the 182
Webster, Captain Robert L. **473**
Weskamp, Captain Bob **545**
Westmoreland, General William C. 40, 48, 91, 137, 151, **209**, **212**
and the ARVN 180
background **62**, 62, **132**
and Con Thien 198
deploys the 4th Infantry Division 106
Honolulu conference 124
and the Ia Drang Valley 65, 73
and Johnson **70-71**
and Khe Sanh 214, 216, 248, 252-253, 329
memoirs 566
and nuclear weapons 214
and the NVA 75
and Operation Junction City 145
and Operation Pegasus 324
and the Paris peace treaty 566
Phase I objectives 86
Phase II 86
plans 50-51
press statements 201
refused permission to enter Cambodia 102
replaced 337
requests increased commitment 321
and the siege of Khe Sanh 329
strategy 45-46, 54, 79, 86, 116, 132, 138-139, 333
suspects NVA return to Ia Drang 98
tactics 62
and Tet 212, 214, 256, 312, 329
and U.S. Marines 73
views on failure 566
Weyand, Major General Frederick C. 86, 212
Wheeler, General Earle G. 214
requests increased commitment 321
Wilder, Lieutenant Colonel Gary 172
"wise men", the 323
women **265**, **340**, **364**, **365**, **419**, **515**, 575
Wood, Sp5 Harris E. **173**

X
Xom Bang 122
Xuan Loc 563

Z
Zais, Major General Melvin 384, 391